Charles Wells

A Practical Grammar

of

the Turkish Language

Elibron Classics
www.elibron.com

تركجهنك صرف و نحوى

تأليف

چارلس ولس

از خواجكان مكتب بحريه‌ٔ شاهانه سابقا

A PRACTICAL GRAMMAR

OF

THE TURKISH LANGUAGE.

تركجهنك صرف و نحوی

تألیف

چارلس ولس

از خواجكان مكتب بحریه٬ شاهانه سابقا

A PRACTICAL GRAMMAR

OF

THE TURKISH LANGUAGE

(AS SPOKEN AND WRITTEN),

WITH EXERCISES FOR TRANSLATION INTO TURKISH, QUOTATIONS FROM TURKISH AUTHORS
ILLUSTRATING TURKISH SYNTAX AND COMPOSITION, AND SUCH RULES OF
THE ARABIC AND PERSIAN GRAMMARS AS HAVE BEEN ADOPTED
BY THE OSMANLIS, THE PRONUNCIATION BEING GIVEN
IN ENGLISH LETTERS THROUGHOUT.

BY

Dr. CHARLES WELLS,

Late Private Secretary to General Sir A. Kemball, on the Turco-Persian Frontier Commission.
Formerly Professor at the Imperial Naval College, Constantinople;
Editor of the New Edition of Redhouse's Turkish Dictionary; Author of علم تدبیر ملك
(An Essay on Political Economy in Turkish), of Mehemet the Kurd, and
other Tales from Eastern Sources, &c.

لوندره شهرنده پیکادیلی صوقاغنده كتابجی قوارپچ افندینك
دكاننده فروخت اولنور

LONDON:

BERNARD QUARITCH, 15 PICCADILLY.

1880.

لوندره شهرنده وایمان افندینك مطبعه سنده
طبع اولنمشدر

INTRODUCTION.

WITHOUT wishing in the least to detract from the labours of my predecessors, I think I may say, without any fear of contradiction on the part of those who are really acquainted with the subject, that all Turkish Grammars which have hitherto appeared in English were extremely defective, and only adapted to give the most rudimentary knowledge of colloquial Turkish. A great number of Arabic and Persian rules of grammar, which have been adopted by all educated Osmanlis, and are indispensable for writing, and even conversing correctly on abstract subjects, were entirely omitted. Moreover, these works were generally crowded with errors, some, it is true, only clerical, but even such mistakes, not to speak of fundamental ones, are very injurious and embarrassing to the student. On the other hand, thoroughly correct native works, published of late years in Turkey, such as the قواعد عثمانيه and others, are either inaccessible or too difficult to be of any use to anyone not already possessing a very considerable knowledge of the language.

I have endeavoured to steer between these two extremes. Having adopted the simplest and plainest style possible in treating so difficult a subject, I flatter myself I am justified in calling the Grammar which I now lay before the English public a practical one; and, having omitted nothing of any value which has been laid down by Turkish grammarians or which is necessary for reading and writing Turkish correctly, I venture to hope that it will also be found complete.

No Turkish grammar in any European language contains exercises,—a great defect. It is not sufficient for the student to read or learn rules. He must practise them, or else they will quickly fade from the memory. The benefit derived from writing exercises is now so universally admitted that all grammars for learning European languages give them, and they are the best preparation for writing and speaking. This want I have endeavoured to supply, and I am convinced that the acquisition of the Turkish language will thereby be greatly facilitated.

Another new feature I have introduced into this volume is the illustration of the rules of Turkish syntax and composition by passages from native authors. Writers on Turkish grammar have hitherto contented themselves with giving one or two short sentences (generally of their own) as examples of the rules of syntax. Quotations from Turkish books are far more interesting and authoritative; and, as they will serve the double purpose of elucidating the rules and introducing the learner to reading Turkish, I have made them long and numerous.

It is almost superfluous for me to enlarge on the vital importance of all Englishmen who proceed to the East, in connection with the reforms in the Ottoman Empire which England has urged on the Porte, being acquainted with Turkish. It is self-evident, as without a proper knowledge of the language of the country their services will be of little or no avail. Ignorance of the vernacular on the part of European officials has been a fruitful source of troubles and misunderstandings in the East; and this evil will never cease until encouragement is given to those who devote themselves to this most arduous study. Appointments in Turkey should be given to those only who have given proof of their ability to acquire Oriental languages. No one should be sent out, even as a student-interpreter, before he has shown that he has an aptitude for learning Turkish. His possessing a generally good education is no criterion of his being able to master Turkish, which is probably the most difficult language in the world except Chinese; but, if Government appointments, and, especially, student-interpreterships, were given only to those who could pass an examination in elementary Turkish, at least, the number of persons who learn the language would be immensely increased, and the probability of the Government obtaining really proficient *employés* would be far greater than at present. Rewarding those who have already acquired Turkish would be a far safer and more economical plan to promote the growth of

Oriental scholars than paying young men to go to Turkey in the hope that they may possibly acquire the language. Were those who were proficient in Turkish sure of encouragement, there would be no lack of Turksh scholars. Such persons having hitherto been neglected may be one cause, and, perhaps, the chief cause, of the extreme scarcity of Englishmen who have mastered Turkish. There was a professorship of English at one of the Turkish Government colleges some years ago, and hundreds of Turkish officers studied English under me there, and those who acquired English were sure of encouragement from their government; but, although England is as much interested in the matter as the Turks, there is no professorship of Turkish in England, and, of course, consequently the number of persons who have attempted to learn Turkish is excessively small. In this the Turks might very well suggest a little reform on our part.

CHARLES WELLS.

8, Prince's Square, W. London,
July 7th, 1880.

CONTENTS.

CHAPTER I.—THE TURKISH ALPHABET.

CHAPTER II.—THE NOUN.

CHAPTER III.—THE ADJECTIVE.

CHAPTER VI.—THE ADVERB.

CHAPTER VII.—PREPOSITIONS OR POSTPOSITIONS.

CHAPTER VIII.—CONJUNCTIONS.

A TURKISH GRAMMAR.

CHAPTER I.

THE TURKISH ALPHABET.

1. THE Turkish Language is of Tartar origin, the Turks having come from Central Asia, and it has a very distinct and peculiar character of its own, which it has never lost, although it has borrowed largely from Arabic and Persian. For many years it was written in characters specially belonging to itself, but they have now become quite obsolete, and the Arabic letters are always employed. The letters of the alphabet are thirty-one in number, and consist of the Arabic letters together with some which the Persians have added. The Turks, as most Oriental nations, read and write from right to left, instead of from left to right as we do, and a book consequently begins where it would end in English. Capital letters and punctuation are unknown, although some unsuccessful attempts have occasionally lately been made to introduce the latter. A great number of the vowel sounds are not written, and, consequently, before knowing a word it is impossible to pronounce it. Turkish writing has, therefore, the advantage of being, so to speak, stenographic, but the frequent omission of the vowels causes great difficulty to the learner. Even a native finds learning to read a slower and more arduous matter than Europeans do, and Europeans experience great hardships in deciphering Turkish writing. Practice and perseverance will always overcome this embarrassment, but there is but little doubt that the stenographic character of the Turkish writing has greatly impeded the general spread of reading and writing in the East, and prevented many Europeans from acquiring the Turkish language. Consequently, many persons have advocated the adoption of the Roman characters by the Turks, but, apart from the fact that our letters are quite unfitted

for the purpose, such a change would lead to utter confusion, both as regards the meaning and derivation of words, and it would be so repugnant to the feelings of most Mussulmans that it stands no chance of being accepted by them. To retain the Turkish characters but write all the sounds would be far better. Nothing new would have to be learnt, and both the native and the foreigner would be able to read correctly immediately on mastering the alphabet. This system, together with some trifling modifications in the way of writing some of the letters, is that advocated and invented by Prince Malcom Khan, the Persian ambassador in London, and would be equally applicable to Persian, Arabic, and Hindustani, &c. Whether his ingenious method will ever be generally accepted I cannot tell, but the adoption of the Roman letters is as improbable as the employment of the phonetic system in England. The acquisition of the Turkish characters is, therefore, indispensably necessary for any one who is desirous of learning Turkish. They are as follows :—

2. The Turkish Alphabet.

Order.	Form.	Name.	Order.	Form.	Name.
1	ا	élif	17	ص	sad
2	ب	bé	18	ض	dad
3	پ	pé	19	ط	tĭ (or ta)
4	ت	té	20	ظ	zĭ (or za)
5	ث	sé	21	ع	ayn
6	ج	jim	22	غ	ghayn
7	چ	chim	23	ف	fé
8	ح	ha	24	ق	káf
9	خ	khĭ	25	ك	kef
10	د	dal	26	ل	lam
11	ذ	zel (or zal)	27	م	mim
12	ر	rĭ (or ra)	28	ن	noun
13	ز	zé (or za)	29	و	vav
14	ژ	zhé	30	ه	hé
15	س	sin	31	ى	yé
16	ش	shin			

The Pronunciation of Turkish in English Characters.

3. In reading the names of the letters in the above table, and whenever Turkish is transcribed into English characters in this volume, the letters must be pronounced as follows:—

*a**	must be pronounced as in the English word "star."		
e	,,	,,	*e* in "perish."
é	,,	,,	*a* in "sand."
i	,,	,,	*i* in "sin" (never as "I").
ĭ	,,	,,	*i* in "bird."
o	,,	,,	*o* in "No."
ou	,,	,,	*oo* in "cool."
u	,,	,,	*u* in the French word *reçu* (there being no equivalent sound in English).
eu	,,	,,	*eu* in the French word *feu*.

The consonants must be pronounced as in English, as they are well fitted for rendering the Turkish. *H* must be aspirated at the beginning, middle, and end of a word. *Ch* must be pronounced as in "chimney;" *kh* as *ch* in German. *Y* must be always looked upon as a consonant. *Ay* or *aï* must be pronounced as *aï* in the French word *haïr; gh* as *g* hard in "game."

4. In giving the letters of the Turkish alphabet in the preceding table (2) we have only shown the shape they have when standing alone. When they are combined with other letters they are sometimes slightly modified, according as they stand at the beginning, in the middle, or at the end of a word. These various changes will be seen from the following table:—

[5. Table

---

* It sometimes, however, represents a broader sound than this French sound of *a*, and is equivalent to the English *aw* in paw, in which case it will be found marked thus *â*.

5. Table showing the shape of the Turkish Letters at the beginning, in the middle, or at the end of a word, and when isolated.

Isolated.	Initial.	Medial.	Final.	Remarks.	Isolated.	Initial.	Medial.	Final.	Remarks.
ا	—	—	ا	This letter is never joined to the one following	ص	صـ	ـصـ	ـص	
ب	بـ	ـبـ	ـب		ض	ضـ	ـضـ	ـض	
پ	پـ	ـپـ	ـپ		ط	طـ	ـطـ	ـط	
ت	تـ	ـتـ	ـت		ظ	ظـ	ـظـ	ـظ	
ة			ـة		ع	عـ	ـعـ	ـع	
ث	ثـ	ـثـ	ـث	Any letter preceding these four must rise above the level of the line.	غ	غـ	ـغـ	ـغ	
ج	جـ	ـجـ	ـج		ف	فـ	ـفـ	ـف	
چ	چـ	ـچـ	ـچ		ق	قـ	ـقـ	ـق	
ح	حـ	ـحـ	ـح		ك	كـ	ـكـ	ـك	
خ	خـ	ـخـ	ـخ		ل	لـ	ـلـ	ـل	
د	—	—	ـد	These five letters are never joined to the following letter.	م	مـ	ـمـ	ـم	The letter preceding م must rise above the line.
ذ	—	—	ـذ		ن	نـ	ـنـ	ـن	
ر	—	—	ـر		و	—	—	ـو	
ز	—	—	ـز		ه	هـ	ـهـ	ـه	The و is never joined to the following letter.
ژ	—	—	ـژ		ى	يـ	ـيـ	ـى	
س	سـ	ـسـ	ـس						
ش	شـ	ـشـ	ـش						

The character ﻻ or ﻷ *la*, called *lam élif*, is the mere combination of the two letters ل and ا.

6. The letters of the alphabet are occasionally used to express numerals. When employed thus their value is as follows :—

ا	ب	ج	د	ه	و	ز	ح	ط	ى	ك	ل	م	ن	س
1	2	3	4	5	6	7	8	9	10	20	30	40	50	60

ع	ف	ص	ق	ر	ش	ت	خ	ذ	ض	ظ	غ
70	80	90	100	200	300	500	600	700	800	900	1,000

7. As stated in the table, seven letters, ا, د, ذ, ر, ز, ژ and و are never joined to the following letter, but they may be joined to the letter preceding them, for example : ماشالله *mashalla* (dear me!), انصاف *insâf* (conscience), رطوبت *routoubet* (damp, humidity), دال *dal* (a branch), روح *rouh* (the

soul, spirit), زیوه zhivé* (mercury), اعتدال itidal (moderation), اعتراض itiráz (an objection).

The Pronunciation of the Turkish Letters.

8..All the letters of the Turkish alphabet are consonants, the vowel sounds either being omitted or indicated by signs above or below the word, of which an explanation will be given hereafter. Four letters, however, are *sometimes* used as vowels, viz.: ١, و, ى, and ى.

9. The ١ *élif* is sometimes a consonant, sometimes a vowel. In Turkish words it is always a vowel, and it may be pronounced as either *á*, *é, i, u,* or *ou*,† when it is at the beginning of any word ; as, اخوت *oukhouvet* (brotherhood), اسرا *ussera* (captives), اسپر *isspir* (a groom), اسان *assan* (easy), استاد *usstad* (a master), ارمود *armoud* (a pear), ارامق *áramak* (to seek), ادب *édeb* (good manners), اسكى *esski* (old). In the middle or at the end of a Turkish word it is sounded like *a*, as باش *básh* (the head), الما *elma* (an apple). As a consonant it is only used in words of Arabic origin, and then only at the end or in the middle of a word. When thus used as a consonant the sign ٔ, called a hemzé, is placed over it, and its pronunciation is then like that of a slight catch in the breath, as تأكيد *te'kid* (confirming).

10. In some words of Persian origin it is silent, as in the words خيرخواه *khaïr-khah* (benevolent), خواجه *khoja* (a teacher), مردمخوار *mer-dumkhor* (a cannibal).

11. The ب *bé* exactly corresponds to our *b*; for example, بركت *beréket* (a blessing), بش *besh* (five), بقال *bákkál* (a grocer), بلا *bela* (a calamity). It is, however, occasionally given the sound of *p*, as مكتوب *mektup* (a letter).

12. پ *pé* is equivalent to our *p*, as پوصو *poussou* (an ambush), پياده *piyadé* (infantry), پيره *piré* (a flea).

13. ث *sé* is pronounced like *s* in Turkish, although its proper pro-

---

* *é* must be pronounced as *é* in the French word *pré*, a meadow.

† ١ combined with و is often used to express *o, ou, eu,* or *u,* as اول *ol* (that), اولمك *eulmek* (to die), اوفاق *oufák* (small), اوكسرك *euksuruk* (a cough), اوشومك *ushumek* (to feel cold). In conjunction with ى it is employed to express the sound of *ay, éy,* or *i,* as ايرى *ayrï* (separate), ايلنجه *éylenjé* (amusement), ايمدى *imdï* (now).

nunciation in Arabic is like our *th* in thin, or the Greek θ. Example,
ثلث *sulss* (a third).

14. ج *jim* has exactly the sound of our English *j ;* for example, تجارت
tijaret (commerce), تاج *taj* (a crown). It is, however, occasionally pronounced like ج *chim.*

15. ج *chim* is the same as *ch* in English, in the word " church "; thus,
قاچ *kach* (how much ?), قیچ *kich* (the stern of a ship).

16. ح *ha* has the sound of a strongly aspirated *h;* as in حاچ *hách* (a
cross), حاجی *hájjï* (a pilgrim).

17. خ *khï* corresponds to *ch* in German, and has no equivalent in
English. It is perhaps best represented by *kh ;* خائن *kha'in* (treacherous),
خبر *kháber* (news), خانم *khanim* (a Turkish lady), خام *khám* (unripe).
In pronunciation it is very often confounded by the Turks with ح, and,
consequently, an Englishman may very well give it the sound of *h,* but
he must be careful not to pronounce it like *k.*

18. د *dál* is our *d.* Example, دال *dál* (a branch), دوشمك *dushmek*
(to fall), دمیر *démir* (iron), دولاب *doláb* (a cupboard). It is sometimes
pronounced like *t,* as دلکی *tilki* (a fox).

19. ذ *zel* is the same as *z.* Example, لذیذ *léziz* (delicious), ذوق
zevk (pleasure, enjoyment).

20. ر *rï* is pronounced as *r.* Example, روح *rouh* (the soul), رحمت
rahmet (mercy), رتبه *rutbé* (rank), رسم *ressm* (a drawing).

21. ز *zé* is another *z.* Example, از *áz* (little), زحمت *zahmet* (trouble).

22. ژ *zhé* is pronounced like *j* in French. Example, ژیوه *zhivé*
(quicksilver).

23. س *sin* is equivalent to our *s,* but must never be sounded like *z,* as
we sometimes pronounce *s.* It is perhaps best represented by *ss* in the
middle or at the end of a word. Example, صحت *sihat* (health), صاعت
saat (a watch, an hour), فس *fess* (a Turkish cap).*

24. ش *shin* is our *sh.* Example, شام *Sham* (Syria), بش *besh* (five).

25. ص *sad* is merely another *s,* and has nearly exactly the same power
as س. Example, مخصوص *makhsouss* (special), صویمق *soïmak* (to strip),
صویش *souyoush* (boiled meat).

26. The ض *dad* is generally pronounced as *z.* Example, ضرر *zarar*
(injury, harm), ضیا *ziya* (light), ضیافت *ziyafet* (a banquet). Occasionally

---

* Called incorrectly by Europeans *fez.*

it has the sound of *d*. · Example, ضرب *darb* (striking, a blow), ضلال *délal* (straying from the right path).

27. The ط *ti* is sometimes pronounced as *t*, and sometimes as *d*. Example, طاغ *dâgh* (a mountain), طويل *tavil* (long), طهارت *taharet* (cleanliness), طولمق *dolmak* (to fill).

28. The ظ *zi* is a hard *z*. Example, ظالم *zalim* (a tyrant), محظوظ *mahzouz* (delighted), حافظ *hafiz* (a protector, preserver).

29. The *aïn* ع has no equivalent in European languages. Its original Arabic pronunciation is extremely difficult and peculiar, and can only be learnt orally from a master; but in Turkish it is most often pronounced like *élif*, or a strong hiatus. It is sometimes distinguished in English by this sign ". Example, زراعت *zira"at* (agriculture), سعادت *sa"adet* (prosperity). Sometimes it is not sounded, as دفع *def"* (repelling), رفع *ref"* (lifting up).

30. The غ *ghaïn* is a hard *g*, best represented by *gh*. Example, غرب *gharb* (the west), غروش *ghouroush* (a piastre), غروب *ghouroub* (the setting of the sun). Sometimes this letter is softened down till it becomes like a *w*; at others it is scarcely heard at all, or is like an *élif*. Example, اغلامق *aghlamak* (to cry), pronounced *aalamak*.

31 The ف *fé* has the same sound as *f*. Example, طرف *taraf* (a side, direction), فقير *fakïr* (poor).

32. The ق *kâf* is a hard and palatal *k*. Example, قولاق *koulâk* (the ear), قولاچ *koulach* (a fathom), قوم *koum* (sand).

33. The ك *kef* in Turkish represents either *k*, *g* hard, or *n*. Its original sound in Arabic is that of *k*, but the Persians adopted it also to represent *gh*. When it has the latter sound, it is sometimes distinguished by a modification in ts shape, thus, گ as, for instance, ایشگذار *ishghiuzar* (energetic).* When it has the sound of *n*, it is sometimes written thus ڭ, with three dots over it to distinguish it; but in general in Turkish the ك alone is used to express all three sounds, and the student can only learn how to pronounce it by practice. When it has its second value of *gh*, it is often so softened down as to closely resemble the sound of *y*. Example, بك *Bey* (a Bey), كله‌جكم *gheléjéyim* (I will come). When having its third value of *n*, it is often

---

* When ك *kef* represents either the sound of *k* or *g* hard, and is followed by an *élif* or a vowel *vav*, the sound of *i* is introduced between those two letters. Example, افكار *efkiar* (ideas), كاه *ghiah* (a place), كون *ghiun* (a day), كور *ghieur* (see).

entirely left out of the pronunciation. Example, صكره *sora* (after) instead of *sonra*.

34. ل *lam* is the same as *l*. Example, لازم *lazim* (necessary), لكن *lakin* (but), مال *mal* (property, wealth).

35. م *mim* is our *m*. Example, ملّت *millet* (a country), مزاد *mezad* (an auction), مسافر *mussafir* (a guest, traveller).

36. ن *noun* is our *n*. Example, اوزون *ouzoun* (long), نتیجه *netijé* (a result), نمونه *noumouné* (an example, pattern).

37. و *vav* is sometimes a consonant and sometimes a vowel. When a consonant it has generally the sound of *v*, but occasionally it is pronounced like *w* in English. Example, وزیر *vézir* (a vizier), واپور *vapor* (a steamboat), والی *wali* (a governor-general), والده *walidé* (mother).

When a vowel it may correspond to either *o*, *ou*, *eu*, or *u*. Example, طوتمق *toutmak* (to hold, seize, &c.), بوش *bosh* (empty), کور *kieur** (blind), کورفز *kieurfez* (gulf, bay), طوز *touz* (salt).

38. In some words of Persian derivation the و is not sounded at all. Example, خیرخواه *khaïr-khah* (benevolent). When used as a conjunction for *and* it is sometimes joined in the pronunciation to the word preceding it and is then sounded like *ou* or *u*. Example, حضر و سفر *hazar-ou-séfer* (peace and war).

39. ه *hé* is sometimes a consonant and sometimes a vowel. When the former it corresponds to *h*, and when the latter, which it generally is at the end of words, it is equivalent to *a* or *é*. Example, هند *hind* (India), هنر *huner* (talent), جمله *jumlé* (all, the whole), پاره *paré* (money), پارچه *parcha* (a piece).

40. The ی *yé* is sometimes a consonant and sometimes a vowel.

As a consonant it corresponds to our English *y*. Example, یمورطه *yĭmourta* (an egg), یمین *yémin* (an oath), یناق *yanak* (a cheek), ینمك *yenmek* (to overcome).

As a vowel it is equivalent to *i* or *ĭ*. Example, این *in* (a cave), الجی *elchi* (an ambassador), ایکنه *ighné* (a needle), فقیر *fakïr* (poor). At the end of some few Arabic words it is pronounced like *a*. Example, اولی *evla* (preferable), بشری *bushra* (good news).†

---

* See note page 7.

† ی is often interchangeable with و. Thus we have طوغری or طوغرو *doghrou* (straight), کندی *kendi* or کندو *kendou* (self).

The Vowel Signs.

41. As has been before stated the vowels in Turkish writing are often omitted. They can, however, be indicated by certain signs above or below the consonants. These signs are as follows :—

42. فتحه *fethé* or اُستون *ustun*, a diagonal stroke drawn from right to left, placed above the letter thus (´), indicates that the letter it is over should be followed by the sound of *a* or *é*. The sound of *a* is given when the letter over which the *fethé* stands or the following letter is hard, that is to say, is either ح خ ص ض ط ظ ع غ or ق. The sound of *é* is given when the letter over which the *fethé* stands or the following letter is soft, that is to say, any other letter of the alphabet. Example, محبّت *mahabet* (love), اَمَك *émek* (labour), كَلَرَك *ghelérek* (coming), يپرَق *yéprák* (a leaf), سبزوَات *sebzévát* (vegetables).

43. اِسرِه *ésseré* or كِسرِه *kessré* is of the same shape as the فتحه *fethé*, but is placed below the letter it affects, to which it gives the sound of *i* in French, or *i* in the English word "bit." Examples, مجيد *mejid* (most glorious), اِصرِدی *issirdi* (he bit), اِستَمَك *isstémek* (to wish).

44. اوتوری *euteuri*, also called ضَمه *damma*, is written thus ُ. It is placed over a letter to show that it must be followed by the sound of either *o, eu, ou,* or *u*. Example, ملحَق *mulhák* (appended), ملتَزِم *multézim* (a farmer of the revenue), ملايِم *mulayim* (mild), مكَلَّف *mukellef* (sumptuous).

45. The above three signs are used considerably in Arabic, but they are scarcely ever employed in Turkish books or writing, except to indicate the pronunciation of some uncommon or foreign word.

46. The sign ً placed over a letter indicates that it should be followed by the sound of *an* or *en*. Example, عِيانًا *ayanan* (clearly), تيمنًا *téyemmunan* (happily, fortunately).

47. The same sign placed below a letter shows that it should be followed by the sound of *in* or *in*. Example, رَجُلٍ *rajolin* (a man, in the genitive, dative, and ablative cases in Arabic).

48. The sign ٌ or ٌ indicates that the letter it surmounts should be

followed by the sound of *un* or *on.* Example, وَاحِدٌ *wahidon* (one, only —in Arabic). This and the preceding sign (47) are very little used in Turkish.

49. The sign ـّ, called *teshdid,* doubles the letter over which it stands. Example, شِدَّت *shiddet* (violence), اَوَّل *evvel* (the first, before).

50. The sign ـْ, called جَزْم *jezm,* is placed over a consonant to show that it is to be followed by no vowel. Example, جَزْم *jezm,* يَوْم *yavm* (a day).*

51. The sign ـٓ, called مَد *med,* placed over an *élif,* shows that its sound must be prolonged. Example, آزَارِش *ázarish* (vexation).

52. The sign *hemzé* (ء) is used in four different ways :—

(1.) Put over an ا thus أ, it indicates that it should be pronounced *éé,* or *é'.* Example, مَأْل *mé'el* (the prophet), تَأْلِيف *té'lif* (writing).

(2.) Standing over a و or a ی it replaces the ا, which undergoes this change in accordance with the rules of Arabic grammar. Example, مُؤَخَّر *mou'akkhar* (posterior, postponed), مُؤَدَّب *mou'eddeb* (well behaved), سَائِل *sa'il* (a beggar, a plaintiff).

(3.) It is occasionally found at the end of a word, taking the place of an ا, a و, or a ی, suppressed in consequence of certain rules of Arabic grammar. Example, جُزء *juz* (a part, portion).

(4.) It is put at the end of a word after ا, ی, and ه, and pronounced as *i* under certain circumstances explained hereafter. Example, بَنْدَهٔ خُدَا *bendé-i-khuda* (the servant of God).

When a *hemzé* is put over a ی the two dots of that letter are left out. Example, غَائِب *gha'ib* (*kaïb*) (lost, absent).

53. The sign ـٓ, called *vasl,* is placed over the ا of the Arabic article اَل to show that it is mute. Example, عَلَی ٱلْحِسَاب *alal-hissab,* كِتَاب ٱللّٰه *kitáb-u-llahi* (the book of God).

The Pronunciation of the Arabic Article.

54. There is no Turkish definite article, but the Arabic article اَل *el* (the) often occurs when Arabic words are used. It is the same in the

---

* In words of Turkish origin and even in Arabic words with Turkish particles added to them, this repetition of a letter is not indicated by this sign. Example, قُوللَر *koullar* (servants), عَقِلْلُو *áklli* (wise).

singular and plural, the masculine and feminine,—in short, never changes; for example, الانسان *el-insan* (the man), العباد *el-ibad* (the servants), الوجوه *el-woujouh* (the faces). When this article is placed before a word and it is preceded by another word, the *élif* of the ال is not pronounced. Example, حياةالانسان *hayat-ul-insan* (the life of man).

55. If the word before which the ال is placed begins with either ت, ث, د, ذ, ر, ز, س, ش, ص, ض, ط, ظ, ل, or ن, the ل is pronounced the same as the first letter of that word, or in other words, it is lost entirely and the first letter of the word is doubled. Example, الشمس (the sun) is pronounced *es-shems*, and not *el-shems;* الصيف (the summer) is pronounced *es-saïf,* not *el-saïf;* النجات *en-nejat* (the salvation), not *el-nejat.*

Of the Laws of Euphony in Pronouncing Turkish.

56. A very remarkable peculiarity of Turkish is the attention paid to euphony in pronunciation, and the changes of the sounds of vowels and consonants which take place in consequence. Thus the collision of hard and soft letters in the same word is always avoided, and when one declines a word or adds a particle or letter to it, whatever be the leading letter the others must be pronounced so as to agree with it. Amongst the consonants, ح, خ, ص, ض, ط, ظ, ع, غ, and ق are considered hard, ت, د, ز, س, ك, and ه soft; the others are neutral. Of the vowels, the sounds *a, ï, o,* and *ou* are hard, and *é, i, eu,* and *u* soft. In words of Turkish origin the vowels in general are either all soft or all hard.

57. If the first syllable of a word contain a soft vowel all the vowels in that word should be soft. Example, پنجره *pénjéré* (a window), اولم *eulum* (death), كورك *kieuruk* (a pair of bellows). If the first vowel be hard then the others should be hard also. Example, طوغرى *doghrou* (right).

58. On the above principle, when one declines a word or adds a particle to it the vowel of the syllable added is generally so pronounced that *ï* comes after *a, i* after *é, ou* after *o, u* after *eu,* and in the same manner, *a* after *o* and *ou, é* after *u* or *eu.* Example, باشك is pronounced *bashïn,* not *bashin* or *bashoun,* because *ï* must follow *a;* موم *moum* makes موموك *moumoun,* not *moumin;* يولى is pronounced *yolou,* not *yoli;* كوزى *gheuzu,* not *gheuzi,* يوزى *yuzu,* not *yuzi.* (See note to 68.)

59. On the same requirements of euphony, words of Turkish origin which end in ق change that letter to غ before the post-positions ك, ى, and

ʻ, and before the pronominal affixes, excepting that of the third person plural ; and Turkish words ending in ٮ or ط change it into د.   Example, قایق *kayïk* (a boat), قایغك *kayïghïn* (of the boat), قایغه *kayïgha* (to the boat), قایغی *kayïghï* (the boat, *accusative*) ; یازمقلق *yazmaklïk* (writing), یازمقلغی *yazmaklïghï* (his writing) ; چبوق *chibouk* (a pipe), چبوغم *chiboughoum* (my pipe) ; قورت *kourt* (a wolf), قوردك *kourdoun* (of the wolf), قورده *kourda* (to the wolf).

60. In the same way *kef* ك must be pronounced as *gh* or *y* under the same circumstances.   Example, كورك *kïeurek** (an oar), كوركك *kïeuréyin** (of the oar).

61. There are, however, a few words which do not make this change. Example, اق *ok* (an arrow), اوقی *okou* (his arrow) ; كوك *kieuk* (a root), كوكی *kieukieu* (its root).

62. The particles affixed to words to form the dative, ablative, and other cases take a hard or soft vowel according as the word itself contains hard or soft vowels.   Example, اوه *evé* (to the house), اودن *avdan* (from the chase).

CHAPTER II.

THE NOUN.

63. There is no definite article in Turkish.   Thus او *ev* may stand either for house or the house, اولر *evler* for houses or the houses, ادم *ádâm* for man or the man.   This seems peculiar at first, but the learner soon becomes accustomed to it.   With Arabic words used in Turkish the Arabic article ال *el* (the) is sometimes employed.   Example, الارض *el-arz* (the earth), الشمس *es-shems*† (the sun).

The Gender of the Noun.

64. As in English, there is no unnatural distinction of gender in Turkish, that is to say, the names of males are masculine, those of females feminine, and those of inanimate objects neuter.   Thus ادم *ádâm* (a man) is masculine, قاری *kárï* (a woman), feminine, قیز *kiz* (a girl), feminine, اوغلان *oghlân* (a boy) masculine ; but numbers of Arabic words being used in Turkish, the rules of Arabic grammar respecting gender are

* See note page 7.   † See page 11, par. 54.

observed in the written language, and even in conversation amongst the better educated classes.

65. In Arabic, as in French, every noun is either masculine or feminine, and it is very requisite in Turkish to know of what gender an Arabic substantive is. As a guide, therefore, it must be borne in mind that all Arabic nouns ending in a ت or ة (when those letters are not radical) are feminine. Example, كتابت *kitabet* (writing, style), ظلمت *zoulmet* (darkness), روضة *revza* (a garden); except علامة *alamé* (a very learned man), خليفة *khalifé* (a caliph).

66. All singular Arabic nouns ending in any other letter but ت or ة (not radical) are masculine. Example, طالب *talib* (a student), طلوع *toulou* (the rising—of the sun, &c.), طعام *taam* (food). Except, أم *um* (a mother), شمس *shemss* (the sun), نفس *nefss* (the soul), يد *yéd* (the hand), which are feminine.

67. The irregular Arabic plurals are all feminine.

The Declension of the Noun.

68. Properly speaking the Turkish noun has no declension, as the word never changes, certain prepositions or post-positions being added to it to show the various cases. The word by itself forms the nominative; the genitive is formed by adding ك *in, in, oun,* or *un,* to the nominative; the dative by adding ه *é* or *a*; and the accusative by adding ى *i* or *ou* or *u* to the original word, as will be seen from the table below. The pronunciation of these terminations is modified according to the predominant vowel of the word.

او *ev,* house.*

	Singular.			Plural.	
Nom.	او	*ev,* house	Nom.	اولر	*evler,* houses
Gen.	اوك	*evin,* of the house	Gen.	اولرك	*evlerin,* of the houses
Dat.	اوه	*evé,* to the house	Dat.	اولره	*evleré,* to the houses
Acc.	اوى	*evi,* the house	Acc.	اولرى	*evleri,* the houses

* There being no article in Turkish, او *ev* corresponds to house, *the* house or *a* house; and this remark holds good with respect to all Turkish nouns in the nominative. *The* with a noun in the accusative is expressed by the accusative termination ى, which is left out if the noun in the accusative be not preceded by "the" in English. Example, كتاب الدم *kitáb áldim* (I bought a book), but كتابى الدم *kitábi áldim* means, I bought *the* book.

موم *moum,* candle.

	Singular.			Plural.	
Nom.	موم	*moum,* candle	Nom.	موملر	*moumlar,* candles
Gen.	مومك	*moumoun,** of the candle	Gen.	موملرك	*moumlarĭn,* of the candles
Dat.	مومه	*mouma,* to the candle	Dat.	موملره	*moumlara,* to the candles
Acc.	مومى	*moumou,** the candle	Acc.	موملرى	*moumlarĭ,* the candles.

69. When the noun ends in a vowel, for the sake of euphony, in the singular, نك is added instead of ك to form the genitive, يه instead of ه to form the dative, and يى instead of ى to make the accusative. Example—

بابا *baba,* father.

	Singular.			Plural.	
Nom.	بابا	*bábá,* father	Nom.	بابالر	*bábálar,* fathers
Gen.	بابانك	*bábánĭn,* of the father	Gen.	بابالرك	*bábálarĭn,* of the fathers
Dat.	بابايه	*bábáya,* to the father	Dat.	بابالره	*bábálara,* to the fathers
Acc.	بابايى	*bábáyĭ,* the father	Acc.	بابالرى	*bábálarĭ,* the fathers

دره *deré,* valley.

	Singular.			Plural.	
Nom.	دره	*deré,* valley	Nom.	درهلر	*deréler,* valleys
Gen.	درهنك	*derénin,* of the valley	Gen.	درهلرك	*derélerin,* of the valleys
Dat.	درهيه	*deréyé,* to the valley	Dat.	درهلره	*deréleré,* to the valleys
Acc.	درهيى	*deréyi,* the valley	Acc.	درهلرى	*deréleri,* the valleys

كدى *kédi,* cat.

	Singular.			Plural.	
Nom.	كدى	*kédi,* cat	Nom.	كديلر	*kédiler,* cats
Gen.	كدينك	*kédinin,* of the cat	Gen.	كديلرك	*kédilerin,* of the cats
Dat.	كدييه	*kédiyé,* to the cat	Dat.	كديلره	*kédileré,* to the cats
Acc.	كديى	*kédiyi,* the cat	Acc.	كديلرى	*kédileri,* the cats.

---

* ك, the sign of the genitive, is pronounced *oun* instead of *in,* for the sake of euphony, if the preceding predominant vowel be *ou* or *o;* it is pronounced *un* if the predominant vowel be *eu.* For the same reason, under similar circumstances ى, the sign of the accusative, is pronounced *ou* or *u* instead of *i.* Thus قوزينك (of the lamb) is read *kouzounoun,* قوزينى (the lamb), accus., *kouzounou;* يولك (of the road), *yoloun,* يولى (the road), accus., *yolou;* چولك (of the desert), *cheulun,* چولى (the desert), accus., *cheulu.* If a word end in *o* the genitive is pronounced *nin,* but the accusative is pronounced *you.* Example, يانقونك *yankonĭn* (of the echo), يانقوبى *yankoyou* (the echo), accus. But these changes in the reading of the words are mere matters of pronunciation and euphony, and no new declensions. (See 58).

70. By exception the noun صو *sou* (water), ending in a vowel, makes صويك *souyoun* instead of صونك *sounoun* in the genitive.

71. If a noun end in a ق that letter changes into غ before a vowel sound, and if it end in ك, that letter before a vowel sound is pronounced like ى *yé*. Example—

قايق *kayïk*, boat.

	Singular.			Plural.	
Nom.	قايق	*kayïk*, boat	Nom.	قايقلر	*kayïklar*, boats
Gen.	قايغك	*kayïghïn*, of the boat	Gen.	قايقلرك	*kayïklarïn*, of the boats
Dat.	قايغه	*kayïgha*, to the boat	Dat.	قايقلره	*kayïklara*, to the boats
Acc.	قايغى	*kayïghï*, the boat	Acc.	قايقلرى	*kayïklarï*, the boats

كوملك *ghieumlek*, shirt.

Nom.	كوملك	*ghieumlek*, shirt	Nom.	كوملكلر	*ghieumlekler*, shirts
Gen.	كوملكك	*ghieumléyin*, of the shirt	Gen.	كوملكلرك	*ghieumleklerin*, of the shirts [shirts
Dat.	كوملكه	*ghieumleyé*, to the shirt	Dat.	كوملكلره	*ghieumlekleré*, to the
Acc.	كوملكى	*ghieumléyi*, the shirt	Acc.	كوملكلرى	*ghieumlekleri*, the shirts.

72. The words اوق *ok* (an arrow), اق *ák* (white), بوق *bok* (excrement), كوك *kieuk* (a root), are exceptions to the above rule, as they do not change ق into غ and ك into the sound of ى *yé*. Example—

اوق *ok*, arrow.

	Singular.			Plural.	
Nom.	اوق	*ok*, arrow	Nom.	اوقلر	*oklar*, arrows
Gen.	اوقك	*okoun*, of the arrow	Gen.	اوقلرك	*oklarïn*, of the arrows
Dat.	اوقه	*oka*, to the arrow	Dat.	اوقلره	*oklara*, to the arrows
Acc.	اوقى	*okou*, the arrow	Acc.	اوقلرى	*oklarï*, the arrows.

73. Nouns ending in ت or ط change that letter into د before ك, ى, and ه, that is to say in the genitive, dative, and accusative singular. Example—

قورت *kourt*, wolf.

	Singular.			Plural.	
Nom.	قورت	*kourt*, wolf	Nom.	قورتلر	*kourtlar*, wolves
Gen.	قوردك	*kourdoun*, of the wolf	Gen.	قورتلرك	*kourtlarïn*, of the wolves
Dat.	قورده	*kourda*, to the wolf	Dat.	قورتلره	*kourtlara*, to the wolves
Acc.	قوردى	*kourdou*, the wolf	Acc.	قورتلرى	*kourtlarï*, the wolves.

74. When a noun is indefinite in the accusative it does not take ـس, but is the same as the nominative. Example, ات يمك *et yémek* (to eat meat), اتى يمك *eti yémek* (to eat *the* meat) ; مكتوبلر يازمق *mektouplar yazmak* (to write letters), مكتوبلرى يازمق *mektouplari yazmak* (to write *the* letters) ; اكمك كسمك *ekmek kessmek* (to cut bread), اكمكى كسمك *ekméyi kessmek* (to cut *the* bread).

75. The ablative is expressed in Turkish by simply adding دن *den* or *dan* after the noun. Example, اودن *evden* (from the house), اوطهدن *odadan* (from the room), يولدن *yoldan* (from the road).

76. The vocative is formed by putting the interjection يا *ya* (oh !) before the noun. Example, يا برادر *ya berader* (oh ! brother), يا بابا *ya bábá* (oh ! father).

The Number of the Noun.

77. As will be seen from the above tables, the plural is formed in Turkish by adding لر *ler* or *lar* to the singular. This is the general and original Turkish mode of showing the plural, and in the ordinary language not only words of Turkish origin, but Arabic and Persian words, are made plural in this way. But in high-flown language, the Arabic and Persian modes of forming the plural are followed, and, consequently, it is necessary for the Turkish student to understand them.

78. The Arabic language has three numbers—the singular, the dual, and the plural.

79. The dual, called تشنيه *tessniyé*, is formed by adding اين *éin* to the singular. Example, كتاب *kitáb* (a book), كتابين *kitábéin* (two books) ; قطب *Kutb* (the Pole), قطبين *Kutbéin* (the two Poles) ; شخص *shakhs* (an individual), شخصين *shakhséin* (two individuals). Sometimes the dual is made by the addition of ان instead of اين. Example, خمس *khumss* (a fifth), خمسان *khumsan* (two-fifths).

80. If the word end in a ة, used instead of ة, the ة must be restored before the dual termination is added. Example, قبله *kiblé*, for قبلة *kiblet*, makes قبلتان *kibletan* (the two kiblas).

81. There are two ways of forming the plural in Arabic, the regular and the irregular.

The Regular Arabic Plural.

82. The plural of masculine Arabic nouns is formed by adding ین *in* or ون *oun* to the singular. Example, طالب *talib* (a student), طالبون *taliboun* or طالبین *talibin* (students); معلم *muallim* (a teacher), معلمین *muallimin* or معلمون *muallimoun* (teachers). This way of forming the plural is only employed in the case of names of reasoning beings.

83. If the masculine noun end in ی, that letter is left out in the plural. Example, ساقی *sakï* (a cupbearer), ساقین *sakïn* (cupbearers).

84. The regular way of forming the plural of feminine Arabic words is by changing the final ة or ت of the singular into ات. Example, عادت *adet* (a custom), عادات *adat* (customs); حرکت *hérékét* (movement), حرکات *hérékiat** (movements); کلمه *kélimé* (a word), کلمات *kélimat* (words).

The Irregular Arabic Plural.

85. The different ways of forming the irregular Arabic plural are so numerous and complex that a separate chapter is requisite to explain them, which will be found farther on. The irregular forms of the plural are used both for masculine and feminine nouns. Example, بیت *béit* (a house), بیوت *bouyout* (houses); عین *aïn* (an eye), عیون *ouyoun* (eyes); یوم *yevm* (a day), ایام *éyyam* (days); طرف *taraf* (a side), اطراف *etraf* (sides).†

86. In Turkish, Arabic words are sometimes made plural by the addition of the Persian sign of the plural, ان *an*. Example, ضابط *zabit* (an officer), ضابطان *zabitan* (officers).

The Persian Mode of Forming the Plural.

87. In the Persian language there are only two numbers, the singular and the plural. If the noun be the name of a human being it forms its plural by taking the termination ان *an*. Example, مرد *merd* (a man), مردان *merdan* (men); زن *zen* (a woman), زنان *zenan* (women).

---

* See note page 7.

† In colloquial language, many of the more commonly used Arabic irregular plurals are regarded as singular, and make their plural in the Turkish way by the addition of لر *ler* or *lar*. Example, فقرا *foukera* (the poor, a poor man), فقرالر *foukeralar* (the poor); کبرا *kubera* (the great, pl. of کبیر *kébir*, a great man), کبرالر *kuberalar* (great people); وزرا *vouzera* (viziers, pl. of وزیر *vézir*), وزرالر *vuzeralar* (viziers); اولاد *evlad* (pl. of ولد *véled*, children, a child), اولادلر *evladlar* (children).

C

88. If the Persian noun be the name of an inanimate object it becomes plural by the addition of ها *ha* to the singular. Example, كل *ghiul** (a rose), كلها *ghiulha* (roses) ; درخت *dirakht* (a tree), درختها *dirakhtha* (trees).

89. The names of animals form their plural by the addition of either ان or ها. Example, اسب *assb* (a horse), اسبان *assban* or اسبها *assbha* (horses) ; شير *shir* (a lion), سيران *shiran* or شيرها *shirha* (lions).

90. Occasionally also the names of inanimate objects become plural by the addition of ان to the singular. Example, درخت *dirakht* (a tree), درختان *dirakhtan* (trees).

91. Persian names of men, animals, or things, which end in ه, form their plural by dropping that letter and taking the termination كان. Example, خواجه *khoja* (a professor), خواجكان* *khojaghian** (professors) ; مرده *mourdé* (a corpse), مردكان *mourdéghian** (corpses).

92. Persian nouns ending in ه, which form their plural by the addition of ها *ha*, omit their last letter in the plural. Example, خانه *khané* (a house), خانها *khanéha* (houses) ; كاسه *kiassé* (a cup), كاسها *kiasséha* (cups); but sometimes the ه is retained to prevent ambiguity. Example, نامها *naméha* (letters, writings), which written نامها *namha* might be mistaken for the plural of نام *nam* (a name).

EXERCISE I.

Of the house. To the man (ادم *ádám*). Of the women (*sing.* قارى *kárï*). Of the wolf. Oh, father. From the road. Of the road. Professors (*sing.* خواجه *khoja*). Of the officer (ضابط *zabit*). To the officers. To the valley. Of the valleys. Of the water. Of the boat (قايق *kayïk*). To the arrow. Arrows. Men. The men (accus.). The woman (accus.). Of the women. Words (*sing.* كلمه *kélimé*). To the words. Of the words. The road (accus.). To the road. Of the shirt. Of the trees (اغاج *ágháj*). Children (*sing.* چوجق *chojouk*).

CHAPTER III.

THE ADJECTIVE.

93. In Turkish, as in English, the adjective precedes the noun, and never varies, being the same whether it qualifies a singular or plural substantive, a

---

* See note page 7.

masculine or a feminine noun. Example, زنكين ادم *zenghin ádám* (the rich man), زنكين ادملر *zenghin ádámlar* (rich men), زنكين قارى *zenghin kári* (the rich woman) ; بيوك او *biyuk ev* (the big house), بيوك اولر *biyuk evler* (big houses). Turkish adjectives, however, not only qualify nouns, but verbs and other adjectives, and, therefore, partake not only of the nature of adjectives, but that of adverbs also. Example, فنا ادم *fena ádám* (the bad man), فنا حركت ايتمك *fena heréket etmek* (to act *badly*) ; چوق كتاب *chok kitáb* (many books), چوق فنا *chok fena* (very bad) ; كوزل يازى *ghiuzel yazi* (beautiful writing), كوزل يازمق *ghiuzel yazmak* (to write *beautifully*).

The Use of Arabic Adjectives.

94. But when Arabic adjectives are used to qualify Arabic nouns they often change in number and gender to agree with the noun, in accordance with the rules of Arabic grammar, and are placed after the noun instead of before it. Example, معلم كامل *muallim-i*-kiamil* (a perfect professor), معلمين كاملين *muallimin-i-kiamilin* (perfect professors).

95. In general an Arabic adjective is made feminine by the addition of 5 to the masculine. Example, جميل *jemil* (beautiful), جميله *jémilé* (beautiful, fem.), عظيم *azim* (great), عظيمه *azimé* (great, fem.), دائرۀ عظيمه *dairé-i-azimé* (a large circle).

96. Strange to say, however, if an Arabic adjective qualify an Arabic plural noun, it is put in the feminine singular. Example, مختلف *mukhtélif* (various), كتب مختلفه *kiutub-i-mukhtélifé* (various books) ; دوائر عظيمه *devair-i-azimé* (large circles) ; قواعد عثمانيه *kavaïd-i-ossmaniyé* (Turkish rules).

The Comparative.

97. The comparative is formed by adding the word دها *daha* (more) to the positive. Example, بيوك *biyuk* (large), دها بيوك *daha biyuk* (larger) ; كوزل *ghiuzel* (pretty), دها كوزل *daha ghiuzel* (prettier) ; فقير *fakïr* (poor), دها فقير *daha fakïr* (poorer).

98. The comparative is often expressed by putting the noun or pronoun in the ablative. Example, بندن بيوك *benden biyuk* (taller than I), بو اندن *bo andan*

---

* This *i* is put after an Arabic or Persian noun when it is *followed* by an adjective, in accordance with rules which will be given hereafter.

ايو دٍر *bou ondan iyi dir* (this is better than that), صو شرابدٍن ايو دٍر *sou sherabdan iyi dir* (water is better than wine), سٍز بندٍن فنا سٍكز *siz benden fena siniz* (you are worse than I).

The Superlative.

99. The superlative is formed by putting the word الك, or بك, before the positive.   Example, الك ايو او *en iyi ev* (the best house), الك فنا ادم *en fena ádám* (the worst man), بك زنكين *pek zenghin* (very rich), چركين *pek chirkin* (very ugly), الك كوتو *en keutu* (the worst), كتابلرك الك ايوسى *kitáblárïn en iyissi* (the best of the books).*

The Persian Comparative.

100.   Occasionally the Persian mode of forming the comparative and superlative by the addition respectively of تٍر *ter* and تٍرين *terin* to the

---

* A kind of superlative is also formed by the repetition of an adjective, as صق صق *sik sik* (very often), چوق چوق *chok chok* (very much), بتون بتون *bitun bitun* (quite), صارى صارى *sárï sárï* (very yellow).

Other superlatives are formed in a way quite peculiar to Turkish, by prefixing to certain adjectives a syllable somewhat similar in sound, commencing with the same vowel and consonants, or the same vowel.   Examples:—

اپ اچق	*áp achïk* .	. Quite open.
اپ اق	*áp ák* .	. Quite white, very white.
اپ اكسز	*áp ansïz* .	. Quite suddenly.
اقرب اقربا	*ákreb ákreba* .	. Very near relations.
بز بتون	*biz bitun* .	. Entirely.
بم بياض	*bem béyáz* .	. Very white.
بوذ بيوك	*buz biyuk* .	. Very large.
بون بوش	*bom bosh* .	. Quite empty.
پر پر پارلر	*per per parlar* .	. Very glittering.
تاز تمام	*taz támám* .	. Quite entire.
تر تب تميز	*ter teb témiz* .	. Very clean.
چر چپلاق	*cher chiplák* .	. Quite naked.
چوب چورك	*cheup churuk* .	. Quite rotten.
دوپ دوز	*deup duz* .	. Quite flat, smooth.
دپ ديرى	*dïp diri* .	. Quite alive.
سب سيجاق	*sib sïják* .	. Very hot.

positive is to be met with. Example, بر *ber* (high), برتر *berter* (higher), برترين *berterin* (highest) ; بد *bed* (bad, ugly), بدتر *bedter* (worse, uglier) ; جوان *jouvan* (young), جوانتر *juvanter* (younger), جوانترين *jouvanterin* (youngest) ; به *beh* (good), بهتر *behter* (better), بهترين *behterin* (best).

101. There is an obsolete mode of forming the comparative by adding the syllable رق or رك to the positive. Example, الجق *âlchak* (low), الجقرق *âlchakrak* (lower) ; بيوك *biyük* (big), بيوكرك *biyukrak* (bigger).

EXERCISE II.

A (بر *bir*) pretty garden (باغچه *bâghché*). My (بنم *benim*) garden is (در *dir*) prettier. Beautiful (كوزل *ghiuzel*) trees (اغاج *âghâj*). Rich men. You (سز *siz*) are (سكز *siniz*) rich, but (لكن *lakin*) my father is richer. Pretty girls (قيز *qïz, sing.*). Your (سزك *sizin*) book (كتاب *kitâb*) is good, but mine is better. The largest house. Very little (كجوك *kiuchuk*). Sensible (عقللى *âkllï*) men. Sensible women

سب سورى	*sip sivri*	. .	Very pointed, very sharp.
سم صوغق	*som soghuk*	. .	Very cold.
سم سياه	*sim siyah*	. .	Very black.
صپا (or صاپه) صاغ	*sapa sagh*	. .	Quite well, healthy.
صب صارى	*sap sârï*	. .	Quite yellow.
صب صقى	*sip sïkï*	. .	Very tight.
صام صافى	*sam sâfi*	. .	Quite pure.
طوب دولو	*top dolou*	. .	Quite full.
طوز طوغرى	*doz doghrou*	. .	Quite straight.
قپ غافل	*kâp ghâfil*	. .	Quite negligent.
قاب قالين	*kâp kâlïn*	. .	Very thick.
قاب قرانلق	*kâp kâranlïk*	. .	Quite dark.
قاب قره	*kâp kâra*	. .	Quite black.
قاب قاينار	*kâp kaïnar*	. .	Quite boiling.
قوب قورى	*koup kourou*	. .	Quite dry.
قيب قرمزى	*kip kïrmïzï*	. .	Quite red.
قوس قوجه	*koss koja*	. .	Thick and fat.
ماس ماوى	*mass mavi*	. .	Very blue.
موس مور	*moss mor*	. .	Quite dark blue.
ياپ يالكز	*yap yalïnïz*	. .	Quite alone.
يام ياش	*yam yash*	. .	Quite wet.
يم (or يپ) يشيل	*yem* (or *yep*) *yeshil*		Quite green.

(قارى *kǎrǐ, sing.*). Pretty children (چوجق *chojouk, sing.*). This child is smaller than that. Useful (فائدەلو *faïdéli*) books. The most useful book. A pretty picture (رسم *ressm*). A prettier picture. The prettiest picture. The richest man. A very small child. A very great man. A long (اوزون *ouzoun*) letter. This is longer than that. It is better to be with friends than enemies. The field (تارلا *tarla*) is quite green. Quite full. Quite dry. Officers. Professors. Trees (Persian). Better (Turkish and Persian). Best (Persian). Very often. Very thick. Quite dry. Quite green. Quite hot. Very tight. A great king. Perfect professors.

Numeral Adjectives.

102. The cardinal numeral adjectives in Turkish are as follows :—

بر	*bir*	One		اوتوز	*otouz*	Thirty
ايكى	*iki*	Two		قرق	*kǐrk*	Forty
اوچ	*uch*	Three		اللى	*elli*	Fifty
درت	*deurt*	Four		التمش	*ǎltmǐsh*	Sixty
بش	*besh*	Five		يتمش	*yetmish*	Seventy
التى	*ǎltǐ*	Six		سكسان	*seksén*	Eighty
يدى	*yédi*	Seven		طقسان	*doksan*	Ninety
سكز	*sékiz*	Eight		يوز	*yuz*	Hundred
طقوز	*dokouz*	Nine		بیك	*bin*	Thousand
اون*	*on**	Ten		یوك	*yuk*	A hundred thousand
يكرمى	*yirmi*	Twenty		ملیون	*milion*	A million.

103. The compound numeral adjectives are formed by simply putting the simple ones together. Example: Eleven, اون بر *on bir*; twelve, اون ايكى *on iki*; thirteen, اون اوچ *on uch*; fourteen, اون درت *on deurt*; fifteen, اون بش *on besh*; sixteen, اون التى *on ǎltǐ*; seventeen, اون يدى *on yédi*; eighteen, اون سكز *on sékiz*; nineteen, اون طقوز *on dokouz*; twenty-one, يكرمى بر *yirmi bir*; twenty-two, يكرمى ايكى *yirmi iki*; twenty-four, يكرمى درت *yirmi deurt*; thirty-one, اوتوز بر *otouz bir*; thirty-two, اوتوز ايكى *otouz iki*; forty-one, قرق بر *kǐrk bir*; fifty-one, اللى بر *elli bir*, &c., &c.; one hundred and fifty, يوز اللى *yuz elli*; one thousand eight hundred and seventy-nine, بیك سكز يوز يتمش طقوز *bin sékiz yuz yetmish dokouz*; five hundred and eighty-five, بش يوز سكسان بش *besh yuz seksén besh*, and so forth.

---

* Pronounced as the English word "own."

104. The Turkish cardinal numbers are indeclinable and prefixed to the substantive, which is put in the singular, as ادم ايكى اون *on iki ádám* (twelve men), عسكر بيڭ اون *on bin asker* (ten thousand soldiers), ليرا يوز اوچ *uch yuz lira* (three hundred pounds), شهر ايكى *iki shehir* (two cities), كتاب بش *besh kitáb* (five books).

105. قاچ *kach?* (how many? how much?) is the interrogative cardinal numeral. It is indeclinable and always accompanied by a noun except in the following four cases:—1st. In asking what number some one has named, as ديدى قاچ *kach dédi?* (how much did he say?) 2nd. In asking the hour, as كلدى قاچه ساعت *saat kacha geldi?* (what o'clock is it?) 3rd. In asking the price of anything, as صاتارسكز قاچه *kacha sátarsiniz?* (how much do you sell it at?) 4th. In asking the day of the month, as بوكون ايڭ قاچيدر *bou ghiun ainyin kachi dir?* (what is the day of the month to-day?)

The Arabic Numbers.

106. The Arabic cardinal numbers are occasionally used in Turkish, especially in writing, and it is therefore necessary for the Turkish student to make himself acquainted with them. We accordingly subjoin them:—

واحد	*wahid*	} One		عشره	*asheré*	Ten
احد	*ahad*			عشرين	*eshrin*	Twenty
اثنين	*essnéin*	} Two		ثلاثين	*selasin*	Thirty
اثنى	*issna*			اربعين	*erbaïn*	Forty
ثلثه	*selasé*	Three		خمسين	*khamsin*	Fifty
اربعه	*erbaa*	Four		ستين	*sittin*	Sixty
خمسه	*khamsé*	Five		سبعين	*sébin*	Seventy
سته	*sitté*	Six		ثمانين	*semanin*	Eighty
سبعه	*seba*	Seven		تسعين	*tisin*	Ninety
ثمانيه	*semanié*	Eight		مأه	*mié*	Hundred
تسعه	*tissa*	Nine		الف	*elf*	Thousand.

107. In forming compound numeral adjectives in Arabic the smaller number always precedes the larger, and و *vé* (and) is used between every number. Example, خمسين و تسع *tissa vé khamsin* (fifty-nine), و اربع erba vé erbaïn vé séman mié vé elf (one thousand الف و ميه ثمان و اربعين eight hundred and forty-four).

The Persian Numeral Adjectives.

108. The Persian numeral adjectives are also sometimes used in written Turkish, but more rarely than the Arabic. They are as follows :—

یك	*yek*	One	بیست ویك	*bisst u yek*	One and twenty
دو	*du*	Two	بیست و دو	*bisst u du*	Two ,,
سه	*séh*	Three	بیست و سه	*bisst u séh*	Three ,,
چهار	{*char* {or *chihar*	Four	سی	*si*	Thirty
پنج	*penj*	Five	چهل	*chihhil*	Forty
شش	*shésh*	Six	پنجاه	*penjah*	Fifty
هفت	*heft*	Seven	شصت	*shast*	Sixty
هشت	*hesht*	Eight	هفتاد	*heftad*	Seventy
نه	*nuh*	Nine	هشتاد	*heshtad*	Eighty
ده	*déh*	Ten	نود	*névéd*	Ninety
یازده	*yazdéh*	Eleven	صد	*sad*	Hundred
دوازده	*duvazdéh*	Twelve	دویست	*duvisst*	Two hundred
سیزده	*sizdéh*	Thirteen	سیصد	*sisad*	Three ,,
چهارده	*chardéh*	Fourteen	چهارصد	*chahr sad*	Four ,,
پانزده	*panzdéh*	Fifteen	پانصد	*pansad*	Five ,,
شانزده	*shanzdéh*	Sixteen	ششصد	*sheshsad*	Six ,,
هفتده	*heftdéh*	Seventeen	هفصد	*hefsad*	Seven ,,
هشت ده or هژده	{*hesht déh* {*hézh déh*	Eighteen	هشصد	*heshsad*	Eight ,,
نوازده	*nuvazdéh*	Nineteen	نهصد	*nuhsad*	Nine ,,
بیست	*bisst*	Twenty	هزار	*hézar*	Thousand
			دو هزار	*du hézar*	Two thousand
			پنج هزار	*penj hézar*	Five ,,

The Arabic Figures.

109. The Arabic figures have been adopted by the Turks and are given below. Although the Turks write from right to left they employ the figures exactly as we do.

1	بر	١	5	بش	٥
2	ایکی	٢	6	التی	٦
3	اوچ	٣	7	یدی	٨
4	درت	۴	8	سکز	٧

9	طقوز	۹	50	اللی	۵۰
10	اون	۱۰	60	التمش	۶۰
11	اون بر	۱۱	70	يتمش	۸۰
12	اون ايكی	۱۲	80	سكسان	۷۰
13	اون اوچ	۱۳	90	طقسان	۹۰
14	اون درت	۱۴	100	يوز	۱۰۰
15	اون بش	۱۵	101	يوز بر	۱۰۱
16	اون التی	۱۶	102	يوز ايكی	۱۰۲
17	اون يدی	۱۸	200	ايكی يوز	۲۰۰
18	اون سكز	۱۷	250	ايكی يوز اللی	۲۵۰
19	اون طقوز	۱۹	300	اوچ يوز	۳۰۰
20	يكرمی	۲۰	1,000	بيك	۱۰۰۰
21	يكرمی بر	۲۱	2,000	ايكی بيك	۲۰۰۰
30	اوتوز	۳۰	10,000	اون بيك	۱۰۰۰۰
40	قرق	۴۰	1879 بيك سكز يوز يتمش طقوز		۱۷۸۹

110. When using a numeral with a noun the Turks frequently introduce a second noun between the two, which is quite superfluous in English, but occasionally employed even by us. For example, the Turks say اوچ نفر ادم *uch néfer âdâm* (three men, literally three (*individual*) men); يوز باش قويون *yuz bâsh koyoun* (a hundred *head* of sheep); يكرمی قطعه كمی *yirmi kita ghémi* (twenty ships, literally twenty *pieces* of ships); اوچ دانه الماس *uch tané elmass* (three diamonds, literally three *berries** of diamonds); يوز پاره شهر *yuz para shehir* (a hundred cities, literally a hundred *pieces* of cities).

The Turkish Cardinal Numbers.

111. The ordinal numeral adjectives are formed by adding نجی *inji* to the cardinal numbers. Example, بر *bir* (one), برنجی *birinji* (first); ايكی (two), ايكنجی *ikinji* (second); اوچ *uch* (three), اوچنجی *uchunji* (third); درت (four), درتنجی *deurdunju* (fourth); بش (five), بشنجی *beshinji* (fifth); التی *alti* (six), التينجی *altïnjï* (sixth), and so forth.

112. First is sometimes expressed by الك *ilk* or اولكی *evvelki*.

113. The word "four," درت *deurt*, makes درتنجی *deurdunju* (fourth),

---

* The word دانه *tané* means one separate grain or unit of anything.

changing the ت into د for the sake of euphony, and its compounds do the same.   Example, اون دردنجى باب *on deurdunju bab* (the fourteenth chapter).

114. The interrogative ordinal numeral, قاچنجى *kâchĭnjĭ?* which is used to ask the numerical order of a thing, has no equivalent in English. Example, بو ادملرك قاچنجيسنى استرسكز *bou âdâmlarĭn kâchĭnjĭssĭnĭ issterseniz?* (which of these men do you want ?) ايكنجيسنى *ikinjissini* (the second).

The Arabic Ordinal Numbers.

115. The Arabic ordinal numbers are very frequently used in writing Turkish, and must, therefore, be understood by the Turkish student.   We subjoin them :—

اول	*evvel*	First	سادس	*sadis*	Sixth
ثانى	*sani*	Second	سابع	*sabi*	Seventh
ثالث	*salis*	Third	ثامن	*samin*	Eighth
رابع	*rabi*	Fourth	تاسع	*tasi*	Ninth
خامس	*khamis*	Fifth	عاشر	*ashir*	Tenth

116. The feminine of اول *evvel* is *oula,* and all the others are made feminine by simply adding *s* to the masculine.   Example, ثانيه *sanié* (second, f.), ثالثه *salissé* (third, f.), رابعه *rabié* (fourth, f.).

The Fractional Numbers.

117. The Arabic fractions are much used.   They are as follows :—

نصف	*nissf*	Half	سبع	*sub* or *subou*	A seventh
ثلث	*sulss* or *suluss*	A third	ثمن	*sumn*	An eighth
ربع	*rub* or *rubou*	A fourth	تسع	*tuss* or *tusou*	A ninth
خمس	*khoums*	A fifth	عشر	*ushr*	A tenth
سدس	*suds*	A sixth			

118. These Arabic fractional numbers up to a tenth are employed with a Turkish cardinal number as the numerator.   Example, بر نصف *bir nissf* (a half), اوچ ربع *uch rub* (three-quarters), درت سبع *deurt sub* (four sevenths), سكز عشر *sekkiz ushr* (eight-tenths).   The Arabic dual ثلثان *soulsan* is used to express two-thirds.

119. Fractions are also formed with words of purely Turkish origin,

and can only be so formed when they are higher than tenths. The denominator of the fraction is expressed by a Turkish cardinal number with the post-position سده *dé* (in) after it, and the numerator by another Turkish cardinal number which follows the other. Example, ايكيده بر *ikidé bir* (the half), التيده ايكى *áltïda iki* (two-sixths), بشده درت *beshdé deurt* (four-fifths), يكرمى درتده بش *yirmi deurtdé besh* (five twenty-fourths). Sometimes one of the words پاى *paï*, جزٔ *juz*, حصه *hissé*, قسم *kïssm*, all meaning a portion, is introduced. Example, يكرمى پايده سكز پاى *yirmi païdé sikkiz paï* (eight-twentieths, literally eight parts in twenty parts).

120. There are three Turkish words for half, viz., يارم *yarim*, بچوق *bouchouk*, and يارى *yarï*. يارم *yarim* is used before a noun like an adjective. Example, يارم ساعت *yarim saat* (half an hour), يارم الما *yarim elma* (half an apple), يارم اكمك *yarim ekmek* (half a loaf). بچوق *bouchouk* is always used in conjunction with a cardinal number. Example, بر بچوق *bir bouchouk* (one and a half), ايكى بچوق *iki bouchouk* (two and a half), اوچ بچوق *uch bouchouk* (three and a half), درت بچوق *deurt bouchouk* (four and a half), بش بچوق *besh bouchouk* (five and a half), and so on. يارى *yarï* is used like a noun, corresponding to the French word *moitié*. Example, المانك يارىسى *elmanin yarïssï* (the half of the apple), يارىسندن زياده *yarïsinden ziadé* (more than the half of it).

121. The Persian fractional number چاريك *charyek* (a quarter), pronounced *chéirek* by the Osmanlis, is used in Turkish to express not only a quarter in general, but also a quarter of an hour. Example, اوچ چاريك *uch chéirek* (three quarters of an hour).

122. When a whole number and a fraction (excepting half) are used together, the conjunction و (and) or the preposition ايله *ilé* (with) is put between them. Example, ايكى و برسبع *iki vé bir sub* (two and a seventh), or ايكى ايله برسبع *iki ilé bir sub* (two and a seventh); درت و بر ربع *deurt vé bir rub* (four and a fourth), or درت ايله بر ربع *deurt ilé bir rub.*

123. In the above case, if the fraction be expressed by Turkish numbers, بر *br* followed by ك *k* or نك *nk* is introduced after و or ايله. Example, التى ايله برك يديده اوچى *alti ilé birin yédidé uchu* (six and three-sevenths).

Distributive Numerals.

124. Distributive numerals are formed by adding ر *ér* to the cardinal numbers ending in a consonant and شر *shér* or *shar* to those ending in a

vowel. Example, برر *birér* (one a-piece), ايكيشر *ikishér* (two a-piece), التيشر
altishér (six a-piece), يديشر *yédishér* (seven a-piece), يكرميشر *yirmishér*
(twenty a-piece).

125. درت makes دردر *deurdér*, changing the ت into a د. Example,
دردر *deurdér* (four a-piece), اوتوز دردر *otouz deurdér* (thirty-four a-piece).

126. When there are hundreds or thousands in the number the ر or the شر
is put after the numeral expressing the number of hundreds or thousands
and nothing is put after يوز or بيك Example, بشر يوز *beshér yuz* (five
hundred a-piece), بيك ايكيشر يوز *bin ikishér yuz* (one thousand two
hundred a-piece), بشر بيك *besher bin* (five thousand a-piece). The ر is
never added to يوز except when it expresses a hundred alone. Example,
يوزر *yuzér* (a hundred a-piece).

127. In numbers composed of hundreds and smaller quantities ر or
شر is added to the word stating the number of hundreds and also at the
end of the whole number. Example, دردر يوز اللى التيشر *deurdér yuz elli
altishér* (four hundred and fifty-six a-piece).

128. When there are thousands, hundreds, and other numbers, ر or
شر is added to the word stating the number of thousands and to the other
two. Example, بشر بيك التيشر يوز اللى برر *bésher bin áltïshér yuz elli birér*
(five thousand six hundred and fifty-one a piece).

129. One by one, two by two, &c., are expressed by برر برر *birér birér,*
ايكيشر ايكيشر *ikishér ikishér*, and so forth.

EXERCISE III.

Three horses (ات *át*), five sheep (قويون *koyoun*), and seven cows (اينك *inek*).
How many chapters are (در *dir*) there (وار *var*) in this (بو *bou*) book? Forty
chapters. Read (اوقو *okou*) the second. What is the day of the month? The
2nd. What do you sell (صاتارسكز *sátarseniz*) this at? Five piastres (غروش
ghroosh). Ten thousand five hundred and sixty-four men. Five head of sheep.
Thirteen villages (كوى *keui*). Two pearls (اينجو *inji*). Two hundred and fifty-
four ships (كمى *ghémi*). The third class (صنف *sinif*). The second day (كون
ghium). The thousand and one nights. The fourth regiment (الاى *álay**). Two-

---

* N.B.—Always pronounce *ay* as *aï* in French.

and-a-half piastres. Five pounds (ليرا *lira*) and a-half. Three-quarters of an hour. Five-sixths. Eleven-twentieths. Two-thirds. Give (ویر *ver*) them (انلره *onlara*) four apples a-piece. Those men received fifty pounds a-piece. Half an hour. The year (سنه *sené*) one thousand eight hundred and seventy-nine. The best scholar (شاكرد *shagird*) will get (اله‌جق *álajak*) twenty pounds. I waited (بكلدم *beklédim*) an hour and a-half.

CHAPTER IV.

PRONOUNS.

Personal Pronouns.

130. The personal pronouns are as follows :—

	Singular.			Plural.	
بن	*ben*	I	بز	*biz* (or بزلر *bizler*)	We
سن	*sen*	Thou	سز	*siz*	You
او	*o*	He	انلر	*onlar*	They

They are thus declined :—

First Person.

Nom.	بن	*ben*, I	بز	*biz* (or بزلر *bizler*), we
Gen.	بنم	*benim*, of me	بزم	*bizim*, of us
Dat.	بكا	*bana*, to me	بزه	*bizé*, to us
Acc.	بنی	*béni*, me	بزی	*bizi*, us
Abl.	بندن	*benden*, from me	بزدن	*bizden*, from us

Second Person.

Nom.	سن	*sen*, thou	سز	*siz* (or سزلر *sizler*), you
Gen.	سنك	*senin*, of thee	سزك	*sizin*, of you
Dat.	سنا	*sana*, to thee	سزه	*sizé*, to you
Acc.	سنی	*seni*, thee	سزی	*sizi*, you
Abl.	سندن	*senden*, from thee	سزدن	*sizden*, from you

Third Person.

Singular.		Plural.	
Nom.	او *o*, he, she, it	انلر *onlar*, they	
Gen.	انك *onoun*,* of him, of her, of it	انلرك *onlarïn*, of them	
Dat.	انا *ana*, to him, to her, to it	انلره *onlara*, to them	
Acc.	انى *onou*,* him, her, it	انلرى *onlarï*, them	
Abl.	اندن *ondan*,* from him, from her, from it	انلردن *onlardan*, from them.	

131. Instead of بز *biz* (we) and سز *siz* (you), بزلر *bizler* and سزلر *sizler* are sometimes used. They are even so used, out of politeness, instead of بن and سن.

132. The genitive of the above pronouns is sometimes used pleonastically before nouns with possessive pronouns. Example, بنم كتابم *benim kitábim* (my book, literally, *of me* my book), سزك اوكز *sizin eviniz* (your house, literally, *of you* your house).

كندى *kendi*, self.

133. Self is expressed by كندو *kendou*, or كندى *kendi*. It is sometimes accompanied by the possessive pronouns. Example :—

Singular.		Plural.	
كندم *kendim*, myself		كندومز *kendimiz*, ourselves	
كندك *kendin*, thyself		كندوكز *kendiniz*, yourselves	
كندى or كنديسى *kendi* or *kendissi*, himself, herself, itself		كندولر or كندولرى *kendiler* or *kendileri*, themselves.	

134. But كندو *kendou* alone can be used, without distinction of gender, for all persons of the singular and plural, when there can be no doubt as to the person it represents. Example, كندو كلورم *kendou ghelerim* (I will come myself), كندو ياپدى *kendou yapdïk* (we did it ourselves).

135. كندو is also used to express the English word " own." Example, كندو كتابم *kendou* (or *kendi*) *kitábïm* (my own book), كندو انام *kendou anam* (my own mother), كندو مملكتكز *kendou memléketiniz* (your own country).

---

* انك انى اندن انلر and انلر are also sometimes pronounced *ánïn, ánï, ándan,* and *ánlar.*

The Demonstrative Pronouns.

136. The Turkish demonstrative pronouns are بو *bou,* شو *shou* (this), and او *or* اول *ol* (that). They are thus declined :—

بو *bou,* this.

	Singular.		Plural.
Nom.	بو *bou,* this	بونلر	*bounlar,* these
Gen.	بونك *bounoun,* of this	بونلرك	*bounlarïn,* of these
Dat.	بوكا *bouna,* to this	بونلره	*bounlara,* to these
Acc.	بونی *bounou,* this	بونلری	*bounlarï,* these
Abl.	بوندن *boundan,* from this	بونلردن	*bounlardan,* from these

شو *shou,* this.

Nom.	شو *shou,* this	شونلر	*shounlar,* these
Gen.	شونك *shounoun,* of this	شونلرك	*shounlarïn,* of these
Dat.	شوكا *shouna,* to this	شونلره	*shounlara,* to these
Acc.	شونی *shounou,* this	شونلری	*shounlarï,* these
Abl.	شوندن *shoundan,* from this	شونلردن	*shounlardan,* from these

او *o,* or اول *ol,* that.

Nom.	او *o,* or اول *ol,* that	انلر	*onlar,* they
Gen.	اونك *onoun,** of that	انلرك	*onlarïn,* of them
Dat.	اکا *ana,* to that	انلره	*onlara,* to them
Acc.	انی *onou,* that	انلری	*onlarï,* them
Abl.	اندن *ondan,* from that	انلردن	*onlardan,* from them.

137. The word اشبو *ishbou* is sometimes used for بو, but only as an adjective, and it never undergoes any change.

Arabic Pronouns.

138. The Arabic pronouns هذا *haza* m., هذه *hazihi* f. (this), and ذلك *zaliké* (that), and the Persian این *in* (this), and آن *an* (that), are occasionally employed in written Turkish.

In Turkish also sometimes, but generally in writing only, one meets with the Arabic personal pronoun of the third person in certain Arabic expres-

---

* See note page 30.

sions adopted by the Osmanlis. To properly understand written Turkish it is requisite to know them. They are as follows :—

Musculine Singular.

ه *hou* or *hi* (according to the rules of Arabic grammar), him, it ; his, its.

Feminine Singular.

ها *ha*, her.

Dual Masculine and Feminine.

هما *huma* or *hima*, them (two).

Plural Masculine.

هم *hum* or *him*, them.

The Interrogative Pronouns.

139. The interrogative pronouns are كم or كيم *kim* (who?), نه *né* (what?), and تنغى *kanghi,* pronounced *hanghi* (which?). They are thus declined :—

Nom.	كيم	*kim,* who ?
Gen.	كيمك	*kimin,* of whom ? whose ?
Dat.	كيمه	*kimé,* to whom ?
Acc.	كيمى	*kimi,* whom ?
Abl.	كيمدن	*kimden,* from whom ?

Nom.	نه	*né,* what ?
Gen.	نه نك	*nénin,* of what ?
Dat.	نيه	*néyé,* to what ?
Acc.	نه يى	*néyi,* what ?
Abl.	نه دن	*néden,* from what ?

Nom.	تنغى	*hanghĭ,* which*
Gen.	تنغينك	*hanghĭnĭn,* of which
Dat.	تنغنه	*hanghĭna,* to which
Acc.	تنغينى	*hanghĭnĭ,* which
Abl.	تنغيندن	*hanghĭndan,* from which

* The strict pronunciation is *kánghĭ,* but it is little used.

كِيم kim and قنغى hánghǐ as Nouns.

140. نه نه, كِيم and قنغى are sometimes used as nouns, and then form their plural like nouns. In this case the ه of نه is generally omitted in the derivatives of that word. Example, كِيملر kimler (what men? who?), نه né (what?), نلر néler (what things?), قنغيلر hanghilar (which? *lesquels* in French).

141. كِيم is used also sometimes to express "some." Example, كِيمِز كتدى كِيمِز كتمدى kimimiz ghitdi kimimiz ghitmédi (some of us went, some of us did not go).

142. The word نصل nassl sometimes means "what kind of?" and then may be considered as an interrogative pronoun. Example, نصل آدم در nassl ádám dǐr (what sort of a man is he?) بو نصل كتاب در bou nassl kitáb dǐr (what sort of a book is this?). نصل nassl in this sense corresponds to the German *was für?*

The Pronominal Affixes.

143. Pronominal affixes are peculiar to Turkish and cognate languages, and are used instead of our possessive pronouns. They consist of syllables added to the end of nouns, have the value of pronouns, and cannot stand alone. These affixes are either possessive or relative.

The Possessive Affixes.

144. The possessive affixes correspond to our possessive pronouns.

م m or *im,* *um* or *oum**	my,	as بابام	*bábám,* my father
ك n or *in,* *un* or *oun*	thy,	„ اوك	*evin,* thy house
ى i or *u, ou*	} his, hers, or its {	قلمى	*kalemi,* his, hers, or its pen
سى *si* or *su, sou* (after a vowel)		اناسى	*anassǐ,* his, hers, or its mother
مز *miz, mouz,* or *imiz* or *oumouz* our,	as مركيمز	*murekkebimiz,* our ink
كز *niz, nouz,* or *iniz* or *ounouz* your,	„ اوكز	*eviniz,* your house
لرى *leri* or *lari,*	their, „ اتلرى	*átlarǐ,* their horse.

---

* Euphonic Pronunciation of the Possessive Affixes.

The possessive affixes are pronounced *im, in, i, imiz, iniz, leri,* if the word to which they are added end in a consonant, as اومز *evimiz* (our house), اوكز *eviniz* (your house), اوى *evi* (his, her, its house); and, consequently, مز and كز are some-

Declension of a Noun with a Pronominal Affix.

145. A noun with one of the pronominal affixes is declinable as follows:—

	Singular.		Plural.
Nom.	كتابم *kitábĭm,* my book	كتابلرم *kitáblarĭm,* my books
Gen.	كتابمك *kitábĭmĭn,* of my book	كتابلرمك *kitáblarĭmĭn,* of my books
Dat.	كتابمه *kitábĭma,* to my book	كتابلرمه *kitáblarĭma,* to my books
Acc.	كتابمى *kitábĭmĭ,* my book	كتابلرمى *kitáblarĭmĭ,* my books
Abl.	كتابمدن *kitábĭmdan,* from my book	كتابلرمدن *kitáblarĭmdan,* from my books

	Singular.		Plural.
Nom.	اغاجى *ághájĭ,* his or her tree	اغاجلر *ághájlarĭ,* his or her trees
Gen.	اغاجنك *ághájĭnĭn,* of his or her tree	اغاجلرينك *ághájlarĭnĭn,* of his or her trees
Dat.	اغاجنه *ághájĭna,* to his or her tree	اغاجلرينه *ághájlarĭna,* to his or her trees
Acc.	اغاجنى *ághájĭnĭ,* his or her tree	اغاجلرينى *ághájlarĭnĭ,* his or her trees
Abl.	اغاجندن *ághájĭndan,* from his or her tree	اغاجلريندن *ághájlarĭndan,* from his or her trees.

times written يمز and أيكز, as پدريمز *péderimiz* (our father), پدريكز *péderiniz* (your father). But, if the preceding predominant vowel in the word be *ou* or *o*, although written the same, they are pronounced *oum, oun, ou, oumouz, ounouz, lari* respectively, as دوستم *dosstoum* (my friend), دوستكز *dosstounouz* (your friend). If the word to which they are appended end in a vowel, they have then only the value of the letters *m, n, si, miz, niz, leri*, as قوزوم *kouzoum* (my lamb), قوزوك *kouzoun* (thy lamb), قوزوسى *kouzousou* (his, her lamb); كديسى *kédissi* (his, her, cat), &c. Remark also that سى is pronounced *sou*, مز *mouz*, كز *nouz*, if the predominant vowel be *ou* or *o*. On the same principle of euphony, if the predominant vowel in the word be *eu* or *u*, the vowel of the possessive affixes is pronounced *u* to agree with it, as كوزك *gheuzun* (thy eye), كوزى *gheuzu* (his eye); يوزك *yuzun* (thy face), يوزى *yuzu* (his face). See page 11 "Laws of Euphony in Pronouncing Turkish."

When the word to which the possessive affixes are attached terminates in اى or وى it must be borne in mind that the ى is in that case not a vowel but a consonant, corresponding to our English *y*. Hence بوى *boï* or *boy*, makes بويم *boyim* (my stature), بويك *boyin* (thy stature), بوىى *boyi* (his, her, stature), &c.; پاى *paï* or *pay*, makes پايم *payim* (my share), پايك *payin* (thy share), پاىى *payi* (his, her, share), &c.

146. After the affixes of the third person, the post-positions ﻩ and ﺱ become ﻥﻩ and ﻰﻧ, and ﻥ is inserted in the ablative.* Example :—

	Singular.			Plural.
Nom.	ﺍﻧﺎﺳﻰ *anassï,* his or her mother		ﺍﻧﺎﻟﺮﻯ *analarï,* their mother
Gen.	ﺍﻧﺎﺳﻴﻨﻚ *anassïnïn,* of his or her mother		ﺍﻧﺎﻟﺮﻳﻨﻚ *analarïnïn,* of their mother
Dat.	ﺍﻧﺎﺳﻴﻨﻪ *anassïna,* to his or her mother		ﺍﻧﺎﻟﺮﻳﻨﻪ *analarïna,* to their mother
Acc.	ﺍﻧﺎﺳﻴﻨﻰ *anassïnï,* his or her mother		ﺍﻧﺎﻟﺮﻳﻨﻰ *analarïnï,* their mother
Abl.	ﺍﻧﺎﺳﻴﻨﺪﻥ *anassïndan,* from his or her mother		ﺍﻧﺎﻟﺮﻧﺪﻥ *analarïndan,* from their mother

Nom.	ﻛﻤﻴﺴﻰ *ghémissi,* his or her ship		ﻛﻤﻴﻠﺮﻯ *ghémileri,* their ship
Gen.	ﻛﻤﻴﺴﻴﻨﻚ *ghémisinin,* of his or her ship		ﻛﻤﻴﻠﺮﻳﻨﻚ *ghémilerinin,* of their ship
Dat.	ﻛﻤﻴﺴﻴﻨﻪ *ghémisiné,* to his or her ship		ﻛﻤﻴﻠﺮﻳﻨﻪ *ghémileriné,* to their ship
Acc.	ﻛﻤﻴﺴﻴﻨﻰ *ghémisiné,* his or her ship		ﻛﻤﻴﻠﺮﻳﻨﻰ *ghémilerini,* their ship
Abl.	ﻛﻤﻴﺴﻴﻨﺪﻥ *ghémisinden,* from his or her ship		ﻛﻤﻴﻠﺮﻧﺪﻥ *ghémilerinden,* from their ship.

---

* In the same way, for euphony's sake, if ﻩﺩ *dé* or *da* (in) be added to a word with the affixes of the third person, that particle must be preceded by a ﻥ ; as, ﺍﻭﻧﺪﻩ *evindé* (in his house), ﺍﻭﻟﺮﻧﺪﻩ *evlerindé* (in their house) ; ﻛﺘﺎﺑﻨﺪﻩ *kitâbïnda* (in his book), ﻛﺘﺎﺑﻠﺮﻧﺪﻩ *kitâblarïnda* (in their book). For such cases the letter ﺱ, indicating his, hers, its, is generally left out, but the sound of *i* is always preserved. The ﺱ also can be omitted in the ablative of a noun followed by the possessive affixes of the third person, as ﻛﺘﺎﺑﻨﺪﻥ *kitâbïndan* (from his book), ﻛﺘﺎﺑﻠﺮﻧﺪﻥ *kitâblarïndan* (from their books).

Most words of Turkish origin ending in ﻕ change that letter into ﻍ before the pronominal affixes. Example, ﺟﻮﺟﻖ *chojouk* (child), ﺟﻮﺟﻐﻢ *chojoughoum* (my child), ﺟﻮﺟﻐﻚ *chojoughoun* (thy child), ﺟﻮﺟﻐﻰ *chojoughou* (his or her child), ﺟﻮﺟﻐﻤﺰ *chojoughoumouz* (our child), ﺟﻮﺟﻐﻜﺰ *chojoughounouz* (your child) ; ﺑﺎﻟﻖ *bâlïk* (a fish), ﺑﺎﻟﻐﻢ *bâlïghïm* (my fish), ﺑﺎﻟﻐﻰ *bâlïghï* (his or her fish). But the ﻕ remains unchanged before ﻟﺮﻯ as ﺟﻮﺟﻘﻠﺮﻯ *chojouklari* (their child), ﺑﺎﻟﻘﻠﺮﻯ *bâlïk-lari* (their fish). In the same way, if the word end with a ﻙ, that letter is

147. When the word صو *sou* (water) takes any of the possessive affixes a س is put between it and the affix, except in the third person plural. Example :—

صویم *souyoum*, my water		صویمز *souyoumouz*, our water	
صویك *souyoun*, thy water		صویکز *souyounouz*, your water	
صویی *souyou*, his or her water		صولری *soularï*, their water.	

148. When any ambiguity is possible the genitive of the personal pronoun is used as well as the possessive affix. For example, اولری *evleri* might be understood either as his houses or their house. To make the meaning quite clear, if the idea to be conveyed be " his houses," انك should be added, and the phrase would then run انك اولری *ánïn evleri*, about which no mistake is possible.

The Relative Pronominal Affix کی *ki.*

149. The relative pronominal affix is کی *ki* (*that of, that which, which*), corresponding to *celui de, celle de,* in French, which sometimes partakes of the nature of an adjective and sometimes of a noun. It is used for all genders. It is attached to nouns and pronouns in two ways :—

1st. By being placed after the genitive form of the noun or pronoun. Thus :—ادمکی *ádámïnki* (that of the man, or the man's, or what belongs to the man), قرنداشکی *karndashïnki* (that of the brother, or the brother's, or what belongs to the brother). Example, کتابم ایو در لکن خواجهنکی دها ایو در *kitábïm iyi dir lakin khojaninki daha iyi dir* (my book is good, but that of the professor, or the professor's, is better). The separate possessive pronouns are accordingly formed by the aid of this particle. Thus, بنمکی *benimki* is (mine), سنکی *seninki* (thine), انکی *ánïnki* (his, hers, its), بزمکی *bizimki* (ours), سزکی *sizinki* (yours), انلرکی *anlerinki* (theirs). Example, کتابم ایو در لکن سزکی اسکی در *kitábïm iyi dir lakin sizinki esski dir* (my book

pronounced like *g* or *y* instead of *k*, and if it end in ت that letter is changed into د before the affixes; as کورك *ghevrek* (biscuit), کورکم *ghevréyim* (my biscuit), کورکمز *ghevréyimiz* (our biscuit) ; کوملك *ghieumlek* (shirt), کوملکم *ghieumléyim* (my shirt), کوملکك *ghieumléyin* (thy shirt), کوملکی *ghieumléyi* (his shirt). The words ' یوك *yuk* (a load), کوت *keuk* (a root), and کورت *kieurk* (a fur) are exceptions to this rule. Hence, کورکم *kieurkum* (my fur), یوکی *yuku* (his load).

is good, but yours is old); سزك الماكز طاتلو در لكن بنمكى اكشى در *sizin elmaniz tâtlï dïr lakin benimki ekshi dïr* (your apple is sweet, but mine is sour).

2nd. By being placed after the preposition دﻩ *dé* (in). Thus, افندﯾﺪﻩﮐﻰ *efendidéki* (that of the gentleman, the gentleman's, that which the gentleman has), صﻧﺪﻗﺪﻩﮐﻰ *sândïkdéki* (that which is in the box), بﻧﺪﻩﮐﻰ *bendéki* (that which is in me, or in my possession).

150. This pronoun is declined like a substantive, when it is used as such. Example:—

	Singular.		Plural.
Nom.	بنمكى *benimki,* mine	بنمكيلر *benimkiler,* mine (the things I possess)
Gen.	بنمكنك *benimkinin,* of mine	بنمكيلرك *benimkilerin,* of mine (of the things I possess)
Dat.	بنمكنه *benimkiné,* to mine	بنمكيلره *benimkileré,* to mine (to the things I possess)
Acc.	بنمكنى *benimkini,* mine	بنمكيلرى *benimkileri,* mine (the things I possess)
Abl.	بنمكندن *benimkinden,* from mine.	بنمكيلردن *benimkilerden,* from mine (from the things I possess).

151. The pronoun is used in combination with a noun without any preposition to form certain adverbial expressions. Example, بو كونكى *bou ghiunki* (that of day, to-day's), دونكى *dounki* (yesterday's, that of yesterday), صباحكى *sabahki* (that of the morning, or the morning's), بو كونكى غزته *bou ghiunki ghazéta* (to-day's newspaper), دونكى حوادث *dounki hawadiss* (yesterday's news).

152. كى *ki* and كيلر *kiler* never vary in their pronunciation for the sake of euphony.

EXERCISE IV.

Who is your friend (دوست *dost*)? Whom did you (كوردكز *gheurdunuz*) see? My father and brother are ill (كيفسز *kéifsiz*). What is your name (اسم *issm*)? This is my own house. Whose house is that? It is my brother's. These flowers are all pretty. Which of them do you prefer (ترجيح ايدرسكز *terjih edérsiniz*)? Give me your knife (بيچاق *bïchâk*) and take (ال *âl*) mine. My knife is sharper (كسكين *kesskin*) than yours. What is the name of your ship? What do you (استرسكز *isstersiniz*) want? He wrote (يازدى *yâzdï*) a letter (مكتوب *mektoub*) to his mother (انا *ana*). What sort of a man is the Professor? He is more learned (معلوماتلو *maloumatli*) than I. You are taller than he. Have you read to-day's newspaper? Do you know what is in the box? Do you know the name of this? What is that? Who is that lady (حانم – *hanim*)?

The Relative Pronoun.

153. In one sense there is no relative pronoun in the original Turkish equivalent to who, which, or that. In English such relatives are always accompanied by a verb, and in Turkish the active or passive participle of the verb expresses both the relative and the verb. This is one of the most curious peculiarities of the Turkish language, and one which foreigners find great difficulty in mastering. Thus, the man who writes is expressed by ادم یازان *yazan ádám*, literally, the writing man; the man you saw, کوردیککز ادم *ghieurduyunuz ádám*, literally, the your having seen man, &c. Still, in vulgar Turkish, the Persian relative pronoun که *ki* (who, which, that) is often used, and the above sentences would be rendered thus, ادم که یازار *ádám ki yazar* (the man who writes), ادم که انی کوردکز *ádám ki ani ghieurdunuz* (the man whom you saw, literally, the man who (him) you saw). This way of speaking or writing, although understood, is extremely inelegant, and quite contrary to the spirit of the Turkish language. To express the dative, genitive, accusative, and ablative, those cases of the pronoun اول are added, and hence که may be said to be declinable as follows:—

که *ki*, who, which, that.

Singular.	Plural.
Nom. که *ki*, who, which, that	که *ki*, who, which, that
Gen. که انک *ki onoun*, of whom, of which, whose	که انلرک *ki onlarïn*, whose, of whom, of which
Dat. که اکا *ki ana*, to whom, to which	که انلره *ki anlara*, to whom, to which
Acc. که انی *ki onou*, whom, which, that	که انلری *ki anlarï*, who, which, that
Abl. که اندن *ki ondan*, from whom, from which	که انلردن *ki anlardan*, from whom, from which

CHAPTER V.

THE VERB.

154. In Turkish the verbs are of two kinds, simple and compound. When simple they are of Turkish origin, when compound they consist of some Arabic or Persian word and one of the auxiliaries ايتمك *etmek,* ايلمك *éilémek,* or قيلمق *kilmak* (all meaning "to do" or "make"), or اولمق *olmak* (to be, or to become).

The Turkish Infinitive.

155. The simple Turkish infinitives always end either in مك *mek* or مق *mak,* as اوقومق *okoumak* (to read), كلمك *ghelmek* (to come), سومك *sevmek* (to love), &c. If you remove this termination مك or مق, you have the root of the verb, which is also the second person singular of the imperative. Example, يازمق *yazmak* (to write), ياز *yaz* (write thou); يوزمك *yuzmek* (to swim), يوز *yuz* (swim thou); كلمك *ghelmek* (to come), كل *ghel* (come thou); سومك *sevmek* (to love), سو *sev* (love thou).

156. By adding to the root of the verb the termination مكلك *meklik* or مقلق *maklik,* or مه *mé,* two other substantive infinitives or verbal nouns are obtained. Example:—

> سومك   *sevmek,* to love.
> سومكلك   *sevmeklik,* to love, loving or the action of loving.
> سومه   *sevmé,* to love, loving or the action of loving.

157. By putting مه *mé* or ما *ma* between the root of the verb and the termination the negative form of the verb is obtained. Example, كلمك *ghelmek* (to come), كلممك *ghelmémek* (not to come); سومك *sevmek* (to love), سوممك *sevmémek* (not to love); يازمق *yazmak* (to write), يازمامق *yazmamak* (not to write).

158. The infinitive forms given above (see 156) can all be declined like substantives when used as such, but they have no plural, and the first form ending in مك or مق has no genitive.

First Form.

Nom.	سومك *sevmek,*	to love, loving
Gen.	Wanting	
Dat.	سومكه *sevméyé,*	to love, to loving
Acc.	سومكى *sevméyi,*	to love, loving

Nom.	يازمق *yazmak,*	to write
Gen.	Wanting	
Dat.	يازمغه *yazmagha,*	to write, to writing
Acc.	يازمغى *yazmaghĭ,*	to write, writing

Second Form.

Nom. سومكلك *sevmeklik,* to love, loving, or the action of loving
Gen. سومكلكك *sevmekliyin,* of loving, &c.
Dat. سومكلكه *sevmekliyé,* to loving
Acc. سومكلكى *sevmekliyi,* loving

Nom. يابمقلق *yapmaklĭk,* to do, doing, or the action of doing
Gen. يابمقلغك *yapmaklĭghĭn,* of doing, &c.
Dat. يابمقلغه *yapmaklĭgha,* to doing
Acc. يابمقلغى *yapmaklĭghĭ,* doing

Third Form.

Nom. كلمه *ghelmé,* to come, coming, or the action of coming
Gen. كلمانك *ghelménin,* of coming
Dat. كلميه *ghelméyé,* to coming
Acc. كلمهيى *ghelméyi,* coming

Nom. يازمه *yazma,* to write, writing, or the action of writing
Gen. يازمانك *yazmanĭn,* of writing
Dat. يازميه *yazmaya,* to writing
Acc. يازمهيى *yazmayĭ,* writing.

159. The two substantive infinitive forms or verbal nouns ending in مكلك *meklik,* مقلق *maklik,* or مه *mé* can take the possessive affixes after them. Example :—

1st person singular		سومكلكم *sevmekliyim,*	my loving
2nd	,,	سومكلكك *sevmekliyin,*	thy loving
3rd	,,	سومكلكى *sevmekliyi,*	his, her, or its loving

1st person plural	سومكلكمز	*sevmekliyimiz*, our loving
2nd ,,	سومكلكز	*sevmekliyiniz*, your loving
3rd ,,	سومكلكلرى	*sevmeklikleri*, their loving

1st person singular	يابمقلغم	*yapmaklïghïm*, my doing
2nd ,,	يابمقلغك	*yapmaklïghïn*, thy doing
3rd ,,	يابمقلغى	*yapmaklïghi*, his, her, or its doing
1st person plural	يابمقلغمز	*yapmaklïghïmïz*, our doing
2nd ,,	يابمقلغكز	*yapmaklïghïnïz*, your doing
3rd ,,	يابمقلرى	*yapmaklarï*, their doing

1st person singular	سومام	*sevmém*, my loving
2nd ,,	سوماك	*sevmén*, thy loving
3rd ,,	سومسى	*sevméssi*, his, her, or its loving
1st person plural	سومامز	*sevméniz*, our loving
2nd ,,	سومكز	*sevméniz*, your loving
3rd ,,	سوملرى	*sevméleri*, their loving

1st person singular	قازمام	*kázmam*, my digging
2nd ,,	قازماك	*kázman*, thy digging
3rd ,,	قازماسى	*kázmassï*, his, her, or its digging
1st person plural	قازمامز	*kázmamïz*, our digging
2nd ,,	قازمكز	*kázmanïz*, your digging
3rd ,,	قازملرى	*kázmalarï*, their digging.

The Causal Form of the Verb.

160. By adding در *or* ت to the root of a verb another verb is formed of a *causal* nature, or if the original verb be passive it is made active. Example, يازمق *yazmak* (to write), يازدرمق *yazdïrmak* (to cause some one else to write); باقمق *bákmak* (to look), باقدرمق *bákdirmak* (to cause some one to look); سونمك *sevinmek* (to rejoice), سوندرمك *sevindirmek* (to cause to rejoice). ت is added when the roots of the verb end with a vowel. Example, اريمك *erimek* (to melt), اريتمك *eritmek* (to cause to melt); سويلمك *suwéylémek* (to speak), سويلتمك *suwéyletmek* (to cause to speak). ديمك *démek* (to say), قومق *komak* (to put, place), and يمك *yémek* (to eat) are exceptions, as they make ديدرمك *dédirmek*, قودرمق *kodourmak*, and ييدرمك *yédirmek*.

ت is also used when the root of the original verb ends either in ل or ر, if the root contain more than two consonants. Example, كتورمك *ghettirmek* (to bring), كتورتمك *ghettirtmek* (to cause some one else to bring); اينجلمك *injelmek* (to grow thin), اينجلتمك *injeltmek* (to cause some one to grow thin); ترلمك *térlémek* (to perspire), ترلتمك *terletmek* (to cause to perspire).

161. There are some verbs, however, which do not follow these rules, such as—

كچمك	*gechmek*, to pass	كچرمك	*gechirmek*, to cause to pass
بتمك	*bitmek*, to finish, to grow	بتورمك	*bitirmek*, to finish, to cause to grow
قاچمق	*kâchmak*, to run away	قاچرمق	*kâchirmak*, to cause to run away
قالقمق	*kâlkmak*, to get up	قالديرمق	*kâldirmak*, to remove
شاشمق	*shashmak*, to be astonished	شاشرمق	*shashirmak*, to astonish
اوچمق	*ouchmak*, to fly	اوچورمق	*ouchourmak*, to cause to fly
ياتمق	*yatmak*, to lie down	ياترمق	*yatirmak*, to cause to lie down
چيقمق	*chikmak*, to go or come out	چيقارمق	*chikarmak*, to cause to go or come out
كورمك	*gheurmek*, to see	كوسترمك	*ghiusstermek*, to show
ايچمك	*ichmek*, to drink	ايچرمك	*ichirmek*, to cause to drink
قوبمق	*kopmak*, to break (*v.n.*)	قوبارمق	*koparmak*, to break (*v.a.*)
ارتمق	*artmak*, to increase (*v.n.*)	ارترمق	*artirmak*, to increase (*v.a.*)
باتمق	*bâtmak*, to sink (*v.n.*)	باترمق	*bâtirmak*, to cause to sink
پشمك	*pishmek*, to cook (*v.n.*)	پشرمك	*pishirmek*, to cook (*v.a.*)
دوشمك	*dushmek*, to fall	دوشرمك	*dushurmek*, to cause to fall
طوغمق	*doghmak*, to be born	طوغرمق	*doghourmak*, to give birth to
اوكرنمك	*eughrenmek*, to learn	اوكرتمك	*eughretmek*, to teach
دويمق	*douïmak*, to feel, to hear	دويورمق	*douyourmak*, to cause to feel or hear.

162. An active verb, or a verb which has been converted into one, according to the above rule, may become doubly and even triply active or causal by adding ت to those which had taken در, and در to those which had taken ت. Example :—

اوطورمق	*otourmak*, to sit	سومك	*sevmek*, to love
اوطورتمق	*otourtmak*, to cause to sit	سودرمك	*sevdirmek*, to cause to love
اوطورتدورمق	*otourtdourmak*, to cause to cause to sit	سودرتمك	*sevdirtmek*, to cause to cause to love.

Reflective and Passive Verbs.

163. A verb is made either reflective or passive by the addition of ن to the root. Example, اوقومق *okoumak* (to read), اوقونمق *okounmak* (to be read) ; يمك *yémek* (to eat), ينمك *yénmek* (to be eaten) ; قومق *komak* (to place), قونمق *konmak* (to be placed) ; بولمق *boulmak* (to find), بولنمق *boulounmak* (to find one's self).

164. Passive verbs are formed by adding ل or ن to the root of a primitive verb. Example, اورمق *wourmak* (to strike), اورلمق *wouroulmak* (to be struck) ; سومك *sevmek* (to love), سولمك *sevilmek* (to be loved) ; اتمق *âtmak* (to throw), اتلمق *âtïlmak* (to be thrown), &c. ن is used when the root of the primitive verb ends in a vowel or ل. Example, اوقومق *okoumak* (to read), اوقونمق *okounmak* (to be read).

165. Reciprocal verbs are made by adding ش to the root of a primitive verb. Example, سومك *sevmek* (to love), سوشمك *sevishmek* (to love one another) ; كورمك *gheurmek* (to see), كورشمك *gheurushmek* (to see one another) ; سويلمك *suwéylémek* (to speak), سويلشمك *suwéyleshmek* (to speak to one another).

The Negative Potential Verbs.

166. Verbs expressing impossibility or incapability are formed by introducing ٥ or ا before the م *mé* or ما *ma* of negative verbs.* Example, يازمق *yazmak* (to write), يازمامق *yazmamak* (not to write), يازەمەمق *yazamamak* (not to be able to write) ; كلمك *ghelmek* (to come), كلممك *ghelmémek* (not to come), كلەممك *ghelémemek* (not to be able to come). If the root of the verb end in a vowel sound, then ي is added to it instead of ٥, for the sake of euphony. Example, ترلمك *terlémek* (to perspire), ترلەيەممك *terléyémemek* (not to be able to perspire).

167. If the root of the verb from which the impossible form is taken end in ت that letter becomes د in the impossible verb. Example, ايتمك *etmek* (to do), ايدەمەمك *edémemek* (not to be able to do).

168. The derivation of Turkish verbs will be seen at a glance from the following table.

---

* See 157.

Table of the Derivation of Turkish Verbs.

Active		سومك	*sevmek,* to love
,,	Negative	سومك	*sevmemek,* not to love
,,	Impossible	سوهمك	*sevémemek,* not to be able to love
Causal		سودرمك	*sevdirmek,* to cause to love
,,	Negative	سودرممك	*sevdirmemek,* not to cause to love
,,	Impossible	سودرهمك	*sevdirémemek,* to be unable to cause to love
Passive		سولمك	*sevilmek,* to be loved
,,	Negative	سولممك	*sevilmemek,* not to be loved
,,	Impossible	سولهممك	*sevilémemek,* not to be able to be loved
Causal		سولدرمك	*sevildirmek,* to cause to be loved
Reflective		سونمك	*sevinmek* (to love one's self), to be delighted
,,	Negative	سونممك	*sevinmemek,* not to be delighted
,,	Impossible	سونهممك	*sevinémemek,* not to be able to be delighted
Causal		سوندرمك	*sevindirmek,* to cause to be delighted
,,	Negative	سوندرممك	*sevindirmemek,* not to cause to be delighted
,,	Impossible	سوندرهممك	*sevindirémemek,* to be unable to cause to be delighted
Reciprocal		سوشمك	*sevishmek,* to love one another
,,	Negative	سوشممك	*sevishmemek,* not to love one another
,,	Impossible	سوشهممك	*sevishémemek,* not to be able to love one another
Passive		سوشلمك	*sevishilmek,* to be loved mutually
,,	Negative	سوشلممك	*sevishilmemek,* not to be loved mutually
,,	Impossible	سوشلهممك	*sevishilémemek,* not to be able to be loved mutually
Causal		سوشدرمك	*sevishdirmek,* to cause to love mutually.

169. All these derived verbs are conjugated in the same way as the primitive verb.

How to Express "to be able" in Turkish.

170. To be able to do an action is expressed by the verb بلمك *bilmek* (to know) put after the root of any verb with *ŝ* joined on to it. Thus :—

يازه بلمك *yaza bilmek* (to be able to write, to know how to write); يوزه بلمك *yuzé bilmek* (to be able to swim, to know how to swim).

171. If the last letter of the root of the verb have a vowel sound يه is added to it instead of ه. Example, اوقويه بلمك *okouya bilmek* (to be able to read), سويليه بلمك *suwéyléyé bilmek* (to be able to speak). The negative of this formation is not used, as there is a special form to express impossibility (see 166).

172. The meaning of the negative form is, of course, in general perfectly clear, but the negative form of the causal verbs, besides its ordinary signification, sometimes expresses prohibiting or preventing the action being done. Thus سوندرمهك *sevindirmemek* means not only " not to cause to rejoice," but also " to prevent some one from rejoicing."

173. All verbs are not capable of all the forms given above. The auxiliary verb ایلهمك *éilémek* (to do), for example, can only make ایلهمك *éilémemek* (not to do) the negative, and ایلیهمهمك *éiléyémemek* (not to be able to do) the impossible form.

The Moods of the Verb.

174. In Turkish the verb has six moods: the infinitive, the indicative, the necessitative, the optative, the conditional, and the imperative. The infinitive, the indicative, and the imperative are the same as in all languages, but the necessitative, optative, and conditional are peculiar to Turkish.

175. The necessitative states than an action *must* or *ought* to take place. Example, يازملويم *yazmaliyim* (I must write, I ought to write, I am to write); يازملوايدم *yazmáli yidim* (I was obliged to write, it was necessary for me to write, or I ought to have written).

176. The optative indicates wishing or desiring, and corresponds to the subjunctive in European languages. Example, يازه *yaza* (that he may write), يازهايدى *yazaydi* (that he might write); كاشكه بلهيدم *keshké biléydim* (oh ! that I knew !) كاشكه كيدهايدى *keshké ghidéydi* (oh! that he would go !)

177. The conditional states the condition on which another action takes place, has taken place, or will take place. Example, كلسه ممنون اولورم *ghelsé memnoun olouroum* (if he come I shall be glad); زنكين اولسهايدم ممنون اولور ايدم *zenghín olsayidim, memnoun olour oudoum* (if I were rich I would be glad).

Conjugation of a Turkish Verb.

178. All Turkish verbs are conjugated in the same way, there being no irregular verbs, except the defective verb "to be;" but there are certain modifications required by the laws of euphony which hold good in the inflexions of verbs as in other things. We subjoin the verb اجمتى *achmak* as a model of the conjugation of all verbs :—

Infinitive Mood.

اجمتى *achmak* (to open).

Indicative Mood.

Present Tense.

Singular.		Plural.	
اجيورم	*achïyorïm,** I am opening†	اجيورز	*achïyorïz,** we are opening
اجيورسن	*achïyorsïn,** thou art opening	اجيورسكز	*achïyorsïnïz,** you are opening
اجيور	*achïyor,* he, she, or it is opening	اجيورلر	*achïyorlar,* they are opening

Imperfect.

اجيور ايدم	*achïyor idïm,‡* I was opening	اجيور ايدك	*achïyor idïk,* we were opening
اجيور ايدك	*achïyor idin,* thou wast opening	اجيور ايدكز	*achïyor idiniz,* you were opening
اجيور ايدى	*achïyor idi,* he, she, or it was opening	اجيور ايديلر	*achïyor idilér,* they were opening

Aorist.

اجارم	*acharïm,* I open (habitually), I shall open	اجارز	*acharïz,* we open, or will open
اجارسن	*acharsïn,* thou openest, thou wilt open	اجارسكز	*acharsïnïz,* you open, or will open
اجار	*achar,* he, she, or it opens, or will open	اجارلر	*acharlar,* they open, or will open

---

* Also pronounced *achïyoroum, achïyorsoun, achïyorouz, achïyorsounouz.*

† Or I open, thou openest, &c. (but not habitually).

‡ Or اجيوردم *achïyordïm,* اجيوردك *achïyordïn,* اجيوردى *achïyordï,* &c.

Past Habitual.

Singular.	Plural.
اجار ايدم *achar-idim,** I used to open, or I would open, or would have opened	اجار ايدك *achar-idik,* we used to open, or would open, or would have opened
اجار ايدك *achar-idin,* thou usedst to open, or would open, or would have opened	اجار ايدكز *achar-idiniz,* you used to open, or would open, or would have opened
اجار ايدى *achar-idi,* he used to open, or would open, or would have opened	اجارلر ايدى *acharlar-idi,* they used to open, or would open, or would have opened

Perfect.

اجدم *achdĭm,* I opened, did open, or have opened†	اجدق *achdĭk,* we opened, did open, or have opened
اجدك *achdĭn,* thou openedst, did open, or hast opened	اجدكز *achdĭnĭz,* you opened, did open, or have opened
اجدى *achdĭ,* he, she, or it opened, did open, or has opened	اجديلر *achdĭlar,* they opened, did open, or have opened

---

* Or اجاردم *achardĭm,* اجاردك *achardĭn,* اجاردى *achardĭ,* &c.

† "I have opened, thou hast opened," &c., are generally considered to correspond to another form which we give below; but this form can only be used correctly when there is doubt or uncertainty, and when the speaker means to state that he believes what he says, but cannot vouch for it.

اجمشم *achmĭshĭm,* I have opened	اجمشز *achmĭshĭz,* we have opened
اجمشسن *achmĭshsĭn,* thou hast opened	اجمشسكز *achmĭshsĭnĭz,* you have opened
اجمش *achmĭsh,* } he, she, or it has opened	اجمشلر *achmĭshlar,* they have opened.
or اجمشدر *achmĭshdĭr,* }	

Hence كلمش *ghelmĭsh* should not be translated "He has come," but "He has come, I believe," &c. كتمش *ghitmish* means not "He has gone," but "I think he has gone, but I cannot vouch for it," and so forth. In fact, the syllable مش *mish* or ايمش *imish,* added to any tense or person of the indicative or necessitative moods, makes the statements doubtful, the speaker intending to convey the idea that what he asserts is only hearsay. Example, اجه جقمش *achajakmĭsh* (he will open, it is said), اجملولر مش *achmalĭlar ĭmĭsh* (they ought to open, it is said).

Pluperfect.

Singular.		Plural.	
اچدیدم	achdidim, I had opened*	اچدیدك	achdidik, we had opened
اچدیدك	achdidin, thou hadst opened	اچدیدكر	achdidiniz, you had opened
اچدیدی	achdidi, he, she, or it had opened	اچدیدیلر	achdidilar, they had opened

or,

اچدم ایدی	achdĭm idi, I had opened	اچدق ایدی	achdĭk idi, we had opened
اچدك ایدی	achdĭn idi, thou hadst opened	اچدكز ایدی	achdĭnĭz idi, you had opened
اچدی ایدی	achdĭ idi, they had opened	اچدیلر ایدی	achdĭlar idi, they had opened

Future.

اچهجغم	achajaghĭm, I shall or will open	اچهجغز	achajaghĭz, we shall or will open
اچهجقسن	achajaksĭn, thou shalt or wilt open	اچهجقسكز	achajaksĭnĭz, you shall or will open
اچهجق	achajak, he, she, or it shall or will open	اچهجقلر	achajaklar, they shall or will open

Past Future.

اچهجق ایدم	achajak idim, I was about to open	اچهجق ایدك	achajak idik, we were about to open
اچهجق ایدك	achajak idin, thou wast about to open	اچهجق ایدكز	achajak idiniz, you were about to open
اچهجق ایدی	achajak idi, he, she or it was about to open	اچهجقلر ایدی	achajakler idi, they were about to open

---

* The pluperfect is also expressed sometimes as follows:—

اچمش ایدم	achmĭsh idim, I had opened	اچمش ایدك	achmĭsh idik, we had opened
اچمش ایدك	achmĭsh idin, thou hadst opened	اچمش ایدكز	achmĭsh idiniz, you had opened
اچمش ایدی	achmĭsh idi, he, she, or it had opened	اچمش ایدیلر	achmĭsh idiler, they had opened

Necessitative Mood.

Aorist.

Singular.

اجملويم *achmalĭyĭm*, I must open, or ought to open, or am to open

اجملوسن *achmalĭsĭn*, thou must open, or ought to open, or art to open

اجملو *achmalĭ*, he, she, or it must open, or ought to open, or is to open

Plural.

اجملوايز *achmalĭyĭz*, we must open, or ought to open, or are to open

اجملوسكز *achmalĭsĭnĭz*, you must open, or ought to open, or are to open

اجملولر *achmalĭlar*, they must open, or ought to open, or are to open

Past.

اجملوايدم *achmalĭyĭdĭm*, I ought to have opened; it was necessary that I opened

اجملوايدك *achmalĭyĭdĭn*, thou ought to have opened; it was necessary that thou openedst

اجملوايدى *achmalĭyĭdĭ*, he ought to have opened; it was necessary that he opened

اجملوايدك *achmalĭyĭdĭk*, we ought to have opened; it was necessary that we opened

اجملوايدكز *achmalĭyĭdĭnĭz*, you ought to have opened; it was necessary that you opened.

اجملولرايدى *achmalĭlarĭdĭ*, they ought to have opened; it was necessary that they opened

Optative Mood.*

Present.

اچهيم *achayĭm*, that I may open

اچه سن *acha sĭn*, that thou mayest open

اچه *acha*, that he, she, or it may open

اچهايز *achayĭz*,† that we may open

اچه سكز *acha sĭnĭz*, that you may open

اچهلر *achalar*, that they may open

---

* Used frequently also instead of the imperative; thus, اچهسن *acha sin* means often " open " (thou), as well as " that thou mayest open."

† Or اچالم *achalĭm*.

E

Past.

Singular.	Plural.
اجه‌ايدم *achaydĭm,* that I had opened, or might open	اجه‌ايدك *achaydĭk,* that we had opened, or might open
اجه‌ايدك *achaydĭn,* that thou hadst opened, or might open	اجه‌ايدكز *achaydĭnĭz,* that you had opened, or might open
اجه‌ايدى *achaydĭ,* that he, she, or it had opened, or might open	اجه‌ايديلر *achaydilér,* that they had opened, or might open

Conditional Mood.

Aorist.

اجسم *achsam,* if I open	اجسق *achsak,* if we open
اجسك *achsan,* if thou openest	اجسكز *achsaniz,* if you open
اجسه *achsa,* if he, she, or it open	اجسه‌لر *achsalar,* if they open

Past.

اجسيدم *achsaydĭm,* if I opened, or had opened	اجسيدق *achsaydĭk,* if we opened, or had opened
اجسيدك *achsaydĭn,* if thou openedst, or hadst opened	اجسيدكز *achsaydĭnĭz,* if you opened, or had opened
اجسيدى *achsaydĭ,* if he, she, or it opened, or had opened	اجسيديلر *achsaydĭlar,* if they opened, or had opened

Imperative Mood.

	اجالم *achalĭm,* let us open
اچ *ach,* or اچك *achĭn,* open thou	اجكز *achĭnĭz,* open you
اجسون *achsĭn,* let him, her, or it open	اجسونلر *achsĭnlar,* let them open

Participles.

Active.

Present.

اجان *áchan,** opening, who or which opens, opened, or will open.

---

* Used both as an adjective and a noun.

Aorist.

اجار *achar*, opening, who or which opens habitually, or will open.

Past.

اجمش *achmĭsh*, who or which has opened.

Perfect.

اجدق *achdĭk*, who or which has opened.

Future.

اجهجق *achajak*, who or which will open.

PASSIVE.

Aorist.

اجدق *achdĭk*, who or which is or has been opened.

Future.

اجهجق *achajak*, who or which will be opened.

Verbal Nouns.

اجمه *achma*, opening, the act of opening

اجدق *achdĭk*, the act of having opened

اجهجق *achajak*, the act of being about to open

Gerunds.

اجوب *achĭp*, opening, having opened

اجهرق *acharak*, opening, continuing to open

اجاجق *achĭjak*, }
اجاجه *achĭnjé*, } as soon as opening, or on opening

اجه اجه *acha acha*, by opening and opening, or repeatedly opening

اجمغين *achmaghĭn*, by reason of opening

اجهلو *achalĭ*, since opening.

Remarks on the Formation of the Tenses and their Value.

179. The characteristic sign of *present of the indicative* is the syllable يور, which, added to the root of the verb, makes the third person singular of this tense. By simply adding سكز ايز سن م and لر to this the other persons are obtained. If the root of the verb end in ت it generally changes into د.

Example, كيتمك *ghitmek* (to go), كيديور *ghidiyor* (he goes); يراتمق *yérât-mak* (to create), يراديور *yérâdïyor* (he creates). This tense is often called by English grammarians the present progressive or second present tense. It indicates that the action is going on at the present moment, while one is speaking; whereas the aorist of the indicative indicates that the action is going on but is not over, and is habitual. Hence the aorist of the indicative has often been regarded as the present tense of that mood; but it is not really so, as it expresses the action in an indefinite way, referring both to the present and the future. Thus, يازيورم *yazïyorïm* means "I write at the present moment, I am writing"; whereas يازارم *yazarïm* means, "I write in general as a habit," or it conveys a promise, and then corresponds to, "I will write."

180. The characteristic sign of the *aorist of the indicative* is the letter ر added to the root of the verb, which forms the third person singular. The other persons are then formed by simply adding سكز ايز سن م and لر. The vowel sound between the ر and the root of the verb varies, being either *a, â, é, ou, eu, u, i* or *ǐ*, and can only be learnt by practice or from a good dictionary, such as Redhouse's, which gives the aorist of each verb with the infinitive. Example, كلمك *ghelmek* (to come), كلور *ghelir* (he comes), كلورم *ghelirim* (I come); قيرمق *kïrmak* (to break), قيرار *kïrar* (he breaks), قيرارسكز *kïrarsïniz* (you break); بلمك *bilmek* (to know), بلور *bilir* (he knows), بلورم *bilirim* (I know); ويرمك *vermek* (to give), ويرر *vérir* (he gives), ويررسكز *vérirsiniz* (you give). If the root of this verb end in ت, that letter generally becomes د in the aorist. Example, كتمك *ghitmek* (to go), كيدر *ghidér* (he goes), كيدرم *ghidérim* (I go), كيدرسكز *ghidérsiniz* (you go).

181. The *imperfect of the indicative* indicates that an action had taken place, but was not finished at a given moment. It is formed by adding دم ايدك ايدم or ديلر دكز دك in the singular, and ايدى ايدك ايدم or دى دك دك ايديلر in the plural, to the third person singular of the present tense. Example, يازيورايدى *yâzïyoridi* (he was writing—then, at that particular time), كيديورايدك *ghidiyoridik* (we were going).

182. The *past habitual* corresponds to the *imparfait* and *conditionnel* tenses in French. It indicates that one was in the habit of doing an action formerly, or that one would do it on condition of something else happening. Thus, كلور ايدم *ghelir idim* signifies either, "I used to come," or, "I would come" (if something else happened). زنكين اولسه ايدم بك ممنون اولور ايدم

zenghin olsaydim pek memnoun olour oudoum* (if I were rich I would be very glad).

183. The *perfect of the indicative* indicates that an action has taken place either a long time ago or quite lately. Hence it not only corresponds to our past tense in English, but to our compound tense formed with the past participle and the auxiliary verb " have." For example, كلدى *gheldi* not only means " he came," but also " he has come "; كزدى *ghézdi,* " he walked," and " he has walked." It may also sometimes be translated by our past formed with *did.* Example, يازديمى *yazdimi* (did he write?), يازدى *yazdi* (he did write). This tense is formed by appending دم دك *dí dk diler* دى دك دلر to the root of the verb. Example, قوبشمق *konoushmak*

---

* The particles which are used to express the different tenses of the verb are subject to the laws of euphony. Therefore *i* generally changes into *ou* when the predominant vowel is *ou* or *o*, and into *u* if the predominant vowel be *eu* or *u*. Thus اولورايدم is pronounced *olour-oudoum* (instead of *olour-idim*); اولدم *oldoum* (I became), اولدك *oldoun* (thou becamest), اولدى *oldou* (he became), اولدك *oldouk* (we became), اولدكز *oldounouz* (you became), اولديلر *oldoular* (they became), اولورم *olouroum* (I become or will become), اولورسن *oloursoun* (thou becomest), اولور *olour* (he becomes or will become), اولويورم *olouyoroum* (I am becoming), اولويورسن *olouyorsoun* (thou art becoming), اولويورز *olouyorouz* (we are becoming), اولويورسكز *olouyorsounouz* (you are becoming), اولويورلر *olouyorlar* (they are becoming). The other tenses are pronounced in a similar way, as اولورايدم *olour oudoum* (I became or would become or be), اولمش ايدى *olmoush oudou* (he had become or he had been). Other verbs the same, as يوريلورم *yoroulouroum* (I am fatigued or shall be fatigued), يوريلورسن *yorouloursoun* (thou art fatigued or wilt be fatigued); اوكسورورم *euksururum* (I cough or will cough), اوكسررسكز *euksurursunuz* (you cough or will cough); بولمشيدم *boulmoushoudoum* (I had found), بولمشيدكز *boulmoushoudounouz* (you had found), بولورايدم *boulouroudoum* (I used to find or would find), بولكز *boulounouz* (find), بولسون *boulsoun* (let him find); كوردم *gheureurum* (I see), كوردم *gheurdum* (I saw), كوردى *gheurdu* (he saw), كورديلر *gheurduler* (they saw), كورمش *gheurmush* (he has seen—they say), كورمش ايسم *gheurmush ussém* or كوررسم *gheurursém* (if I see), كوردم *geururdum* (I would see). These euphonic changes are not different conjugations, and are best learnt by reading and speaking with a good teacher; and, although the laws of euphony given in a preceding chapter will serve generally as a guide and help, considerable latitude is allowed, giving rise often to slight differences of pronunciation, as, for instance, اچيورم *achïyorïm* and *achïyaroum*, which are both allowable.

(to talk), قوكشدق *konoushdouk* (we talked); كولمك *ghiulmek* (to laugh), كولدم *ghiuldum* (I laughed).

184. The *pluperfect* is formed by adding دى or ايدى to the perfect. Example, كلدى ايدى *gheldi idi* (he had come).

185. The *future* corresponds to the future in English, with this difference that it simply asserts what will happen without making a promise, which is always expressed by the aorist. The third person singular of this tense is formed by adding جق or جك preceded by ه to the root of a verb. The other persons are then obtained by appending م سن ايز سكز لر to the third person singular. Example, اوره‌جق *wourmak* (to strike), *wourajak* (he will strike); كسمك *kessmek* (to cut), كسه‌جكم *kessejéyim* (I will cut), كسه‌جكز *kesséjéyiz* (we shall cut), &c. If the root of the verb end in ت it generally changes into د in this tense. Example, كتمك *ghitmek* (to go), كيده‌جكم *ghidéjéyim* (I shall go); ايتمك *etmek* (to do), ايده‌جكم *edéjéyim* (I shall do). In the first person singular and plural the ق changes into غ and the ك is pronounced like *y*, for the sake of euphony, as يازه‌جغم *yazajaghim* (I will write).

186. The *future past* of the indicative signifies that an action was going to take place in the past, present, or future. It is formed by adding دم دك دى دكز ديلر or ايدم, &c., to the third person singular of the future. Example, كله‌جك‌ايدم *geléjek-idim* (I was about to come), ياپه‌جق‌ايدى *yapajak-idi* (he was about to do it), اوله‌جك ايديلر *euléjek idiler* (they were about to die).

187. The characteristic sign of the *present of the necessitative* is ملي *méli* or *mali*, which, added to the root of the verb, forms the third person singular of this tense. The other persons are then obtained by adding ايم سن, &c. It serves to express a present necessity or duty. Example, بو كون چالشملويم *bou ghiun châlïshmalïyim* (I must work to-day, or I ought to work to-day, or I am to work to-day).

188. The *past necessitative* expresses that it was necessary or right that an action should have taken place, or that one was forced to perform some act. It is formed by adding ايدك ايدم &c. to the root of the verb, with ملو added to it. Example, دون چالشملو ايدم *doun châlïshmalïyidim* (I ought to have worked yesterday, or I was compelled to work, or I was to work), محاربه‌يه كيتملو ايدكز *mouharebéyé ghitméliyidiniz* (you ought to have gone to the war, or you were obliged to go to the war, or you were to go to the war, or you should have gone to the war). It is the past tense of

" must," which is wanting in English, and corresponds to the German
musste.

189. The *present of the optative* serves to indicate a wish or desire that
some action may be performed. Its characteristic sign is ٵ, added to the
root of the verb, which forms the third person singular, from which the other
tenses are formed by the addition of م سن لم سكزلر. If the root of the verb
end in ت, that letter most often changes into د in this tense. Example,
كيدەايم *ghidéyim* (that I may go), كيدەلم *ghidélim* (let us go).

190. The past optative either expresses a wish that some action may
take place, although one scarcely expects it, or indicates regret that some
action has not taken place in the past. It is formed by adding ايدم ايدك
&c. to the third person singular of the present optative. Example, كاشكه
كلەايدى *keshké ghuléydi* (Oh, that he would come, or might come !), كاشكه
تركجه بلەايدم *keshké turkché biléydim* (Oh, that I knew Turkish ! or, Oh,
that I had known Turkish !).

191. The characteristic sign of the optative, ٵ *é*, is pronounced like *a*
when the verb is composed of hard letters, and sometimes even it is replaced
by an *élif*. Example, اچالم *achalim* (let us open), instead of اچەلم ; اولا instead
of اولە *ola* (it may be). Sometimes even the ٵ and ا are omitted altogether.
Example, كسيدى *kesséydi* (that he might cut); اچيدم *achaydim* (that I
might open), اچيدق *achaydik* (that we might open).

192. The *present or aorist of the conditional* states the condition on
which some other action takes place or will take place. Example, كلسه بن
ghelsé ben ghiderim (if he come, I shall go); هوا كوزل ايسه كزرم *hawa
ghiuzel issé ghézerim* (if the weather be fine, I shall take a walk). It is
formed by adding سم سن سه or لر كرسق to the root of the verb.

193. The past conditional states the condition on which, if something had
happened, some other action would have taken, or would take place still.
It casts doubt on the performance of some condition in the past, present,
or future. Example, كلسەايدى كزر ايدم *ghelséydi ghézér idim* (if he came, I
would take a walk); ياپسيدى بن دخى ياپار ايدم *yapsaydi ben dakhi yapar
idim* (if he did it, I would do it also). The past and present conditional
correspond to the present and past subjunctive in European languages.
The preposition " if " is, so to speak, included in this mood, but it can and
is often used together with it. Example, اكر زنكين اولسەايدم كتابلر الور ايدم
eyer zenghin olsaydim kitâblar âlir idim (if I were rich I would buy
books). The conditional mood is often used for the optative ; thus, كلسيدى

ghelséydi is the same as كليدى *gheléydi* (Oh, that he would come, or that
he had come!) The past conditional is formed by adding ايدك ايدم
ايدى &c. to the third person singular of the present conditional.

The Number and Person of the Verb.

194. Verbs, like nouns, have two numbers, the singular and the plural.
They have three persons, which remain invariable, whatever may be the
gender of the nominative.

The persons of each number are formed from the third person singular,
to which certain endings are added.

The *first person singular* of *all tenses* is formed by adding م or يم to the
third person singular. If the third person singular end with a ى or a s, the
ى is always left out, and the s left out or retained at pleasure. Example,
يازار *yazar* (he writes), يازارم *yazarim* (I write); اتايور *átáyior* (he is throwing), اتايورم *átáyiorim* (I am throwing); يازدى *yazdi* (he wrote), يازدم
yazdim (I wrote); اتار دى *átar idi* (he used to throw, or would throw),
اتار ايدم *átár idim* (I used to throw, or would throw); اتسه *átsa* (if he
throw), اتسم or اتسهم *atsam* (if I throw).

195. In the first person singular of the optative, the م is sometimes
preceded by a ى. Example, كيدهيم or كيدهيم *ghidéyim* (that I go), كلهيم or
كلهيم *gheléyim* (that I come).

196. In the *first person singular of the indicative mood of the negative
or impossible form* of a verb, the ز of the third person singular is generally
omitted, but it is occasionally retained, and always so in the interrogative.
Example, يازمز *yazmaz* (he does not write), يازمم *yazmam* (I do not write),
or, more rarely, يازمزم *yazmazim* (I do not write), يازمزميم *yazmazmiyim*
(do I not write?); سويلمز *suwéyléméz* (he does not speak), سويلمم
suwéylémem or سويلمزم *suwéylémazim* (I do not speak), سويلمزميم
suwéylémézmiyim (do I not speak?)

197. The *second person singular* is formed by adding س to the third
person singular; but if the third person end with دى or سه, a surd ك
(pronounced like *n*) is appended instead. In this case the ى is always
left out, and the s can be omitted or retained. Example, كيدر *ghider* (he
goes), كيدرسن *ghidersin* (thou goest); كليور *ghelior* (he comes), كليورسن
gheliorsin (thou comest); كيتدى *ghitdi* (he went), كيتدك *ghitdin* (thou
wentest); كيتسه *ghitsé* (if he go), كيتسهم *ghitsém* (if I go), or كتسك *ghitsen*
(if thou go).

198. The *second person singular of the imperative* is an exception to this rule, for it consists simply of the root of the verb, without any addition. Example, يابمق *yapmak* (to do, to make), ياپ *yap* (do, make); قاچمق *kàchmak* (to run away), قاچ *kàch* (run away).

199. There is another form of the imperative second person singular which is used to give greater force or emphasis to the command. It consists of the root of the verb with a surd ك *n* added to it. Example, يابك *yapïn* (do it, then); قاچك *kàchïn* (run away, then, or do run away); يازك *yazïn* (do write).

200. If the root of the verb end in a vowel, يك is added instead of ك to form the emphatic imperative. Example, باشلا *bàshla* (begin thou), باشلايك *bàshlayïn* (do thou begin).

201. The *first person plural* is obtained by adding ز or يز to the third person singular; but if the latter end in دى or ـه, then ق or ك (according as it is a verb containing hard or soft letters) is employed, in which case the ى is always left out, and the ه sometimes. Example, چكر *cheker* (he draws), چكرز *chekeriz* (we draw), چكدى *chekdi* (he drew), چكدك *chekdik* (we drew), چكسه *cheksé* (if he draw), چكسك or چكسهك *cheksek* (if we draw).

202. In the present of the indicative of the negative and impossible forms the general rule is occasionally followed for forming the first person plural, and it is always in the interrogative; but in general the ز of the third person singular is omitted, and the يز then added. Example, يازمز *yazmaz* (he does not write), يازميز *yazmayiz* (we do not write), instead of يازمزيز *yazmaziz*, rarely used ; يازمزميز *yazmazmiyiz* (do we not write?); كسهمز *kessémaz* (he cannot cut), كسهميز *kesséméyiz* (we cannot cut), *kessémazmiyiz* (cannot we cut?)

203. The *first person plural* of the *imperative* is exceptional. It is formed by adding a ه (pronounced *a* or *é* according as the preceding letters are hard or soft) to the root of the verb, if that end in a consonant, and also the syllable لم ; but if the root of the verb end with a vowel sound then a ى is put before the ه. Example, كل *ghel* (come), كلهلم *ghelélim* (let us come) ; چق *chïk* (go out), چقهلم *chïkàlim* (let us go out) ; چالش *chàlïsh* (work, study), چالشهلم *chàlïshàlim* (let us work, study); باشلا *bàshla* (begin), باشلايهلم *bàshlayalïm* (let us begin) ; سويله *suweylé* (speak, talk), سويليهلم *suwéyléyélim* (let us speak, talk).

204. In the *present of the optative* the vowel و is sometimes prefixed to the j of the first person plural. Example, اولەيز instead of اولەيز *olayïz* (that we may be) ; قيلاوز instead of قيلەيز *kïlâyïz* (that we may make).

205. The *second person plural* is formed by adding سكز *seniz* to the third person singular; but if that end in دى or سه, كز is used instead, in which case ى and ه can be omitted. Example, چقارسكز *chïkar* (he goes out), چقارسكز *chïkârsïnïz* (you go out), چقه *chïka* (that he may go out), چقەسكز *chïka-sïnïz* (that you may go out), چقدى *chïkdï* (he went out), چقدكز *chïkdïnïz* (you went out).

206. The *second person plural* of the imperative is irregular, for it is formed by adding كز to the root of the verb, or يكز if the root end in a vowel sound. Example, ياپ *yap* (make thou), ياپكز *yapiniz* (make you) ; باشلا *báshla* (begin thou), باشلايكز *báshlayïnïz* (begin you).

207. The *third person plural* is always formed by adding لر to the third person singular. Example, چقار *chïkâr* (he goes out), چقارلر *chïkârlar* (they go out), چقدى *chïkdï* (he went out), چقديلر *chïkdïlar* (they went out); ايتدى *etdi* (he did), ايتديلر *etdilér* (they did) ; چقسه *chïksa* (if he go out), چقسەلر *chïksalar* (if they go out), چقسون *chïksïn* (let him go out), چقسونلر *chïksïnlar* (let them go out).

208. The syllable لر in the compound tenses may either precede or follow the termination دى or ايدى. Example, سوردى *severdi* (he loved), سورلرايدى *severler idi* or سور ايديلر *sever idiler* (they loved).

EXERCISE V.

I will make him write. He writes. I wrote. You wrote. I walk (يوريمك *yurumek*). I shall walk. You walked. I must walk. I ought to have walked. If you walk you will be (اوله‌جقسكز *olajaksiniz*) tired (يورغون *yorghoun*). If you walked. Open the window (پنجره *penjéré*). I have opened it. Begin thou. Begin you. I have begun. Run (قوشمق *koshmak*) thou. Run you. Let him run. I must run. You must run. He ought to have run. If he run. If you run. If they ran. It is (در *dir*) necessary (كرك *gherek*) that they run. I would run. We shall see (كورشمك *ghieurushmek*) one another again. We saw one another. Make him read (اوقوتمق *okoutmak*) his lesson (درس *derss*). I made him read. He ought to read every day. Hold your tongue.* I will hold my

---

* To hold one's tongue in Turkish is صوصمق *soussmak*.

tongue. He ought to have held his tongue. Ask (صورمق *sormak*) what o'clock (ساعت قاچ در *saat kach dir*) it is. I have asked. I had asked. If you ask him, he will tell you. If you asked me, I would tell you. If you study, you will learn. Where is your brother. He* has gone out. When will he come back (كيرو *ghéri*). He will come at five o'clock. Tell him I came. I will tell him. I will wait (بكلهمك *beklémek*) an hour. Wait. If you wait. I have waited in vain (بيهوده *bihoudé*). Come to-morrow (يارين *yarin*). I cannot come. I cannot wait. You ought to wait. I cannot see. I must read. Sit down. Make him sit down. I will make him sit down. Let them sit down. Let him get up (قالقمق *kálkmak*). Get up. At what o'clock do you get up. I rose this morning at six o'clock. You must rise to-morrow at five. Go to bed (ياتمق *yatmak*) early. If you go to bed early you will get up early. He has gone to bed. Oh, that I knew Turkish ! Let us go. Let us run. We have run. If we study, we shall learn. I wish (استمك *isstémek*) to study. He wanted (استمك *isstémek*) to walk. If he wishes, let him walk. The Pasha has come (they say). If you wish, we will go out. You heard the news (خبر *khábr*) yesterday. I heard it last (كچن *ghechen*) week (هفته *hafta*). I ought to have heard it also. If the post arrive to-day let me know (بلدرمك *bildirmek*). If the post had arrived I should know it. It will come next (كلهجك *geléjek*) week. The man who brought† the news is dead (اولمك *eulmek*, to die). The man who wrote the letter is alive (صاغ *sagh*). Who knows ? I saw him yesterday. He introduced (كورشدرمك *ghieurushdurmek*) me to his friend. He can speak English very well. You can speak to him. Let us talk (قونوشمق *konoushmak*) Turkish every day. You speak very well. I can write it better.

The Participles.

209. A participle, as its name implies, partakes both of the nature of a verb and an adjective, and in Turkish it is sometimes used as a noun, in which case it is declinable and can take affixes.

210. There are *five active participles* in Turkish, the **present**, the *aorist*, the *past*, the *perfect*, and the *future*, and two *passive*, the *aorist* and the *future*.

211. The *present active participle* is formed by adding أن or ن *en* to the root of the verb, according as that consists of hard or soft letters.   If

---

* The personal pronouns are generally omitted in Turkish, except when the meaning would not be clear without them.

† See 156.

the root of the verb end in a vowel sound, یان or یین is added instead of ان or ن. Example, یازان ادم *yazan âdâm* (the writing man, or the man who writes, wrote, or will write); سون قارى *seven kârï* (the loving woman, or the woman who loves, loved, or will love); اوقویان چوجق *okouyan chojouk* (the child who reads, read, or will read); سویلین قیز *suwéyléyen kiz* (the girl who speaks, spoke, or will speak).

212. If the root of the verb end in ت, that letter changes into د to form this participle. Example, کیدن *ghiden* (who goes), from کتمك *ghitmek* (to go); ایدن *eden* (who does), from ایتمك *etmek* (to do).

213. With causal verbs ending in ت, the ت can be retained or a د substituted for it at pleasure. Example, چاغرتمق *chaghïrtmak* (to cause to call), چاغرتان *chaghïrtân* or چاغردان *chaghïrdân* (causing to call, who causes to call).

214. This participle is applicable either for the present, past, or future. Example, کلان ادم *ghelan âdâm* means either " the coming man, the man who comes, the man who came, or the man who will come."

215. It can be used as a noun, and can then be declined as such. Example, یازانلر *yazanlar* (writers, or those who write), اوقویانلر *okouyanlar* (readers, or those who read). This participle thus replaces the relative pronoun with a verb in European languages.*

216. The *aorist active participle* is very similar in its meaning to the preceding, but it indicates that the action is habitual, whereas the present active participle merely asserts that the action is performed only once, or just at present. It is formed by adding ر to the root of the verb, and inserting a vowel between them, which varies according to the laws of euphony, or, in other words, it is the same as the third person singular of the aorist of the indicative. What vowel sound must be given can only be learnt by practice, or the use of a good dictionary which gives the aorist participle with every infinitive. Example, چیچکلر دکر ادم *chichekler dikér âdâm* (the flower-planting man, or the man who plants flowers (habitually), or will plant flowers); کولر قارى *ghiulér kari* (the laughing woman, or the woman who laughs); باشنى کسدرمکدن اجتناب ایدر بر ادم دکلم *bâshïnï kessdirmekden ijtinab edér bir âdâm déilim* (I am not a man *who avoids* having his head cut off); هر نوع حوادثدن بحث ایدر غزته در *her nev-i*

* See 156.

héwadissden bahss edér ghazeta dir (it is a newspaper *treating* (or *which treats*) of every kind of news).

217. This participle is generally used as an adjective, but can be employed as a noun.

218. With negative verbs or those signifying impossibility, this participle is formed by putting ماز or مز after the root of the verb, according as that contains hard or soft letters. Example, یازماز *yazmaz* (not writing, who does not write, or will not write); كلمز *ghelmez* (not coming, who does not come, or will not come); كورمز *ghieurmez* (not seeing, who does not see, or will not see). Thus it always corresponds to the third person singular of the aorist of the indicative.

219. Most verbs ending in ت change that letter into د to make this participle. Example, كیتمك *ghitmek* (to go), كیدر *ghider* (going, who goes, or who will go).

220. The *past active participle* is formed by adding مش (pronounced *mish, mĭsh, mush,* or *moush,* according to the letters preceding it) to the root of the verb. Example, اوقومش *okoumoush* (who has read), اوقومش ادم *okoumoush ádâm* (a man who has read, *i.e.,* a learned man), قیرلمش بر فنجان *kĭrĭlmĭsh bir finjan** (a broken cup, or a cup that has been broken).

221. In European languages the past participle and the passive participle are alike, but in Turkish the passive participle is expressed by the active participle of the passive form of the verb. Example, یازمش *yazmish* (who has written), یازلمش *yazĭlmĭsh* (which has been written).

222. This participle is almost always used as an adjective.

223. The *perfect active participle* consists of دق or دك added to the root of the verb. Example, باقدق *bâkdĭk* (who has looked). This form is but little used.

224. The *future active participle* is formed by adding جق or جك to the root of the verb; that is to say, it corresponds exactly to the third person singular of the future indicative. Example, كله‌جك هفته *gheléjek hafta* (the week which will come, *i.e.* next week).

225. When the active participles are employed as adjectives, they always refer to the noun which is the subject of the verb to which they belong. Example, یازلمش مكتوب *yazilmish mektoup* (the letter which has

---

* Commonly pronounced *filjan.*

been written); قوشان آدم *koshan ádám* (the running man, or the man who runs, ran, or will run); كورمدك آدم *ghieurmadik ádám* (the man who has not seen); چقهجق قارى *chĭkájak kárĭ* (the woman who will come out).

226. The *aorist passive participle* is formed exactly the same as the *perfect active participle,* and is generally confounded with it, although perfectly distinct. Example, باقدق *bákdĭk* (who is or has been looked at), كسدك *kessdek* (which is cut). Example, اوقودیغم كتاب *okoudoughoum kitáb* (the book *which has been read* by me, or which I read); كسديك ات *kessdiyin et* (the meat which *has been cut* by thee).

227. The noun which a Turkish passive participle qualifies when it is used as an adjective, or for which it stands when it is used as a noun, is the direct or indirect object of the verb of which the participle is a part, *if that verb be transitive,* and therefore there must be a doer. This doer of the action which the participle expresses is indicated by the pronominal affixes or the genitive* case of the noun which is the nominative of the verb of which it forms part. Example, يازدیغم كتاب *yazdĭghĭm kitáb* (the book which *I* wrote); بكا ویردیكی چیچك *bana vérdighi chichek* (the flower which *he* gave to me); سویله‌دیكی طوغرى در *suwéylédiyi doghrou dour* (what *he* says is true); قرنداشكزك يازدیغى كتاب *karndashinizin yazdĭghĭ kitáb* (the book which *your brother* wrote); ات كسديكى بیچاق *et kessdiyi bĭchák* (the knife with which *he* cut the meat).

228. If the verb from which the passive participle is formed be either neuter or passive, then the noun which it qualifies, or for which it stands, when used substantively, is the indirect object of the verb. The nominative of the verb in this case also is indicated in the same way by the pronominal affixes, or the genitive of the noun which is the nominative of the verb. Example, كلدیكى سبب بو در *gheldiyi sebeb bou dour* (the reason for which he came is this); استانبوله كيتدیكم سنه *Istanbola ghitdiyim sené* (the year in which I went to Constantinople); قتل اولندیغى محل *kátl oloundoughou mahal* (the place where he was killed); سزه راست كلدیكم كون *sĭzé rasst gheldiyim ghiun* (the day on which I met you); استانبولك فتح اولندیغى سنه *Isstanboloun feth oloundoughou sené* (the year in which Constantinople was conquered).

<hr>

* The noun is generally, but not always, put in the genitive. Thus you can say, باباكك يازدیغى مكتوب *bábániz yazdĭghĭ mektoub* or باباكز يازدیغى مكتوب *bábánĭzin yazdĭghĭ mektoub,* but the meaning of the latter is more unmistakable.

229. The *future passive participle* has the same form as the future active participle. Example, باقه‌جق *bákajak* (who will be looked at); اله‌جغم پاره *álajaghim para* (the money which will be received by me, or which I shall receive).

EXERCISE VI.

I received letters by the mail (پوسته *posta*) which came* yesterday. Eat the bread which you have cut. I have bought the horses which your father sold (صاتمق *sátmak*). He has sold the houses your brother gave him. I heard that he died. The town I lived (اوطورمق *otourmak*) in. The town where I shall live. The man who wrote this book is alive. He is a very learned man (a man who has read). What I have heard is this. You know what I have done. This is the picture I spoke of. The merchant who sends goods (امتعه *emtia*) to foreign (اجنبیه *ejnebiyé*) countries (ممالك *memalik*). The gardener who plants flowers. The flowers which are being planted in the Emperor's (پادشاه *padishah*) garden (باغچه *bághché*) are very beautiful. The year in which I was born. The place where he died. The houses which are being pulled down (یقلمق *yïklïmak*). He is a man who has seen a thousand troubles (بلا *bila*). He is a man who has done† a great deal of work. I know what you want. I ate the fruit (یمش *yémish*) your father sent. The year in which Constantinople was conquered (اولنمق *olounmak* فتح *feth*).

The Gerunds.

230. There are seven gerunds in Turkish.

231. The *first gerund* is characterised by the termination وب *ip, eup*, or *oup* added to the root of the verb, or یوب *yip, yeup*, or *youp* if the root of the verb end with a vowel. Example, سووب *sevip* (loving), اوقویوب *okouyoup* (reading), صوروب *soroup* (asking).

232. If the root of the verb end with a ت that letter changes into د before وب. Example, ارادب *áradïp*, from اراتمق *áratmak* (to cause to seek).

233. This gerund is equivalent to a verb followed by the conjunction "and," and always indicates that a sentence is finished or one member of it. Example, باقوب کتدی *bakïp ghitdi* (looking he went, *i.e.*, he looked and (then) went away); عجله ایدوب وقتله کلدی *ajelé edip wákïtilé gheldi* (making haste he arrived in time, *i.e.*, he made haste and arrived in time);

---

* See 156 and 211.   † Say " seen."

يازارم اوقويوب *okouyoup yazarïm* (reading I write, *i.e.*, I read and write);
ايشم اوقويوب يازمقدر *ishim okouyoup yazmak˚ dïr* (my work is reading to write, *i.e.*, to read and write).

234. The *second gerund* is formed by adding رق or رك to the root of the verb, but if that end in a vowel then a ى must be introduced. Example, كلهرك *ghelérek* (coming, while coming), باشلايهرق *bâshlayarak* (beginning, while beginning). It is used to express a subordinate action which takes place at the same time as that stated by the verb it accompanies. Example, اغلايهرق قاچدى *âghlayarak kâchdï* (he ran away crying). It is used also in the same way as the first gerund to prevent the too frequent repetition of the latter.

235. The *third gerund* is formed by putting the termination يجق or يجك to the root of the verb; but if the latter end with a vowel then a ى must be introduced between them. It corresponds to "as soon as," or "on." Example, بوخبرى الجق كتدى *bou khâbrï âlïjak ghitdi* (as soon as he received this news he went away); مكتوبم واصل اوليجق *mektoupoum vassil oloujak* (as soon as my letter arrives, or on my letter arriving); باقيجق طانيدى *bâkïjak tânïdï* (as soon as he looked he recognised him).

236. The *fourth gerund* is formed by adding نجه to the root of the verb, or ينجه if the root of the verb end with a vowel. It sometimes has the same meaning as the third gerund, that is to say, it corresponds to "as soon as," or "on," but when it is negative it signifies "until." Example, مكتوبم واصل اولنجه *mektoupoum vassil olounja* (on my letter arriving, or as soon as my letter arrives); بن كلمينجه كتمه *ben ghelméyinjé ghitmé* (do not go till I come); او كتمينجه بكلرم *o ghitméyinjé beklerim* (I will wait until he goes); بابام يازمينجه بورادَه قالورم *bâbâm yazmayïnja bourada kâlïrïm* (I shall remain here until my father writes).

237. The *fifth gerund* consists of ه added to the root of the verb, but if the root of the verb end with a vowel, then يه must be used instead of ه or, in other words, it is precisely the same as the third person singular of the present optative. It generally indicates the repetition of an action by means of which another action is performed which is expressed by the verb it precedes. It is generally repeated twice. Example, قوشه قوشه كلدك *kosha kosha gheldik* (we have come running, or by running and running), اوقويه اوقويه اوكرندم *okouya okouya eughrendim* (I learnt it by reading it again and again).

238. The *sixth gerund* is formed by adding ين *in* to the infinitive. If

the verb end in مق, then the ق is changed into a غ, and, if it end in مك,
then the ك is pronounced like *y*. It expresses an action by reason of which
another act occurs, stated by the verb which it precedes. Example, دوستم
يازمغين كتدم *dostoum yazmaghïn ghitdim* (I went owing to my friend having
written.)*

239. The *seventh gerund* is formed by adding لو *lou, lu,* or لى *li* or *lï,* to the
third person singular of the present of the indicative. It indicates the
length of time since which another action expressed by the verb with which
it is connected in the same sentence has taken place, and thus corresponds
to "since." Example, سن لوندرەيه كلەلى قاچ سنه در *sen Londraya gheléli kach
sené dir* (how many years is it since you came to London?) او كلەلى *o gheléli*
(since he has come); دوستك يازدلى قاچ كوندر *dostoun yazélï kach ghiun
dir* (how many days is it since thy friend wrote?) استانبول فتح اولنەلى درت
يوز سنه در *Istanbol feth olounalï deurt yuz sené dir* (it is four hundred years
since Constantinople was conquered). دنبرى *denbéri*, which also means
"since," is sometimes added to this termination ەلى. Example, او كيدەلى
دنبرى چالشيورم *o ghidéli denbéri châlïshïyoroum* (I have been working since
he has gone).

Gerund-like Expressions.

240. Besides the above gerunds there are several gerund-like expressions. These expressions are formed with the infinitive or a participle, and
certain prepositions or post-positions.

241. The preposition له *lé* put after the infinitive forms a kind of gerund
which indicates the reason for which some other action is performed. In
this case the final ق must be changed into غ, and the ك pronounced like *y*.
Example, سومكيله *sevméyilé* (by reason of loving, on account of loving);
اورمغيله *wourmaghilé* (by reason of striking, or on account of striking).

242. The post-position دن appended to the perfect participle ending in
دق or دك, or rather to the verbal noun of the same form, also gives a kind
of gerund, indicating the reason why some other action is preformed. The
doer of the first action is indicated by the pronominal affixes. Example,
كتابى المديغندن كوندرەمدم *kitâbi âlmadïghïndan ghiunderémadïm* (owing to
his not having bought the book, I could not send it); سويلەمديككردن بلمدم
suwéylémediyinizden bilmédim (owing to you not telling me, I did not

---

* *i.e.,* I was able or obliged to go, owing to my friend having written.

know); اشیتمدیکندن جواب ویرمدی *ishitmadiyinden jawab vermédi* (owing to his not having heard he did not answer).

243. By adding جه *jé* instead of دن to the same participle or verbal noun ending in دك or دق, another kind of gerund is made which corresponds to "in proportion as," "the more." Example, چالشدقجه ایلرولرسكز *chálishdïkjé ilérilersiniz* (you will progress in proportion as you study, or the more you study the more you will progress). In its negative form it expresses "until." Example, او صورمدقجه بن سویلمم *o sormadïkja ben suwéylémem* (I shall not tell him until he asks).

244. Another expression is formed by adding ده *da* or *dé* to this same participle or verbal noun, which indicates when an action is performed. Example, مسافرلر كلدكده یمك یدك *musafirler gheldïkdé yémek yédik* (when the guests arrived we dined; or, the guests having arrived, we dined; or, on the guests arriving we dined); یاز كلدكده *yaz gheldïkdé* (on summer coming, or, when summer comes).

245. Such English expressions as "before coming," "before going," &c., consisting of "before" with a participle, are rendered in Turkish by the verbal noun ending in مه *mé* followed by دن, and the word اول *evvel* or مقدم *moukáddem*. Example, یازمدن اول *yazmadan evvel* (before writing). The ه is often omitted. Example, كلمدن مقدم *ghelméden moukáddem* (before coming).

246. The same thing is expressed by putting دن and اول or مقدم after the third person singular of the aorist indicative, negative form. Example, یازمزدن اول *yazmazdan evvel* (before writing), اوقومزدن اول *okoumazdan evvel* (before reading).

247. "After," with a participle, is rendered in Turkish by the ablative of the participle or verbal noun ending in دق or دك, followed by the word صكره *sora* (after). Example, یازدقدنصكره اوقودق *yazdïkdan sora okoudouk* (after having written, we wrote); سودگدنصكره *sevdikden sora* (after having loved). The person who performs the action can be indicated by the pronominal affixes. Example, پاره الدیغكزدنصكره *para áldïghïnizdan sora* (after your having received the money, or, after you have received the money); ترکچه تحصیل ایتدیکندنصكره *Turkché tahsíl etdiyinden sora* (after his acquiring Turkish, or, after he had acquired Turkish).

248. Some one being just about to perform some action is expressed by the future active participle ending in جق or جك followed by ایكن (being). Example, یازهجق ایكن *yazajak iken* (while just about to write). This form

of the verb sometimes indicates a duty. Example, قوكشه‌جق ايكن يازيور *konoushajak iken yazïyor* (he writes while he ought to talk, or should talk).

249. "While," accompanied by a participle in English, is rendered in Turkish by the active aorist participle ending in ر followed by ايكن *iken.* Example, بن اوقور كن* سز سويلرسكز *ben okour ken siz suweylersiniz* (you talk while I am reading).

250. By putting ايكن after the past active participle ending in مش another gerund-like form is obtained which expresses "while being in the state of one who has done some action." It corresponds to the English expression, "having done so-and-so." Example, كلمش ايكن *g̈elmish iken* (having come), بن سزه سويلمشيكن اونوتدكز *ben sizé suweylémish iken ounout-dounouz* (I having told you, you forgot—nevertheless).

EXERCISE VII.

I read and† write. He came and went. He mounted his horse and went into the country (كوى *keuy*).‡ The man mounted a tree and began to cut the branch (دال *dal*) on which he sat. One day while walking I met a friend and brought him to my house. The woman coming home and knocking at the door, on her husband coming to the door and saying, "what do you want?" she flew into a passion. Having received your letter, I immediately wrote an answer. Do not go until I come. He came laughing. He laughed and laughed till he cried (laughing and laughing, he cried). As soon as I saw him, I was astonished (شاشمق *shashmak*). As soon as my letter arrives, send me a telegram (تلغرافنامه *télégrafnamé*). You cannot start until you receive the money. I fell (اولمق *olmak*) ill, owing to my father dying. How long is it since you came to Constantinople? How many years is it since Constantinople was taken by the Turks? My servant having acted (ايتمك *etmek* ‎ حركت *haréket*) very badly, I dismissed (صاومق *sawmak*) him. The streets (صوقاق *sokák*) being very muddy (جامورلى *chamourli*), I cannot walk. Before my coming, you used to talk. Before his coming. While speaking. He talked when he ought to have studied. I having told you so often, still you forget. On your seeing him, he ran away (قاچمق *káchmak*). The more he studies, the more progress he makes. I am comfortable since he has gone.

---

* كن *ken* is used sometimes for ايكن *iken.* † See 233. ‡ See 228.

Verbal Nouns.

251. Three simple verbal nouns can be formed from every Turkish verb.

252. The first is formed by adding the termination مه *ma* or *mé* to the root of the verb, and may be called the present verbal noun.   It expresses in a general way the action indicated by the verb from which it comes. The *s* can be dropped or retained according to the requirements of euphony. Example, يازمه *yazma* (the action of writing, or writing), اوقومه *okouma* (the action of reading, or reading), يازمانز *yazmanĭz* (your writing), سومسى *sevméssi* (his loving), سوملرى *sevméleri* (their loving).

253. Another verbal noun is formed by adding دق *dĭq* or دك *dĭk* to the root of the verb, that is to say, it corresponds in form to the perfect active participle and the aorist passive participle. It may be called, as it expresses an action performed in the past, the perfect verbal noun.   Being a noun it can be declined and take the pronominal affixes, and when it does this it changes ق into غ and ك is pronounced *y*.   Example, باقدق *bâkdĭk* (the action of having looked), باقديغى *bâkdĭghĭ* (his having looked); يازديغم *yazdĭghĭm* (my having written), كلديكمى بلدكز *gheldiyimi bildiniz* (you knew that I had come—my having come), سويلديكنى اكلادم *suweylédiyini annadĭm* (I understood what he said), تركجه اوكرنديكنى بلمدم *turkjé eurendiyini bilmédim* (I did not know that he learnt Turkish or his having learnt Turkish).

254. Another verbal noun, which may be called the future verbal noun as it refers to future time, has the same form as the future active participle, that is to say, it consists of جق *é* or جك *é* added to the root of the verb.   It states an action which will také place at some future time.   Example, كله جكم *gheléjéyim* (the action of my coming—in future), كله جكنى بلورميسكز *ghelé-jéyini bilirmisiniz* (do you know that he will come—his coming in future); پاره ويره جكنى ظن ايتدم *para veréjéyini zan etdim* (I thought he would pay; literally, I thought he *will* pay).

EXERCISE VIII.

My father's dying caused me to fall ill.   I did not know that he was ill.   I have expected that he would die* for a long time.   His coming to Constantinople

---

جوق وقتدن برو * *chok vakitdanbéri.*

was the cause of his illness. My writing is useless (فائده‌سز *faïdésiz*). You thought he would get better. Did you hear what I said ? I did not hear what you said. Do not pay attention to what he says, but pay attention to what your father says. He did what I wanted (استمك *isstémek*). I hope he will come. Read what I have written. What they have written is incorrect (یاكلش *yanïsh*). What he says is true (طوغری *doghrou*). What you wish is impossible (غیر ممكن *ghaïri mumkin*). Our walking in the garden is forbidden (یساق *yassák*). I did not know that he went to Bagdad (بغداد *baghdad*). What you have seen is very strange (عجائب *ajaïb*). His loving his country is very proper. Having received your letter I read what you wrote.

The Dubitative Form of the Verb.

255. Every tense of the indicative and necessitative moods can be made dubitative by simply putting مش or ایمش after the tenses which do not end in دی or ایدی; and those tenses (except the perfect of the indicative) which end with that syllable are made dubitative by مش or ایمش being put before the دی or ایدی. Subjoined are some examples.

Indicative Mood.

Present Tense.

یازیور ایمش *yaziyor ïmïsh*, I think, or I have heard, that he writes.

Imperfect.

یازیور مش ایدی *yaziyor mïsh idi*, I think, or I have heard, that he wrote, or was writing.

Perfect.

یازمش *yazmish*, I think, or I have heard, that he wrote, or has written.

Pluperfect.

یازمش ایدی *yazmïsh idi*, I think, or I have heard, that he had written.

Necessitative.

یازملو ایمش *yazméli ïmïsh*, I think, or I have heard, that he must or ought to write.

EXERCISE IX.

Has the Pasha (پاشا *pasha*) come (كلدیمی *gheldimim*)? He has come, I think. He has given some orders (امر *emr*), I believe. They say he has brought some

books. Yes, he has brought some books. I have heard that you were writing.
Has your salary (ايلتی *aïlìk*) come? I believe it has come. Yes, it has come.
He has received (المتی *álmak*)· his salary, I have heard. I think he ought to
receive it. I believe he will come. Did he understand (اكلاديمی *annadimmi*)
what I said? He understood, I think. Yes, he understood very well. I believe
·that he had started (قالقمتی *kálkmak*). On hearing that his father had died, he fell
ill, I think. Yes, he fell ill.

The Three Complex Conjugations of the Verb.

256. The conjugation of a Turkish verb has been given at 178 ; but
besides the simple tenses there given, and which are those generally in use,
there are three sets of complex tenses, formed by adding the aorist past
and future participles to the various tenses of the verb اولمتی *olmak* (to be,
or to become).

First Complex Conjugation.

The first complex conjugation is formed by putting the various tenses of
اولمتی after the aorist participle.

Present.

يازار اوليور *yazar oliyor*,* he writes, or he is or becomes one who writes
habitually.

Imperfect.

يازار اوليوردی *yazar oliyordi*,† he was writing, or was becoming one who writes
habitually.

Aorist.

يازار اولور *yazar olour*, he writes, or will write, or he will become one who
writes.

Perfect.

يازار اولدی *yazar oldou*, he wrote, or he became one who writes habitually.

&c. &c. &c.

Second Complex Conjugation.

257. The second complex conjugation is formed by putting the various
tenses of اولمتی after the past participle ending in مش. Example :—

---

* Also pronounced *olouyor*.   † Also pronounced *olouyordou*.

Second Complex Conjugation.

Present.

يازمش اوليور *yazmïsh oliyor*, he has written, or he is, or is becoming, one who has written.

Imperfect.

يازمش اوليور ايدى *yazmish oliyor idi*, he had written, or he was becoming one who had written.

Aorist.

يازمش اولور *yazmish olour*, he will have written, or he will become one who has written.

&c. &c. &c.

258. The third complex conjugation is formed by putting the various tenses of اولمتى after the future active participle. Example :—

Third Complex Conjugation.

Present.

يازه‌جتى اوليور *yazajak oliyor*, he is about to write, or he becomes one who will write.

Past.

يازه‌جتى اوليور ايدى *yazajak oliyor idi*, he was about to write, or he was becoming one who would write, or should write.

Aorist.

يازه‌جتى اولور *yazajak olour*, he will be one who will write.

Perfect.

يازه‌جتى اولدى *yazajak oldou*, he was about to write, or he became one who will write, or ought to write.

&c. &c. &c.

259. The distinction between the simple conjugation of the verb and the first complex conjugation being very trifling, the latter is not much used, but the two other complex conjugations are employed considerably. These three complex conjugations consisting simply of the various tenses of the verb "to be" put after the three participles, I have only given examples, instead of the complete conjugations through all the moods and tenses.

Conjugation of a Passive Verb.

260. As a general rule, a verb is made passive by inserting ل after its root, and it is then conjugated exactly as the active verb. Example :—

سولمك *sevilmek*, to be loved.

Indicative.

Present.

Singular.		Plural.	
سوليورم *seviliyorĭm*, I am loved		سوليورز *seviliyorĭz*, we are loved	
سوليورسن *seviliyorsĭn*, thou art loved		سوليورسكز *seviliyorsĭnĭz*, you are loved	
سوليور *seviliyor*, he, she, or it is loved		سوليورلر *seviliyorlar*, they are loved	

Imperfect.

سوليورايدم *seviliyoridim*, I was loved		سوليورايدك *seviliyoridik*, we were loved	
سوليورايدك *seviliyoridin*, thou wast loved		سوليورايدكز *seviliyoridiniz*, you were loved	
سوليورايدى *seviliyoridi*, he, she, or it was loved		سوليورلرايدى *seviliyorlaridi*, they were loved	

Aorist.

سولورم *sevilirim*, I am loved (habitually), I shall be loved		سولورز *seviliriz*, we are loved, or shall be loved	
سولورسن *sevilirsin*, thou art loved, thou wilt be loved		سولورسكز *sevilirsiniz*, you are loved, or will be loved	
سولور *sevilir*, he is loved, or he will be loved		سولورلر *sevilirler*, they are loved, or will be loved	

Past.

سولورايدم *seviliridim*, I was loved, I would be loved		سولورايدك *seviliridik*, we were loved, or would be loved	
سولورايدك *seviliridin*, thou wast loved, or would be loved		سولورايدكز *seviliridiniz*, you were loved, or would be loved	
سولورايدى *seviliridi*, he was loved, or would be loved		سولورلر ايدى *sevilirler idi*, they were loved, or would be loved	

Perfect.

Singular.	Plural.
سولدم *sevildim*, I was loved, or I have been loved	سولدك *sevildik*, we were loved, or we have been loved
سولدك *sevildin*, thou wast loved, or thou hast been loved	سولدكز *sevildiniz*, you were loved, or you have been loved
سولدى *sevildi*, he was loved, or he has been loved	سولديلر *sevildiler*, they were loved, or they have been loved

Pluperfect.

سولدم ايدى *sevildim idi*, I had been loved	سولدك ايدى *sevildik idi*, we had been loved
سولدك ايدى *sevildin idi*, thou hadst been loved	سولدكزايدى *sevildiniz idi*, you had been loved
سولدى ايدى *sevildi idi*, he had been loved	سولديلرايدى *sevildiler idi*, they had been loved

Future.

سوله جكم *seviléjéyim*, I shall be loved	سوله جكز *seviléjéyiz*, we shall be loved
سوله جكسن *seviléjeksin*, thou wilt be loved	سوله جكسكز *seviléjeksiniz*, you will be loved
سوله جك *seviléjek*, he will be loved	سوله جكلر *seviléjekler*, they will be loved

Future Past.

سوله جك ايدم *seviléjek idim*, I was about to be loved	سوله جك ايدك *seviléjek idik*, we were about to be loved
سوله جك ايدك *seviléjek idin*, thou wast about to be lóved	سوله جك ايدكز *seviléjek idiniz*, you were about to be loved
سوله جك ايدى *seviléjek idi*, he was about to be loved	سوله جكلر ايدى *seviléjekler idi*, they were about to be loved

Necessitative.

Present.

سولملويم *sevilméliyim*, I must or ought to be loved	سولملويز *sevilméliyiz*, we must or ought to be loved
سولملوسن *sevilmélisin*, thou must or ought to be loved	سولملوسكز *sevilmélisiniz*, you must or ought to be loved
سولملو *sevilméli*, he must or ought to be loved	سولملولر *sevilméliler*, they must or ought to be loved

Perfect.

Singular.	Plural.
سولملوايدم *sevilméliyidim,* I ought to have been loved, or must have been loved	سولملوايدك *sevilméliyidik,* we ought to have been loved, or must have been loved
سولملوايدك *sevilméliyidin,* thou oughtest to have been loved, or must have been loved	سولملوايدكز *sevilméliyidiniz,* you ought to have been loved, or must have been loved
سولملوايدى *sevilméliyidi,* he ought to have been loved, or must have been loved	سولملوايدلر *sevilméliyidiler,* they ought to have been loved, or must have been loved

Optative.

Present.

سولهيم *seviléyim,* or سولهم *sevilem,* } that I may be loved	سولهيز *seviléyiz,* that we may be loved
سولهسن *sevilésin,* that thou mayest be loved	سولهسكز *sevilésiniz,* that you may be loved
سوله *sevilé,* that he may be loved	سولهلر *seviléler,* that they may be loved

Perfect.

سوليدم *seviléydim,* that I might be loved, or might have been loved	سوليدك *seviléydik,* that we might be loved, or might have been loved
سوليدك *seviléydin,* that thou mightest be loved, or mightest have been loved	سوليدكز *seviléydiniz,* that you might be loved, or might have been loved
سوليدى *seviléydi,* that he might be loved, or might have been loved	سوليديلر *seviléydiler,* that they might be loved, or might have been loved

Conditional.

Aorist.

سولسم *sevilsém,* if I be loved	سولسك *sevilsék,* if we be loved
سولسهك *sevilsén,* if thou be loved	سولسكز *sevilséniz,* if you be loved
سولسه *sevilsé,* if he be loved	سولسهلر *sevilséler,* if they be loved

Perfect.

<table>
<tr><td colspan="2" align="center">Singular.</td><td colspan="2" align="center">Plural.</td></tr>
<tr><td>سولسيدم</td><td>*sevilséydim*, if I were loved, or if I had been loved</td><td>سولسيدك</td><td>*sevilséydik*, if we were loved, or had been loved</td></tr>
<tr><td>سولسيدك</td><td>*sevilséydin*, if thou wert loved, or if thou hadst been loved</td><td>سولسيدكز</td><td>*sevilséydiniz*, if you were loved, or had been loved</td></tr>
<tr><td>سولسيدی</td><td>*sevilséydi*, if he were loved, or had been loved</td><td>سولسيديلر</td><td>*sevilséydiler*, if they were loved, or had been loved</td></tr>
</table>

Imperative.

سول *sevil* or ⎫
سولك *sevilin,* ⎬ be thou loved

سولسون *sevilsin*, let him be loved

سولهلم *sevilélim*, let us be loved

سولكز *seviliniz*, be you loved

سولسونلر *sevilsinler*, let them be loved

Participles.

ACTIVE.

Present.

سولان *sevilan*, being loved; who or which is loved, was loved, or will be loved.

Aorist.

سولور *sevilir*, being loved; who or which is loved, or will be loved.

Past.

سولمش *sevilmish*, who or which has been loved.

Perfect.

سولدك *sevildik*, who or which has been loved.

Future.

سولهجك *seviléjek*, who or which will be loved.

PASSIVE.

Aorist.

سولدك *sevildik*, by, with, in, or to which one has been loved.

Future.

سولهجك *seviléjek*, by, with, in, or to which one will be loved.

Verbal Nouns.

سولمه *sevilmé,* the action of being loved

سولدك *sevildik,* the action of having been loved

سوله‌جك *seviléjik,* the action of being about to be loved.

Gerunds.

سولوب *sevilip,* being loved or having been loved

سوله‌رك *sevilérek,* being loved

سولیجك *sevilijek,* on being loved

سولنجه *sevilinjé,*   ,,

سوله سوله *sevilé sevilé,* by dint of being loved

سولمكین *sevilméyin,* by reason of being loved, having been loved

سوله‌لو *seviléli,* since being loved.

EXERCISE X.

We are loved. He was struck (اورلمق *wouroulmak*). I was struck. He was killed (اولدیرلمك *euldurulmek*) in the battle (محاربه *muharebé*). The whole regiment (الای *álaï*) was killed. Your brother was wounded (یارلنمك *yarélenmek*). The officers (ضابطان *zabitan*) will be wounded. His foot (اياق *ayak*) was cut off (كسلمك *kessilmek*). The order was given (ویرلمك *verilmek*) and sent (كوندرلمك *ghieundurulmek*). The cannon (طوب *top*) were sent to the officers, but they did not receive them. The letter which was written. The firman which was sent from the Sublime Porte (باب عالی *Báb-ali*). We shall be killed. Let the servant be sent. Let them be loved. He ought to be loved. He will be loved, if he behave well (ایتسه *etsé* حركت *hareket* ایو *iyi*). The houses were pulled down (یقلمق *yïkïlmak*). I bought the houses which were pulled down. The stone with which he was struck. The battle in which he was wounded. The books which are being printed (باصلمق *bássïlmak*). My book has been printed, but yours will never be printed.

Conjugation of the Defective Verb ایم *im* (I am).

261. There is a verb in Turkish which in general corresponds to our verb "To be," but it is defective, having no infinitive mood, &c. The following are all the tenses it has :—

Indicative Mood.

Present.

Singular.	Plural.
م ايم *im* } I am or يم *yim**	ايز ز *iz*† } we are or يز *yiz*
سن *sin*, thou art	سكز *siniz*, you are
در *dir*, He is	درلر *dirler*, they are

Perfect.

ايدم *idim*, I was or have been	ايدك *idik*, we were or have been
ايدك *idin*, thou wast or hast been	ايدكز *idiniz*, you were or have been
ايدى *idi*, he was or has been	ايدىلر *idiler*, they were or have been

Conditional.

Aorist.

ايسم ايسم } *issèm*, if I be	ايسك *issèk*, if we be
ايسك ايسەك } *issèn*, if thou be	ايسكز *isséniz*, if you be
ايسە *issé*, if he be	ايسەلر *isséler*, if they be.

Perfect.

ايسيدم *isséydim*, if I were or have been	ايسيدك *isséydik*, if we were or have been
ايسيدك *isséydin*, if thou wert or have been	ايسيدكز *isséydiniz*, if you were or have been
ايسيدى *isséydi*, if he were or have been	ايسيديلر *isséydiler*, if they were or have been

Verbal Noun.

ايدك *idik*, the action of already being.

Gerund.

ايكن *iken*, being, while being.

---

* يم *yim* after a word ending in a vowel, as انا يم *ana yim* (I am a mother).

† يز or ييز *yiz* after a word ending in a vowel, as جسارتلييز *jessaretliyiz* (we are courageous).

The deficient tenses are expressed by the corresponding tenses of the verb اولمق *olmak* (to become), and any part of the verb is made negative by putting دكل *diyil* before it.   Example :—

NEGATIVE FORM.

Indicative Mood.

Present.

Singular.	Plural.
دكليم *déylim,* I am not	دكليز *déyliz,* we are not
دكلسن *déylsin,* thou art not	دكلسكز *déylsiniz,* you are not
دكلدر *deyldir,* he, she, or it is not	دكلدرلر *déyl dirler,* they are not

Perfect.

دكل ايدم *déyl idim,* I was not	دكل ايدك *déyl idik,* we were not
دكل ايدك *déyl idin,* thou wast not	دكل ايدكز *déyl idiniz,* you were not
دكل ايدى *déyl idi,* he, she, or it was not	دكل ايديلر *déyl idiler,* they were not

Conditional Mood.

Present.

دكل ايسم *déyl issém,* if I be not	دكل ايسك *déyl issek,* if we be not
دكل ايسك *déyl issén,* if thou be not	دكل ايسكز *déyl isseniz,* if you be not
دكل ايسه *déyl issé,* if he, she, or it be not	دكل ايسهلر *déyl isséler,* if they be not

Perfect.

دكل ايسيدم *déyl isséydim,* if I were not	دكل ايسيدك *déyl isséydik,* if we were not
دكل ايسيدك *déyl isséydin,* if thou wert not	دكل ايسيدكز *déyl isséydiniz,* if you were not
دكل ايسيدى *déyl isséydi,* if he, she, or it were not	دكل ايسيديلر *déyl isseydiler,* if they were not

Gerund.

دكل ايكن *déyl iken,* while not being.

EXERCISE XI.

He is a soldier (عسكر *assker*).   We are brothers.   I was very ill last (كچن *gechen*) week (هفته *hafta*).   He was celebrated (مشهور *meshour*).   I am very sorry that I cannot come.   They are very glad (ممنون *memnoun*).   While he was in the garden. He was French ambassador (ايلچى *elchi*) in Constantinople (استانبول *Isstanbol*) in the year 1850.   Who is English ambassador now ?   If he is your brother I would like (حظ ايتمك *haz etmek*) to be introduced (كورشدرمك *ghieurushdurmek*) to him. He is a very learned (اوقومش *okoumoush*) man, but he is not so learned as (قدر *kadar*) your father.   Where is my watch (ساعت *saat*) ?   It is on (اوزرينده *uzerindé*) the table (تربزه *trebézé*).   He was in Smyrna (اسمير *essmir*), but he is now in England (انكلتره *Inghilterra*).   I am very glad that you have learned Turkish.   It is a very pretty language (لسان *lissan*), but it is more difficult (كوچ *ghuch*) than English (انكليزجه *inglizché*).   If he is a good doctor (حكيم *hékim*) he can give you a remedy (علاج *ilaj*).   He is an excellent soldier but not a doctor.   I am not well since I have been in London.

Conjugation of the Verb "To Have."

262. There is no verb in Turkish corresponding to our word "have." Possession is expressed by putting the adjective وار *var* (existing) after the noun possessed.   If the possessor in English be a pronoun it is indicated by a pronominal affix, and if it be another noun, that noun is put in the genitive.   Example, مركبم وار در *murekkebim var dir* (I have ink, literally, "my ink existing is").   The verb "to be" after وار can be used or left out in the present, but must be used in the other tenses.   Example, ادامك آدامڭ پاره‌سى وار *âdâmin parassi var* (the man has money, literally, of the man his money existing is).   The negative is expressed by putting the word يوق *yok* after the noun possessed.   Example, اينه‌م يوق *ainém yok* (I have not a mirror).   The ق of يوق is changed into غ when it comes before ى.   Example, اينه‌م يوغيدى *ainém yoghoudou** (I had not a mirror). We subjoin some of the leading tenses of the verb "to have" with their Turkish rendering as examples.

---

* See 58.

Indicative Mood.

Present.

Singular.	Plural.
اوم وار *evim var*, I have a house	اومز وار *evimiz var*, we have a house
اولك وار *evin var*, thou hast a house	اوكز وار *eviniz var*, you have a house
اوى وار *evi var*, he, she, or it, has a house	اولرى وار *evleri var*, they have a house

Negative.

اوم يوق *evim yok*, I have not a house	اومز يوق *evimiz yok*, we have not a house
اولك يوق *evin yok*, thou hast not a house	اوكز يوق *eviniz yok*, you have not a house
اوى يوق *evi yok*, he, she, or it has not a house	اولرى يوق *evleri yok*, they have not a house

Past.

اوم وار ايدى *evim var idi*, I had a house	اومز وار ايدى *evimiz var idi*, we had a house
اولك وار ايدى *evin var idi*, thou hadst a house	اوكز وار ايدى *eviniz var idi*, you had a house
اوى وار ايدى *evi var idi*, he, she, or it had a house	اولرى وار ايدى *evleri var idi*, they had a house

Negative.

اوم يوغيدى *evim yoghoudou*, I had not a house	اومز يوغيدى *evimiz yoghoudou*, we had not a house
اولك يوغيدى *evin yoghoudou*, thou hadst not a house	اوكز يوغيدى *eviniz yoghoudou*, you had not a house
اوى يوغيدى *evi yoghoudou*, he, she, or it had not a house	اولرى يوغيدى *evleri yoghoudou*, they had not a house

Dubitative.

اوم وار ايمش *evim var imish*, I had a house (I think)	اومز وار ايمش *evimiz var imish*, we had a house (I think)
اولك وار ايمش *evin var imish*, thou hadst a house (I think)	اوكز وار ايمش *eviniz var imish*, you had a house (I think)
اوى وار ايمش *evi var imish*, he, she, or it had a house (I think)	اولرى وار ايمش *evleri var imish*, they had a house (I think)

Negative.

Singular.	Plural.
اوم يوغيمش *evim yoghoumoush,* I had not a house (I think)	اومز يوغيمش *evimiz yoghoumoush,* we had not a house (I think)
اوڭ يوغيمش *evin yoghoumoush,* thou hadst not a house (I think)	اوكز يوغيمش *eviniz yoghoumoush,* you had not a house (I think)
اوک يوغيمش *evi yoghoumoush,* he had not a house (I think)	اولرى يوغيمش *evleri yoghoumbush,* they had not a house (I think)

Future.

اوم اوله‌جق *evim olajak,* or اولور *olour,*	} I shall have a house	اومز اوله‌جق *evimiz olajak,* or اولور *olour,*	} we will have a house
اوڭ اوله‌جق *evin olajak,* or اولور *olour,*	} thou shalt have a house	اوكز اوله‌جق *eviniz olajak,* or اولور *olour,*	} you will have a house
اوک اوله‌جق *evi olajak,* or اولور *olour,*	} he, she, or it will have a house	اولرى اوله‌جق *evleri olajak,* or اولور *olour,*	} they will have a house

Conditional.

Present.

اوم وار ايسه *evim var ĭssa,* if I have a house	اومز وار ايسه *evimiz var ĭssa,* if we have a house

&c. &c.

Negative.

اوم يوغ ايسه *evim yogh oussa,* if I have not a house	اومز يوغ ايسه *evimiz yogh oussa,* if we have not a house

Past.

اوم وار ايسه‌ايدى *evim var ĭssaydĭ,* if I had a house	اومز وار ايسه‌ايدى *evimiz var ĭssaydĭ,* if we had a house

Negative.

اوم يوغ ايسه‌ايدى *evim yogh oussaydĭ,* if I had not a house	اومز يوغ ايسه‌ايدى *evimiz yogh oussaydĭ,* if we had not a house

Optative.

Present and Perfect.

Singular.	Plural.
اوم اوليدی *evim olaydĭ,* Oh! that I had a house; that I had had a house	اومز اوليدی *evimiz olaydĭ,* Oh! that we had a house; that we had had a house

Imperative.

	اومز اولسون *evimiz olsoun,* let us have a house
اوك اولسون *evin olsoun,* have thou a house?	اوكز اولسون *eviniz olsoun,* have a house
اوی اولسون *evi olsoun,* let him, her, or it have a house	اولری اولسون *evleri olsoun,* let them have a house

Gerund.

اوم وار ايكن *evim var iken,* while I had a house.

اوم يوغيكن *evim yogh iken,* while I had not a house.

263. "Have" can also be expressed in Turkish by putting ده *dé* (in) after the personal pronouns, and adding وار *var.* Example:—

Singular.	Plural.
بنده وار *bendé var,* I·have	بزده وار *bizdé var,* we have
سنده وار *sendé var,* thou hast	سزده وار *sizdé var,* you have
انده وار *ondé var,* he, she, or it has	انلرده وار *onlarda var,* they have
بنده يوق *bendé yok,* I have not	بزده يوق *bizdé yok,* we have not
سنده يوق *sendé yok,* thou hast not	سزده يوق *sizdé yok,* you have not
انده يوق *onda yok,* he, she, or it has not	انلرده يوق *onlarda yok,* they have not.

264. The name of the thing possessed is put before وار. Example, بنده الما وار *bendé elma var* (I have an apple), سنده قلم وار ايدی *sendé kalem var ĭdĭ* (thou hadst a pen), انلرده كتابلر وار ايسه *onlarda kitáblar var ĭssa* (if they have books).

EXERCISE XII.

Turkey (دولت عليه *devleti-aliyé*) has a large fleet. Germany has the largest army in Europe, but she has not a very large fleet. You have pens (قلم *kalem*), ink, and paper (كاغد *kiaghid*). He has very beautiful pictures (رسم *ressm*). Your friend has a large garden. I had a penknife (چاقی *chakĭ*). You had a pencil (قورشون قلم *kourshoun kalem*). The tree has leaves (يپراق *yaprăk*). If you have not a book you cannot read. He has great wealth (مال *măl*). We have no* money. He has no sense (عقل *akl*). He had no patience (صبر *sabr*). You have no paper, but you have pens and ink. My friend has a farm (چفتلك *chiftlik*) near (قربنده *kourbĭnda*) Smyrna. I have two houses in Constantinople. That poor woman had many children, but most (اكثر *ekser*) of them have died. How many children have you? I have none (هيچ *hich*). My brother had a beautiful sword (قلج *kĭlĭj*), which he brought from Damascus (دمشق *damashk*). You have not a good sword, but you have a very good gun (تفنك *tufek*). We have not time to read. That boy is very industrious, but he has not any† capacity (اقتدار *iktidar*). You have capacity, but you are not industrious.

Conjugation of a Negative Verb.

265. A verb is made negative by simply putting م after the root. It is then conjugated in the same manner as any other verb quite regularly, except in the aorist, as will be seen from below.

Infinitive Mood.

يازممق *yazmamak*, not to write.

Indicative Mood.

Present.

Singular.	Plural.
يازميورم *yazmayoroum*, I do not write	يازميورز *yazmayorouz*, we do not write
يازميورسن *yazmayorsoun*, thou dost not write	يازميورسكز *yazmayorsounouz*, you do not write
يازميور *yazmayor*, he does not write	يازميورلر *yazmayorlar*, they do not write

---

* Say we have not money.　　　† Say he has not capacity.

Imperfect.

Singular.	Plural.
يازميور ايدم *yazmayor oudoum,* I did not write or was not writing	يازميور ايدق *yazmayor oudouk,* we did not write or were not writing
يازميور ايدك *yazmayor oudoun,* thou didst not write or wast not writing	يازميور ايدكز *yazmayor oudounouz,* you did not write or were not writing
يازميور ايدى *yazmayor oudou,* he did not write or was not writing	يازميور ايديلر *yazmayor oudoular,* they did not write or were not writing

Aorist.

يازمم *yazmam,* I do not write or shall not write	يازميز *yazmayïz,* we do not write or shall not write
يازمزسن *yazmazsïn,* thou dost not write or shalt not write	يازمازسكز *yazmazsïnïz,* you do not write or will not write
يازماز *yazmaz,* he does not write or will not write	يازمازلر *yazmazlar,* they do not write or will not write

Past.

يازماز ايدم *yazmaz ïdïm,** I used not to write or would not write	يازمازدق *yazmazdïk,* we used not to write or would not write
يازماز ايدك *yazmaz ïdïn,* thou usedst not to write or would not write	يازمازدكز *yazmazdïnïz,* you used not to write or would not write
يازماز ايدى *yazmaz ïdï,* he used not to write or would not write	يازمازديلر *yazmazdïlar,* they used not to write or would not write

Perfect.

يازمدم *yazmadïm,* I did not write, I have not written	يازمدق *yazmadïk,* we did not write, we have not written
يازمدك *yazmadïn,* thou didst not write, thou hast not written	يازمدكز *yazmadïnïz,* you did not write, you have not written
يازمدى *yazmadï,* he did not write, he has not written	يازمديلر *yazmadïlar,* they did not write, they have not written

---

* One can say يازماز ايدم *yazmaz ïdïm* or يازمازدم *yazmazdïm,* يازمازدك *yazmazdïn* or يازماز ايدك *yazmaz ïdïn,* and so on.

Future.

Singular.	Plural.
يازميه‌جغم *yazmayajaghĭm*, I shall or will not write	يازميه‌جغز يازميه‌جغز *yazmayajaghĭz*, we shall or will not write
يازميه‌جقسن *yazmayajaksĭn*, thou shalst or wilst not write	يازميه‌جقسكز يازميه‌جقسكز *yazmayajaksĭnĭz*, you shall or will not write
يازميه‌جق *yazmayajak*, he shall or will not write	يازميه‌جقلر يازميه‌جقلر *yazmayajaklar*, they shall or will not write

Necessitative.

Present.

يازمه‌ملييم *yazmamalĭyĭm*, I must or ought not to write	يازمه‌مليِيز *yazmamalĭyĭz*, we must or ought not to write
يازمه‌مليسن *yazmamalĭsĭn*, thou must or ought not to write	يازمه‌مليسكز *yazmamalĭsĭnĭz*, you must or ought not to write
يازمه‌ملى در *yazmamalĭ dĭr*, he must or ought not to write	يازمه‌ملى درلر *yazmamalĭ dĭrlar*, they must or ought not to write

Perfect.

يازمه‌ملى‌ايدم *yazmamalĭyĭdĭm*, I ought not to have written, and so on.

Conditional.

Present.

يازمه‌سم *yazmasam*, if I do not write, and so on.

Perfect.

يازمه‌سيدم *yazmasaydĭm*, if I did not write, &c.

Optative.

Present.

يازميه‌يم *yazmayayĭm*, that I may not write, and so on.

Past.

يازميه‌يدم *yazmayaydĭm*, that I might not write.

Imperative.

Singular.	Plural.
	يازميـيهلم *yazmayalĭm,* let us not write
يازمه *yazma,* write thou not	يازميكز *yazmayĭnĭz,* write not
يازمسون *yazmasĭn,* let him not write	يازمسونلر *yazmasĭnlar,* let them not write.

EXERCISE XIII.

He does not read well, but he writes pretty well (ايوجه *éyjé*). He will not go to London. We shall not travel this year, but we travelled a great deal last year. Do not write a very long (اوزون *ouzoun*) letter. We have not seen each other for (برو *béri*) a long time. Let him not speak till I come. Do not let us speak. He ought not to have spoken. Oh, that I had not seen him! We do not know when the steamer (وابور *vapor*) will start (قالقمق *kálkmak*). It will start to-morrow morning (صباحلبن *sabahléin*), but I do not know at what o'clock. You do not know the name of the vessel (كمى *ghémi*). Do not start before the post arrives (كلمك *ghelmek*). We do not write. He did not run (قوشمق *koshmak*). He would not run. We do not walk every day. He used not to rise (قالقمق *kálkmak*) early. He does not sleep well. We shall not go (ياتمق *yatmak*) to bed. He has not gone to bed. We do not swim. If you do not study you will never learn Turkish, for it is a very difficult language. You ought not to be (اولمق *olmak*) idle (تنبل *tenbel*). He did not work. Light (ياقمق *yakmak*) a candle (موم *moum*). Do not light a candle. Let him light it. Do not put (سوندرمك *seundurmek*) it out. You will put it out, if you do not take (صاقنمق *sakĭnmak*) care. I shall not put it out.

The Interrogative Form of the Verb.

266. A verb is conjugated interrogatively by the use of the particle مى (pronounced *mi, mĭ, mou,* or *mu,* according to the vowels soft or hard by which it is preceded—see 58 and 68). It is generally placed before the characteristic endings of the different *simple* tenses, except in the third person, and before the termination ايدى *idi* of the *compound* tenses, even in the third person, as الورميـيم *alĭrmĭyĭm* (do I take?), الورمسن *alĭrmĭsĭn* (dost thou take?), الورمى *alĭrmĭ* (does he take?), اليورميـيوم *aliyormouyoum* (am I taking?), اله جقمـيم *alajakmĭyĭm* (shall I take?), الملوميـيم *almalĭmĭyĭm* (ought I to take?), الملوميـيدم *almalĭmĭyĭdĭm* (ought I to have taken?); باقدى مـيدى *bákdĭ mĭdĭ* (had he looked?). But in the perfect of the indicative, and in the optative* and imperative, it comes completely at the

---

* Except in the second person singular and plural,

end of the verb; as سودممى *sevdimmi* (did I love?), كلديمى *gheldimmi* (did he come?), يازدقمى *yazdĭkmĭ* (did we write?), طوردكزمى *dourdou-nouzmou* (did you remain?), ويرهيمى *véréyimmi* (shall I give, or may I give?), يازسونمى *yazsinmĭ* (may he write, or shall he write?).

Conjugation of a Verb Interrogatively.

المتى *almak* (to take).

Indicative Mood.

Present.

Singular.	Plural.
اليورميم *alĭyormouyoum*, do I take? am I taking?	اليورميز *alĭyormouyouz*, do we take? are we taking?
اليورميسن *alĭyormousoun*, dost thou take? art thou taking?	اليورميسكز *alĭyormousounouz*, do you take? are you taking?
اليورمى *alĭyormou*, does he take? is he taking?	اليورلرمى *alĭyorlarmĭ*, do they take? are they taking?

Aorist.

الورميم *alĭrmĭyĭm*, do I take? shall I take?	الورميز *alĭrmĭyĭz*, do we take? shall we take?
الورميسن *alĭrmĭsĭn*, dost thou take? wilt thou take?	الورميسكز *alĭrmĭsĭnĭz*, do you take? will you take?
الورمى *alĭrmĭ*, does he take? will he take?	الرلرمى *alĭrlarmĭ*, do they take? will they take?

Past.

الورميدم *alĭrmĭdĭm*, } used I to take?	الورميدق *alĭrmĭdĭk*, used we to take?
or الورميديدم *alĭrmĭyĭdĭm*, }	
الورميدڭ *alĭrmĭdĭn*, usedst thou to take?	الورميدكز *alĭrmĭdĭnĭz*, used you to take?
الورميدى *alĭrmĭdĭ*, used he to take?	الورميديلر *alĭrmĭdĭlar*, used they to take?

Perfect.

الدمى *aldĭmmĭ*, did I take, or have I taken?	الدقمى *aldĭkmĭ*, did we take, or have we taken?
الدكسمى *aldĭnmĭ*, didst thou take, or hast thou taken?	الدكزمى *aldĭnĭzmĭ*, did you take, or have you taken?
الدىمى *aldĭmmĭ*, did he take, or has he taken?	الديلرمى *aldĭlarmĭ*, did they take, or have they taken?

Future.

Singular.	Plural.
الله‌جقمييم *alajakmĭyĭm*, shall I take?	الله‌جقمييز *alajakmĭyĭz*, shall we take?
الله‌جقميسن *alajakmĭsĭn*, shalt thou take?	الله‌جقميسكز *alajakmĭsĭnĭz*, shall you take?
الله‌جقمى *alajakmĭ*, shall he take?	الله‌جقلرمى *alajaklarmĭ*, shall they take?

Necessitative.

Present.

الملیمییم *almalĭmĭyĭm*, ought I to take, or must I take?	الملیمییز *almalĭmĭyĭz*, ought we to take, or must we take?
الملیمیسن *almalĭmĭsĭn*, oughtst thou to take, or must thou take?	الملیمیسكز *almalĭmĭsĭnĭz*, ought you to take, or must you take?
الملیمى *almalĭmĭ*, ought he to take, or must he take?	الملیلرمى *almalĭlarmĭ*, ought they to take, or must they take?

Perfect.

الملیمییدم *almalĭmĭyĭdĭm*, ought I to have taken, or was I obliged to take?	الملیمییدق *almalĭmĭyĭdĭk*, ought we to have taken, or were we obliged to take?
الملیمییدك *almalĭmĭyĭdĭn*, oughtest thou to have taken, or wast thou obliged to take?	الملیمییدكز *almalĭmĭyĭdĭnĭz*, ought you to have taken, or were you obliged to take?
الملیمییدى *almalĭmĭyĭdĭ*, ought he to have taken, or was he obliged to take?	الملیمییدیلر *almalĭmĭyĭdilar*, ought they to have taken, or were they obliged to take?

Optative.

الله‌یمى *alayĭmmĭ*, may I take, or shall I take?	الله‌لمى *alalĭmmĭ*, may we take, or shall we take?
الله‌میسن *alamĭsĭn*, mayst thou take, or shalt thou take?	الله‌میسكز *alamĭsĭnĭz*, may you take, or shall you take?
الله‌مى *alamĭ*, may he take, or shall he take?	الله‌لرمى *alalarmi*, may they take, or shall they take?

Imperative.

السونمى *alsĭnmĭ*, may he take, or shall he take?	السونلرمى *alsĭnlarmĭ*, may they take, or shall they take?

EXERCISE XIV.

Do you know Turkish? I know it pretty well. Did your friend come yester-day? He did not come yesterday, but he will come to-day. Will you write to me every week? Ought I to have written? You ought not to have written. Shall I read? Shall* we take (كزمك *ghézmek*) a walk? Did they take a walk? Did you run? Shall I call (چاغرمق *chaghïrmak*) the servant (خدمتكار *hizmetkiar*)?† Do not call him, he will come. What ‡ is he doing? Is he reading? Shall (كلسونمی *ghelsinmi*) he come? Does he study (چالشمق *chálïshmak*)? Used he to study? Shall I finish (بتورمك *bitirmek*) this letter? Do you swim? Does he give lessons (درس *derss*)? He used to give lessons. Do you know his name? I do not know it, but cannot you ask (سورمق *sormak*)? Is the weather fine? Has it cleared up (أچلمق *achïlmak*)? No, it has not cleared up yet (دها *daha*). Have you read the newspaper to-day? No; did you see it? I did not see it; but cannot you tell me the news? Have you received (المق *álmak*) a telegram (تلغرافنامه *telégrafnamé*)? Who§ sent it? Mr. So-and-so (فلان افندی *filan effendi*) sent it. What does he say?

Conjugation of " To be Able."

267. To express being able to do anything in Turkish, the verb بلمك *bilmek* is used and placed after the other verb, the root only of which is taken and a ه added to it. Some of the most important tenses are subjoined as an illustration.

Indicative Mood.

Present.

Singular.	Plural.
سوه بیلیورم *sevé biliyoroum*, I can love	سوه بیلیورز *sevé biliyorouz*, we can love
سوه بیلیورسن *sevé biliyorsoun*, thou canst love	سوه بیلیورسکز *sevé biliyorsounouz*, you can love
سوه بیلیور *sevé biliyor*, he can love	سوه بیلیورلر *sevé biliyorlar*, they can love

---

* Use the interrogative of the optative.

† The proper pronunciation of this word would, according to the spelling, be *khidmetkiar*, but it is usually pronounced *hizmetkiar.*

‡ When "what" is used, می is not required to show interrogation.

§ When the interrogative pronoun كيم is used, می is not required.

Aorist.

Singular.	Plural.
سوه بلورم *sevé bilirim*, I can love, or I shall be able to love	سوه بلورز *sevé biliriz*, we can love, we shall be able to love
سوه بلورسن *sevé bilirsin*, thou canst love, thou wilt be able to love	سوه بلورسكز *sevé bilirsiniz*, you can love, you will be able to love
سوه بلور *sevé bilir*, he can love, he will be able to love	سوه بلورلر *sevé bilirler*, they can love, they will be able to love

Perfect.

سوه بلدم *sevé bildim*, I could love, or I have been able to love*	سوه بلدك *sevé bildik*, we could love, or we have been able to love
سوه بلدك *sevé bildin*, thou couldst love, thou hast been able to love	سوه بلدكز *sevé bildiniz*, you could love, you have been able to love
سوه بلدى *sevé bildi*, he could love, he has been able to love	سوه بلديلر *sevé bildiler*, they could love, they have been able to love

Future.

سوه بله‌جكم *sevé biléjéyim*, I shall or will be able to love	سوه بله‌جكز *sevé biléjéyiz*, we shall or will be able to love
سوه بله‌جكسن *sevé biléjeksin*, thou shalt or wilt be able to love	سوه بله‌جكسكز *sevé biléjeksiniz*, you shall or will be able to love
سوه بله‌جك *sevé biléjek*, he shall or will be able to love	سوه بله‌جكلر *sevé biléjekler*, they shall or will be able to love

Necessitative.

سوه بلمليم *sevé bilméliyim*, I ought or must be able to love	سوه بلمليز *sevé bilméliyiz*, we ought or must be able to love

Optative.

سوه بله‌يم *sevé biléyim*, that I may be able to love

&c. &c. &c.

268. "Not to be able," is expressed by the negative potential form of the verb. Example, سوه‌ممك *sevémemek* (not to be able to love), سوه‌مم

---

* And also, I would be able to love.

sevémem (I cannot love), سوه‌مدم *sevémadim* (I could not love); اوقومتی
okoumak (to read), اوقویامامك *okouyamamak* (not to be able to read), اوقویاماز
okouyamaz (he cannot read); كیده‌مز *ghidémez* (he cannot go); كله‌مز
ghelémez (he cannot come); and so forth.

EXERCISE XV.

Can you read Turkish? I can read a little (بر از *bir áz*). I wish (كاشكه *keshké*)
I could write well. He cannot swim. I cannot go out (چقمتی *chikmak*) to-morrow.
They can go out. Can you give lessons in English (انكلیزچه *inglizché*)? I cannot.
Birds (قوش *koush*) can fly (اوچمتی *ouchmak*). He ought to be able to write. He
cannot write, but he can read. Can you see? I cannot see. I could not sleep.
I could not write to you, because I had no paper. He could not find my book. I
can find it. Where is it? I cannot tell you, because it is a secret (سر *sir*). My
horse cannot run. He ought to be able to run. Can you send me my box (صندوق
sandik)? I cannot send it. Can you play (اویناماتی *oinamak*) chess? I can play a
little, but I cannot play well. Can you lend (اورد نج ویرمك *eurdunj vermek*) me a
book (كتاب *kitáb*)?

Compound Verbs.

269. Compound verbs are formed by employing Arabic, Persian, and
occasionally Turkish words with the Turkish auxiliary verbs.

Compound *active* verbs are constructed with nouns of action (generally
of Arabic origin) and one of the Turkish auxiliaries, ایتمك *etmek*, ایلمك
éylémek, قیلمتی *kilmak*, بیورمتی *bouyourmak*, all meaning "to do,"* but the
first is most frequently used; as قتل ایتمك *katl etmek* (to kill), from the
Arabic verbal noun قتل *katl* (the action of killing); رجا ایتمك *rija etmek*
(to request), from رجا *rija* (requesting); رسم ایتمك *ressm etmek* (to draw),
from رسم *ressm* (drawing); تكلم ایتمك *tékellum etmek* (to converse, talk);
تشریف ایتمك *teshrif etmek* (to honour, visit); درج ایتمك *derj etmek* (to
insert).

Compound *passive* verbs are constructed with the same words and the
passive form of the auxiliary verbs ایدلمك *edilmek*, قیلنمتی *kilinmak*, and
بیورلمتی *boyouroulmak*, or, more frequently, with the passive form of the
verb اولمك *olmak*; viz., اولنمتی *olounmak*, a passive form of the verb
"to become," to which we have nothing corresponding in English; as
قتل اولنمتی *katl olounmak* (to be killed), تشریف اولنمتی *teshrif olounmak* (to

---

* The original meaning of بیورمتی *bouyourmak* is "to deign," "to be kind enough."

be honoured), درج اولنمق *derj olounmak* or درج ا يديلملك *derj edilmek* (to be inserted).

Compound *neuter* verbs are obtained by uniting Arabic or Persian active and passive participles to the neuter verb اولمق *olmak* (to be); as, راضى اولمق *razï olmak* (to consent), from راضى, an Arabic word meaning "consenting, who consents," literally, to be a consenter, or one who consents.

Model of the Conjugation of a Compound Active Verb.

قتل ايتملك *katl etmek*, to kill.

Indicative Mood.

Present.

Singular.	Plural.
قتل ايديورم *katl ediyoroum*, I kill	قتل ايديورز *katl ediyorouz*, we kill
قتل ايديورسن *katl ediyorsoun*, thou killest	قتل ايديورسكز *katl ediyorsounouz*, you kill
قتل ايديور *katl ediyor*, he kills	قتل ايديورلر *katl ediyorlar*, they kill

Imperfect.

قتل ايديوردم *katl ediyordoum*, I was killing	قتل ايديوردق *katl ediyordouk*, we were killing

&c. &c.

Aorist.

قتل ايدرم *katl ederim*, I kill (habitually), or I shall kill	قتل ايدرز *katl ederiz*, we kill (habitually), or shall kill
قتل ايدرسن *katl edersin*, thou killest, or wilt kill	قتل ايدرسكز *katl edersiniz*, you kill, or will kill
قتل ايدر *katl eder*, he kills, or will [kill	قتل ايدرلر *katl ederler*, they kill, or will

Past.

قتل ايدرايدم* *katl eder idim*, I used to kill, or would kill	قتل ايدردك *katl ederdik*, we used to kill, or would kill
قتل ايدردك *katl eder din*, thou usedst to kill, or wouldst kill	قتل ايدردكز *katl ederdiniz*, you used to kill, or would kill
قتل ايدردى *katl eder di*, he used to kill, or would kill	قتل ايدرديلر *katl ederdiler*, they used to kill, or would kill

* Or قتل ايدردم *katl ederdim*, &c.

Perfect.

Singular.	Plural.
قتل ايتدم *katl etdim,* I killed, or have killed	قتل ايتدك *katl etdik,* we killed, or have killed
قتل ايتدك *katl etdin,* thou killedst, or hast killed	قتل ايتدكز *katl etdiniz,* you killed, or have killed
قتل ايتدى *katl etdi,* he killed, or has killed	قتل ايتديلر *katl etdiler,* they killed, or have killed

Future.

قتل ايده جكم *katl edéjeyim,* I shall or will kill	قتل ايده جكز *katl edejéyiz,* we shall or will kill
قتل ايده جكسن *katl edéjeksin,* thou shalt or wilt kill	قتل ايده جكسكز *katl edéjeksiniz,* you shall or will kill
قتل ايده جك *katl edéjek,* he shall or will kill	قتل ايده جكلر *katl edejekler,* they shall or will kill

Necessitative.

Present.

قتل ايتملييم *katl etméliyim,* I must kill, or ought to kill	قتل ايتملييز *katl etméliyiz,* we must kill, or ought to kill
قتل ايتمليسن *katl etmélisin,* thou must kill, or ought to kill	قتل ايتمليسكز *katl etmélisiniz,* you must kill, or ought to kill
قتل ايتملى (در) *katl etméli (dir),* he must kill, or ought to kill	قتل ايتمليدرلر *katl etmélidirler,* they must kill, or ought to kill

Perfect.

قتل ايتملييدم *katl etméliyidim,* I ought to have killed, or I was obliged to kill	قتل ايتملييدك *katl etméliyidik,* we ought to have killed, or were obliged to kill
قتل ايتملييدك *katl etméliyidin,* thou oughtest to have killed, or thou wast obliged to kill	قتل ايتملييدكز *katl etméliyidiniz,* you ought to have killed, or were obliged to kill
قتل ايتملييدى *katl etméliyidi,* he ought to have killed, or was obliged to kill	قتل ايتملييديلر *katl etméliyidiler,* they ought to have killed, or were obliged to kill

Conditional.
Aorist.

Singular.	Plural.
قتل ايتسم *katl etsém*, if I kill	قتل ايتسك *katl eték*, if we kill
قتل ايتسك *katl etsén*, if thou kill	قتل ايتسكز *katl etséniz*, if you kill
قتل ايتسه *katl etsé*, if he kill	قتل ايتسهلر *katl etséler*, if they kill.

Perfect.

قتل ايتسيدم *katl etséyidim*, if I killed or had killed	قتل ايتسيدك *katl etséyidik*, if we killed or had killed
قتل ايتسيدك *katl etséyidin*, if thou killed or had killed	قتل ايتسيدكز *katl etséyidiniz*, if you killed or had killed
قتل ايتسيدى *katl etséyidi*, if he killed or had killed	قتل ايتسيديلر *katl etséyidiler*, if they killed or had killed

Optative.
Present.

قتل ايدهيم *katl edéyim*, that I may kill	قتل ايدهوز* *katl edéyiz*, that we may kill
قتل ايدهسن *katl edésin*, that thou mayest kill	قتل ايدهسكز *katl edéseniz*, that you may kill [kill
قتل ايده *katl edé*, that he may kill	قتل ايدهلر *katl edéler*, that they may

Perfect.

قتل ايدهايدم *katl edéyidim*, that I might kill, or might have killed	قتل ايديدك *katl edéyidik*,† that we might kill, or might have killed
قتل ايديدك *katl edéyidin*,† that thou mightst kill, or mightst have killed	قتل ايديدكز *katl edéyidiniz*,† that you might kill, or might have killed
قتل ايديدى *katl edéyidi*,† that he might kill, or might have killed	قتل ايديديلر *katl edéyidiler*,† that they might kill, or might have killed

Imperative.

	قتل ايدهلم *katl edélim*, let us kill
قتل ايت *katl et*, kill thou [kill	قتل ايدكز *katl ediniz*, kill you
قتل ايتسون *katl etsin*, let him, her, or it	قتل ايتسونلر *katl etsinler*, let them kill

---

* Also written ايدهيز.

† Also *sometimes*, but not generally, written قتل ايدهايدى, قتل ايدهايدك, قتل ايدهايدكز, and قتل ايدهايديلر, قتل ايدهايدك.

Participles.

ACTIVE.

Present.

قتل ايدن *katl eden,* killing, who or which kills, killed, or will kill.

Aorist.

قتل ايدر *katl eder,* killing, who or which kills habitually, or will kill.

Past.

قتل ايتمش *katl etmish,* who or which has killed.

Perfect.

قتل ايتدك *katl etdik,* who or which has killed.

Future.

قتل ايده‌جك *katl edéjek,* who or which will kill.

PASSIVE.

قتل ايتدك *katl etdik,* who or which is or has been killed

قتل ايده‌جك *katl edéjek,* who or which will be killed.

Verbal Nouns.

قتل ايتمه *katl etma,* the action of killing

قتل ايتدك *katl etdik,* the action of having killed

قتل ايده‌جك *katl edéjek,* the action of being about to kill.

Gerunds.

قتل ايدوب *katl edip,* killing, having killed

قتل ايده‌رك *katl edérek,* killing, continuing to kill

قتل ايديجك *katl edijek* ⎫
قتل ايدنجه *katl edinjé* ⎬ on killing, as soon as killing occurs

قتل ايده ايده *katl edé edé,* by dint of killing, by repeatedly killing

قتل ايتمكين *katl etméyin,* by reason of killing

قتل ايده‌لى *katl edéli,* since killing.

EXERCISE XVI.

Can you draw (رسم ايتمك *ressm etmek*)? I can draw a little. My brother draws very well, and he will help (يارد‌م ايتمك *yardĭm etmek*) you. You must make haste (عجله ايتمك *ajelé etmek*). Let us make haste. I must make haste, because I am very tired (يورغون *yorghoun*). You must sign (امضا ايتمك *imza etmek*) this paper. I signed it yesterday. The letter I signed was very important (مهم *muhim*). The enemy (دشمن *dushmen*) destroyed (تلف ايتمك *télef etmek*) several towns and killed the inhabitants (سكنه *sekéné*). Will you help me? I will always help you. I thank (تشكر ايتمك *téshekkiur etmek*) you. He promised (وعد ايتمك *vad etmek*) to lend me a book. If you promise, you must perform (اجرا ايتمك *ijra etmek*). He has performed what he promised. I cannot promise. We promise. They promised, but they did not perform. Did the gardener (باغچوان *bághchéwán*) send (ارسال ايتمك *irsal etmek*) the fruit (يمش *yémish*)? He has not sent it. You ought not to delay (تأخر ايتمك *téékhkhur etmek*). He always delays. Did you visit (زيارت ايتمك *ziyaret etmek*) your friend? I have not visited him lately (كچنلرده *gechenlerdé*). I regret (تأسف ايتمك *téessouf etmek*) it. Do you regret it? We shall regret it. I do not regret it. We do not regret it. Have you lost (غائب ايتمك *kaïb etmek*) your money? Yes, I have lost it. He has lost his handkerchief (منديل *mendil*)? We lost our books. He has lost nothing (هيچ *hich*). Did your friend preach (وعظ ايتمك *vaz etmek*) last (كچن *gechen*) Sunday (بازاركونى *bazar ghiunu*)? No, but he will preach next (كله جك *ghéléjek*) Sunday. Make haste, it is late (كچ *ghech*). We made haste. He did not make haste. You must make haste. He ought to have made haste. Shall we make haste? Having written the letter, he sent it at once (اول ساعت *ol saat*).

Conjugation of a Neuter Compound Verb.

270. Neuter compound verbs are formed by putting اولمق *olmak* after Arabic or Persian participles. Example, راضى اولمق *razï olmak* (to consent, literally, to become one who consents).

Indicative Mood.

Present.

Singular.	Plural.
راضى اوليورم *razï olïyorĭm*,* I consent	راضى اوليوريز *razï olïyorĭz*, we consent
راضى اوليورسن *razï olïyorsĭn*, thou consentest	راضى اوليورسكز *razï olïyorsĭnĭz*, you consent
راضى اوليور *razï olïyor*, he consents	راضى اوليورلر *razï olïyorlar*, they consent

* Or *razï olouyoroum, olouyorsoun, olouyor, olouyorsounouz,* &c.

Imperfect.

Singular.	Plural.
راضی اوليوردم *razĭ olĭyordĭm,** ⎱ I or راضی اوليورايدم *razĭ olĭyorĭdĭm,* ⎰ was consenting	راضی اوليوردك *razĭ olĭyordĭk,* we were consenting
راضی اوليوردن *razĭ olĭyordĭn,* thou wast consenting	راضی اوليوردكز *razĭ olĭyordĭnĭz,* you were consenting
راضی اوليوردی *razĭ olĭyordĭ,* he was consenting	راضی اوليورديلر *razĭ olĭyordĭlar,* they were consenting

Aorist.

راضی اولورم *razĭ olouroum,* I consent (habitually), or will consent	راضی اولورز *razĭ olourouz,* we consent (habitually), or will con- sent
راضی اولورسن *razĭ oloursoun,* thou con- sentest (habitually), or wilt consent	راضی اولورسكز *razĭ oloursounouz,* you con- sent (habitually), or will consent
راضی اولور *razĭ olour,* he consents (habitually), or will consent	راضی اولورلر *razĭ olourlar,* they consent (habitually), or will con- sent

Past.

راضی اولوردم *razĭ olourdoum,* ⎱ I or راضی اولورايدم *razĭ olour-oudoum,* ⎰ would consent, or used to consent	راضی اولوردق *razĭ olourdouk,* ⎱ we or راضی اولورايدق *razĭ olour-oudouk,* ⎰ would consent, or used to consent
راضی اولوردك *razĭ olourdoun,* ⎱ or راضی اولورايدك *razĭ olour-oudoun,* ⎰ thou wouldst con- sent, or usedst to consent	راضی اولوردكز *razĭ olourdounouz,* ⎱ or راضی اولورايدكز *razĭ olour-oudounouz,* ⎰ you would consent, or used to consent
راضی اولوردی *razĭ olourdou,* ⎱ he or راضی اولورايدی *razĭ olour-oudou,* ⎰ would consent, or used to consent	راضی اولورديلر *razĭ olourdoular,* ⎱ or راضی اولورايديلر *razĭ olour-oudoular,* ⎰ they would consent, or used to consent

---

* Or *olouyordoum* or *olouyor oudoum,* &c.

H

Perfect.

Singular.	Plural.
راضى اولدم *razĭ oldoum*, I consented, or have consented	راضى اولدق *razĭ oldouk*, we consented, or have consented
راضى اولدك *razĭ oldoun*, thou consentedst, or hast consented	راضى اولدكز *razĭ oldounouz*, you consented, or have consented
راضى اولدى *razĭ oldou*, he consented, or has consented	راضى اولديلر *razĭ oldoular*, they consented, or have consented

Future.

راضى اوله جغم *razĭ olajaghĭm*, I shall or will consent	راضى اوله جغز *razĭ olajaghĭz*, we shall or will consent
راضى اوله جقسن *razĭ olajaksĭn*, thou shalt or wilt consent	راضى اوله جقسكز *razĭ olajaksĭnĭz*, you shall or will consent
راضى اوله جق *razĭ olajak*, he shall or will consent	راضى اوله جقلر *rāzĭ olajaklar*, they shall or will consent

Necessitative.

Present.

راضى اولملويم *razĭ olmalĭyĭm*, I must or ought to consent	راضى اولملويز *razĭ olmalĭyĭz*, we must or ought to consent
راضى اولملوسن *razĭ olmalĭsĭn*, thou must or ought to consent	راضى اولملوسكز *razĭ olmalĭsĭnĭz*, you must or ought to consent
راضى اولملو *razĭ olmalĭ*, he must or ought to consent	راضى اولملولر *razĭ olmalĭlar*, they must or ought to consent

Perfect.

راضى اولملوايدم *razĭ olmalĭyĭdĭm*, I ought to have consented, or was obliged to consent	راضى اولملوايدق *razĭ olmalĭyĭdĭk*, we ought to have consented, or were obliged to consent
راضى اولملوايدك *razĭ olmalĭyĭdĭn*, thou oughtest to have consented, or wast obliged to consent	راضى اولملوايدكز *razĭ olmalĭyĭdĭnĭz*, you ought to have consented, or were obliged to consent
راضى اولملوايدى *razĭ olmalĭyĭdĭ*, he ought to have consented, or was obliged to consent	راضى اولملوايديلر *razĭ olmalĭyĭdĭlar*, they ought to have consented, or were obliged to consent

Optative.

Present.

<table>
<tr><td colspan="2">Singular.</td><td colspan="2">Plural.</td></tr>
<tr><td>راضی اولهیم</td><td>*razĭ olayĭm*, that I may consent [consent</td><td>راضی اولهیز *</td><td>*razĭ olayĭz*, that we may consent [consent</td></tr>
<tr><td>راضی اولهسن</td><td>*razĭ olasĭn*, that thou mayest</td><td>راضی اولهسکز</td><td>*razĭ olasĭnĭz*, that you may</td></tr>
<tr><td>راضی اوله</td><td>*razĭ ola*, that he may consent</td><td>راضی اولهلر</td><td>*razĭ olalar*, that they may consent</td></tr>
</table>

Perfect.

<table>
<tr><td>راضی اولهیدم</td><td>*razĭ olaydĭm*, that I might consent, or might have consented</td><td>راضی اولهیدق</td><td>*razĭ olaydĭk*, that we might consent, or might have consented</td></tr>
<tr><td>راضی اولهیدك</td><td>*razĭ olaydĭn*, that thou mightest consent, or might have consented</td><td>راضی اولهیدکز</td><td>*razĭ olaydĭnĭz*, that you might consent, or might have consented</td></tr>
<tr><td>راضی اولهیدی</td><td>*razĭ olaydĭ*, that he might consent, or might have consented</td><td>راضی اولهیدیلر</td><td>*razĭ olaydĭlar*, that they might consent, or might have consented</td></tr>
</table>

Conditional.

Aorist.

<table>
<tr><td>راضی اولسم</td><td>*razĭ olsam*, if I consent</td><td>راضی اولسق</td><td>*razĭ olsak*, if we consent</td></tr>
<tr><td>راضی اولسك</td><td>*razĭ olsan*, if thou consentest</td><td>راضی اولسکز</td><td>*razĭ olsanĭz*, if you consent</td></tr>
<tr><td>راضی اولسه</td><td>*razĭ olsa*, if he consent</td><td>راضی اولسهلر</td><td>*razĭ olsalar*, if they consent</td></tr>
</table>

Perfect.

<table>
<tr><td>راضی اولسیدم</td><td>*razĭ olsaydĭm*, if I consented, or if I had consented</td><td>راضی اولسیدق</td><td>*razĭ olsaydĭk*, if we consented, or had consented</td></tr>
<tr><td>راضی اولسیدك</td><td>*razĭ olsaydĭn*, if thou consentedst, or hadst consented</td><td>راضی اولسیدکز</td><td>*razĭ olsaydĭnĭz*, if you consented, or had consented</td></tr>
<tr><td>راضی اولسیدی</td><td>*razĭ olsaydĭ*, if he consented, or had consented</td><td>راضی اولسیدیلر</td><td>*razĭ olsaydĭlar*, if they consented, or had consented</td></tr>
</table>

* Also spelt اولهوز. In common conversation, too, the first person plural of the imperative اولهلم *olalĭm* is used instead of اوله یز *olayĭz*.

Imperative.

<table>
<tr><td align="center">Singular.</td><td align="center">Plural.</td></tr>
<tr>
<td>راضی اول razï ol, consent thou</td>
<td>راضی اوله لم razï olalïm, let us consent</td>
</tr>
<tr>
<td>راضی اولسون razï olsoun, let him, her, or it consent</td>
<td>راضی اولكز razï olounouz, consent you</td>
</tr>
<tr>
<td></td>
<td>راضی اولسونلر razï olsounlar, let them consent</td>
</tr>
</table>

Participles,

Active.

راضی اولان <i>razï olan</i>, consenting, who or which consents, consented, or will consent

راضی اولور <i>razï olour</i>, consenting, who consents or will consent

راضی اولمش <i>razï olmoush</i>, who has consented

راضی اولدق <i>razï oldouk</i>, who has consented

راضی اوله جق <i>razï olajak</i>, who will consent

Passive.

راضی اولدق <i>razï oldouk</i>, which is consented to

راضی اوله جق <i>razï olajak</i>, which will be consented to.

Verbal Nouns.

راضی اولمه <i>razï olma</i>, the act of consenting

راضی اولدق <i>razï oldouk</i>, the act of having consented

راضی اوله جق <i>razï olajak</i>, the act of being about to consent.

Gerunds.

راضی اولوب <i>razï oloup</i>, consenting (first consenting then)

راضی اوله رق <i>razï olarak</i>, consenting, continuing to consent

راضی اولیجق <i>razï olïjak</i>, ⎫
راضی اولنجه <i>razï olounja</i>, ⎬ on consenting, as soon as consenting

راضی اوله اوله <i>razï ola ola</i>, by dint of consenting

راضی اولمغین <i>razï olmaghin</i>, by reason of consenting

راضی اوله لو <i>razï olálï</i>, since consenting.

EXERCISE XVII.

I shall be a soldier. He has become a soldier. Did he consent? He did not consent. When did that happen (واقی اولمق *vakï olmak*)? It happened last week. We shall repent (پشیمان اولمق *pishmán* olmak*) (it). He repented (it). I am very glad (ممنون *memnoun*) that I have seen you. I have not seen you for (برو *beri*) a long (چوقدن *chokdan*) time. You will dine (طعام ایتمك *taam etmek*) with us? I cannot dine with you to-day. He disappeared (نا پیدا اولمق *na péyda olmak*). We prevailed (غالب اولمق *ghalib olmak*). You prevailed. They must prevail. He will profit (فائدهمند اولمق *faïdémend olmak*) by this experience (تجربه *tejribé*). You profited by what you saw. We have succeeded (مظهر توفق اولمق *mázhari-tevfik olmak*). Oh! that I might succeed. I shall be very grieved (متأسف *mutéssif*) if you go. You must not be sorry, because I shall return (عودت ایتمك *avdet etmek*) soon (عن قریب *an karib*). Has your brother returned? Yes. I was not aware (خبردار اولمق *khabrdar olmak*) of it. You must have been aware of it. If we had been aware of it.

Conjugation of a Compound Passive Verb.

271. Passive compound verbs are formed by putting اولنمق *olounmak*, the passive form of the auxiliary verb اولمق *olmak* (to become), after Arabic verbal nouns (see 269). Example,—

قتل اولنمق *katl olounmak*, to be killed.

Indicative Mood.
Present.

Singular.	Plural.
قتل اولنیورم *katl olounouyouroum*,† I am being killed	قتل اولنیورز *katl olounouyorouz*, we are being killed
قتل اولنیورسن *katl olounouyoursoun*, thou art being killed	قتل اولنیورسکز *katl olounouyorsounouz*, you are being killed
قتل اولنیور *katl olounouyor*, he is being killed	قتل اولنیورلر *katl olounouyorlar*, they are being killed

---

* The original Persian pronunciation is *peshiman*, but the Turks say *pishmán*.

† Or *olouniyorïm*, &c.

Imperfect.

Singular.	Plural.
قتل اولنيور ايدم *katl olounouyor ou-* doum,* I was being killed	قتل اولنيور ايدق *katl olounouyor ou-* douk, we were being killed
قتل اولنيور ايدك *katl olounouyor oudoun,* thou wast being killed	قتل اولنيور ايدكز *katl olounouyor ou-* dounouz, you were being killed
قتل اولنيور ايدى *katl olounouyor oudou,* he was being killed	قتل اولنيورلر ايدى *katl olounouyorlar ou-* dou, they were being killed

Aorist.

قتل اولنورم *katl olounouroum,* I am killed, or shall be killed	قتل اولنورز *katl olounourouz,* we are killed, or shall be killed
قتل اولنورسن *katl olounoursoun,* thou art killed, or wilt be killed	قتل اولنورسكز *katl olounoursounouz,* you are killed, or will be killed
قتل اولنور *katl olounour,* he is killed, or will be killed	قتل اولنورلر *katl olounourlar,* they are killed, or will be killed

Past.

قتل اولنوردم *katl olounourdoum,*† I was killed, or would be killed	قتل اولنوردق *katl olounourdouk,* we were killed, or would be killed
قتل اولنوردك *katl olounourdoun,* thou wast killed, or would be killed	قتل اولنوردكز *katl olounourdounouz,* you were killed, or would be killed
قتل اولنوردى *katl olounourdou,* he was killed, or would be killed	قتل اولنورديلر *katl olounourdoular,* they were killed, or would be killed

---

* Or قتل اولنيوردم *katl olounouyordoum,* &c.
† Or قتل اولنور ايدم *katl olounour oudoum,* &c.

Perfect.

Singular.	Plural.
قتل اولندم *katl oloundoum,* I was killed, or have been killed	قتل اولندق *katl oloundouk,* we were killed, or have been killed
قتل اولندك *katl oloundoun,* thou wast killed, or hast been killed	قتل اولندكز *katl oloundounouz,* you were killed, or have been killed
قتل اولندى *katl oloundou,* he was killed, or has been killed	قتل اولنديلر *katl oloundoular,* they were killed, or have been killed

Future.

قتل اولنه‌جغم *katl olounajaghĭm,* I shall or will be killed	قتل اولنه‌جغز *katl olounajaghĭz,* we shall or will be killed
قتل اولنه‌جقسن *katl olounajaksĭn,* thou shalt or wilt be killed	قتل اولنه‌جقسكز *katl olounajaksĭnĭz,* you shall or will be killed
قتل اولنه‌جق *katl olounajak,* he shall or will be killed	قتل اولنه‌جقلر *katl olounajaklar,* they shall or will be killed

Necessitative.

Present.

قتس اولنملوايم *katl olounmalĭyĭm,* I must or ought to be killed	قتل اولنملويز *katl olounmalĭyĭz,* we must or ought to be killed
قتل اولنملوسن *katl olounmalĭsĭn,* thou must or ought to be killed	قتل اولنملوسكز *katl olounmalĭsĭnĭz,* you must or ought to be killed
قتل اولنملو *katl olounmalĭ,* he must or ought to be killed	قتل اولنملولر *katl olounmalĭlar,* they must or ought to be killed

Perfect.

قتل اولنملو ايدم *katl olounmalĭ idim,* I was obliged to be killed, or ought to have been killed, &c., &c.

Optative.

Present.

قتل اولنه‌يم *katl olounayĭm,* that I may be killed, &c.

Perfect.

قتل *اولنيدم *katl olounaydĭm,* that I might be killed, or might have been killed, &c.

---

* Also spelt اولنه‌ايدم.

Conditional.

Aorist.

قتل اولنسم *katl olounsam*, if I be killed, &c.

Perfect.

قتل *اولنسيدم* *katl olounsaydim*, if I were killed, or if I had been killed, &c., &c.

Imperative.

Singular.	Plural.
	قتل اولنه‌لم *katl olounalĭm*, let us be killed
قتل اولن *katl oloun*, be thou killed	قتل اولنكز *katl olounouz*, be killed
قتل اولنسون *katl olounsoun*, let him, her, or it be killed	قتل اولنسونلر *katl olounsounlar*, let them be killed

Participles.

Active.

قتل اولنان *katl olounan*, being killed, who or which is, was, or will be killed

قتل اولنور *katl olounour*, being killed, who or which is or will be killed

قتل اولنمش *katl olounmoush*, who or which has been killed

قتل اولندق *katl oloundouk*, who or which has been killed

قتل اولنه‌جق *katl olounajak*, who or which will be killed

Passive.

قتل اولندق *katl oloundouk*, by which, with which, where, &c., one has been killed

قتل اولنه‌جق *katl olounajak*, by which, with which, where, &c., one will be killed.

Verbal Nouns.

قتل اولنمه *katl olounma*, the action of being killed

قتل اولندق *katl oloundouk*, the action of having been killed

قتل اولنه‌جق *katl olounajak*, the action of being about to be killed.

Gerunds.

قتل اولنوب *katl olounoup*, being killed

قتل اولنه‌رق *katl olounarak*, being killed

قتل اولنيجق *katl olounoujak*, } on being killed
قتل اولنجه *katl olounja*, }

---

* Also spelt اولنسه‌ايدم.

قتل اولنهاولنه *katl olouna olouna*, by dint of being killed

قتل اولنهمغين *katl olounmaghĭn*, by reason of being killed

قتل اولنهلو *katl olounalĭ*, since being killed.

EXERCISE XVIII.

If you do not learn your lesson you will be punished (مجازات اولنمتى *mujazat olounmak*). He was punished yesterday. If you act (حركت ايتمك *héreket etmek*) well, you will be rewarded (مكافات اولنمتى *mukiafat olounmak*). It is a shame (عيب *aïb*) that he has not been rewarded. Has the letter been sent (ارسال *irsal*)? Was it corrected (تصحيح اولنمتى *tásshĭh olounmak*) before it was sent? It ought to have been corrected. It was corrected. If it was not corrected it was not my fault (قباحت *kábahat*). When was Constantinople conquered (فتح اولنمتى *feth olounmak*) by the Turks? Were the walls repaired (تعمير اولنمتى *tamir olounmak*)? They ought to have been repaired. The newspaper you speak of has been suppressed (محو اولنمتى *mahv olounmak*). Why was it suppressed? It was suppressed because it wrote against (عليهنده *aleyhindé*) the Government (حكومت *hukiumet*). Where was the book you speak of printed (طبع اولنمتى *tab olounmak*)? It was printed in Smyrna (ازمير *Ezmir*). When was that town built (بنا اولنمتى *bina olounmak*)? It was built three thousand years ago.

CHAPTER VI.

THE ADVERB.

272. AN adverb is a word which qualifies a verb, an adjective, or another adverb. Example, دوستكز كوزل يازار *dostounouz ghiuzel yazar* (your friend writes *beautifully*); تركجه پك تكميل سويلرسكز *Turkjé pek tekmil suweylérsiniz* (you speak Turkish *very perfectly*); هوا پك لطيف در *hawa pek latif dir* (the weather is *very* agreeable).

273. In Turkish, adjectives are very often used as adverbs. Example, پك فنا حركت ايتدى *pek féna héreket etdi* (he acted very *badly*); پك كوزل يازارسكز *pek ghiuzel yazarsĭnĭz* (you write very *beautifully*).

274. There are adverbs of manner, number, time, place, and order, and there are also affirmative and negative adverbs.

Adverbs of Manner.

275. The principal adverbs of manner are :—

كوزل *ghiuzel*, beautifully, prettily

ايو *éï*, well

فنا *fena,* } badly
بد *bed,* }

كنه or ينه *yiné (ghené)*, } again
يكيدن *yéniden,* }

اويله *euïlé,* } so, in that manner.
بويله *beuïlé,* }

276. Adverbs of this kind are often formed by adding the Persian termination انه *ané* or يانه *yané* to nouns. Example, دوست *dost* (a friend), دوستانه *dostané* (friendly, in a friendly manner); بابا *bâbâ* (a father), بابايانه *bâbáyané* (fatherly, in a fatherly manner).

The Particle جه *jé.*

277. Adverbs are also formed by adding the syllable جه *jé* to adjectives. Example, ترك *turk* (Turkish), ترکجه *turkjé* (in a Turkish way); سويلمك turkjé *turkjé suweylémek* (to talk Turkish—*i.e.*, after the manner of the Turks); فرانسز *fransïz* (French), فرانسزجه *fransïzjé* (after the manner of the French); فيلسوفجه يشاييورم *féïlésoffjé yashayoroum* (I live philosophically).

278. This particle, جه *jé*, can also be added to nouns and pronouns, to form a kind of adverb or adverbial expression. Example, سزجه *sizjé* (in your opinion, after your way), بنجه *benjé* (in my opinion, in my way); ياشجه بندن دها بيوك سنز *yashjé benden daha biyuk sunuz* (you are greater than I as regards age—*i.e.*, you are older than I); بوحسابجه يارين آى باشى در *bou hissabja yarïn aï bâshï dïr* (according to this calculation, to-morrow is the first of the month).

279. جه *jé* added to adjectives has also sometimes the meaning of "pretty," or "a little," "passably." Example, فرانسزجه ايوجه سويلر *Fransïzjé éïjé suwéyler* (he speaks French pretty well); خسته‌جه در *khastaja dïr* (he is a little ill).

280. جه *jé*, when added to nouns, and having the meaning of "as," "after the manner of," sometimes takes the syllable سنه after it. Example, انسانجه‌سنه حرکت ايتملیدر *insanjésené héréket etmélidir* (one ought to act like a man).

281. Adverbs of Number.

چوق *chok,* } much
وافر *wafir,* }

از *áz,* little

بر از *bir áz,* a little

ازاجق *ázajīk,* a very little (*un petit peu*)

دخی *dakhi,* or دها *daha,* } more
زیاده *ziadé,* }

پك *pek,* very.

282. Adverbs of Place.

نره ده *nerédé,* }
نه یرده *né yerdé,* } where? in what place?
قانی or قنی *kánï (hanï),* }
قنده *kándé,* }

نره یه *neréyé,* } whither? to what place?
نه یره *né yeré,* }

نره دن *neréden,* }
نه یردن *né yerden,* } whence? from what place?
نردن *nérden,* }

بوراده *bourada,* }
بورده *bourda,* } here
بونده *bounda,* }
شونده *shounda,* }

اوراده *orada,* } there
اورده *orda,* }

بورایه *bouraya,* } hither
بویره *bou yeré,* }

اورایه *oraya,* thither

بورادن *bouradan,* } hence, from here
بویردن *bou yerden,* }

اورادن *oradan,* from there, thence

هر یرده *her yerdé,* everywhere

هیچ بر یرده *hich bir yerdé,* nowhere

صاغه *sagha,* to the right

صوله *sola,* to the left.

283.   Adverbs of Time.

شمدی   *shimdi,** now

شمدییه دك   *shimdiyé dek,* until now, hitherto

نه‌زمان or نزمان   *né zeman,*
قیچان   *káchán,* } when?
نه‌وقت or نوقت   *né wákït,*

دمین   *demin,* just now, a minute ago

چوقدن   *chokdan,* a long while ago, for a long time

بو کون   *boughïun,* } to-day
امروز   *imrouz,*

دون   *dun,* } yesterday
دیروز   *dirouz,*

اولسی کون   *evvelsi ghiun,* } the day before yesterday
اوته کون   *euté ghiun,*

یارین   *yarïn,* to-morrow

اول بر کون   *o bir ghïun,* the day after to-morrow

ارته   *erté,* } the day following
فردا   *ferda,*

دائما   *daïma,* always

هیچ   *hich,* } never
اصلا   *asla,*

کوندز   *ghiunduz,* in the daytime

کیجه   *ghejé,* at night

ارکن   *erken,* early

کیچ   *ghech,* late

اخشام   *akhsham,* at evening, of an evening

صباح   *sabah,* in the morning, of a morning

اولین or اویلن   *euïlen* or *euïléin,* at midday

بهارین   *baharïn,* in the spring

یازین   *yazïn,* in the summer

قیشین   *kïshïn,* in the winter

کوزین   *ghiuzun,* in the autumn

صباحلین   *sabahléin,* early in the morning

اخشاملین   *akhshamléin,* in the evening

کوندزین   *ghiunduzun,* in the daytime

---

* Generally pronounced *shindi.*

كيجه‌لين *ghejéléin*, in the night

انسز *ansïz,* انسزين *ansïzin,* اب انسزين or *áp ansïzin,* } suddenly

بولدر *bouldour*, last year

كچنلرده *ghechenlerdé,*
كچنده *ghechendé,*
اوته كونلرده *euté ghiunlerdé,* } lately

تيز *tiz (téz),*
جابك *chabik,* } soon, quickly

بعضى كره *bázï kérré,*
احياناً *ahyanan,*
بعضى وقت *bazï wákit,* } sometimes

اول *evvel,*
مقدم *mukaddem,* } before

صكره *sonra (sora)*, afterwards, by-and-bye.

284. Adverbs of Order.

اول *evvel,* اولا *evvela,*
ابتدا *ibtida,* } first of all, firstly, in the first place

ثانيا *saniya,*
ايكنجى يرده *ikinji yerdé,* } in the second place

عاقبت *akïbet*, at last, at length.

285. Adverbs of Interrogation.

نه *né*, what ?

نيچون *nichun (nichin)*, why ?

نه سببدن *né sébebden*, for what reason ?

نصل *nassl,*
نيجه *nijé,* } how ? in what manner ?

قاچ *kach*, how many ?

نه قدر or نقدر *né kádar*, how much ?

286. Adverbs of Affirmation.

اوت *evvet,*
بلى *béli,* } yes

كرچك *gerchek*, truly, really

بلكى *belki*, perhaps

حقيقت *hakikkat,* } truly
حقا *hakka,*

سبهەسز *shubhésiz*, no doubt, doubtlessly

واقعا *wakĭa*, really, in fact.

287. Negative Adverbs.

يوق *yok,* } no
خير *khaïr,*

دكل *déïl*, not

كوجله *ghiujilé*, hardly, with difficulty

كوچ بلا *ghiuch bela*, hardly, only just

انجق *anjak*, only, hardly, just.

Miscellaneous Adverbs.

288. The other Turkish adverbs most in use are:—

كبى *ghibi*, as, like

نتەكم *nété kim*, as, in like manner as

أشته *ishté*, behold

تك *tek*, only, merely

كوره *gheuré*, according

بيله *bilé*, even

طولايى *dolayĭ,* } concerning, on account of.
يكا *yana,*

289. The following Persian words are used as Turkish adverbs:—

هنوز *henuz (héniz)*, only just this moment

هنوز (with a negative), not yet

هركز *herghéz*, never

چون *choun*, as

كاه *ghiah*, sometimes

همیشه *hemishé*, always.

290. Any masculine Arabic noun or adjective may be made into a Turkish adverb by an ۱ being put after it; and any Arabic noun or adjective

of the feminine form may be changed into a Turkish adverb by the final ة
being written thus : ت and the sign ˝ added. Example, ‫حق‬ *hak* (truth),
‫حقا‬ *hakka* (in truth, in justice); ‫اول‬ *evvel* (first), ‫اولا‬ *evvela* (firstly); ‫ثانی‬
sani (second), ‫ثانیا‬ *sania* (secondly, in the second place); ‫ملت‬ *millet*
(people, nation), ‫ملة‬ *milletan* (as regards the people, nation). With masculine words thus converted into Turkish adverbs, the sign ˝ is sometimes
prefixed to the ‫ا‬, thus, ‫ثانیا‬ ‫اولاحقا‬, and they are pronounced accordingly as
if they ended with the sound of *an*; but it is generally omitted, and the
words pronounced as if ending with the sound of *a*.

The Interrogative Particle ‫می‬ *mi.*

291. To show that a sentence is interrogative, the Turks make use of
the adverbial particle ‫می‬ *mi, mĭ, mou,* or *mu,* corresponding to the Latin
ne, an. Example, ‫اسممی بلورمیسکز‬ *issmimi bilirmisiniz* (do you know my
name?), ‫کلدیمی‬ *gheldimmi* (did he come?), ‫یاغمور یاغهجقمی‬ *yaghmour*
yaghajakmĭ (will it rain?)

292. This particle is placed after the word to which the question chiefly
refers. Example, ‫لوندرادن کلدیمی‬ *Londradan gheldimmi* (has he *come* from
London?), ‫لوندرادنمی کلدی‬ *Londradanmi gheldi* (has he come from
London?), ‫لوندرادن بو کونمی کلدی‬ *Londradan bou ghĭunmu gheldi* (did he
come from London *to-day*?).

293. In asking a question, if an interrogative pronoun, such as ‫کیم‬ *kim,*
‫قنغی‬ *hanghĭ,* ‫قاچ‬ *kach,* ‫قاچنجی‬ *kăchĭnjĭ,* or ‫نصل‬ *nassl,* be used, then ‫می‬
is not employed. Example, ‫نه استرسکز‬ *né isstersiniz* (what do you want?);
‫نصل سکز‬ *nassl siniz* (how are you?); ‫کیم بلور‬ *kim bilir* (who knows?);
‫نیچون یاپدك‬ *nichin yapdĭn* (why didst thou do it?). In short, ‫می‬ must
always be used unless the interrogative nature of the sentence is clearly
indicated by some other word.

EXERCISE XIX.

Where are you going to? You are walking very quickly. Why are you
hurrying (‫عجله ایتمك‬ *ajelé etmek*)? If I do not hurry I shall be late. My sister
has been ill lately, but now she is better. When did you see the Emperor? I saw
him the day before yesterday on the Bosphorus (‫بوغاز‬ *Bogház*). Where does he

live? Do you know his name (اسم *issm*)? I know it very well. Will you tell it me? Yes, I will tell it you by-and-bye. You must get up early to-morrow. I never get up early. Do you go to (ياتمق *yatmak*) bed late? Sometimes I go to bed late. It is good to get up early in the summer. Did he send a present (هديه *hédiyyé*)? Perhaps. Do you not know? No, I do not know. Will you ask?

CHAPTER VII.

PREPOSITIONS OR POSTPOSITIONS.

294. In the Turkish language there are no prepositions, properly so called, but their place is supplied by words or syllables, called postpositions, placed after the words to which they refer.

295. Some postpositions are joined to words, others are written separately.

The following postpositions are joined to the words to which they refer :—

296. ك, which corresponds to *of* in English. Example, اوك *evin* (of the house), ادمك *ádámĭn* (of the man), اغاجك *ághájĭn* (of the tree). If the word to which it is attached end in a vowel, then ك becomes نك. Example, بابانك *bábánĭn* (of the father), قارينك *kárĭnĭn* (of the woman), الماتك *elmanĭn* (of the apple).

297. The word صو *sou* (water) is an exception to the rule, as it forms its genitive by the addition of يك instead of نك. Example, صو *sou* (water), صويك *souyoun* (of the water).

298. ى placed after a noun or pronoun indicates that it is the direct object of a transitive verb, *i.e.*, that it is in the accusative case. Example, ادمى كوردم *ádámĭ ghieurdum* (I saw the man).

299. When the word to which it is attached ends in a vowel, it becomes بى. Example, الماىى يدم *elmayi yédem* (I ate the apple), كوپرىبى تعمير ايتديلر *kieupruyu tamir etdiler* (they repaired the bridge).

300. After the relative pronominal affixes, and after the possessive affixes of the third person singular or plural, this postposition changes into نى for the sake of euphony.

The final ى of the different singular affixes is then omitted if it be connected with the letter preceding it. Example, مكتوبنى اوقودم *mektoubounou okoudoum* (I read his letter).

301. But the final ى of the plural affix is always retained, and also that of the singular affix if it be not connected with the letter preceding it. Example, مكتوبلرينى اوقودم *mektoublarïni okoudoüm* (I read their letter); برادرينى سورميسكز *beradérini severmisiniz* (do you like his brother?); پدرينى بلورم *péderini bilirim* (I know his father).

302. ه corresponds to "to" in English, and serves to indicate that the word to which it is joined is in the dative case. Example, اوه كيت *evé ghit* (go to the house), استانبوله كيتدى *Istanbola ghitdi* (he went to Constantinople).

303. But if the word to which it is joined end in a vowel, it changes into یه. Example, لوندریه كيتمليسكز *Londraya ghitmélisiniz* (you ought to go to London); خواجهیه ویردم *khojaya vérdim* (I gave (it) to the professor).

304. When this postposition is joined to a word having the relative pronominal affix كى *ki,* or the possessive affix of the third person singular or plural, it takes an ن *n* before it, to prevent the clashing of the vowels; and in this case the singular affixes كى and سى lose their final ى. Example, برادرینه سویلدم *beradériné suwéylédim* (I told his brother), باباسنه یازدم *bâbâsina yazdïm* (I wrote to his father), دوستلرینه هدیه ویردى *dostlarina hédiyé vérdi* (he gave a present to their friends), مملكتارینككنه *memléketlérininkiné* (to him of their country, or belonging to their country).

305. If the singular affix ى be joined to the letter preceding, it is omitted before this postposition. Example, مملكتنه كتدى *memléketiné ghitdi* (he went to his country).

306. If the ى be not joined to the letter preceding it, it is retained. Example, شهرینه *shehiriné* (to his city), پدرینه *péderiné* (to his father).

307. Joined to a future verbal noun followed by a pronominal possessive affix this postposition corresponds to our expressions "instead of," "rather than." Example, یازه‌جغمه بر از كزرم *yazajaghïma bir âz ghézerim* (rather than write, or instead of writing, I will walk a little).

308. ده *da, dé,* corresponds to "in" or "at," and indicates where one is or where something happens. Example, اوده در *evdé dir* (he is in the house or at the house, *i.e.,* at home), ازمیرده اوطوریور *Ezmirdé otouriyor* (he lives in Smyrna).

I

309. The possessive pronominal affixes of the third person singular and plural, as well as the relative pronominal affix, change their final ی into ن before دە, but retain the sound of it. Example, اوطەسندە *odasinda* (in his room), اطەلرندە *ádalerĭnda* (in their island), اولرندە *evlerindé* (in their house), بابامكندە *bábámĭnkĭnda* (in that of my father).

310. Joined to an infinitive or verbal noun this postposition corresponds to " engaged in," " busy with " in English. Example, اوقومقدە در *okou-makda dir* or اوقومدە در *okoumada dĭr* (he is reading or busy with writing), چالشمقدە ایدی *chálishmakda idi* or چالشمدە ایدی *chálishmada idi* (he was studying or occupied in studying),

311. دن *den, dan*, is equivalent to " from," and shows that the word to which it is appended is in the ablative case. Example, ادرنەدن کلدی *Edir-néden gheldi* (he has come from Adrianople).

312. The rules given above with regard to دە when preceded by the final ی of the possessive and relative pronominal affixes apply also to دن. Example, مملکتندن *mémléketinden* (from his country), بابەسندن پارە الدی *bábásĭndan para áldĭ* (he has received money from his father), دوستلرندن *dostlarĭndan* خبر الدیلر *khábr áldĭler* (they received news from their friends), بابامكندن *bábámĭnkindan* (from that of my father).

313. دن sometimes means " by " or " through," or " of." Example, قرەدن *karadan* (by land), دکزدن *dénizden* (by sea), قپودن کیردك *kápĭdan ghirdik* (we entered through or by the gate), زهردن اولمك *zéhirden eulmek* (to die of poison or by poison).

314. After past verbal nouns with a pronominal affix it means " owing to," " by reason of." Example, سویلدیکمه دقت ایتمدیکندن *suvéylédiyimé dĭkkat etmédiyinden* (owing to his not paying attention to what I said), ایشتمدیکمدن *ishitmédiyimden* (by reason of my not having heard, as I did not hear), کلدیکمدن *gheldiyimden* (as I have come, &c.).

315. It is also used to express " than." Example, بندن بیوك سز *benden biyuk siniz* (you are taller than I).

316. It indicates also the material of which anything is made and then corresponds to " of." Example, کارکیردن *kiavghirden* * (of brick), التوندن *altĭndan*† (of gold), اغاجدن *ághájdan* (of wood), دمیردن *démirden* (of iron), بو ساعت التوندن در *bou saat áltĭndan dir* (this watch is

---

* Generally pronounced by the Turks *kiavghir*, although, according to the spelling, it ought to be *kiarghir*,   † Or *áltoundan*.

of gold), دمیردن یاپیلمش بر کوپری *démirden yapïlmïsh bir keupru* (a bridge made of iron), اوكز كاركيردن در *eviniz kiavghirden dir* (your house is of brick).

317. سز *siz, sïz, suz*, or *souz*, " without," corresponds to the termination " less " in English. Example, شبهه‌سز *shubhésiz* (doubtless), تأخیرسز *téékh-khoursouz* (without delay).

318. له *lé* instead of ايله *ilé* corresponds to " with " or " by." Example, قورشون قلم ايله واپور ايله كلدی *vapor ilé gheldi* (he came by the steamer), يازدم *kourshoun kalem ilé yazdïm* (I wrote (it) with a pencil).

319. When ايله or له is used after personal, interrogative, or demonstrative pronouns they must be put in the genitive, except the third person plural. Example,—

> بنم ايله *benim ilé* or بنمله *benimlé*, with me
> سنكله *seninlé*, with thee
> انكله *onounla*, with him, her, it
> بزمله *bizimlé*, with us
> سزكله *sizinlé*, with you
> انلرله *onlarla*, with them.

320. له *lé* is joined to infinitives and then means "because." Example, سز سومكله *siz sevmek-lé* (because you have loved), انلر چالشمقله *onlar châlishmak-la* (because they have studied, or, they having studied).

321. له is sometimes used as a conjunction and corresponds to " and." Example, بیلمکله بیلمامك بر دكل در سزكله بن *sizinlé ben* (you and I), *bilmek-lé bilmémek bir déil dir* (to know and not to know are not the same), مركب ايله قلم ویر بكا *murekkeb ilé kalem vér bâna* (give me a pen and ink).

322. The other postpositions are always written as separate words.

323. These postpositions are either variable or invariable.

The Invariable Postpositions.

324. The invariable postpositions are the real ones and correspond to prepositions in other languages. Amongst these are, ايچون *ichun, ichïn* (for, owing to), كبی *ghibi* (like), كوره *ghieuré* (according to), دكین *déyin* (as far as), صكره *sora* (after).

325. When ايچون is joined to personal, interrogative, or demonstrative

pronouns they must be put in the genitive, except the third person plural. Example,—

بنم ايچون   *benim ichin,* for me
سنك ايچون   *senin ichin,* for thee
انك ايچون   *onoun ichin,* for him, her, or it
بزم ايچون   *bizim ichin,* for us
سزڭ ايچون   *sizin ichin,* for you
انلر ايچون   *onlar ichin,* for them.

نه نڭ ايچون *nénin ichin* (for what?), كيمڭ ايچون *kimin ichin* (for whom?). But كيم and نه may be used in the nominative when followed by ايچون, and one may therefore correctly say كيم ايچون *kim ichin,* نه ايچون *né ichin* (what for?). In the same way كيم and نه, when followed by ايله or ل, may be put either in the nominative or genitive. Example, كيم ايله *kim ilé* or كيمڭ ايله *kimin ilé* (with whom?), نه نڭ ايله *nénin ilé* or نه ايله *né ilé* (with what?).

326. The variable postpositions are mostly nouns which are used in connection with other nouns or pronouns to supply the place of prepositions in European languages. Their use will be best understood from examples. Thus ارا *ara* means "the midst"; ارامزده *aramizdé,* in the our midst, *i.e.,* between us; ارالرنده *aralerindé,* in their midst, *i.e.,* between them. ارد *ard* means the space at the back side of anything, or the back; اردمده *ardimdé,* in my back, *i.e.,* behind me. اوڭ *eun* means the space in front of anything, the front; اوكمده *eunumdé,* in my front, *i.e., before* me; اوكڭزده *eununuzdé,* in your front, *i.e., before* you; اوڭ اوكنده *evin eunindé,* in the front of the house, *i.e., before* the house. اوزر *uzer* means the space over anything; اوزرمده *uzerimdé,* in the space over me, *i.e.,* over or upon me; اوزرلرنده *uzerlerindé,* in the space over them, *i.e.,* over them or upon them.

327. The words thus employed and the prepositions in European languages which they supply the place of are as follows :—

ارا	*ara,*		
اورته	*orta,*	the midst	Between, amongst
بين	*béyn,*		
ميان	*miyan,*		
ارد	*ard,* the back, the space behind . .		Behind
اشاغه	*áshagha,*	the lower part	Below, under
اشاغى	*áshaghï,*		
الت	*ált,* the space under		Under

اوزر *uzer,* the space over . . . . . Over

است *ust,* ,, ... ,, on

ایچ *ich,* } the inside . . . . . . Inside
ایچرو *ichéri,* }

اوك *eun,* the front . . . . . . Before, in front of

طشره *táshra,* } the outer part (of anything) Out of, outside
or طشرى *dïsharï,* }

یقین or یاقین *yakïn,* the space near . . . . . Near

اوزاق *ouzák,* the space far away . . . . Far

یان *yan,* the side . . . . Near

یوقارى *youkarï,* the top of anything . . . Above

قارشو *karshï,* the space opposite . . . . Opposite

دیب *dib,* the bottom of anything . . . Under.

328. The postpositions دك *dek,* دكین *déyïn* (as far as, until), طوغرى *doghru* (towards), یاقین *yakïn,* قریب *karib* (near), قارشو *karshï* (opposite), and كوره *ghieuré* (according to) require the noun they refer to to be put in the dative case. Examples, كیجه‌یه‌دك *ghejéyédek* (until night), ازمیره طوغرى *Ezmiré doghrou* (towards Smyrna), سویلدیككزه كوره *suwéylediyinizé ghieuré* (according to what you say), اومه یاقین *evimé yakïn* (near my house).

329. صكره *sora* (after), اوترو *euturu* (with regard to), یكا *yana* (with respect to), برو *béri* (on this side of, since), اوته *euté* (on the other side of), اول *evvel,* اقدم *ákdém,* مقدم *moukáddem* (before), غیرى *ghaïri,* ماعدا *maada,* بشقه *báshka* (except, besides), طشره *táshra* (out of), ایچرو *ichéri* (inside), اشاغى *áshaghï* (under), یوقارى *youkarï* (above) require the ablative. Examples, یازدیغمدن صكره *yazdiyimdan sora* (after my writing), كلدیكندن اول *gheldiyinden evvel* (before his coming), شهردن طشره *shehirden táshra* (outside the town), بندن بشقه كمسه بلمز *benden báshka kimsé bilmaz* (no one knows except me).

330. In written Turkish some Persian and Arabic prepositions are used.

The Persian Prepositions.

The Persian prepositions are as follows :—

ب or به *bé* corresponds to "to," "in," or "with." Example, بدست *bé desst* (in the hand), بشمشیر انتقام *bé shimshir-i-intikam* (with the sword of vengeance), بشهر رفته است *bé shehir refté esst* (he is gone to the town), بامید خدا (with the hope of God).

331. بی *bi* (without). Example, بیباك *bibak* (without fear, fearless), بینظیر *binazïr* (without equal, peerless), بیچاره *bi charé* (without resource), بیوفا *bi véfa* (without fidelity).

332. با *ba* (with). Example, با خدا *ba khuda* (with God), با من *ba men* (with me), با حرمت *ba hurmet* (with respect).

333. بر *bér* (on, in, to, according). Example, بر عكس *bér akss* (on the contrary), بر طرف *bér taraf* (on one side), بر سر *bér sér* (on the head), بریك *bér yek kiushé-i-chimen* (in one corner of the garden), بر منوال *bér minval-i-mouharrér* (in the way mentioned), بر وجه مشروح *bér vejhi meshrouh* (in the said manner).

334. زیر *zir* (under). Example, زیر زمین *ziri zémin* (under the earth, subterranean).

335. در *dér* (in). Example, در بوستان *dér bosstan* (in a garden), در این عالم *dér in* alem* (in this world), در دست *dér desst* (in hand). It also sometimes signifies about or on. Example, در بیان فتح هندستان *dér béyan-i-feth-i-hindisstan* (about the conquest of India).

336. ز or از *éz* (from, of, by, through, over, under). Example, از دست *éz desst* (out of hand, from the hand), از سر نو *éz sér-i-nev* (again), از هر جهت *éz hér jihet* (from every side, in every respect, in every way).

337. تا *ta* (as far as, until) always requires another preposition like دك ب or قدر with it. Example, تا بصباح *ta bé sabah* (until the morning) or تا صباحه دك *ta sabaha dek*.

338. برای *beraï* (for). Example, برای مصلحت *beraï maslahat* (for a piece of business).

The Arabic Prepositions.

339. The Arabic prepositions are much used in Turkish, but only in connection with Arabic words. Those most frequently met with are the following :—

ب *bi* (with, by, in, on). Example, بسم اللّه *bissm-illah* (in the name of God), باجمعهم *bi ejmaihim* (with the whole of them, *i.e.*, all together), بالجمله *bil jumlé* (all, every one), بالاتفاق *bil itifak* (with agreement, *i.e.*, unanimously), باللّه *billahi* (by God!).

---

* " *i* " in Arabic and Persian words, when corresponding to a vowel ى or اى, is generally a long vowel and must be pronounced like *i* in French or *ee* in English.

340. بلا *bila* (without). Example, بلا شبهة *bila shuphé* (without doubt), بلا رخصت *bila roukhsât* (without permission), بلا فائض *bila faïz* (without interest).

341. الى *ila* (to, towards, as far as, until). Example, الى الآن *ilé-'l-an* (until this moment, hitherto), الى الابد *ilé-'l-ébed* (until eternity, to all eternity), الى اخره *ila-akhirih* (until the end).

342. عن *an* (from, of, out of). Example, عنه *anhu* or *anh* (from him, from it), عنها *anha* (from her), عن قصد *an-kassdin* (on purpose), لا عن قصد *la-an-kassdin* (accidentally), عن صميم القلب* *an-samimi-l-kalb* (from the bottom of the heart).

343. من *min* (from, of, out of). Example, من القديم *min-el-kâdim** (from ancient times).

344. على *ala* (on, upon, according to, in, to). Example, على العموم *alé-'l-oumoum* (generally), على التحقيق *alé-t-tahkïk* (assuredly, really), على وجه التفصيل *ala-vejhi-t-tâfsïl* (in a detailed manner), على التوالى *alé-t-tévali* (successively), على اى حال *ala-éyi-hal* (in whichever way), على كلا التقديرين *ala-kéla-t-tâkdïréïn* (in either of the two cases), على الصباح *alé-s-sabah* (early in the morning).

345. فى *fi* (in, to, concerning). Example, فى الحقيقه *fi-'l-hâkika* (in truth, in fact, really), فى الحال *fi-'l-hal* (instantly, at once), فى الجبر *fi-'l-jebr* (about algebra).

It is also used in the sense of at, when stating a price. Example, فى يكرمى غروش *fi yirmi ghroush* (at the rate of twenty piastres).

346. ل *li* (for, to). Example, لمصلحت *li-mâslahat* (for business), عبرة للسائرين *ibreten-li-ss-saïrin* (as an example to others), حبة لله *hubbetan-li'llah* (for God's sake).

This letter is sometimes used combined with the word اجل *ejl* (cause, reason). Example, لاجل المصلحت *li-ejl-il-mâsslahat* (for business).

347. لدى *léda, lédé* (immediately after—in time, quite near—in space, on). Example, لدى الوصول *lédé-l-vussoul* (on arrival), لدى السؤال *lédé-ss-sual* (when asked), لدى الاقتضا *lédé-'l-iktiza* (in case of need, when requisite).

EXERCISE XX.

Last year a great many travellers (يولجى *yoljou*) came from England to Turkey. My servant has gone to France to see his family. I paid him his salary (أيلق

aïlĭk) before he departed (قالقمق *kálkmak*), but he spent (خرج ايتمك *kharj etmek*) it all except five pounds. It is very inconvenient to be amongst strangers (يبانجى *yabánjĭ*). Your house is amongst trees. My house is in front of the castle (قلعه *kala*). The book is under the table. The ink is in the cupboard (دولاب *doláb*). He has gone to his country. Did you bring this rose for me? For whom is this money? For him or for them? I do not know, but probably it is for you. For God's sake! The king (قرال *kral*) punished the murderer (قاتل *kátil*) as an example to others. She is without equal. He killed his brother on purpose. In Constantinople there is an underground railway (دمير يول *démir yol*). He lent me the money without interest. That is beyond doubt. The council unanimously resolved (قرار ويرمك *karar vermek*) to declare war (علان حرب ايتمك *ilan-i-harb etmek*). He found a treasure (خزينه *khaziné*) at the bottom (ديب *dib*) of the tree in his garden. He related (نقل ايتمك *nákl etmek*) all he had seen in a detailed manner. In the name of God. Here, we are arrived.* Where does your friend live? Out of the town. In case of need the police (ضبطيه مامورى *zábtïyé mamourou*) must help (اعانه ايتمك *iané etmek*) and protect (حمايت ايتمك *himayet etmek*) him.

CHAPTER VIII.

CONJUNCTIONS.

348. THERE are very few conjunctions of Turkish origin, the nature of the language being such that it scarcely requires them. Many Persian and Arabic conjunctions, however, are used in written Turkish.

349. Copulative Conjunctions.

و *vé, u* or *ou*, and

هم هم *hem, hem,* } both, also
هم وهم *hem, vé hem,* }

ده *da, dé,* } also, and, even
دخى *dakhi,* }

حتى *hatta,* so much so that, even

نه نه *né, né,* neither, nor.

---

* Say, Behold! we have come.

Pronunciation of و.

349. و *vé* is pronounced *ou* or *u* when it connects two synonymous words, or words which are a contrast to each other or usually coupled together. Example, ليل و نهار *léil u nahar* (night and day), كاغد و قلم *kiagad u kalem* (pen and paper). If it come after a word ending in a vowel it is pronounced *vu*. Example, صفا و جفا *sâfa vu jefa* (pleasure and pain). In short sentences و *vé* is often omitted. Example, انا بابا *ana bâbá* (father and mother), اوقور يازار *okour yazar* (he reads and writes).

350. هم *hem* must be repeated. Example, هم بن هم سن *hem ben hem sen* (both you and I), هم نازك هم اوقومش برادم در *hem nazik hem okoumoush bir âdâm dir* (he is both an affable and a learned man).

351. ده *dé* or دخی *dakhï* is always placed after the word which one wishes to emphasize, and it is sometimes repeated. Example, بن ده سن ده *ben dé sen dé* (I and you also), كتديسه ده كلمش در *ghitdisé dé ghelmish dir* (if even he went, he has returned).

352. و *vé* is often replaced by ايله *ilé*. Thus, صو ايله شراب *sou ilé sherab* (wine and water).

353. حتی *hatta* (even, so much so that) introduces a phrase which corroborates what precedes it. Example, حتی او دخی راضی اولدی *hatta o dakhï razï oldou* (so much so that he also has consented).

354. نه *né*, نه *né* or ونه *né*, *véné* (neither, nor). Example, نه يرنه ايچر *né yér né ichér* (he neither eats nor drinks), نه اوقور نه يازار *né okour né yazar* (he neither reads nor writes).

Disjunctive Conjunctions.

355. The disjunctive conjunctions are the following :—

يا *ya,*
ياخود *yakhod,* } or

يا يا *ya ya,* either, or

كرك *gherek,*
استر *isstér,* } whether, or whether
ها *ha,*

يوخسه *yokhsa,*
يوقسه *yoksa,* } or else, otherwise, or (after or before a negative sentence)

الّا *illa,* or otherwise, but, except, only that, saving that.

356. كرك ها and استر are put before two opposite words or phrases to state an alternative. They require the verb to be in the conditional or imperative, but with استر it can only be in the imperative. Example, ها يازسه ها يازمسه *ha yazsa ha yazmassa* or ها يازسون ها يازمسون *ha yazsïn ha yazmasïn* (whether he write or not), كرك كلسه كرك كلمسه *gherek ghelsé gherek ghelmessé* (whether he come or not).

Contrasting Conjunctions.

357. The conjunctions used for making contrasts are as under :—

اما *amma,*
لكن *lakin,* } but
و لكن *vé lakin,*

و الّا *vé illa,* otherwise, or if not, and if not

اكرچه *éyérché,* } although.
كرچه *gherché,*

Conditional Conjunctions.

358. The conjunctions which serve to state a condition are the following :—

اكر *éyér,* if
صانكى *sanki,* as if, as though, supposing it were
فرض ايدەلم كه *farz edélim ki,*
طوت كه *tout ki,*
طوتەلم *toutalïm,*
طوتەلم كه *toutalïm ki,* } supposing that
فرضا كه *faraza ki,*
فرض ايدەلم كه *farz edélim ki,*
كويا كه *ghïouya ki,* as if, as it were
مكر *méyér,* } unless, and still, and yet
مكر كه *méyér ki,*
مكر سه *méyér sé,* while, and yet.

359. اكر requires the verb to be in the conditional. Example, اكر يابمز *éyér yapmaz-issé mujazat ederim* ايسه مجازات ايدرم (if he does not do it, I will punish him), اكر چالشسه اوكرنەجك *éyér châlïshsa eurenéjek* (if he studies he will learn). It is very often omitted, especially in conversation, the sense being sufficiently indicated by the conditional mood of the verb.

Miscellaneous Conjunctions.

360. The remaining conjunctions are as under :—

اويله كه *euilé ki,* ⎫
بويله كه *beuilé ki,* ⎬ so that
شويله كه *sheuilé ki,* ⎭

ايمدى *imdi,* now, therefore, wherefore

انك ايچون *anïn ichin,* ⎫
اول سببدن *ol sebebden,* ⎬ therefore

يعنى *yani,* that is to say

خصوصا *khousoussa,* ⎫
على الخصوص *al elkhousouss,* ⎬ especially, particularly

زيرا *zira,* ⎫
زيرا كه *zira ki,* ⎬ because

چونكه *chunku* or *chunki,* as, because

كه *ki,* that, for, because

تا كه *ta,* تا كه *ta ki,* as far, in order that

مادام *madam,* as long as

مادامكه *madamki,* since, as

كاشكه or كاشكى *kiashki (keshki),* would to God that!

شايد كه *shayed ki,* may be that, peradventure lest

مبادا كه *mebada ki,* for fear that, God forbid that

الحاصل *el hássïl,* ⎫
ولحاصل *vé el hássïl,* ⎪
حاصل كلام *hássïlï kélam,* ⎬ finally, in a word
نتيجهٔ كلام *netijé-i-kélam,* ⎪
خلاصهٔ كلام *khoulassa-i-kelam,* ⎪
القصة *el-kïssa,* ⎭

پس *pess,* then, moreover

پس ايمدى *pess imdi,* well then

فقط *fakát,* only

بعده *badahu,* then, afterwards.

361. مكر *or* مكركه begins a phrase expressing an exception. Example, اورايه كيدهمزسكز مكر كه *بارگير ايله اوله *oraya ghidémezsiniz méyér ki béghir ïlé ola* (you cannot go there unless with a horse).

---

* The original Persian pronunciation of this word is *barghir,* but in Turkish it is pronounced *béghir.* It originally meant a pack-horse, but is now often used for any horse.

362. مگر *méyér*, or مگر سه *méyér sé* begins a phrase containing a state-ment contrasting with what has been asserted previously.   Example, ایكی ساعتدن بری قلمنی برو ارایور مكرسه تربزه اوزرینه دوریور *iki saatdan béri kalemini arayor méyérsé tirébezé uzeriné douriyor* (he has been looking for his pen for two hours, and yet it was on the table all the while).

363. شايد كه *shayed ki* is used to express a contingency desired or anticipated.   Example, شايد كه قرال اولور *shayed ki kral olour* (peradventure he will become king).

364. مبادا كه *mébada ki* is used to express a contingency one fears but hopes to avoid.   Example, مبادا كه قرال اولور *mébada ki kral olour* (for fear that he may become king, God forbid that he become king !).

365. " Or " between numbers is omitted in Turkish.   Example, ایكی اوچ الما *iki uch elma* (two *or* three apples), بش التی اى *besh áltï aï* (five or six months), قرق اللی لیرا *kïrk elli lira* (forty or fifty pounds).

EXERCISE XXI.

He neither reads nor writes. Both you and I are English. I went, but I did not see the pasha, because he was not at home. Although he is rich he is not happy (ممنون *memnoun*). He is neither rich nor poor (فقیر *fakïr*).   Whether it rain or not, I shall go out. Whether he like (استمك *isstémek*) it or not, do not do it again (بردها *bir daha*). She is both beautiful and amiable (نازك *nazik*). If you do not obey (اطاعت ایتمك *itaat etmek*) you will be punished. I will help (يارديم *yardïm etmek*) you, as you have helped me. Would to God I had known ! As if he had been mad (دلی *déli*). You will regret it as long as you live. God forbid that she hear it ! I will not tell her, as I have promised (سوز ویرمك *seuz vermek*). We go and come every day. You must take care or else you will lose your money. I shall neither take care nor lose my money. As you are so obstinate (عنادجی *inadjï*) you deserve to lose your money. Give me a pen and paper.

CHAPTER IX.

INTERJECTIONS.

366. INTERJECTIONS are words which express a sudden and violent emotion.

Sometimes they are used alone, and sometimes accompanied by the word to which they refer, which in Turkish is generally put in the dative. Example, افرین *aferin* (bravo! well done!), افرین سزه *aferin sizé* (bravo you!); يازق *yazïk* (it is a pity!), يازق سكا *yazïk sana* (it is a pity for thee!); واى *waï* (woe!), واى سزه *waï sizé* (woe to you!).

367. ى *éi* (O! eh! holloa!), and يا *ya* (O!) are used simply to call attention, or to express some emotion. Example, يا قارى *ya karï* (O woman!), اى *éi* (holloa! ahoy!), اى كميدن *éi ghémiden* (ship ahoy!), يا هو *ya hou* (holloa!), برو *bré* (fellow!), and باق سكا *bak sana* (I say!), are used for the same purpose.

368. ايواه *éiwah* or واه هى *héi wah* (alas!), مدد *méded* (alas! help!), امان *aman* (mercy! help!), express pain and trouble.

369. يازق *yazïk*, حيف *haïf* (pity! it is a pity!), نه يازق *né yazïk* (what a pity!) express regret.

370. واى *waï* (woe!), واى باشكه *waï bashïna*, واى سكا *waï sana* (woe to thee!), express a threat.

371. ماشاالله *mashalláh* (dear me!—literally, what great things God has willed!—wonderful!) expresses admiration or surprise.

372. صاقن *sakïn* (take care, now! mind what you are about!), كوزكى اچ *ghieuzunu ach* (be attentive! keep your eyes open! be sharp! take care!), زنهار *zinhar* (Persian) (take care! beware!), express a warning.

373. صاول *sawoul* (get out of the way! clear the road!), هايده كيت *haïdé ghit* (be off!), are used to drive any one away.

374. There is a species of interjection of Persian origin which consists of ا added to a word. Example, شاه *shah* (a king), شاها *shaha* (O king!) مهربان *mihriban* (a friend), مهربانا *mihribana* (O friend!).

375. There is also a Turkish interjection consisting of the same letter, only it is put at the end of a sentence instead of being added to a noun. Example, او بنمدر ا *o benim dir a* (that is mine, mind!). Instead of the letter ا, the syllable ها is sometimes used. Example, او بنمدر ها *o benim dïr ha*.

376. The other interjections most used are the following:—

هله *helé*, now! look there! well, did you ever!

دى بقالم *dé* or *di bâkâlïm,* ⎫ now then! well, go on!
دى امدى *dé imdi (déindik),* ⎭

هايدى *haïdi*, come!

عجائب *ajaïb*, wonderful! dear me!

اى وللّه   *éi wallâh,* thanks (good, by God!) !

هاى هاى   *haï haï,* to be sure ! yes, certainly !

استغرالله   *esstaghfrullâh,* God forgive me ! (used when one is praised, or when one has committed a fault)

نعوذ بالله   *nauzu-billâh,* God preserve us ! (we take refuge in God)

معاذلله   *maazallâh,* God forbid! (God is our only refuge in such an event)

حاشا   *hasha,* God forbid !

ان‌شاالله   *inshallâh,* please God ! (if God wish !)

والله   *wallâhi,*

تالله   *tallâhi,*   } by God!

بالله   *billâhi,*

واخ   *wakh,* alas ! woe !

وآ ويلا   *wa véïla,* Oh ! alas !

صوص   *souss,* hush ! hold your tongue !

دی‌ها or دیها   *di ha,* come now, what's that !

مرحبا   *mérhaba,* hail ! (used only between Mussulmans)

لبیك   *lebbik,* holloa ! here I am ! what are your commands ?

اوخ   *okh,* Oh, I am glad !

اوف   *ouf,* ah, what a bother !

EXERCISE XXII.

Thanks ! Please God we shall see each other again soon. What a pity ! Bravo you ! O king ! I say ! Be off ! Get out of the way ! Come, be quick ! Hush ! the professor is coming. Oh, I am glad ! By God I do not know ! Mercy ! Sir, I did not do it. Is this correct ? To be sure ! That is my box, mind ! I thought you had forgotten me. God have mercy on me ! (what an idea !) Woe to them ! Will your friend come to Turkey ? Please God ! (I hope so) for he is a very affable (نازك *nazik*) man.

CHAPTER X.

THE FORMATION OF TURKISH WORDS.

1. Turkish Nouns.

377. By the addition of the syllable جی to a noun another noun is formed indicating the individual who exercises a trade or calling connected with the first noun. Example, توتون *tutun* (tobacco), توتونجی *tutunju*

(a tobacconist); تنكه‌جی *tenéké* (tin), تنكه‌جی *tenékéji* (a tinman); شكر *sheker* (sugar), شكرجی *shekerji* (a confectioner); اتمك *ekmek** (bread), اتمكجی *ekmekji* (a baker); تیمور *démir* (iron), تیمورجی *démirji* (a smith); صو *sou* (water), صوجی *soujou*† (a water-seller).

378. The termination جی is also used for making nouns designating persons who practise something expressed by the noun to which it is appended. Example, دعا *doua* (a prayer), دعاجی *duaji* (one who prays); یلان *yalán* (a lie), یلانجی *yalánji* (a liar); لطیفه *latifé* (a joke), لطیفه‌جی *latiféji* (a joker).

379. By adding یجی *iji* to the root of a verb a noun is formed designating a person who habitually performs the action expressed by the verb. Example, سومك *sevmek* (to love), سویجی *seviji* (a lover); صاتمق *sátmak* (to sell), صاتیجی *satíji* (a seller); یازمق *yazmak* (to write), یازیجی *yazíji* (a writer); المق *álmak* (to buy), الیجی *áliji* (a buyer).

380. If the root of the verb end in a vowel then ییجی *yiji* must be added instead of یجی *iji*. Example, اوقومق *okoumak* (to read), اوقویوجی *okouyoujou* (a reader).

381. If the root of the verb end in ت quiescent it generally changes into د before جی. Example, یراتمق *yerátmak* (to create), یرادیجی *yerádíji* (a creator).

382. An enormous number of Turkish nouns are formed by the help of the termination لق or لك *lik, lík, louk,* or *luk.* In the first place, names of abstract qualities are obtained by adding it to adjectives. Example, كوزل *ghiuzel* (beautiful), كوزللك *ghiuzellik* (beauty); اوفاق *oufak* (small), اوفاقلق *oufaklík* (smallness); دوز *douz* (smooth), دوزلك *douzlouk* (smoothness); زنكین *zenghin* (rich), زنكینلك *zenghinlik* (opulence); كبرلی *kibrlí* (proud), كبرلیلك *kibrlilik* (pride).

383. Names of trades or professions are also formed by adding جی to the nouns designating the persons who exercise them. Example, تیمورجیلق *démirjilik* (the trade of a smith), اتمكجیلك *ekmekjilik* (the trade of a baker), قایقجی *káïkjí* (a boatman), قایقجیلق *káïkjílik* (the trade of a boatman).

384. The same termination added to a noun designates a place where

---

* Written *etmek*, but pronounced *ekmek*.

† The termination جی is pronounced *ji, jí, jou,* or *ju* according to the preceding predominant vowel. See 58.

something (expressed by the noun) is found or fit for that thing. Example, اورمان *ormán* (a wood or forest), اورمانلنی *ormánlik* (a place full of forests); ساز *sáz* (a reed), سازلنی *sázlik* (a place full of reeds); چیبوق *chibouk* (a pipe), چیبوقلق *chibouklouk* (the place where the pipes are kept); طوز *touz* (salt), طوزلق *touzlouk* (a saltcellar). لك or لق also indicate quantity, as بش غروشلق *besh ghroushlouk* (five piastres' worth), ایكی غروشلق *iki ghroushlouk* (two piastres' worth).

385. Verbal nouns are formed by adding لق or لك to infinitives. Examples, یازمق *yazmak* (to write), یازمقلق *yazmaklik* (the action of writing, or writing); اوقومقلق *okoumaklik* (the action of reading, or reading), سومكلك *sevmeklik* (the action of loving, or loving).

386. Nouns are also obtained by putting the termination ش to the roots of verbs. Examples, المق *álmak* (to buy), الش *álish* (a purchase, buying); ویرمك *vérmek* (to give), ویرش *vérish* (giving, a gift); الش ویرش *álish-vérish* (giving and taking, commerce); بیلمك *bilmek* (to know), بیلش *bilish* (knowing).

387. If the root of the verb end in a vowel, then یش *yish* must be added instead of ش. Example, سویلمك *suwéylémek* (to speak), سویلیش *suwéyléyish* (speaking, or way of speaking); اوقومق *okoumak* (to read), اوقویش *okouyoush* (reading, or way of reading). This kind of substantive generally expresses the way of doing anything. Example, بویله اوقویش اولمز *beuïle okouyoush olmaz* (such a way of reading is not permissible).

388. If the root of the verb end in a quiescent ت, it generally changes into د before this termination. Example, یراتمق *yerátmak* (to create), یرادش *yerádish* (creating, the action of creating).

389. Some few nouns are also made by adding the letter ج, instead of ش, to the roots of reflective verbs. Example, سونمك *sevinmek* (to be glad), سونج *sevinj* (gladness); قزانمق *kázánmak* (to win, gain), قزانج *kázánj* (gain, profit, earnings).

390. A noun is likewise formed by the addition of كو or كی *ghi* or *ghu* to the root of a verb. Example, ویركو *virghiou* or *vérghi* (giving, a gift, a tribute—from ویرمك), سوكی *sevghi* (love, loving—from سومك), بیلكو *bilghu* (knowing, knowledge—from بیلمك).

391. Sometimes the termination كیج *ghij* or غیج is used instead of كو or كی. Example, بلكیج *bilghij* (knowing, knowledge).

392. By affixing م *im, ïm, oum,* or *um* to the root of a verb a few nouns

are formed. Example, اولم *eulum* (dying, death—from اولمك *eulmek*, to die), اتم *átïm* (a cast, a throw, throwing) from اتمق *átmak* (to throw).

393. This termination sometimes indicates quantity. Example, اتم *átïm* (a charge of powder, *i.e.*, the quantity that one can throw, the distance one can throw); يوتم *youtoum*, from يوتمق *youtmak* (to swallow) (the quantity one can swallow); ايچم *ichim*, from ايچمك *ichmek* (to drink) (the quantity one drinks at one time).

Diminutive Nouns.

394. Diminutive nouns are constructed by adding جق *jïk* or جك *jik* and جغز *jaghaz** or جكز *jéyéz*,* as euphony requires,† to other nouns. Example, او *ev* (a house), او جكز *evjéyéz* (a little house); آدم *ádám* (a man), ادمجغز *adamjaghaz* (a little man;) قوى *keuï* (a village), كريجك *keuïjuk*† (a little village); قوزو *kouzou* (a lamb), قوزوجق *kouzoujouk*‡ (a little lamb).

395. If the noun end in ك, that letter is omitted or changed into *s* in the diminutive. Example, كوپك *kieupek* (a dog), كوپجك or كريهجك *kieupéjik* (a little dog).

396. The above rule holds good with respect to some adjectives ending in ك and ق. Example, كجوك *kuchuk*, كجوجك *kuchujuk* (rather small); سيجاق *sïjâk* (hot), سيجاجق *sïjâjïk* (rather hot).

397. از *áz* (little) and چوق *chok* (much) do not conform to this rule, for their diminutives are respectively ازهجق *ázajïk* (a very little), چوغجق *choghoujak* (rather much).

398. Names of languages are formed by adding جه *jé, ja,* to the names of nations. Example, انكليز *inghlïz* (English), انكليزجه *inghlïzjé* (the English language); فرانسز *fransïz* (French), فرانسزجه *fransïzja* (the French language); عربجه *arabja* (the Arabic language).

399. This same termination is used to express the way of doing anything. Example, جوجقجه *chojoukja* (in a childish way), قاريجه *kárïja* (in a womanish way), فيلسوفجه *féilésoffa* (in a philosophical way), سزجه *sïzjé* (in your way), بنجه *benjé* (in my way).

---

* Also pronounced *jaghïz* and *jéyiz*.

† *I.e.*, جغز *jaghaz* is added to nouns in which hard vowels preponderate, and جكز *jéyéz* to nouns in which soft vowels are predominant.

‡ جق and جك are euphonic and are pronounced *jik, jïk, jouk,* or *juk* according to the preceding predominant vowel. See 58.

400. A diminutive of the above termination is formed by omitting the final ه and adding لین *léyn*. Example, قاریجلین *kárïjaléyin* (somewhat in a womanish way).

EXERCISE XXIII.

Give me five piastres' worth of tobacco. Seamanship is a useful art. Bring the saltcellar. Is your brother a smith or a sailor? He is neither a sailor nor a smith; he is a soldier (عسكر *assker*). That little lamb is very pretty. What a pretty little girl! Is it proper to talk thus? There is no commerce in this country. God is the creator of all things. Has the boatman come? Do you know Turkish as well as (قدر *kádar*) French? I both read it and speak it. In my opinion, in order to learn French well you must go to France. You are (حقكز وار *hákïnïz var*) right, but one can learn it pretty well in Turkey. Where did you learn Arabic? I learnt it in Constantinople, but I only speak a very little. You ought to act like a philosopher. He acted like a man. You must not act like a woman. Were you not writing while I was speaking? No, Sir, I was listening. Is the garden in which you were walking your property (مال *mál*)? No, I have sold it to the baker whom I told you of. Have you seen his little daughter?

2. Turkish Adjectives.

401. By adding لو *lou, lu, li,* or *lï* to a noun an adjective is formed indicating possession of the thing designated by the noun or connection with it. Example, عقل *ákl* (sense), عقللو *áklli* (sensible, possessed of sense); جان *ján* (a soul), جانلو *jánlï* (living, possessed of a soul); كريد *Ghirid* (Crete), كريدلو *Ghiridli* (Cretan); لوندره *Londra* (London), لوندرهلو *Londralï* (of London); بچ *Bech* (Vienna), بچلو *Bechli* (Viennese).

402. The termination سز *siz, sïz, souz,* or *suz,* corresponding to "less" in English, when added to a noun, forms an adjective expressing the want or absence of the thing designated by the noun. Example, عقلسز *áklsiz* (foolish, senseless), مناسبتسز *munasébetsiz* (improper, *i.e.,* without (مناسبت) propriety), پارهسز *parasïz* (penniless, without money), اوسز *evsiz* (homeless, houseless), دقتسز *dikkátsïz* (careless), عارسز *arsïz* (impudent, without (عار) shame).

403. Some few adjectives are formed by adding ق or ك *ik* or اق *ak* to the root of a verb. Example, قیرمق *kirmak* (to break), قیریق *kïrïk* (broken); جاتلمق *chatlamak* (to crack, split), جاتلاق *chatlák* (cracked, split); اوطورمق *otourmak* (to sit); اوطوراق *otourák* (stationary, applied to

troops in garrison); دورمق *dourmak* (to stop), دوراق يری *dourák yéri* (a stopping place).

404. Some adjectives are also derived from verbs by the addition of غون, غين *ghin* or قبن *or* قون to the root. Example, شاشمق *shashmak* (to be bewildered), شاشقین *shashkĭn* (stupid, bewildered); قیزمق *kĭzmak* (to get hot, to get angry),' قیزغین *kĭzghĭn* (hot, angry, in heat); قبرمق *kĭrmak* (to break), قبرغین *kĭrghĭn* (hurt, vexed, grieved). دارغبن *darghĭn* (passionate, angry), derived from دارلمق *dárĭlmak* (to get angry), is somewhat irregular.

405. جه *jé, ja*, which in this case corresponds to "ish" in English, added to an adjective, forms a sort of diminutive adjective. Example, قره *kára* (black), قراجه *káraja* (blackish, rather black); خسته *khássta* (ill), خستهجه *khásstaja* (rather ill); ایو *éi* (good, well), ایوجه *éijé* (pretty well); کوزل *ghiuzel* (pretty), کوزلجه *ghiuzéljé* (rather pretty); شاشقین *shashkĭn* (stupid), شاشقبنجه *shashkĭnja* (rather stupid); بیوك *biyuk* (big), بیوکجه *biyukjé* (rather big); دوز *douz* (smooth), دوزجه *douzja* (pretty smooth).

EXERCISE XXIV.

Are you a Constantinopolitan? No, I was born (طوغمق *doghmak*) in Smyrna. He is a Bosnian (بوسنهلو *Bossnali*), but he speaks Turkish pretty well. The Herzegovinians (هرسكلو *Herseklí*) are a brave (شجاعتلو *shejaatli*) nation (ملت *millet*), but they are very lazy. The Montenegrins (قره طاغلو *Kára dághlĭ*) are very cruel (انسانيتسز *insaniyyetsiz*). If you were born in Constantinople, you must be a Constantinopolitan. This cup is broken. He is a very passionate man. What is your trade (صنعت *sanat*)? I am a sailor (کميجی *ghémiji*) at present, but formerly I was a shopkeeper (دكانجی *dukkianjĭ**). I wish I were a soldier (عسكر *assker*). Did you not know that my father was a bookseller (كتابجی *kitábjĭ*)? I thought so. This is a very useful (فائدهلو *fa'idéli*) book. Some of your pupils are very stupid. Our professor is a very learned (معلوماتلو *maloumatli*) man. You ought not to be so careless. The weather (هوا *hawa*) is very damp (رطوبتلو *routoubetli*) in England. I prefer (ترجيح ايتمك *térjih etmek*) the climate (هوا *hawa*) of Constantinople, because it is not so damp.

3. Turkish Verbs.

406. Transitive verbs are formed from nouns and adjectives by the addition of لمق, لمق *lamak* to those containing hard letters, and لمك *lémek*

---

* دكان *dukkian* (a shop), originally an Arabic word, is sometimes pronounced *dukén* by the Turks.

to those containing soft. When this termination is added to a noun, it has the meaning of "to provide with," and when added to an adjective it signifies "to render." Example, باغ *bâgh* (a tie, a knot, string), باغلامق *bâghlamak* (to tie, fasten, bind); صو *sou* (water), صولامق *soulamak* (to water —a garden, flowers, &c.); نشان *nishân* (a mark, a pledge, token given to a girl at a betrothal), نشانلمق *nishânlamak* (to betroth); مهر *muhur* (a seal), مهرلمك *muhurlémek* (to seal); حاضر *hâzïr* (ready), حاضرلمق *hâzïrlamak* (to prepare); تميز *témiz* (clean), تميزلمك *témizlémek* (to clean).

407. Passive and neuter verbs are formed by the addition of لنمق *lanmak* or لنمك *lenmek*. Example, اكشى *ekshi* (sour), اكشيلنمك *ekshilenmek* (to become sour); خسته *khâssta* (ill), خستهلنمق *khâsstalanmak* (to grow ill, fall ill); صاغر *saghïr* (deaf), صاغرلنمق *saghïrlanmak* (to become deaf); كوزل *ghiuzel* (pretty), كوزللنمك *ghiuzellenmek* (to grow pretty, become beautiful).

408. Some neuter verbs are formed from adjectives by the addition of لشمق or لشمك *leshmak* or *leshmek*. Example, اكشيلشمك *ekshileshmek* (to get sour), كوزللشمك *ghiuzelleshmek* (to become beautiful).

409. This same termination, however, added to *nouns* produces reciprocal verbs. Example, مكتوب *mektoub** (a letter), مكتوبلشمك *mektupleshmek* (to correspond).

410. A few neuter verbs are formed from adjectives by the addition of المق *âlmak*. Example, جوغالمق *choghâlmak* (to increase—from چوق *chok*, much), ازالمق *âzalmak* (to diminish—from از *âz*, little).

411. Other neuter verbs are formed by the addition of رمق. Example, قره *kâra* (black), قرارمق *kârarmak* (to get black, dark, or lowering); اق *âk* (white), اغرمق *âgharmak* (to grow white, to break—the day).

EXERCISE XXV.

Did you seal the letters? I forgot to seal them, but I tied them. He has fallen ill. Have you watered the garden? I watered it yesterday. Have you prepared the dinner? They corresponded for many years, but they never saw each other. My money has diminished. I awoke when it began to dawn (اغرمغه باشلامق *âgharmagha bâshlamak*). Did you get up? No, I went to sleep again. The state of the country has grown worse. The revenue of Turkey has diminished since the war. Perhaps it will increase next year. I hope so, but it is not probable (احتمال *ihtimâl*), as she has lost several provinces (ولايت *vilayet*).

---

* Or *mektup*.

Russia is a powerful (قوتلو *kouvvetli*) enemy. Can you speak Russian? Pretty well. How long have you been learning it? Two years and a-half. Then (اويله أيسه *euïlé issé*) you must speak it very well. I should have learnt it very well, if I had studied properly. Laziness is a bad thing.

CHAPTER XI.

THE CONSTRUCTION OF PERSIAN WORDS.

1. The Persian Noun.

412. ABSTRACT nouns and names of professions are formed in Persian by adding ى, which corresponds to لن or لك in Turkish, to nouns and adjectives. Example, خوب *khoub* (beautiful), خوبى *khoubi* (beauty); دردمند *dérdmend* (afflicted), دردمندى *dérdmendi* (affliction); آهنگر *ahengher* (a smith), آهنگرى *ahengheri* (the trade of a smith); زرگر *zergher* (a goldsmith), زرگرى *zergheri* (the trade of a goldsmith); سفيد *séfid* (white), سفيدى *séfidi* (whiteness).

413. If the word from which the abstract noun is formed end in ا, then the ى is doubled. Example, گدا *ghéda* (a beggar), گدايى *ghédayi* (beggary).

414. If it end in a vowel ه گ *gh* is introduced instead of ى, but the sound of *é* is retained. Example, بنده *bendé* (a servant, a slave), بندگى *bendéghi* (slavery, servitude).

2. The Persian Adjective.

415. Persian adjectives are formed from nouns by the addition of ى or انه *ané*. Example, ادم *adam* (a man), ادمى *adami* or ادمانه *adamané* (human); پادشاه *padishah* (an emperor), پادشاهانه *padishahané* (imperial).

416. If the noun end in a vowel ه, that letter is omitted before انه *ané* and a گ *gh* preceded by the sound of *é* put in its place. Example, بنده *bendé* (a slave), بندگانه *bendéghiané* (humble).

417. Persian adjectives are also formed by appending the terminations مند *mend*, ناك *nak*, وار *var*, or ور *ver* to nouns. Example, درد *dérd* (grief), دردمند *dérdmend* (afflicted, full of grief); زخم *zakhm* (a wound), زخمناك *zakhmnak* (wounded, full of wounds); هنر *huner* (talent), هنرمند *hunermend* (talented); اميد *eumid* (hope), اميدوار *eumidvar* (hopeful, hoping); هول *hevl* (terror), هولناك *hevlnak* (terrible, terrific); خطر *khatr* (danger), خطرناك *khatrnak* (dangerous).

418. Adjectives describing one's nationality or place of birth are formed by the addition of ى. Example, اصفهانى *Issfahan* (Ispahan), اصفهانى *Issfahani* (of Ispahan); عرب *Arab* (an Arab), عربى *Arabi* (Arabic, Arabian); ايران *Iran* (Persia), ايرانى *Irani* (Persian).

419. If the substantive from which such an adjective is formed end in a vowel ه or ا the ى must be preceded by a و. Example, بروسه *Broussa* (the town of Broussa), بروسهوى *Broussavi* (belonging to the town of *Broussa*); بصره *Bassra* (the town of *Bassora*), بصرهوى *Bassravi* (belonging to the town of Bassora); نمسه *Nemsé* (Germany), نمسهوى *Nemsévi* (German).

420. Adjectives stating the material of which a thing is made are formed by affixing ين *in* to the name of the substance. Example, سيم *sim* (silver), سيمين *simin* (of silver); زر *zer* (gold), زرين *zerin* (golden); اهن *ahen* (iron), اهنين *ahenin* (of iron).

3. The Persian Participles.

421. Persian infinitives are not used in Turkish, but Persian present or active participles, and past or passive participles, frequently are, especially in the formation of compound words; and they are sometimes used as nouns. Example :—

دارنده *darendé*, holding, who holds; a bearer, holder, possessor (of a letter, &c.)

اينده *ayendé*, coming, who comes, future

رونده *revendé*, going, who goes

خواننده *khanendé*, singing, reading; a singer, reader

خواه *khah*, desiring, wishing

خيرخواه *khair-khah*, a well-wisher

بد خواه *bed-khah*, an evil-wisher

خوانده *khandé*, called, invited

ديده *didé*, seen

امور ديده *umour didé*, who has seen business, experienced

شكسته *shikessté*, broken

دل شكسته *dil shikessté*, heart-broken

نما *nouma*, showing

رهنما *rahnuma*, showing the road, a guide

كير *ghir*, taking, holding, conquering

جهانكير *jihan-ghir*, world-conquering

باز *baz*, playing, risking

جانباز *janbaz*, who risks his life; an acrobat, a horse-breaker, horse-dealer.

422. The Persian active participles are either regular or irregular. The regular active participles are divided into two classes, those which end in ز, and those which end with any other letter.

423. The passive of a regular active participle ending in ز is formed by removing that letter, and putting خَتَهٔ in its stead. Example, سوز *souz* (burning), سوختهٔ *soukhté* (burnt). (This word is also used as a noun, meaning one whose heart is inflamed with the love of God or science. Hence it also signifies a student of law and divinity.) ساز *sáz* (making, fabricating), ساختهٔ *sakhté* (made, fabricated, spurious, forged). Hence the Turkish word ساختهٔکار *sakhté-kiar** (a forger).

424. The passive of the regular active participles which do not end in ز is obtained by the addition of یدهٔ *idé*. Example, پسند *pésend* (approving), پسندیدهٔ *pessendidé* (approved) ; رس *ress* (bringing, causing anything to reach its destination†), رسیدهٔ *ressidé* (arrived, matured), نو رسیدهٔ *nev-ressidé* (newly-arrived, just come to maturity).

425. The passive of irregular active participles ends always in تهٔ *té* or دهٔ *dé*. Example, بستهٔ *bessté* (tied), دیدهٔ *didé* (seen), گفتهٔ *ghiufté* (said), داشتهٔ *dashté* (had).

426. Another kind of Persian active participle, ending in ندهٔ *endé* or ایندهٔ is much used in Turkish as a noun. Example, دارندهٔ *darendé* (having, bearing, carrying, the bearer), خواننده *khanendé* (singing, a singer, a reader).

427. The Persian active participle which ends in ان *an*, instead of ندهٔ or یندهٔ, is also much used in Turkish as an adjective. Example, سوزان *suzan* (burning), گویان *ghuyan* (speaking), روان *reván* (flowing, moving), رخشان *rakhshan* (flashing, brilliant).

CHAPTER XII.

THE FORMATION OF ARABIC WORDS.

428. THOUSANDS of Arabic words being constantly used in Turkish some knowledge of the formation of Arabic words is indispensable, and is a great assistance to the memory. There is, strictly speaking, no limit to the words

---

* See note page 7.

† Hence, نامهٔ رس *namé ress* (an envoy who brings a letter).

which the Turks borrow from Arabic, and the number of Arabic words to be learnt would thus be a great difficulty were it not that they are all derived from certain roots which are, of course, very much less numerous. If the learner get a proper insight into the system of Arabic derivation of one word from another his labour is vastly diminished.   After acquiring a certain number of roots he will at once recognise and remember a large number of words formed from them.   This system of derivation is extremely regular, logical, and beautiful, although, at first, it appears complicated.

429. The number of Arabic verbal nouns in use in Turkish, in parti-cular, is extremely large.   Every Arabic verb has a large number of verbal nouns derived from it, but there are twenty-four different forms which are most met with in Turkish.   Of course these twenty-four forms of every root are not in use.

430. Every Arabic root in general consists of three letters only, to which a vast number of derivates can be traced.*   Example, كَتَبَ *kétéb* in Arabic means "he wrote," which is the third person singular, past tense of the verb, which corresponds to our infinitive, which does not exist in Arabic. From this we have the active participle كَاتِب *kiatib*,† writing, one who writes, hence a writer, a clerk.   مَكْتُوب *mektoub* is the past participle meaning written ; hence, something written, a letter.   مَكْتَب *mekteb* is what is called the noun of place formed by prefixing م to any root, and signifies the place where writing goes on ; hence a school, an office. Almost every root has all these kinds of derivatives, or most of them.

431. There are a few Arabic roots consisting of four letters, as دَحْرَج *dahraj* (to roll, he rolled), and even some of five, but they are extremely rare.

432. There are a great number of nouns of action which are derived directly from the root, but twenty-four are most in use in Turkish.   The word فعل *fal* (doing) is taken as the model which is supposed to have all these twenty-four forms and more, although they are all not in use, and every other root is supposed to have the same number of derivatives, although, in fact, they have a few only.   By studying the following table the learner will soon be able on meeting with an Arabic word to tell

---

* ʼSome words are derived from roots which are lost or out of use.

† The sound of *i* is introduced into the pronunciation by the Turks.   See note page 7.

whether it is one of these forms, which are called primitive, to distinguish them from others termed derived forms, of which we shall speak further on.

433. Table of the Primitive Forms of an Arabic Root of Three Letters.

1.	فَعَل *fal*	ضبط	*zábt*, holding, seizing
2.	فِعَل *fil*	فسق	*fissk*, sin, wickedness
3.	فُعَل *foul*	حزن	*huzn*, sadness
4.	فَعَل *fael*	طلب	*taleb*, demanding
5.	فِعَل *fial*	صغر	*sïghar*, smallness
6.	فَعَال *féaal*	سلام	*sélam*, salutation, peace
7.	فِعَال *fiaal*	حجاب	*hijab*, shame
8.	فُعَال *fuaal*	بخار	*bukhar*, exhalation, vapour
9.	فُعُول *fuoul*	دخول	*dukhoul*, entering
10.	فَعُول *féoul*	قبول	*káboul*, accepting
11.	فَعْلَى *fala*	دعوى	*dawa*, asserting a claim, lawsuit
12.	فُعْلَى *foula*	سكنى	*sukna*, habitation
13.	فِعْلان *filan*	حرمان	*hirman*, disappointment, being disappointed
14.	فُعْلان *foulan*	بطلان	*boutlán*, being unfounded, absurdity
15.	فَعَلان *faalan*	لمعان	*leméan*, shining
16.	فَعْلَة *falet*	زحمت	*zahmet*, trouble
17.	فِعْلَت *filet*	فطنت	*fitnet*, quickness of intelligence
18.	فُعْلَت *foulet*	حرمت	*hurmet*, respect, prohibitedness
19.	فَعَلَت *faalet*	غلبت	*ghalabet*, victory
20.	فَعَالَت *féaalet*	سعادت	*saadet*, happiness, felicity
21.	فِعَالَت *fiaalet*	درايت	*dirayet*, ability
22.	فُعُولَت *fuoulet*	سهولت	*suhoulet*, ease

23. مَفْعَلَتْ *mefalet*　مرحمت *merhamet,* mercy

24. مَفْعِلَتْ *méfilet*　محمدت *mahmidet,* a praiseworthy point of character, glory.

434. Every word in the second column is derived from a root corresponding in form to فعل *fal,* which is supposed to have all the other twenty-four forms and more. Example, رحمت *rahmet* is derived from رحم (having mercy), and مرحمت from the same; قبول from قبل (accepting), and so on, but frequently the roots are not adopted in Turkish, while the derivatives are.

The Arabic Active and Passive Participles.
1. The Active Participle.

435. The active participle of an Arabic verb of three letters is formed by inserting an ا between the first and second letter. The second letter of the root is then followed by a *kessré,* or the sound of *i.* Example, كتب **keteb* (he wrote), كاتب †*kiatib* (writing, one who writes, a writer), طلب *taleb* (he demanded, desired), طالب *talib* (desiring, one who desires, seeks, a seeker; hence, a student, a seeker after knowledge); نصر *nassar* (he helped), ناصر *nassir* (helping, one who helps, a helper).

436. The plural of these participles used as nouns is formed by putting a ʼ after the first letter of the root and inserting an ا after the second, thus :—

Singular.	Plural.
طالب *talib*	طلاب *toulab,* students, seekers
كاتب *kiatib*	كتاب *kiuttáb,*† writers
حاكم *hakim*	حكام *hukkiam,* judges, rulers.

437. The plural of these nouns may also be formed as follows :—

---

* This third person singular of the past tense, corresponding to our infinitive (which does not exist in Arabic), is never used in Turkish.

† The sound of *i* is introduced by the Turks, but does not exist in the original Arabic pronunciation. See note page 7.

Singular.	Plural.
طالب *talib*	طَلَبَه *talebé*, students
كاتب *kiatib*	كَتَبَه *ketébé*, writers.

438. If the second letter of the root be a و or a ى it changes into a ٔ in the active participle. Example:—

| سوق *sevk*, pushing | سائق *sa'ik*, who pushes, a pusher |
| ميل *méil*, inclination, inclining | مائل *ma'il*, who inclines, inclining. |

439. There are three forms of the Arabic verb, corresponding to فعيل *fail*, فعول *faoul*, and فعال *faaal*, which are like active participles or adjectives. Example:—

رحم *rahm*, pity, pitying   رحيم *rahim*, who pities, has mercy, merciful, compassionate

كتم *ketm*, being discreet, discretion, concealing   كتوم *kétoum*, who is discreet, prudent, who conceals

حمل *haml*, a burthen, bearing, carrying   حمال *hámmál*, one who carries, a porter.

2. The Passive Participle.

440. The passive participle of a verb of three letters is formed by putting a م followed by a ٔ, or the sound of *a* or *é*, before the first letter of the root, and a و after the second. Example :—

كتب *ketb*, writing	مكتوب *mektoub*, written, what has been written, a letter
نصر *nássr*, helping, aid	منصور *mánsour*, helped, assisted (by God)
نظر *názr*, looking	منظور *mánzour*, looked at, seen, examined
نظم *názm*, putting into metre, versifying	منظوم *mánzoum*, ranged in metre, metrical
نسخ *nesskh*, abolishing	منسوخ *mensoukh*, abolished
نقل *nákl*, narrating, transporting	منقول *menkoul*, narrated, transported
طلب *taleb*, desiring, demanding	مطلوب *matloub*, desired, a desideratum.

441. The plural of these participles, when used as nouns, is formed after the model of those following.

Singular.	Plural.
مكتوب *mektoub*, a letter	مكاتيب *mékiatib*, letters
مطلوب *mátloub*, a desideratum	مطلوبات *mátloubat*, desiderata.

The Arabic Comparative and Superlative.

442. The Arabic comparative and superlative are formed by putting an ا before the root of the word and writing a ´ after the second letter, or rather giving it the vowel *a* or *é* after it. Example :—

رحم *rahm*, mercy

أرحَم *erham*, more merciful or most merciful

فضل *fazl*, excellence, virtue

افضل *efzal*, more excellent or most excellent, more or most virtuous.

Or, in other words, it always corresponds to the form اَفعَل. Example, اَكبَر *ekber* (greater, or the greatest).

443. The plural form of these words, when used as nouns, which is most common, is always on the model of افَاعَل *éfail*. Example :—

افضل *efzal*, most excellent

اكبر *ekber*, greatest

احسن *ahsan*, most beautiful

افاضل *éfazil*, most excellent people

اكابر *ékabir*, the aristocracy, the greatest

احاسن *ahasin*, the most beautiful.

444. The feminine of these superlatives is always shaped on the model of فُعلَى *foula*. Example :—

Masculine.	Feminine.
اعلى *ala*, the highest	علیا *ulya*, the highest
اكبر *ekber*, the greatest	كبرى *kubra*, the greatest.

The Noun of Place.

445. Nouns indicating a place or locality where any action takes place are formed in Arabic by putting a م, followed by *ustun* or the sound of *a* or *é*, before the root of the verb expressing that action. Thus كتب *ketb* means writing ; put a م, followed by the sound of *é*, before it, and you have

the word مكتب *mekteb,* which in Turkish means a school (a place where writing goes on). In Arabic it also means an office. Example:—

Root.	Noun of place.
خرج *kharj,* going out	مخرج *makhrej,* an outlet, issue
جمع *jem,* collecting	مجمع *mejma,* a place where things are collected together, a junction
طبخ *tábkh,* cooking	مطبخ *mátbákh,** a kitchen; a place where cooking goes on
طبع *táb,* printing	مطبع *mátba,* a printing-office
دخل *dakhl,* entering	مدخل *medkhal,* an entry, inlet.

446. Sometimes the second vowel of the noun of place is *i* instead of *a* or *é.* Example :—

Root.	Noun of place.
نزل *nezl,* descending, alighting	منزل *menzil,* a station (where one alights)
جلس *jelss,* sitting	مجلس *mejliss,* a council, company
سجد *sejd,* worshipping	مسجد *messjid,* a mosque (a place where one worships)
شرق *shark,* rising (as the sun)	مشرق *meshrik,* the place where the sun rises, the east
غرب *gharb,* setting (as the sun)	مغرب *maghrib,* the place where the sun sets, the west.

447. The plural of nouns of place is formed on the model of منازل *menazil* (stations), which is the plural of منزل *menzil.* Example :—

Singular.	Plural.
مكتب *mekteb,* a school	مكاتب *meki†atib,* schools
مجلس *mejliss,* a council	مجالس *mejaliss,* councils
مسجد *messjid,* a mosque	مساجد *messajid,* mosques
مسكن *messken,* an habitation	مساكن *messakin,* habitations
مسلك *messlek,* a road, path, career	مسالك *messalik,* roads, paths, careers.

448. A *s* is sometimes found at the end of a noun of place, as مدرسة *medressé* (a college) from درس *derss* (a lesson, teaching), محكمة *mehkemé* (a court of justice) from حكم (judging, decreeing).

---

* Vulgarly pronounced by the Turks *moutfák.*

† See note page 7.

The Noun of Instrument.

449. By prefixing م, followed by a *kessré*, *i.e.*, the sound of *i*, and by putting a (´) or ١, *i.e.*, the sound of *é* or *a*, after the second letter of the root, the name of the instrument is obtained used to perform the action designated by the verb.   Examples :—

Root.	Noun of Instrument.
فَتْح *feth*, opening	مِفْتاح *miftah*, a key
نَشْر *neshr*, sawing	مِنْشار *minshar*, a saw
سَطْر *setr*, a line, ruling with lines	مِسْطَر *misstar*, a ruler
صَقْل *sákl*, polishing	مَصْقَل { *másskál* } anything used to { *misskal* } polish with.

450. Sometimes the noun of instrument ends with a ة.   Example :—

Root.	Noun of Instrument.
كَنْس *kenss*, sweeping	مَكْنَسَة *miknesset*, a broom.

451. If the noun of instrument take a (´) after the second letter of the root it forms its plural thus,—

Singular.	Plural.
مِسْطَر *mistar*, a ruler	مَساطِر *messatir*, rulers.

452. If it take an ١ after that letter, then it forms its plural thus,—

Singular.	Plural.
مِفْتاح *miftah*, a key	مَفاتيح *méfatih*, keys
مِصْباح *missbah*, a lamp	مَصابيح *massabih*, lamps.

Derivative Forms of an Arabic Root of three Letters.

453. By certain variations in the root, and the addition of certain letters, according to regular rules, other verbs and verbal nouns are formed, having slightly different meanings from the root.   These are called the derivative forms.   Thus :—

454. By putting ١ with a *kessré* under it, *i.e.*, with the sound of *i*, before the root, and another ١ between the second and third letters of the root, a verbal noun is obtained which has a causal or a transitive meaning Example :—

Root.	Derived Form.
غفل *ghafl*, being careless, negligent	اغفال *ighfal*, putting one off one's guard, making one negligent
فهم *fehm*, understanding	افهام *ifham*, causing one to understand
عزم *azm*, starting, departing	اعزام *izam*, causing to start, depart
عدم *adm*, not existing	اعدام *idam*, annihilating, destroying
نزل *nezl*, descending	انزال *inzal*, causing to descend.

455. If the second letter of the primitive root be a و or a ى, that letter is omitted, and a ه is added at the end of the word. Thus :—

Root.	Derived Form.
عون *avn*, help	اعانه *iané*, helping
ميل *méil*, inclination	اماله *imalé*, to cause to incline.

456. Transitive and causal verbs are also formed from the root by prefixing the letter ت to it and putting a ى before the last letter. Example :—

Root.	Derived Form.
شكل *shékl*, a form, shape	تشكيل *teshkil*, forming, shaping
شرف *sheref*, an honour	تشريف *teshrif*, honouring
كدر *kédr*, grief	تكدير *tekdir*, causing grief, grieving
حمل *haml*, bearing	تحميل *tahmil*, loading.

457. Sometimes this form conveys the meaning of considering something to be what the root refers to. Example :—

Root.	Derived Form.
عظم *azam*, being great	تعظيم *tazĭm*, considering one as great, making much of
كرم *kerem*, nobility, grandeur, being noble	تكريم *tekrim*, considering one as noble, and therefore honouring him.

458. If the last letter of the root be a و or an ا, it changes into a ى, and a ه is added to the end of the word. Example :—

Root.	Derived Form.
صفو *sáfv*, pureness, being pure	تصفيه *tássfiyé*, purifying
رضاء *réza*, being satisfied, consenting	ترضيه *tarziyé*, satisfying
ربو *rebv*, growing, rising, making enquiry	تربيه *terbiyé*, educating.

459. Passive or intransitive words are formed from the root by prefixing a تـ to it and doubling the middle letter, which is then followed by a ٔ, or the sound of *u*. Example, تعلم *téallum* (the action of learning or being taught), from علم *ilm* (knowing, or knowledge); تعظم *téazzum* (false greatness, growing big in one's own esteem), تقطر *tékáttur* (dripping, falling in drops, being distilled), from قطر *katr* (dropping—as water).

460. If the syllable اِن *in* be put before the root, and an ا after its second letter, a passive verbal noun is obtained. Examples:—

Root.	Derived Form.
كسر *kessr*, breaking	انكسار *inkissar*, being broken
جذب *jezb*, attracting	انجذاب *injizab*, being drawn or attracted, affection
دفع *def*, repulsing	اندفاع *indifa*, being repelled, repulsion
كشف *keshf*, discovering, detecting	انكشاف *inkishaf*, detection, being discovered
قطع *kát*, cutting	انقطاع *inkĭta*, being cut off, being interrupted
قبض *kábz*, seizing	انقباض *inkĭbáz*, being laid hold of, costiveness
قسم *kĭssm*, dividing, a part	انقسام *inkĭssam*, being divided, division
عقد *ákd*, tying	انعقاد *inĭkád*, being tied, a knot, a contract.

461. If an ا (pronounced as *i*) be prefixed to the root, a تـ put after its first letter, and an *élif* before its last, a verbal noun is constructed of an intransitive nature. Example:—

Root.	Derived Form.
جنب *jenb*, a side	احتناب *ijtinab*, avoiding
فخر *fakhr*, glorying, a cause of just pride	افتخار *iftikhar*, to be proud of
نقم *nákém*, vengeance, anger, hatred	انتقام *intikám*, taking vengeance
عذر *uzr*, an excuse	اعتذار *itizar*, asking to be excused.

462. A verbal noun expressing reciprocity is formed by prefixing a مُ (followed by the sound of *u*) to the root, putting an ا after its second letter and a ى at the end. Thus:—

Root.	Derived Form.
جدل *jedl,* disputing, a dispute	مجادله *mujadelé,* disputing with one another [ling one another
قتل *kátl,* killing	مقاتله *moukátélé,* mutual slaughter, kil-
كلمه *kélimé,* a word	مكالمه *mukialemé,* talking to one another, conversation [one another
كتب *ketb,* writing	مكاتبه *mukiatebé,* corresponding with
جذب *jezb,* drawing, attracting	مجاذبه *mujazebé,* attracting one another
قسم *kissm,* dividing	مقاسمه *moukássemé,* sharing, partitioning.

463. Verbal nouns of the above form sometimes do not express reciprocity, but are simple active verbs. Example, مشاهده *mushahedé* (looking, beholding, witnessing), ملاحظه *mulahazé* (considering, examining cautiously), ملازمت *mulazemet* (attending any one constantly, following any one).

464. Reciprocal verbal nouns are also formed by putting a ت before the root, ا after its first letter, and the sound of *u* after its second letter. Thus:—

Root.	Derived Form.
ضرب *zarb,* striking	تضارب *tézarub,* striking one another
قبل *kábl,* the front	تقابل *tékábul,* being opposite to one another
عقب *akeb,* the time or space immediately following anything, the heel	تعاقب *taakub,* succeeding one another.

465. This form is sometimes neuter, as تزايد *tézayud* (increasing), تدافع *tédafu* (defence), تقاعد *tékaud* (being pensioned), from قعد *kad* (sitting down, resting).

466. It sometimes signifies pretending to be or to do something referred to by the root. Thus:—

Root.	Derived Form.
جهل *jehl,* ignorance	تجاهل *téjahul,* pretending ignorance
مرض *maraz,* disease	تمارض *témaruz,* pretending to be ill.

467. By putting the syllable است *isst* before the root, and an *élif* before its last letter, a verbal noun is constructed which expresses asking for or demanding something designated by the primitive Arabic word. Example:—

Root.	Derived Form.
نطق *noutk*, speaking	استنطاق *isstintâk*, interrogating
علم *ilm*, knowledge, knowing	استعلام *isstilam*, enquiring, asking for knowledge
خرج *kharj*, going out	استخراج *isstikhraj*, extracting, deducing
حكم *hukm*, power, being strong	استحكام *isstihkiam*,* fortifying, strength-
رحم *rahm*, pitying, mercy	استرحام *isstirham*, asking mercy [ening
جلب *jelb*, drawing, attracting	استجلاب *isstijlab*, trying to attract.

468. Sometimes this form indicates considering a thing to be something expressed by the root. Thus, استحقار *isstihkar* (considering a thing mean or low), from حقير *hakir* (low, vile); استثقال *isstisskál* (deeming any one a bore), from ثقيل *sakil* (disagreeable, heavy); استحسان *isstihsan* (approving), from حسن *hussn* (beauty, agreeableness).

469. If the middle letter of the root be a و or a ى it is omitted in this form of verbal noun, and a ه is added to the end of the word. Thus, استعانه *isstiané* (asking help), from عون *avn* (help); استماله *isstimalé* (causing to incline—to one's self), from ميل *méil* (inclination).

470. Table of the Derivative Forms obtained from an Arabic Root of Three Letters.

	Model.	Example. Meaning.	Letters added.
1.	انفعال *ifal*	اخراج *ikhraj*, extracting	ا ا
2.	تفعيل *téfil*	ترتيب *tertib*, arranging	ت ى
3.	تفعل *téfaoul*	تعلّم *taalum*, learning	ت ع
4.	انفعال *infiaal*	انكسار *inkissar*, being broken	ان ا
5.	افتعال *iftiaal*	اجتناب *ijtinab*, avoiding	ا ت ا
6.	مفاعله *mufaalé*	مقاتله *moukâtélé*, mutually killing	م ا ا ة or ت ة
7.	تفاعل *téfaaoul*	تجاهل *téjahul*, feigning ignorance	ت ا
8.	استفعال *isstifaal*	استنصار *isstinsar*, asking for help	ا س ت ا

* See note page 7.

471. It must be borne in mind that all Arabic roots of three letters cannot assume all the eight forms given above. Many have only a few of them.

The Active and Passive Participles of an Arabic Root of Four Letters.

472. The active and passive participles of an Arabic verb of four letters are not formed in the same way as those of a verb of three letters.

473. If an Arabic verb have more than three letters in its root its active participle is formed by prefixing a م, followed by an *euturu, i.e.,* by the sound of *u* or *ou*, to the root. The second syllable of the word thus formed has an *ustun* for its vowel and the last syllable a *kessré*. Example:—

Root.	Active participle.	Model.
ترجم *terjem,* translating	مترجم *muterjim,* a translator (translating)	مفعلل

474. The passive participle is formed in the same way, only the last syllable has an *ustun* for its vowel. Example:—

Root.	Passive participle.	Model.
ترجم *terjem,* translating	مترجم *muterjem,* translated	مفعلل

475. The active and passive participles of the derivative forms (see 470) are formed nearly in the same way, with slight variations which will be shown by the examples given below:—

Verbal noun.	Passive participle.	Active participle.
استحسان *isstihsan,* approving	مستحسن *musstahsen,* approved	Not in use
استحقاق *isstihkák,* a just claim	مستحقّ *musstahákk,* deserved	مستحقّ *musstahik,* deserving
استناد *isstinad,* relying, leaning on	مستند *musstèned,* relied on, leant on	مستند *musstènid,* relying on, leaning on

L 2

Verbal noun.	Passive participle.	Active participle.
ترتيب *tertib*, arranging, composing (as a printer)	مرتّب *muretteb*, set in order, arranged, composed	مرتّب *murettib*, a compositor
تجاهل *tejahul*, feigning ignorance	Not in use	متجاهل *mutéjahil*, who feigns ignorance
تجاسر *téjassur*, daring	,, ,,	متجاسر *mutéjassir*, one who dares, bold
انكسار *inkissar*, being broken	Wanting	منكسر *munkessir*,* broken, grieved
انهدام *inhidam*, demolishing	,,	منهدم *munhédim*,* demolished
انهزام *inhizam*, being defeated	Not in use	منهزم *munhézim*,* defeated
انكساف *inkissaf*, being eclipsed	,, ,,	منكسف *munkessif*,* eclipsed
انكشاف *inkishaf*, being discovered	,, ,,	منكشف *munkeshif*,* discovered
التزام *iltīzam*, contracting, farming the revenue	,, ,,	ملترم *multézim*, who farms the revenue, a farmer of the revenue
تكبر *tekebbur*, being proud, pride	,, ,,	متكبر *mutékebbir*, proud
تسلط *tésallut*, arrogating power to one's self	,, ,,	متسلط *mutéssalit*, who arrogates to himself power
محاربه *mouharrebé*, making war, war	,, ,,	محارب *muharrib*, belligerent, making war
محاصره *mouhâsseré*, besieging, a siege	,, ,,	محاصر *mouhassïr*, a besieger.

* The active participles of forms having a passive meaning have a passive signification in English.

CHAPTER XIII.

THE ARABIC IRREGULAR PLURALS.

476. The method of forming the regular plural of Arabic words has been explained in a previous chapter (see 82). The irregular plurals are extremely difficult; but as they are much used in written Turkish, and to some extent in conversation, it is indispensable for the student to learn them. The following rules will serve to help him to acquire them and to impress them on the memory, although there are many exceptions.

477. There are two kinds of irregular plurals: one called the *plural of scarcity*, and the other the *plural of multitude* (in Arabic جمع القلة and جمع الكثرة). The first is used when only a few things or people are meant, from three to ten. The second applies to all higher numbers. There is also what is called the *plural of plurals* (جمع الجموع), applying to very high numbers. The numerical difference between the two first kinds of plural is more imaginary than real, especially in Turkish, in which language the distinction is scarcely recognised.

478. The *plural of paucity* assumes four shapes, corresponding to أفعُل أفعال أفعِلة and فِعلة.

479. (1) Words which form their plural according to the form أفعُل.

Words in the singular shaped like

Singular.	Plural.
نفس *nefss*, the soul	أنفس *enfuss*, souls
رجل *rijl*, the foot	ارجل *erjul*, feet
عناق *anak*, a kid	أعنق *anuk*, kids
يمين *yémin*, an oath	ايمُن *éimun*, oaths
ذراع *zira*, the fore-arm, a cubit, the fore-leg of an animal	أذرع *azru*, fore-arms, cubits, fore-legs.

(2) Words which form their plural according to the form أفعال.

Singular.	Plural.
لوح *levh*, a table, tablet, flat surface, board	الواح *elvah*, tables, tablets, flat surfaces, boards
ملك *milk*, dominion, territory	املاك *emlak*, dominions, territories

Singular.	Plural.
حكم *hukm*, a decree	احكام *ahkiam*, decrees
بطل *bétel*, a hero	ابطال *abtal*, heroes
عقب *akeb*, the heel	اعقاب *akab*, heels
عنق *unk* or *unuk*, the neck	اعناق *anak*, necks.

(3) Words which form their plural after the form اَفْعِلَة.

Singular.	Plural.
طعام *taam*, food	اطعمه *atimé*, foods
عمود *amud*, pillar	اعمده *amidé*, pillars
حمار *himar*, an ass	احمره *ahmiré*, asses
غراب *ghurab*, a crow, a raven	اغربه *aghribé*, crows, ravens.

(4) Words which form their plural according to the form فُعَلَة.

Singular.	Plural.
ثور *sawr*, a bull	ثِيرة *siret*, bulls
غزال *ghazal*, a gazelle	غزلة *ghizlet*, gazelles
ولد *wéled*, a child	ولدة *wildet*, children
غلام *ghoulam*, a boy	غلمة *ghilmet*, boys.

480. The *plural of multitude* has nineteen forms, given below.

(1) Words which form their plural after the form فُعْل.

Singular.	Plural.
اسد *essed*, a lion	اسد *usd*, lions
احمر *ahmer*, red	حمر *humr*, red (pl.)

(2) Words which form their plural according to the form فُعُل.

Singular.	Plural.
سفينه *sefiné*, a ship	سفن *sufun*, ships
كتاب *kitab*, a book	كتب **kiutub*, books
رسول *resul*, an apostle, prophet	رسل *russul*, apostles, prophets.

(3) Words which form their plural according to the form فُعَل.

Singular.	Plural.
قريه *kariyé*, a village	قرا *kura*, villages
لحيه *lihyé*, the beard	لحى *luha*, beards.

---

* See note page 7.

(4) Words which form their plural according to the form فِعَل.

Singular.	Plural.
نعمة *nimet*, benefit, comfort, blessing	نعم *niém*, benefits, comforts, blessings.

(5) Words which form their plural according to the form فَعَلَة.

Singular.	Plural.
طالب *talib*, a student	طلبه *talebé*, students
سيد *séïd*, a lord	سادة *sadet*, lords
خبيث *khabiss*, bad	خبثه *khabésé*, bad people, villains.

(6) Words which form their plural according to the form فُعَلَة.

Singular.	Plural.
قاضى *kázï*, a judge	قضاة *kouzat*, judges
كمى *kémi*, a warrior (not used in Turk- [ish)	كماة *kumat*, warriors.

(7 and 8.) These forms are فَعَلَة and فُعَّل, but there are scarcely any Arabic words used in Turkish which form their plurals according to them.

(9.) The ninth form is فُعَّال, according to which the word تاجر *tajir* (a merchant) makes تجار *tujjar* in the plural, merchants.

(10.) The tenth form is فِعال, according to which numerous words used in Turkish form their plural.

Singular.	Plural.
عبد *abd*, a servant	عباد *ibad*, servants
ذئب *ziib*, a wolf	ذئاب *ziab*, wolves
رمح *rumh*, a lance	رماح *rimah*, lances.
نقطه *nokta*, a point	نقاط *nikát*, points
جبل *jebel*, a mountain	جبال *jibal*, mountains
رجل *rajol*, a man	رجال *rijal*, men
كريم *kerim*, a noble, great person	كرام *kiram*, the noble, the great.

(11.) The eleventh form is فُعول, in accordance with which a great number of words used in Turkish shape their plural, as,—

Singular.	Plural.
قلب *kálb*, the heart	قلوب *kouloub*, hearts
علم *ilm*, knowledge, science	علوم *ouloum*, sciences
برج *bourj*, a tower, a sign of the zodiac	بروج *burouj*, towers
ملك *mélik*, a king	ملوك *mulouk*, kings.

(12.) Words which form their plural according to the form فُعْلان.

Singular.	Plural.
راهب *rahib*, a Christian monk	رهبان *ruhban*, Christian monks
اسود *eswed*, a negro, Ethiopian	سودان *soudan*, negroes, Ethiopians.

(13.) Words which form their plural according to the form فِعْلان.

Singular.	Plural.
نور *nur*, light	نيران *niran*, lights
غلام *ghoulam*, a boy, page	غلمان *ghilmán*, boys, pages
صبى *sébi*, a boy	صبيان *sibian*, boys
ضيف *zaif*, a guest	ضيفان *zifan*, guests.

(14 and 15). These forms are respectively فَعْلى and فِعْلى, but they are not used in Turkish.

(16.) This form is فُعَلاء, according to which we have several words in Turkish.

Singular.	Plural.
فقير *fakĭr*, a poor man (poor)	فقرا *foukéra*, the poor
خليفه *khalifé*, a successor to Mahomet, a caliph	خلفاء *khoulefa*, successors, caliphs.

(17.) Some words in Turkish form their plural according to this form أَفْعِلاء.

Singular.	Plural.
نبى *nébi*, a prophet	انبياء *enbiya*, prophets.

(18.) Words which form their plural according to the form فَعَالى.

Singular.	Plural.
يتيم *yetim*, an orphan [*mufti*	يتامى *yetama*, orphans
فتوى *fetwa*, a legal opinion given by a	فتاوى *fetawa*, legal opinions.

(19.) There are scarcely any Arabic words used in Turkish which form their plural according to this form فُعالى.

481. All original quadriliteral and the most of those forms of words in which the triliteral root is increased by one or more letters have the same kind of irregular plural consisting of three syllables. The first of these

syllables has an *ustun* for its vowel sound, the second takes an ١ or the sound of *a*, and the third has a *kessré* for its vowel sound. Examples:—

Singular.	Plural.
رسالة *risalé*, a treatise, pamphlet	رسائل *ressail*, treatises, pamphlets
دعوى *dawa*, a lawsuit, claim	دَعَاوى *daawi*, lawsuits, claims
جوهر *jevher*, a jewel	جواهر *jevhahir*, jewels
قافله *káfilé*, a caravan	قوافل *kawafil*, caravans
قانون *kanoun*, a law	قوانين *kawanin*, laws
اكبر *ekbér*, the greatest	اكابر *akabir*, the greatest
اقليم *iklim*, a district, climate	اقاليم *akálim*, districts, climates
مطبخ *mátbákh*, a kitchen	مطابخ *matábih*, kitchens
سلطان *sultan*, a sovereign	سلاطين *salatin*, sovereigns
تجربه *tejribé*, an experiment, a trial	تجارب *tejarib*, experiments, trials
تصوير *tassvir*, a picture	تصاوير *tessavir*, pictures
دفتر *defter*, a list, register	دفاتر *defatir*, lists, registers.

482. Sometimes this form of irregular plural has a ه at the end of it. Example:—

Singular.	Plural.
كشميرى *Kishmiri*, an inhabitant of Cashmere	كشامره *Keshamiré*, inhabitants of Cashmere
افغان *Afghán*, an Afghan	افاغنه *Afaghiné*, Afghans.

EXÉRCISE XXVÍ.

Unless (اولمدقجه *olmadoukja*) affection (محبت *mahabet*) be mutual (ايكى باشدن *iki báshdan*) it does not (ثبوت بولمق *subout boulmak*) last. I regret (تأسف ايتمك *tééssuf*) that I cannot help your friend. He has acted so badly that no one will help him. Is he not ashamed? No, he is proud (افتخار ايتمك *ifitkhar*) of what he has done. He ought to be punished. No doubt he will be punished. Has your friend been rewarded (مكافات اولنمق *mukiafat-olounmak*)? When did he acquire Turkish? He speaks it very well. He acquired it in London, before coming to Constantinople. You gave him letters of recommendation (توصيه نامه *tavsiyé-namé*). They will be very useful to him. Has he seen the grand vizier? Yes, he had an interview with him last week. That is a very important thing. Will he see him again (بر دها *bir daha*)? I think so. If he wish to speak Turkish well, he must have intercourse (اختلاط ايتمك *ikhtilat*) with the Turks (عثمانلو *Ossmanli*). Have you any Turkish friends ? I have both Turkish and Christian friends. Do you think the promised reforms (اصلاحات *isslahát*) in Turkey will be carried (اجرا اولنمق *ijra olounmak*) out ? I hope so. The consolation (تسليه *tessliyé*) of the poor is to die (اولمك *eulmek*) (Turkish proverb). One ought to respect (رعايت ايتمك *riayet*) the customs (عادت *adet*) of the country in which he lives. You are quite right. What are you going to do to-day ? I am going to the watchmaker. Are you not pleased (خوشنود *khoshnud*) with the watch you bought ? No. I am astonished (تعجب ايتمك *taajub*) at that, for it was very dear. Have the kindness (تأليف ايتمك عنايت ايدوب *inayet*) to give me pen and ink. Are you writing (تأليف ايتمك *té'lif etmek*) a book ? No, I am not an author (مولف *mu'ellif*). Your father is a celebrated author. I am much honoured by what you say. It is a pity that of late years the arts (فنون *fenoun*) and sciences (علوم *uloum*) have been neglected (مهمل *muhmel*) and abandoned (متروك *metruk*) in Mussulman (اسلامى *Esslami*) countries.

CHAPTER XIV.

TURKISH COMPOUND WORDS.

483. THERE are scarcely any compound words of Turkish origin.

484. Compound words, on the contrary, abound in Persian and form a special beauty of that tongue. The Turks have adopted a very large number of these words, and although they are not understood by the uneducated, they are in constant use in written Turkish, and especially in poetry. The number of these compounds is almost unlimited, but still it must not be supposed that they can be coined *ad libitum*. Even native Turkish and Persian writers in general only employ those which usage has sanctioned. As, however, scarcely any dictionary is large enough to contain them all, it is very important for the student to understand their construction, not merely to facilitate his acquisition of them, but to enable him to understand such as may not be found in the dictionary, which he will easily do after a little experience, and when he has a certain stock of Persian and Arabic roots which enter into their composition.

485. Persian compound words are generally formed either of (1) a noun

and a participle, (2) an adjective and a noun, (3) or two nouns. Others are constructed by the use of particles.

486. They may consist of two Persian words, or an Arabic and a Persian word, or two Arabic words.

487. The Persian participles which are most frequently employed in the formation of these compound words are the following, which the learner will do well to commit to memory, as they constantly recur in words used in Turkish :—

اور *avér*, bringing, possessing

ارا *ara*, ornamenting

ازار *azar*, tormenting

افزا *efza*, increasing

باز *báz*, playing

بار *bar*, pouring forth

رو *rev*, going, running

بر *ber*, carrying

بر *bur*, cutting

بخش *bakhsh*, giving

پر *per*, flying

پسند *pésend*, approving

آشام *asham*, drinking

آفرین *aferin*, creating

افراز *efraz*, raising

افروز *efrouz*, illuminating

رس *ress*, arriving, attaining

رسان *ressan*, causing to reach

رسیده *ressidé*, reached, ripe

كداز *ghiudaz*, melting

دان *dan*, knowing

ده *dih*, giving

ریز *riz*, shedding

كشا *kusha*, opening

كن *ken*, digging

كوب *koup*, striking

مال *mal*, rubbing

نشین *nishin*, sitting

نما *numa*, showing

زن *zen*, striking

ساخته *sakhté*, made, fabricated

ساز *sáz*, fabricating, making

سوز *souz*, burning

شكسته *shikessté*, broken

شكن *shiken*, breaking

كش *kesh*, drawing

كش *kush*, killing

بند *bend*, tying

بسته *bessté*, tied

پیرا *pira*, ornamenting

بین *bin*, seeing [ing

تاب *tab*, illuminating, burning, twist-

تاز *taz*, running, rushing

خور *khour*, eating

روب *roup*, sweeping

خوان *khan*, reading

خراش *khirash*, tearing

دار *dar*, holding, having

انكیز *enghiz*, exciting

كیر *ghir*, seizing, taking

فریب *firib*, deceiving

نویس *nuviss*, writing

نه *nih*, placing [ing

دوز *douz*, sewing, embroidering, stitch-

ربا *ruba*, carrying off or away

ران *ran*, giving course to anything

یاب *yab*, finding

انداز *endaz*, casting, throwing.

488. I.—Words formed from a Noun and a Participle.

کل افشان *ghiul efshan*, rose-scattering ; from کل *ghiul*, a rose

در افشان *dur-efshan*, pearl-scattering ; from در *dur*, a pearl

خون افشان *khoun-efshan*, shedding blood ; from خون *khoun*, blood

دل ازار *dil-azar*, heart-tormenting ; from دل *dil*, the heart

جان ازار *jan-azar*, soul-tormenting ; from جان *jan*, the soul

جهان ارا *jihan-ara* ⎱
عالم ارا *alem-ara* ⎰ ornamenting the world (عالم *alem*)

روح افزا *rouh-efza*, soul-refreshing ; from روح *rouh*, the soul

سر افراز *ser-efraz*, raising the head ; سر *sér*, the head

فتنه انکیز *fitné-enghiz*, exciting rebellion ; فتنه *fitné*, rebellion

دلبر *dilber*, heart-ravishing, lovely

دل فریب *dil-firib*, heart-deceiving, seductive

عالمتاب *alemtab*, illuminating the world

جهاندار *jihan-dar*, possessing the world

کامران *kiamran*, successful, obtaining his wishes, mighty ; from کام *kiam*, a wish

خونریز *khounriz*, shedding blood

رهزن *rahzen*, infesting the road, a robber

دلسوز *dilsouz*, heart-inflaming

پرتو انداز *pertev-endaz*, casting rays

جگر کداز *jigher ghiudaz*, heart-melting

جها نکیر *jihan-ghir*, world-conquering

دلکشا *dil-kiusha*, heart-rejoicing

می آشام *méi-asham*, wine-drinking, who drinks wine (می *méi*)

جزیره نشین *jeziré-nishin*, inhabiting an island

اورك نشین *evrengh-nishin*, sitting on a throne (اورك *evrengh*)

ویرانه نشین *virané-nishin*, inhabiting a desert (ویرانه *virané*)

رهنما *reh-numa*, showing the way, a guide

کامیاب *kiamyab*, finding his wish, successful

کهربار *ghiuher-bar*, scattering pearls or precious stones (کهر *ghiuher*).

489. II.—Words formed of an Adjective and a Noun.

خوب روی *khob-rouï*, with a pretty face ; from خوب, pretty

پاکدامن *pak-damen*, virtuous (the skirt of whose garment is clean) ; from دامن *damen*, a skirt

خوش رفتار *khosh-reftar,* walking gracefully ; from رفتار *reftar,* walking
ساده دل *sadé-dil,* simple-hearted
سیاه چشم *siyah-cheshm,* black-eyed ; from سیاه *siyah,* black, and چشم *cheshm,* the eye
شیرین دهن *shirin-dihen,* sweet-mouthed ; from شیرین *shirin,* sweet
سبكپای *sébuk poï,* quick-footed ; from سبك *sébuk,* quick
تیز فهم *téz-fehm,* of quick understanding
شكسته دل *shikesté-dil,* broken-hearted.

490. III.—Words formed of two Nouns.

پری روی *péri-rouï,* ⎫
پری پیكر *péri-péïker,* ⎭ with the face of a fairy
پری رخسار *péri-roukhsar,* with the cheeks of a fairy
ماه پرتو *mah-pertev,* shining like the moon
خوش صحبت *khosh-sohbet,* of agreeable conversation
شكر لب *shéker-leb,* with lips of sugar
كلرخ *ghiulroukh,* ⎫
كلرخسار *ghiulroukhsar,* ⎬ rosy-cheeked
كلعذار *ghiulizar,* ⎭
كلروی *ghiulrouï,* whose face is like a rose
سمن بوی *sémen-bouï,* having the perfume of jasmine (سمن)
مشكبوی *mushk-bouï,* smelling of musk (مشك)
یاقوت لب *yakout-leb,* ruby-lipped ; from یاقوت, a ruby
شیر دل *shir-dil,* lion-hearted ; from شیر, a lion
غنچه دهان *ghunché-dihan,* with a mouth like a rose-bud (غنچه *ghunché*)
دولتمآب *devlet-mab,* the resort of fortune (دولت *devlet*), fortunate
عدالت دستكاه *adalet-desstghiah,* the bench of justice, just
انجم سپاه *enjum-sipah,* whose armies are numerous as the stars (انجم *enjum*)
أصف تدبیر *Asaf-tedbir,* as able in management (تدبیر) as Asaf[*]
عالمپناه *alem-penah,* the asylum of the universe
زهرة جبین *zuhré-jebin,* with a forehead like that of Venus (زهرة *zuhré*)
سمین بر *simin-ber,* silver-breasted ; from بر, the breast
طوطی كفتار *touti-ghiuftar,* talking like a parrot (طوطی *touti*)
سمن بر *sémen-bér,* with a breast like jessamine

---

[*] Asaf is supposed to have been the name of Solomon's grand vizier.

حمشید کلاه *Jemshid-kiulah*, with the diadem of Jemshid

دارا حشمت *dara-hashmet*, with troops (or pomp) of Darius.

491. A number of these compound words will be found in the following
Persian couplet :—

ماه روی مشکبوی دلکشی
جان فزای دلفریبی مهوشی

which means : " A beauty with a face like the moon, odoriferous as musk,
attracting the heart, delighting the soul, and seducing one's affection." The
word for a " beauty" (مهوش *mehvesh*) is derived from two words, meaning
" resembling the full moon." This word, and all the others applying to it,
are used in Turkish.

Words formed by the use of Particles.

492. The particle هم *hem* prefixed to a noun produces a compound word
expressing companionship or intimacy.   Example :—

همشهری *hem-shehri*, fellow-townsman, fellow-countryman

همفراش *hem-firash*, a bed-fellow

همراه *hem-rah*, fellow-traveller ; from راه, a road

همجنس *hem-jinss*, of the same species (جنس)

همشیره *hem-shiré*, of the same milk, a sister ; from شیر *shir*, milk

همراز *hem-raz*, having the same secrets (راز), an intimate friend

هماشیان *hem-ashiyan*, of the same nest (اشیان)

همدم *hem-dem*, one breathing the same breath (دم), an intimate associate

همدل *hem-dil*, of the same heart, unanimous

همسال *hem-sal*, of the same year (*i.e.*, age)

همکتب or } *hem-mekteb*, a schoolfellow
هممکتب }

همپستر *hem-pisster*, sleeping on the same pillow

همخوابه *hem-khabé*, sleeping together—of the same sleep (خوابه)

هماهنك *hem-aheng*, of the same inclination (اهنك)

493. Adjectives denoting the want or absence of something are framed
by using the particles نا *na* (not, without), equivalent to the syllables "less"
or " un " in English ; بی *bi* (without), and کم *kem* (little).   Examples :—

نا اميد *na-eumid*, hopeless ; from اميد *eumĭd*, hope

نا شناس *na-shinass*, ⎫

نا اشنا *na-ashina*, ⎬ ignorant (not knowing)

نا دان *na-dan*, ⎭

نا مرد *na-mérd*, unmanly ; from مرد *mérd*, a man

نا باك *na-pak*, impure ; from باك *pak*, pure

نا شكفته *na-shukiufté*, not full blown

بی امان *bi-aman*, unmerciful

بی باك *bi-bak*, fearless ; from باك *bak*, fear

بی تأمل *bi-taamul*, inconsiderate

بی ترتیب *bi-tertib*, irregular ; from ترتیب *tertib*, arrangement

بی خرد *bi-khiréd*, senseless ; from خرد *khiréd*, sense

بی دین *bi-din*, without religion (دین *din*)

بی ادب *bi-édeb*, unmannerly

كمبها *kem-baha*, of little value (price)

كمعقل *kem-akl*, of small intelligence

كمتجربه *kem-tejribé*, of little experience, inexperienced

كمٮایه *kem-mayé*, of little capital (*i.e.*, poor in resources); from مایه *mayé*, capital, ferment, stock.

494. Compound nouns designating the people who exercise any trade or profession, or perform some action habitually, are formed by adding the syllables دار *dar* (having), كار *kiar* or كر *ghér* (doer, maker), بان *ban* (keeper), to the substantives. Examples ;—

دربان *dér-ban*, a door-keeper, porter

زندانبان *zindan-ban*, a turnkey, warder

اهنگر *ahen-ghér*, a smith (a worker of iron)

زرکر *zer-ghér*, a goldsmith (a worker of gold)

سلحدار *silah-dar*, an esquire (who carries arms)

كناهكار *ghiunah-kiar*,* an evil-doer, a sinner ; from کناه *ghiunah*, sin.

495. Nouns indicating place are formed by adding the syllable کاه *ghiah* (meaning " place " or " time ") to a substantive. Thus we have خوابکاه *khab-ghiah* (a bed—the sleeping-place), اردوکاه *ordon-ghiah*, لشكركاه *leshkér-ghiah* (a camp—a place where soldiers are), مخیمکاه *mukhayem-ghiah* (a camp—a place under canvas).

---

* See note page 7.

496. The words ستان *isstan* (a country), زار *zar* (a plot or bed), كده *ghedé* or *kedé* (a house), دان *dan* (a holder, case), سار *sar* (a country, land), لاخ *lakh* (a place), are also used to form compound nouns of place. Thus we have;—

كلستان *ghiulisstan*, the country of roses, a rose-garden

داغستان *daghisstan*, a mountainous country

خارستان *kharisstan*, a thorny place; from خار *khar*, a thorn

نكارستان *nighiarisstan*, a place where pictures are, a picture gallery; from نكار

بهارستان *baharisstan*, the abode of spring (بهار *bahar*)   [*nighiar*, a picture*

كلزار *ghiulzar*, a bed of roses

لالهزار *lalézar*, a bed of tulips; from لاله *lalé*, a tulip

سنكزار *senghsar*, }

سنكلاخ *senghlakh*, } a stony place; from سنك *sengh*, a stone

سنكبار *senghbar*, }

شورهزار *shorézar*, } a salt-desert, a salt-works; from شوره *shoré* and نمك

نمكزار *nemekzar*, }   *nemek*, salt

چشمهزار *cheshmézar*, a place full of springs

بتكده †*poutghédé*, an idol temple; from بت *pout*, an idol

اتشكده *ateshghédé*, a fire temple

قلمدان *kalemdan*, a pen-case; from قلم *kalem*, a pen

شمعدان *shemadan*, a candlestick; from شمع *shema*, a candle

كوهسار *kiuhsar*, a mountain district; from كوه *kiuh*, a mountain

ديولاخ *divlakh*, a place inhabited by demons; from ديو *div*, a demon.

497. Adjectives expressing similarity are made by adding آسا *asa*, or سا *sa* or وش *vesh* to substantives.   Example :—

عنبرآسا *anbér-asa*, like ambergris ; from عنبر, ambergris

مشكآسا *muskh-asa*, like musk

جنتآسا *jennet-asa*, like paradise (جنت)

مهوش *mévesh*, like the moon, a beautiful woman

قمروش *kamr-vesh*, like the moon

سحرسا *sihr-sa*, like magic ; from سحر *sihr*, magic

غنچهوش *ghiunché-vesh*, like a rose-bud

پریوش *péri-vesh*, like a fairy, fairy-like.

---

* To help the learner, I give the meaning of those Persian words which have not occurred before in this grammar.

† بت an idol, is pronounced *pout* by the Turks, although written with a ب.

498. The termination فام *fam* (coloured), كون *ghiun* (colour), رنك *rengh* (colour), are used to form epithets expressing colour. Example :—

گلكون *ghiulghiun*, rose-colour

گلفام *ghiulfam*, rose-coloured

زمردفام *zumrud fam*, emerald-coloured, green

سبزرنك *sebz rengh*, the colour of verdure (سبز), green.

499. Some adjectives which express fulness, completeness, or multifariousness, are constructed by the repetition of the noun and an ١ being inserted in the middle. Example :—

لبالب *lebaleb*, full to the brim; from لب *leb*, the lip or brim

سراسر *sérasér*, from end to end ; from سر *sér*, a head

كوناكون *ghiunaghiun*, of many colours ; from كون *ghiun*, colour

رنگارنك *rengharengh*, ,, ,, from رنك *rengh*, colour.

500. Adjectives expressing possession and fulness are made by adding the termination سار *sar* (abounding in, full of), كین *ghin* or اكین *eghin* (full), مند *mend* (full, or the termination "ish" in English), ناك *nak* (full), and وار or ور *vér* (like, possessing).

غمکین *ghemghin*, full of grief (غم *ghem*)

شرماکین *shermeghin*, full of shame (شرم *sherm*)

امیدوار *eumidvar*, hopeful

پروانهوار *pervané-var*, like a moth (پروانه *pervané*)

بهرهور *behrévér*, a participator ; from بهره *behré*, a share

شرمسار *shermsar*, full of shame ; from شرم *sherm*, shame

دانشمند *danishmend*, learned ; from دانش *danish*, learning

زهرناك *zéhirmak*, poisonous ; from زهر *zéhir*, poison

دانشور *danishvér*, learned ; from دانش *danish*, learning

خردمند *khirédmend*, intelligent ; from خرد *khiréd*, sense.

501. The termination انه *ané* appended to a noun indicates resemblance or forms an adverb. Example :—

مردانه *merdané*, like a man, manly, courageously

درویشانه *dervishané*, like a dervish

ستمکارانه *sitemkiarané*, unjustly ; from ستمکار *sitemkiar*, unjust.

502. If the word to which this termination is added end in an ١ or و, then a ی must be put between them. Example :—

كدايانه *ghedayané*, beggarly; from كدا *gheda*, a beggar

عدويانه *adouyané*, hostile, or in a hostile way; from عدو *adou*, an enemy

دانايانه *danayané*, prudently; from دانا *dana*, prudent, wise.

503. If the word to which انه *ané* is appended end with a ه, a ك, preceded by the sound of *é*, is substituted for it; as, بندكانه *bendéghiané* (humble, humbly), from بنده *bendé* (a servant).

504. Some Persian nouns ending in اه are sometimes written without the ا. Example:—

راه or ره *rah*, a road

شاه or شه *shah*, a king

كناه or كنه *ghiunah*, a sin.

505. These words thus shortened are used to form compound nouns. Example :—

رهكذار *rehghiuzar*, who passes (كذار) the road, a traveller

رهزن *rehzen*, who strikes (زن) the road, a highwayman

شهزاده *shehzadé*, begotten (زاده) of a king, a prince

رهبر *rehbér*, who brings (بر) the road, a guide

رهدار *rehdar*, who has (دار) the road, a collector of toll or merchandise.

506. Some abstract nouns are formed by adding ا to adjectives; as كرم *gherm* (hot), كرما *gherma* (heat).

Arabic Expressions used as Turkish Compound Words.

507. There are no compound nouns in Arabic; but certain Arabic expressions have been adopted by the Turks, and are regarded as compound words by them. The words most commonly met with used in this way are as follows :—

ولى *véli*, a master, saint, patron, servant, next of kin

ولى نعمت *véli-nimet*, a benefactor, (a master of favour, نعمت)

ولى عهد *véli-ahd*, the heir-apparent

صاحب *sahib*, possessor

صاحب جمال *sahib-jimal*, possessor of beauty (جمال)

صاحبقران *sahib-kïran*, a lord of the age

صاحب *sahib*, possessor

صاحب خروج *sahib-khurouj*, a great but cruel conqueror, like Jenghiz Khan or Timur

أهل *ehl*, people

أهل عرض *ehl-i-irz*, honest, honourable (*i.e.*, people of honour, عرض)

أهل حكمت *ehl-i-hikmet*, (people of wisdom, حكمت)

ذات *zat*, possessor of, endowed with (fem. singular)

ذات الجنب *zat-ul-jenb*, pleurisy (*i.e.*, possessor of the side, جنب)

ذو *zou*, possessor of (singular masculine)

ذو ذوابه *zu-zuabé*, possessor of flowing locks, *i.e.*, a comet

ذو اربعة الاضلاع *zu-erbaat-ulazla*, a possessor of four sides, a quadrilateral figure

ذوى *zévi*, plural of ذو, possessors (plural masculine)

ذوات *zewat*, plural of ذات, possessors (feminine plural)

ذوى العقول *zévi-ul-oukoul*, the possessors of senses, sane persons

ارباب *erbab*, plural of رب *rab*, owners of, endowed with, competent persons, people belonging to, Lord

رب الارباب *rab-ul-erbab*, the Lord of Lords, God

ارباب تغلب *erbabi-téghallub*, superiors, conquerors (the possessors of power, predominance)

ارباب مسند *erbabi-messned*, the holders of office of high distinction (مسند), dignitaries

غير *ghaïr*, not, " un " at the beginning of English words

غير متساوى *ghaïri-mutéssavi*, unequal

غير معلوم *ghaïri-maloum*, unknown

لا *la*, not (used with the third person singular of an Arabic verb)

لا يموت *la yémut*, immortal (literally he does not die)

لا يحصى *la yuhsa*, innumerable

لا *la,* not

لا بَأْس *la-bess,* harmless

لا أُبالى *la-ubali,* careless, free-and-easy (literally, I do not care)

لا جرم *la-jerem,* without fail (literally, no fault, (جرم).

508. Another kind of Arabic expression used as a compound word in Turkish consists of an adjective followed by a noun with the definitive article. Example :—

قوى البنيان *kavi-ul-bunyan,* robust (*i.e.,* strong in construction)

ضعيف الأياد *zaïf-ul-éyad,* weak in the hands (أياد)

ابدى الدوام *ébedi-ud-déwâm,* eternal in duration (دوام).

509. Compound nouns in Turkish are treated just the same as simple ones, and governed by the same rules. Example :—

ولى نعمتم سكز *véli-nimetim siniz,* you are my benefactor

ولى نعمتمى كوردم *véli-nimetimi ghieurdum,* I saw my benefactor.

EXERCISE XXVII.

He saw a beautiful girl, with a face like the moon, smelling of musk.* The governor of the town acted very unjustly. The prince admired (بكنمك †*béyenmek*) the picture (رسم *ressm*) very much, and could not believe (اينانمق *inanmak*) that it was a soulless figure (تصوير *tassvir*). We saw a splendid (دلكشا *dilkiusha*) garden (باغ *bâgh*). Where are the candlesticks? Bring me a candle (موم *moum*). Put it in a candlestick. I have lost the case for my pens. You left it at school. It is a pity you forgot it. We are fellow countrymen. Is your servant honest (اهل عرض *ehl-i-irz*)? I believe so. Honest servants are very rare (نادر *nadir*). We are all sinners. The mighty (كامران *kiamran*) (successful) king (پادشاه *padishah*) was disappointed (محروم كالمق *mahroum kâlmak*). I did not know that your sister was ill. I hope she will soon be better (كچمش اولسون *ghechmish olsoun*). Has she taken any medicine (علاج *ilaj*)? Yes. What is the matter (نه سى وار *né si var*) with her? She has pleurisy. May God give her health (شفا *shefa*)! Where is the printing-office of the *Jeridé-Hawadiss* (جريدهٔ حوادث *Jeridé-i-héwadiss*) newspaper (غزته *ghazéta*).

---

* I write here such English as will suggest the Turkish.

† See page 7, paragraph 33, with reference to the pronunciation of ك.

Tell the cook (اشجِی *áshjĭ*) to go to the kitchen and cook (پِشورمك *pishirmek*) the dinner (یمك *yémek*). He has gone to the market (چارشو *charshi*). I fear he is very lazy (تنبل *tenbel*). Have you given him his wages (ایلتی *aĭlĭk*)? I gave them to him last week. You ought not to have given them to him so soon.

CHAPTER XV.

TURKISH ORTHOGRAPHY.

510. THE orthography of words of purely Turkish origin unfortunately is not fixed. The same word is often met with spelt in two or three different ways by writers of equal ability and repute. This is especially the case in old books, and more particularly in manuscripts, which are, hence, very difficult to decipher. Some attempt has been made of late years to reduce Turkish orthography to a system; but it has not been attended with much success, and writers still allow themselves the greatest latitude. Consequently, we find a word like "iron" written in Turkish either تیمور or دمیر *démir*, whereas, according to its pronunciation, it should certainly always be written in the latter way. Again, ترزی *térzi* (a tailor) is quite as often written درزی; and تلكی *tilki* (a fox) is often written دلكی, and so on.

511. Words of Arabic and Persian origin, however, nearly always retain their original spelling, which is invariable. This is, no doubt, one reason why such a large number of Arabic and Persian words are used in documentary Turkish, in which the double meanings to which uncertain spelling gives rise are thus, to some extent, obviated.

512. The modern writers who endeavoured to improve the state of Turkish orthography, amongst other things, set the example of expressing the vowel sounds more frequently by the letters ا, و, ه ی,—decidedly a step in the right direction; for the omission of the vowels in oriental writing has undoubtedly been a great obstacle to the spread of education amongst the natives, and to the acquisition of oriental languages by Europeans. As, however, this system was not carried out consistently, and as it has not been generally adopted—other authors of equal authority still adhering to the old system—Turkish spelling still remains so unsettled that it is difficult to give many rules respecting it. Yet as, notwithstanding the latitude natives allow themselves, one cannot spell as he pleases, the following rules may be serviceable.

513. In general, the broad vowel sounds *a, ï, o,* and *ou* are expressed by ای و د ی, especially if they are accompanied by a soft consonant.* Example, یازمق *yazmak* (to write), باقمق *bâkmak* (to look), بولمق *boulmak* (to find), بیلمك *bilmek* (to know).

514. If the soft consonants, however, be followed immediately by a hard one, the vowel is not written. Thus, بغدای *boghdaï* (corn), بغرصاق *baghïrsak* (the intestine). Still, in words of one syllable the vowels are written; as in باغ *bâgh* (a vineyard), باص *bâss* (tread), صوص *souss* (hold your tongue); and in words of two syllables, also, when the last syllable contains two hard consonants, as لحتق *lahïk* (joined, touching).

515. If a word contain different broad vowel sounds, then they are generally written, as صاری *sarï* (yellow), صالی *Sâlï* (Tuesday), صانجی *sânjï* (the cholic), قولای *kolaï* (easy), قوله *koulé* (a tower, steeple), قومسال *koumsâl* (a sandy beach), قوناق *konak* (a mansion), قیراچ *kïrach* (of the nature of sterile moorland), تازی *tâzï* (a greyhound), تابوت *tabout* (a coffin), پویراز *poïraz* (the north-east wind).

516. The grammatical terminations are an exception to the above rule, as they always remain without the vowels being written, whatever word they may be appended to. Example, قوچلر *kochlar* (rams), عقلسز *âklsïz* (foolish).

517. The letters ش د ر and ن, when used to make causal, reciprocal, or passive verbs, are also an exception to the above (515), as they do not have this vowel written in words when there are different vowel sounds. Examples, یاپدرمق *yapdïrmak* (to have made), باصدرمق *bâssdïrmak* (to have printed), یاغدرمق *yaghdïrmak* (to cause to fall like rain, to pour out), سونمك *sevinmek* (to be glad, to rejoice). Still, in the new system spoken of above we meet with ین and یش.

518. The sound of *a* or *é* at the beginning of a word is expressed by ا, and at the end of a word by ه. Example, ال *âl* (take—thou), اغ *âgh* (a net), اق *âk* (white), اغاج *âghâj* (a tree), اغر *âghïr* (heavy), اطه *adа* (an island), پاره *para* (money).

519. If the same vowel sound be repeated in one word it need only be written once. Thus we have یلان *yalân* (a lie), ادم *âdâm* (a man), درلو *turlu* (a kind, sort), درد *deré* (a valley), چوللق *choullouk* (a woodcock), چقور *choukour* (a hole), چقال *chakâl* (a jackal), چقرق *chïkrïk* (a spinning

---

* The hard consonants are ح خ ص ض ط ظ ع غ and ق; the rest are soft.

wheel), نمسه *Nemsé* (Germany), خسته *khássta* (ill), چكه *chene* (the chin), اودنج *eudunj* (borrowed money), صيغر *sighír* (an ox), صيرق *sírík* (a small pole), صيغرتماج *sighírtmaj* (a drover, herdsman), صيقندت *síkíndí* (trouble, bother, uneasiness), يناق *yanak* (a cheek), يواش *yawásh* (slow, gentle; gently !)

520. In particles like ايم *im* (am), ايز *iz* (are), when they are appended to an unalterable active participle, the diphthong اى can be left out, but need not necessarily. Hence we see both يازارايم and يازارم *yazarim* (I write), يازارايز and يازارز *yazaríz* (we write), سورم and سوراىم *severim* (I love), and سورز or سوراىز *severiz* (we love).

521. When a word beginning with the letters اى follows a word ending in ٯ or ى, the اى can be left out. Thus, اوغلى ايله *oghlouyoula* can be also written اوغليله (with his son), كورمه اىله can also be written كورمهله *ghieurmé-lé* (with the seeing, on seeing).

522. When a word ending in ٯ comes before a word beginning with اى or او, the ٯ may be left out and the ا at the beginning of the following word also. Thus we have نيچون *nichin* instead of نه ايچون *né ichin* (why ?), نولدى for نه اولدى *né oldou* (what has happened ?) [the form نولدى, however, is not to be recommended], باقيدم *bakaydim* instead of باقه ايدم (that I might look), سويدك *sevéydik* instead of سوه ايدك (that I might love).

523. ى when used to express the accusative is sometimes left out, especially in old books; but if it be so, it ought to be written before the ن. Hence in old works we see باباسين or even باباسن instead of باباسنى *bábásíní* (his father) (accusative), as in باباسنى كوردم *bábássíní gheurdum,* which might be written باباسين كوردم (I saw his father). An instance of this will be found in the following passage from the طوطى نامه "*Touti-namé*" :—

لايقميدر كه مسلمانلرك دعواسنى (دعواسنى) شرع اوزره فصل ايتميوب خاتونه علاقه پيدا ايدوب جبرا بنم جاريهم در ديوب المزدن المق استرسن.

Láyik mídír ki moussoulmánlarín dawassini shér uzeré fassl etméyíp khátouna alaka péída edip jebran benim jariyém dír déyup elimizden álmak isstérsin?

(Translation.)

" Is it proper that, not deciding a dispute between Mussulmans according to the law, and making out some connection with the lady, you wish to take her out of our hands by force, pretending that she is your slave ?"

I refer to this mode of spelling, because, if the student met with it, it might puzzle him ; but it is by no means to be recommended.

EXERCISE XXVIII.

Do you know that the ship will start to-morrow at eleven o'clock in the morning (صبالین *sabáhléyin*) ? Yes, I know it. At what o'clock does the boat (واپور *vapor*) start for Pringipo (بوك اطه *Biyuk Ada*) ? I cannot tell you exactly (تمام *tamam*), but I think it starts at nine. That is very early (ارکن *erkcn*). What (قاچه *kacha*) do you sell these apples (الما *elma*) at ? At nine piastres (غروش *ghroush*). That is very dear. Where does this street go to ? Out (طشره *tashra*) of (دن *den*) the town. Is it far to the market (چارشو *charshï*) ? Which is the nearest road to go to the market ? You must go straight on (طوغری طوغرویه *doghrou doghrouya*). Where do you live ? I live at the English Embassy (سفارت *Séfaret-khanéssi*). خانه‌سی Do you know Mr. So-and-so (فلان افندی *Filán*) ? I will show you his house. I am much obliged (تشکر ایتمك *téshekkiur etmek*). The weather is very bad. Can you tell me what o'clock (ساعت قاچ *saat kach*) it is ? It is eleven o'clock. What (نصل *nassl*) sort of weather (هوا *hawa*) is it ? It is cold (صوغوق *soghouk*). It is hot (سیجاق *sïják*). It is foggy (طومان *domán*). The weather has cleared (اچیلمك *achilmak*) up. Do you think it will clear up ? I think so. It is very windy (پك روزگاروار *pek rouzghiar var*). A cold wind is blowing (اسمك *essmek*). Have you seen his father lately (کچنلرده *ghechenlerdé*) ? I saw him last week. What is the matter (نه اولدی *né oldou*) ? He did not tell me (dative). Is it raining (یاغمور یاغمق *yaghmour yaghmak*) ? It is raining very hard (شدتلو *shiddetli*). It is a pity (یازق *yazïk*). As we live (نصل که یشامق *nassl ki yashamak*), so shall we die (اولمك *eulmek*). He is the most fortunate (بختلو *bakhtli*) of all (هب *hep*). God makes the nest (یوا *yiwa*) of the blind (کور *kieur*) bird (قوش *koush*).* An old fox does not fear (قورقمق *korkmak*) the net (ablative).* He who wishes (استمك *isstémek*) for a faultless (عیبسیز *aïpsiz*) friend (یار *yar*) remains friendless (یارسز *yarsiz*).* The tongue (دل *dil*) kills (اولدرمك *euldurmek*) more (چوق *chok*) than (دن *dan*) the sword (قلیج *kïlïj*).* Two captains (رئس *réis*) sink (باترمق *bátïrmak*) a ship. Man (انسان *insan*) proposes (تدبیر ایتمك *tedbir etmek*), God disposes (تقدیر ایتمك *tákdïr etmek*). He who gives (ویرن *veren*) to the poor (فقیرلر *fakïrlar*) gives to God. He who (کیدن *ghiden*) goes quickly (تیز *téz*) is quickly tired (یورلمق *yoroulmak*). If we have not wealth (مال *mál*), let us have honour (عرض *irz*).

---

* Turkish proverb.

CHAPTER XVI.

THE SYNTAX.

The Noun.

524. A TURKISH noun, when the subject of a sentence, is equivalent either to a noun alone in English or to a noun with the definitive article " the " or with the indefinite article " a." Example :—

ياتان ارسلاندن دری تلكی یكدر *yatan arsslandan diri tilki yek dir,* a live fox is better than *a* dead lion

یوركدن یوركه یول وار *yurekden yuréyé yol var,* there is *a* road from heart to heart

ایت حولر كاروان كچر *it havlar, kiarwan ghecher, the* dog barks (but) *the* caravan passes on

استدیكز او صاتلدی *isstédiyiniz ev sátïldï, the* house you want has [been sold

دل قلیجدن چوق اولدرر *dil kïlïjdan chok euldurur, the* tongue kills more than *the* sword.

525. A singular noun has also very often a plural signification. Examples :—

شهرده اغاج یوق	*Shehirdé ágháj yok*	There are no trees in the town
چارشوده آلما یوق	*Charshïda elma yok*	There are no apples in the market
اسكی چینی فنجان	*Esski chini filjan birdé*	He sells things like old china
برده اسكی خنجر كبی	*esski khanchar ghibi shéi*	cups, and also old daggers
شی صاتار	*satar*	[things.
چلیك شفالو شی ده	*Chilek shifali shéi dir*	Strawberries are wholesome

The Construction of Nouns in Conjunction.

526. The possession or connection of one thing or person with another; or, in other words, the possessive case is expressed in Turkish by the name of the possessor being put first and that of the thing possessed second ; the affix ی (or سی if the word end in a vowel) his, hers, or its, being appended to the second noun. Example :—

پاشا اوغلی *pasha oghlou,* a pasha's son
قاری یوزی *kárï yuzu,* a woman's face.

Literally, a pasha *his* son, a woman *her* face.

527. This construction of noun with noun is used to indicate not only possession but also genus and species, the name of the species coming first, as طاغ كچيسى *dâgh kéchissi* (a mountain goat, or the mountain goat), يبان اوردكى *yabán eurdéyi* (the wild duck, or a wild duck).

528. The names of rivers, mountains, lakes, &c., are formed in this manner.   Example :—

آزاق دكزى *Azak dénizi*, the Sea of Azof

تن صويى *Ten souyou*, the River Don

بچ شهرى *Bech shehiri*, the town of Vienna

بالقان طاغلرى *Bálkán dághlarï*, the Balkan mountains

طونا صويى *Touna souyou*, the River Danube.

529. Sometimes in addition to the pronominal affix ى or سى (after a word ending with a vowel) being added to the second noun, the first is put in the genitive.   Example :—

كمينك رئيسى در *gheminin réissi dir*, he is the captain of *the* ship*

پاشانك اوغلى در *pashanïn oghlou dir*, he is *the* pasha's son.*

This latter construction is definite, and is generally used when the article *the* would be put before the first noun in English. The former construction (see 526) is somewhat indefinite and is generally used when the article *a* would be put before the first noun in English.   Example :—

او طامى *ev dámï*, the roof of *a* house

اوك طامى *evin dámï*, the roof of *the* house

بغچه قپوسى *bághché kápoussou*, the gate of *a* garden

بغچه نك قپوسى *bághchénin kápoussou*, the gate of *the* garden.

530. When two nouns come together in English with the word " of " between them, the first expressing the quantity of the second, the phrase is translated into Turkish by simply putting the name of the quantity before the other noun and omitting " of," as in German, they say "*Ein Glas Wein*," &c.

بر پارچه اكمك *bir parcha ekmek*, a piece *of* bread

ايكى قيه ات *iki kïyyé (oka) et*, two okes† *of* meat

بر قدح شراب *bir kadéh sherab*, a glass *of* wine

بر فنجان چاى *bir filján chaï*, a cup *of* tea.

---

* Literally, *Of* the ship *its* captain, *Of* the Pasha *his* son.

† An *oke* is a Turkish measure of 2¾ lbs.

531. There are two ways of expressing the material of which a thing is made :

(1.) The noun, which is the name of the material, is simply put, like an adjective, before the other substantive. Example :—

دمير زنجير *demir zinjir*, an iron chain

ايپلك چوراب *iplik chorab*, cotton stockings

التون قوطى *altoun koutou*, a gold box

كومش قاشق *ghiumush káshik*, a silver spoon

التون كوستك *altoun kieustek*, a gold chain.

(2.) Or the noun expressing the material is put in the ablative. Example :—

دميردن زنجير *démirden zinjir*, an iron chain (or a chain of iron)

التوندن قوطى *altoundan koutou*, a gold box (or a box of gold)

كومشدن قاشق *ghiumushden káshik*, a silver spoon (or a spoon of silver).

In the latter construction one of the words معمول *mamoul* or ياپلمش *yapilmish* (made), or مصنوع *massnou* (fashioned, manufactured) is understood. It is sometimes also written. Example :—

دميردن ياپلمش كوپرى *demirden yapilmish kieupru*, an iron bridge

دميردن معمول زنجير *démirden mamoul zinjir*, an iron chain.

The Persian Mode of Connecting Noun with Noun.

532. In books and in conversation also, sometimes when elegance is studied, instead of the Turkish way of indicating possession of one thing by another, or of rendering " of " in English (see 526, 529), the Persian method is used, especially when the words employed are either Arabic or Persian.

533. This consists simply in putting the name of the possessor first, and the name of the thing possessed after it. In pronouncing these nouns the sound of *i* is introduced after the first, if its end is a consonant. Example :—

پادشاه زمين *padishah-i-zémin*, the king *of* the earth

درخت باغ *dirakht-i-bágh*, the tree *of* the garden

پدر دختر *péder-i-dukhter*, the father *of* the girl

اصحاب سيف *ashab-i-séif*, companions *of* the sword (military men)

دار بقا *dar-i-báka*, the abode *of* permanency (future life)

آب حیات نوش ایتمدی *áb-i-hayat noush etmadi,* he did not drink the water
    of life

حضور باریده نه جواب ویررسن *houzour-i-baridé né jewáb verirsin,* what answer
    will you give in the presence *of* God ?

534. If the first noun end with an ا and be of Persian, Turkish, or
foreign origin, a consonant ی is written at the end of it followed by the
sound of *i* or *ĭ*. Example :—

جای پدر *jayĭ-péder,* the place *of* this father

بالای خانه *balayĭ-khané,* the top *of* the house

پای تخت *payĭ-takht,* the foot *of* the throne.

535. If it end in ا and be of Arabic origin, either a ی is added to it, or
a *hemzé* (pronounced with the vowel sound of *i*). Example :—

بقای عمر *bakayi-umr,* length of life

بناء بیت *bina-i-béit,* the building *of* the house.

536. If it end with a و pronounced as a vowel a ی is added to it, and
if it end with a vowel ه or ی a *hemzé* is appended to it, pronounced like
i or *ĭ.*

روی زمین *rouyi zémin,* the face *of* the earth

بوی کول *bouyi ghiul,* the smell *of* the rose

قاضی قضات *kázĭ-i-kouzát,* the judge *of* judges

خانه پدر *khané-i-péder,* the father's house

ماهی دریا *mahi-i-derya,* the fish *of* the sea

نشئه می *neshé-i-méi,* the gaiety *of* wine.

537. When the Persian construction is used, it may be either definitive
or indefinite ; that is to say, in English the second noun may have either
the definitive article " the," or the indefinite " a " before it. Thus, بناء بیت
bina-i-béit may mean either the building of *the* house, or the building of *a*
house ; بوی کل *bouyi-ghiul* the scent of *a* rose, or the scent of *the* rose, and
so on.

538. When several nouns follow each other in English, with the preposition " of " repeated several times between them, and the Turkish
construction is used to render them, the sign of the genitive (ک or نک)
may be omitted after one or more of them. Example :—

عراق شهرى وزيرينك بر شوريده مشرب اوغلى وار ايدى	Irak shehiri vézirinin bir shouridé meshreb oghlou var idi	The vizier of the city of Irak had a good-for-nothing son
كيمدر بسوأل ايلدكده شهرمز بادشاهنك قيزيدر ديديلر	Kim dir sual éilédekdé shehirimiz padishahinin kïzï dïr dédiler	On his asking "Who is she?" they said, "She is the daughter of the king of our city"
قصاب حضر محلهسى ساكنلرندن	Kássáb Hazr mahalléssi sakinlerinden	One of the inhabitants of the parish of Kassab Hazr.

539. When several nouns follow each other in English, with "of" between them, when rendered into Turkish the "of" is often translated partly in the Persian way and partly in the Turkish, to prevent monotony. Example :—

تحصيل علم فايدهسى	Tahsïl-ï-ilm fa'idéssi	The advantage of the acquisition of knowledge
فن جغرافيابى تحصيلنه مدار	Fen-i-jagrafiyayi tah-sïlïna médar	A means for the acqui-sition of the science of geography
هر برى شمس حسننك پروانهسى اولوب مابينلرنده عظيم غوغا و نزاع واقع اولدى	Her biri shemss-i hus-sunun pervanési oloup ma-béinlerindé azim kawgha vu niza wáki oldou	Every one of them becoming the moth of the sun of her beauty, a great quarrel and dispute arose between them*
شجره محبت ثمهسى	Shejéré-i-mahabet semé-réssi	The fruit of the tree of affection.

The Use of Synonymous Words in Couples.

540. As most Persian and Arabic words have various meanings, it is customary, to prevent any mistake, to use synonymous words in pairs, the second noun confirming the meaning of the first. Thus :—

---

* See طوطى نامه.

نیازورجا ایدرم	*Niaz-u-rija ederim*	I *beg* and *request* (you)
کمال لطف و کرملری ثمرهسندن	*Kémal lutf-u-kéremleri sémerésinden*	From the fruits of your perfect *grace* and *favour*
شاهك بر مقبول و مرغوب و محبوب بر مصاحبی وار ایدی	*Shahïn bïr makboul vé merghboub vé mahboub bir musahibi var idi*	The king had a *pleasant* and *agreeable* and *beloved* companion
عشاق صادقلری خأیب و خاسر قالدیلر	*Oushak sadikleri kha'ib-ou-khasir kaldïlar*	Her sincere lovers remained *disappointed* and *hopeless***
اى قادر و توانا	*Ei kádir-u-tewana*	Oh, Almighty and Powerful One (God) !*
اى علیم و دانا	*Ei alim-u-dana*	Oh, Omniscient and Wise One (God) !
راویان اخبار و ناقلان آثار اداى شیرین و الفاظ سكرین برله نقل ایدرلر که زماناولده پیلسان شهرنده علماى عصرىن برفاضل محقق وار ایدى اسمنه ابوالمجد دیرلریدى صفحهٔ درونی زیورعلوم ایله آراسته و لسان خوش بیانى انواع فصاحت و بلغت ایله پیراسته ایدى	*Raviyan-i-akhbar u-nakilan-i-asar eday-i-shirin vé elfaz-i-sukkerin birle nâkl ederlér ki zeman-i-evveldé Pilsan shehirindé ulemay-i assrden bir fázïl mouhákkak var-idi issminé Ab-ul-Mejd derleridi - safha - i derounou zivér-i uloum ilé arassté vé lissân-i-khosh béyani envaï fássahat-u-belaghat ilé pirassté idi*	*Relators of news* and *narrators of events*, with *sweet* grace and *sugary* words report that in olden times there was a man of proved excellence, one of the learned men of the age, in the city of Pilsan. They called him Ab-ul-Mejd. The space of his interior† (his mind) was *embellished* with the ornaments of science, and his tongue of sweet explanation was *adorned* with *eloquence* and *fluency*.

541. There being no capital letters to distinguish proper names from others the Turks very often use the word نام *nam* (name) or نامِدہ *namindé* (in the name) for the purpose. Example:—

احمد نام كمسنه *Ahmed nam kimessné*, the person called Ahmed

لیورپول نام شهر *Liverpool nam shéhir*, the town called Liverpool

---

* See طوطی نامہ (''Tales of a Parrot''). These pairs of words in the original language have exactly the same meaning.　† I translate literally intentionally.

بو شهرك اعيانندن	*Bou shehirin ayanïndan*	Amongst the chief men
سعيد نامنده بر بازرگان	*Saïd namindé bir bázïr-*	of this city was a merchant
وار ايدى	*ghian var idi*	*of the name* of Said.

Modes of Address in Turkish.

542. The words حضرتلرى *hazretleri* (their excellency, majesty, high-ness) and جنابلرى *jenábleri* (their honour) are titles equivalent to " his majesty," " his lordship," " his excellency," but they are placed after instead of before proper names. Examples:—

محمود تاشا حضرتلرينه *Mahmoud Pasha Hazretleriné*, to his Excellency Mahmoud
Pasha

بادشاه حضرتلرى *Padishah hazretleri*, his Majesty the Emperor

ألچى حضرتلرى *Elchi hazretleri*, his Excellency the Ambassador.

543. In addressing any dignitary it is a great mistake to use this word حضرت with the pronominal affix ك or كز, that is to say, to employ the expression حضرتك *hazretin* or حضرتكز *hazretiniz* (thy or your excellency, majesty, &c.) The simple pronoun thou or you must be used, or the expression ذات عاليلرى *zat-i-alileri* (your high person, or literally their high persons). ذات عاليكز *zat-i-aliniz* (your high person) is also used, but is not so respectful, as it is considered more polite to address any one in the third person plural. Example, ذات عاليكزه خيلى زحمت ويردم *zat-i-alinizé khaïli zahmet vérdim* (I have given your excellency much trouble).

The use of the Singular after Cardinal Numbers.

544. If a noun is preceded by a cardinal number it must remain in the singular. Example —

بو دورت رفيق كورديلر	*Bou deurt refik geur-*	These *four companions* saw
كه قاضى بونلرك باشنه	*dulér ki kazi bounlarïn*	that the Cadi would bring
قضاى اسمانى و بلاى	*báshïna kâzayi assimani*	a judgment from heaven and
ناكهانى كتورجك كه	*vu belayi naghehani ghe-*	a sudden calamity on their
بروجهمله دفعى ممكن	*tiréjek ki bir vejhilé defi*	heads which could not be
دكل	*mumkin diyil*	averted in any way
ايكى رئس بر كمى باترورلر	*Iki réiss bir ghémi báti-*	*Two captains* sink a ship
	rïrlar	

دروش دخی میر کلام اولمغین بونلره حکایات غریبه و تمثیلات عجیبه نقل ایتدی هر نکتهیی بیك باب و هر بابی بیك کتاب ایتمکین اهل مجلس تمام مرتبه ذوقیاب اولدی	*Dervish dakhi mir-i-kelâm olmaghïn bounlara hikiayat gharibé vé temsilat ajibé nâkl etdi hér nuktéyi bin bâb ve hér bâbï bin kitâb etméyin ehli-mejliss tamam mertébé zevkyab oldou*	The dervish also being an eloquent man related to them strange tales and wonderful examples, and making every piece of wisdom a *thousand chapters* and every chapter a *thousand books*, the company were perfectly delighted
ایکی باصمه کتاب الدم	*Iki bassma kitâb âldïm*	I have bought *two* printed books
پارهسی نقدر	*Parassi nékâdar ?*	How much are they ?
اللی غروشه	*Elli grousha*	(At) *fifty piastres*
یوز ییمورطه	*Yuz yïmourta*	A *hundred* eggs
طربزوندن ارضرومه ایکی یول وار در	*Trebzoundan Erzrouma iki yol var dïr*	There are *two* roads from Trebizond to Erzroum.

EXERCISE XXIX.

Have you bought silver spoons ? Have you ever seen the island (جزیره *jéziré*) of Crete (کرید *ghirid*) ? The king arrived last night. There are no gardens (باغچه *bâghché*) in the town of Brighton. Do you like (بکنمك *béyenmek*) china cups (ablative) ? I like them very much, but they are very dear (پهالو *pâhâlï*). There are a great many wild ducks in that country (مملكت *memléket*). Do you know the name of the landlord (او صاحبی *ev-sahibi*) ? I have heard it, but have forgotten (اونوتمق *ounoutmak*) it. Buy six okes of grapes (اوزوم *uzum*) for me, and two okes of potatoes (پاتاتس *patatass*). The Danube is a very large river. Have you seen my brother's portrait (رسم *ressm*) ? I saw it at the photographer's (فوطوغرافیهجی *fotografïyajï*) house. There is now a fine iron bridge at Constantinople. I wrote to His Excellency Fuad Pasha, but I have not yet (دها *daha*) received an answer (جواب *jawab*). I am very much obliged (تشکر ایتمك *teshekkiur etmek*) to your Excellency. The company (مجلس اهل *ehl-i-mejliss*) enjoyed themselves (ذوقیاب *zevkyab*). He was one of (دن *den*) the learned (علما *ulema*) men of the age (عصر *assr*). He gave a feast (ضیافت *zïyafet*) to the principal (اعیان *ayan*) men of his country (ولایت *vilayet*). In that city there was a merchant who had three sons. This book contains (حاوی اولمق *havi olmak*) fifty-two chapters. Have you read the tale (حکایه *hikiayé*) of the Dervish Hawayi ? I have only read the first and second chapters (باب *báb*) of it. The people (خلق *khalk*) of the city heard (دكلمك *dinlémek*) the dispute (دعوا *dawa*). As soon (كمى *ghibi*) as the king saw the girl's beauty (جمال *jemal*), he was smitten (عشقنه كرفتار اولمق *áshkina ghiriftar olmak*) with her. Go to the mayor (صوباشى *sou-báshï*) of the town (شهر *shéhir*) and tell him the circumstances (أحوالكز *ahwaliniz*) (you are in). This woman is the wife (خاتون *khatoun*) of my elder (بيوك *biyuk*) brother. They appealed (دعوت ايتمك *davet*) to the law (شرع شريف *sher-i-sherif*) and went into the presence (حضور *houzour*) of the Cadi (قاضى *kázï*). The Cadi looked at the old (أختيار *ikhtiyar*) man's face (يوز *yuz*). Four persons (كش *kishi*) agreed (اتفاق ايتمك *ittifák etmek*) to travel (سياحت ايتمك *séyahét etmek*). For fear (خوفندن *khav-findan*) of wild (موذى *muezzi*) animals (جانوار *janvar*) they agreed to sleep (ايومق *ouyoumak*) by turns (نوبتله *nubetlé*). They approved (تحسين ايتمك *tahsin etmek*) and applauded (* أقرين ايتمك *aferin etmek*) the carpenter's (دولكر *dulghér*) skill (هنر *huner*) (ablative). Have you written to His Excellency the Prince (شهزاده *shehzadé*)? There were formerly (سابقا *sabïka*) two brothers of mine in the king's service (خدمت *khidmet, hizmet†*). They were young men (تازه جوان *tazé juwan*), but in sense (عقل جهتندن *akl jihetinden*) and intelligence (فراست *feraset*) they were old (پير *pir*).

THE ADJECTIVE.
Adjectives of Turkish Origin.

545. In an ordinary way, especially when the words used are of Turkish origin, the adjective in Turkish, as in English, is put before the noun, and is invariable, whether the noun be masculine or feminine, singular or plural. Example :—

كوزل ادم	*Ghiuzel ádám*	A handsome man
كوزل قارى	*Ghiuzel kárï*	A pretty woman
كوزل ادملر	*Ghiuzel ádámlar*	Handsome men
كوزل قاريلر	*Ghiuzel kárïlar*	Pretty women
بيوك ادم	*Biyuk ádám*	A great man
بيوك ادملر	*Biyuk ádámlar*	Great men
بر ايو شراب و دلبر	*Bir éi sherab vé dilber*	A good wine and a
عورت ايكى طاتلو زهر در	*avret iki tátlï zéhir dir*	fascinating woman are two
		sweet poisons [slaves.
وافر كوزل جاريهلر	*Wafir ghiuzel jariyélér*	Many beautiful (female)

---

* It is not requisite to repeat ايتمك *when writing the Turkish sentence.
† The latter is the usual pronunciation in Turkish, although incorrect.

N

546. When the adjective is the predicate of a sentence it still remains invariable. Example :—

قیز دلی در	*Kïz déli dir*	The girl is mad
دلی اولدر که زنکین در	*Déli ol dir ki zenghin dir*	He is mad who is rich
* ولكن فقرا كبي كچنور	*vé foukera ghibi ghechenir*	and yet lives like the poor
بو چیچك كوزل در	*Bou chichek ghiuzel dir*	This flower is pretty
بو چیچكلر كوزل در	*Bou chichekler ghiuzel dir*	These flowers are pretty
خواجهمز پك معلوماتلو در	*Khojamïz pek maloumátlï dïr*	Our professor is very learned
خواجه لرمز معلوماتلو در	*Khojalarimiz maloumátlï dïr*	Our professors are learned
دوستكز كیفسز در	*Dosstounouz kéifsiz dir*	Your friend is ill
قیزی كیفسز در	*Kïzï kéifsiz dir*	His daughter is ill
شاكرد تنبل در	*Shaghird tenbel dir*	The pupil is lazy
شاكردان تنبل در	*Shaghirdan tenbel dir*	The pupils are lazy
قاری چركین در	*Kárï chirkin dir*	The woman is ugly
قاریلر چركین در	*Kárïlar chirkin dir*	The women are lazy.

The Persian Mode of Connecting Noun and Adjective.

547. In books, and in conversation when elegance is studied, the Persian mode of connecting the adjective is often adopted. This consists in putting the adjective *after* the noun, and joining the two vocally by pronouncing an *i* between them. Example :—

باغ دلكشا	*Bágh-i-dilkiusha*	A delightful garden
لسان تركی یی اوكرنملو سكز	*Lissan-i-turkiyi eughrenméli siniz*	You ought to learn the Turkish language
اول مملكتده بر شهر عظیم وار ایدی	*Ol memléketdé bir shehir-i-ázïm var-idi*	There was a great city in that country
مزاج شریفكز نصل در	*Mizaj-i-sherifiniz nassl dir ?*	How is your (noble) health ?
كچن كون ازمیره تشریف عالیلرنده سپارش عاجزی واقع اولمش	*Ghechen ghiun Ezmiré teshrif-i-alilerindé siparish-i-ajizi váki olmoush*	The other day, on your sublime visit to Smyrna, I gave you a humble commission.

---

* "And" and "but" are often thus found together in Turkish.

548. The rules with regard to the connection of the two nouns after the Persian fashion (see 533, 534, 535, 536) apply also to a noun and an adjective connected in the Persian way. Example:—

والئ عادل	*Vali-'i-adil*	A just governor
بناى استوار	*Binayi-ustuvar*	A solid building
موى سياه	*Mouyi-siyah*	Black hair
خانه دلكشا	*Khané-'i-dilkiusha*	A delightful house
جاى جانفزا	*Jayi-janfeza*	A delicious place
دعاى خير	*Duayi-khaïr*	A good prayer
ميوهٔ شيرين	*Méivé-'i-shirin*	Sweet fruit [Persia
دولت بهيهٔ ايران	*Devlet-i-béhiyé-i-iran*	The beautiful State of
وكلاى سلطنت سنيهدن	*Vukelayï - saltanat - i -*	A letter of thanks for one
برى مكتبهٔ زيارتسه	*seniyéden* biri mektebé*	of the ministers of the
كلديكندن تشكر نامه	*ziyareté gheldiyinden tésh-*	Turkish Government com-
	ekkiur-namé	ing to visit a school.

The Use of Arabic Adjectives.

549. When an Arabic adjective is placed before a noun it generally is invariable, applying both to masculine and feminine, singular and plural substantives. Example:—

عظيم وزير	*Azïm vézir*	A great vizier
عظيم دولت	*Azïm devlet* (feminine)	A great state
ناظر و خواجهمز بو	*Nazïr vé khojamiz bou*	My principal and pro-
شاكرد قوللرينه تركى	*shaghird koullarïna turki*	fessor on their beginning
لسانى اوكرتمكه بدأ و	*lissânini eurutméyé bed u*	to teach this pupil your
مباشرت بيوردقلرنده اولا	*mubashiret bouyourdouk-*	(humble) servant the *Turk-*
وحى ربانيدن خبر ويرن	*larïnda evvela vahï rabba-*	*ish language* having first of
عربى حروفاتنى تعليم	*nïdan khabr veren Arabi*	all taught me the *Arabic*
بيوردقلرندن	*huroufâtïnï talim bou-*	*letters* which inform one of
	yourdouklarïndan	the Divine inspiration.†

550. If the Arabic adjective, however, follows the noun it agrees with it in number and gender.

---

* This word literally means "splendid," but is used for "Turkish."

† This means that the Koran is written with Arabic letters.

دولت علیه	*Devlet-i-aliyé*	The sublime* nation (Turkey)
دولت بهیهٔ ایران	*Devlet-i-behiyé-i-iran*	The beautiful* state of Persia
سنهٔ جدیدۀ دخول ایتدیکندن	*Sené-'i-jédidé doukhoul etdiyinden*	As the new year has commenced
ذات سنیهٔلرینه علاقهٔ ازلیهم و اخوت ابدیهم	*Zat-i-seniyéleriné ala-ka-'i-ézeliyém u oukhou-vet-i-ébediyém*	My eternal love and ever-lasting brotherhood to your brilliant† person.

551. An Arabic irregular plural noun requires the adjective following it to be an irregular plural or feminine singular (regular). Example :—

خطوط متوازیه	*Khoutout-i-mutévaziyé*	Parallel lines
وكلای فخام	*Vukelayi-fékham*	Noble ministers
قواعد عثمانیه	*Kawaid-i-ossmaniyé*	Turkish rules
جماهیر مجتمعهٔ امریقا	*Jemahir-i-mujtémié-'i--Amérika*	The United States (re-publics) of America
قلاع ایرانیهدن برٔ در	*Kïla-i-iraniyéden biri dir*	It is one of the Persian fortresses
انبیاء عظام	*Enbiya-'i-ïzâm*	Great prophets.

552. When the adjective is put after the noun in the Persian way it takes the affixes which would be added to the noun were the adjective put before it. Example :—

قبر شریفی اوراده در	*Kâbr-i-sherifi orada dir*	*His* holy tomb is there
بر شهر عظیمه كلدك	*Bir - shehir - i - azimé gheldek*	We came *to a large* city
كیف شریفكز نصل در	*Keïf-i-sherifiniz nassl dir?*	How is *your noble* health (how do you do) ?
مزاج والالری استفسارنده شقهٔ تحریر و تسییر قلندی	*Mizaj-i-valaleri isstif-sarindé shoukké tahrir u tessyir kïlïndï*	The note was written and sent to inquire after *your* "*exalted*" health.

---

* These are stereotyped epithets in continual use.

† The example I have taken to illustrate the rules are often taken from Turkish standard works. They are thoroughly Turkish, of course, and therefore the English of them will sound peculiar to English ears.

كلام ثريا نظامكله خلتى	*Kelam - i - surreya - ni-*	With *thy brilliant** dis-
عالمى طريق حقه دلالت	*zăminlé khalk - i - alemi*	course you guide the people
ايدرس	*tariki-hăkka delalet edér-*	of the world into the path
	sen	of truth.

553. When adjectives are put before the noun in the Turkish way they are generally not joined together by the conjunction و *vé* (and), but they are sometimes and very often in writing. Example:—

كوزل ادبلو ادم	*Ghiuzel édepli ădăm*	A *handsome and polite*
or كوزل و ادبلو ادم	*Ghiuzel vé edepli ădăm*	man
كوزل محجوب قيز	*Ghiuzel mahjoub kĭz*	A *pretty and modest* girl
or كوزل ومحجوب قيز	*Ghiuzel vé mahjoub kĭz*	
برغايت كوزل ومرغوب كتاب	*Bir ghayet ghiuzel vé merghoub kităb*	An extremely *beautiful and popular* book
مبارك و مسعود خاكياى مراحم آلود همايوندن رجاى كمترانهم در	*Mubarek vé messoud khakipayi merahim-aloud humayoundan rijayi kemtaraném dir*	It is my humble request to your *blessed and happy* Imperial Majesty, who are noted for mercy
بر عاقل و دانا وزيرت وار ايدى	*Bir akil u dana véziri var idi*	He had an *intelligent and wise* vizier
چوق كوزل و مرغوب شاعر	*Chok ghiuzel vé merghoub shair*	A very *beautiful and popular* poet.

554. When there are several adjectives put *after* the noun in the Persian way they are never connected by و, but they are joined to each other by the sound of *i*, according to the rules given for connecting nouns with nouns and nouns with adjectives in the Persian fashion (see 533, 534, 535, 536). Example:—

| فرماننامهٔ مكارم علامهٔ خديوانهلرى | *Fermăn - name - 'i - mekiarim alamé-'i-khidivanéleri* | Your *noble and princely* letter |
| مراحم عليهٔ اصفانهلرى | *Merahim - i - aliyé -'i - assefanéleri* | Your *high and* states-man-like† acts of grace. |

555. An adjective, or a possessive pronominal affix when used as an adjective, may refer to several nouns without being repeated. Example:—

---

*The expression ثريا نظام *suréyya-nizam* literally means, "arranged like the Pleiades."

† The word اصفانه is derived from اصف, the name of Solomon's grand vizier.

صحت و عافيتلرى
خبريله بزلرى فرحان و
دلشاد ايتملرى تمناسنده

*Sïhat-u-afiyetleri khab-
rilé bizleri férhan u dilshad
etméleri témennasindé*

Requesting you to make
us glad and joyful with the
news of *your health* and
immunity from sickness

لطف و احسان كريمانه
لرينه متشكرم
واشبوتبريك وتهنيت
عاليلرندن معظوظيت و
ممنونيت عاجزانهم تعر
يفدن ازاده اولديغى
بياننده و مبارك مزاج
دولتلرى استفسارنده
نميقه ثناورى تحرير
قلندى

*Loutf-u-ihsan kerima-
néleriné mutéshekkir im*

*Vé ishbou tebrik u-
tehniyet - i - alilérinden
mahzouziyet u-memnouni-
yet - i - ajizaném tarifden
azadé oldoughou béyanindé
vé mubarek mizaj-i-dev-
letléri isstifsarindé ne-
miké - i - senavéri tahrir
kïlïndï*

I thank you for *your
gracious favour* and *kindness*

My letter (the letter of
him who prays for you) has
been written to explain that
my humbler joy and *delight*,
owing to *your sublime con-
gratulation* and *felicitation*,
are beyond expression, and
to enquire after your blessed health*

ما بينلرنده عظيم
مباحثه و منازعه واقع
اولدى

*Ma - béinlerindé ázïm
mubahessé vu munazéa
wáki oldou*

*A great discussion and
great quarrel* arose between
them.

556. If two nouns be joined in the Persian way, and the first is
described by one or more adjectives, simple or compound, they must be
put after the first noun. Example :—

خبر مسرت اثر جلوس
همايونلرى

*Khabr-i-mésseret essr-
i-julouss-i-humayounlarï*

The *joyful* tidings of his
imperial accession

فلان كمسنه سايه
شوكتوايةحضرتشاهانده
بر قطعه سفينه بنا و انشا
ايدهحكى بيانيله اذن و
رخصت ويرلمسنى با
عرضحال التماس ايتمش

*Filán kimessné sayé-'i-
shevketvayé-'i-hazret-i-
shahanédé bir kïta séfiné
bina vu insha edéjéyi
béyanilé izn-u roukhsát
vérlilmassi bé arzuhal
iltimass etmish*

A certain person, stat-
ing that he will construct
and build a vessel under the
mighty† shadow of (his)
imperial majesty, has re-
quested by a petition that
permission be given (him).

557. Adjectives which require some other word or words to complete
their meaning must be put after those words when Turkish construction is
used. Example :—

---

* This is the style usual in Turkish letters, and is extracted verbatim from one.

† This is the style adopted in Government documents.

شراب ايله طولو	*Sherab ilé dolou*	*Full of* wine
محاربهیه قادربر پادشاه	*Mouharebéyé kádïr bir padishah*	A king *able in* war [*dir* [*arts*
صنايع عجيبه يه قادر در	*Sanai-i-ajibé yé kádir*	He is *skilful in* strange
كلماتـه قـادر بـر	*Kélimaté kádïr bïr*	He is a companion *able*
مصاحب در كه مثلى كورلمش دكك	*mussahib dir ki messli ghieurulmush déil*	*in speech* whose like is not seen.

558. With the Persian construction, the adjective always precedes the word it requires to complete its meaning. Example :—

قادر مباحثه	*Kádïr-i mubahessé*	Able in controversy.

The Use of بر *bir*, " A," with an Adjective.

559. When the word بر *bir*, " one" or " a," is used with an adjective qualifying a noun, it is generally put immediately before the noun, and not before the adjective, as in English; but it can also be put before the adjective. Thus :—

اِيو بر ادم در *éi bir ádám dïr*, he is a good man

فأيدهلى بر كتاب الدم *faïdé'li bir kitáb áldïm*, I have bought a useful book

بر اِيو شراب *bir éi sherab*, a good wine

انصافسز بر ادم سن *insáfsïz bir ádám sïn*, thou art a dishonest man

تميز بر اُستاد بلورميسكز *témiz bir ustad bilirmisiniz?* do you know a good workman ?

طاتلو بر الما *tátlï bir elma*, a sweet apple.

The Turkish Adjective كبى *ghibi.*

560. The Turkish adjective كبى *ghibi* (like) comes after nouns and pronouns, instead of before them, as in English.

طورپ كبى *tourp ghibi*, like a radish

الماس كبى *élmáss ghibi*, like a diamond

كمى كبى *ghémi ghibi*, like a ship

ارسلان كبى *arsslan ghibi*, like a lion.

When used thus with a noun, or with the personal pronoun third person plural, with the plural demonstrative pronouns, or with interrogative or relative pronouns, it requires no change in those words. Example :—

سرو كبى رفتاره و طوطى كبى كَفتاره باشلادى	*Serv ghibi reftaré vé touti ghibi ghiuftaré básh-ladï*	She began to walk *like* a *cypress tree** and talk *like* a *parrot*
طوطى كبى سويلر	*Touti ghibi suwéylér*	He talks *like a parrot*
انلر كبى يازه بلورميسكز	*Anlar ghibi yazé bilir-misiniz ?*	Can you write *like them ?*
بونلركبى كوزل كتابلركز وارمى	*Bounlar ghibi ghiuzel kitáblarïnïz var mi ?*	Have you pretty books *like these ?*

561. When used with any other pronoun than those stated above, كبى requires the pronoun to be in the genitive. Example:—

بنم كبى	*Benim ghibi*	Like me
سزك كبى	*Sizin ghibi*	Like you
انك كبى	*Anin ghibi*	Like him
سكا بو حكايه‌ى ابراز ايتمكدن مرادم بو در كه بنم كبى برمحرم اسرار اله كيرمش ايكن مشاوره‌ده اهمال ايتميه‌سن	*Sána bou hikiayéyi ibraz etmekden mouradim bou dïr ki benim ghibi bir mahremi-i-issrar elé ghir-mish iken mushaverédé ihmal etméyésin*	My object in telling you this tale is that, having got a confidant *like me,* you may not neglect me in consultation.

Adjectives Requiring the Dative Case.

562. Many adjectives require the noun or pronoun to which they refer to be in the dative case. Those most in use which do so are the following :—

لازم	*Lazïm*	Necessary
فأيده‌لو	*Fa‘idéli*	Useful
مالك	*Malik*	Possessing
مأيل	*Ma‘il*	Inclined
محتاج	*Muhtáj*	In need of, wanting, requir-[ing
مغاير	*Moughayir*	Contrary to
مناسب	*Munassib*	Fit, proper for
لايق	*Layïk*	Fit, worthy of

---

* See طوطى نامه. The cypress is regarded in the East as the symbol of gracefulness.

مقید	Moukayyéd	Attentive to
یاقشق	Yakïshïk	Suitable, fitting, seemly
یرار	Yarar	Useful
یارامز	Yaramaz	Useless
واقف	Wâkïf	Aware of
مطلع	Moutâlï	Cognisant of, aware of.

Examples :—

اصوله مغایر نا لجا و نا سزا حرکت	Ousoula-moughayir na--béja-vu-na-seza héréket	Unseemly and improper conduct, *contrary* to custom.
کتاب سپارشنه دائر بر مکتوب	Kitâb siparishiné da'ir bïr mektoup	A letter *about* ordering a book
مدحه لایق	Medhé layïk	*Worthy of* praise
نیه یارار	Néyé yarar ? [dir	What is it *useful for ?*
همتکزه محتاج در	Himmetinizé muhtdj	It *requires* your influence
قتل نفس خصوصنده عجله ایتمك پادشاهلره مناسب دکلدر	Kdtl-i-nefss khoussous-sïnda ajelé etmek padishaleré munassib déil dir	In the matter of taking life it is not *proper for* kings to be in a hurry
فقیر ابوالمجد ایسه بر فیل یوكی التون دکل بر حبیه مالك دکل ایدی	Fakïr Abul-Mejd issé bir fil yuku âltoun déil bir habbéyé malik déil idi	As for poor Abul Mejd, he did not only not *possess* an elephant load of gold, but not even a grain
حق سبحانه و تعالی حضرتلری درونم حالنه واقف در	Hâkk subhanahu vé taala hazretleri derounoum haliné wâkïf dïr	His Majesty God (to whom be praise, and whose name be exalted!*) is *aware of* the state of my interior (soul)
شاه بهواج بو احواله مطلع اولدیغی کمی کمال سفقتندن اغلیوب و بی توقف بر فیل یوكی التون خزینهسندن چیقاردوب بر بیاض فیله یوکلیوب ابوالمجده تسلیم ایتدیلر	Shah Behvaj bou ah-walé moutâlï oldoughou ghibi kemal shéfakâtïndan âghlayïp vé bi tévakouf bir fil yuku altoun khazi-nésinden chïkardïp bir béyaz filé yukléyip Abul Mejdé tesslim etdiler	As soon as Shah Behvaj became *cognisant of* this state (of things) he cried from his perfect commiseration, and, without delay having an elephant load of gold taken out of his treasury, and put on a white elephant, they delivered it to Abul Mejd

---

* These two Arabic expressions are continually used after the name of God.

بادشاهلر كندی قوللرینی اولدرمکده بر علته محتاج دکل در	*Padishahlér kendi koul-larĭnĭ euldurmekdé bir illeté muhtáj déil dir*	Kings do not *need* a pretext for killing their servants.

Adjectives Requiring the Ablative.

563. Some adjectives require the ablative, the following amongst the number :—

ممنون	*Memnoun*	Glad
خوشنود	*Khoshnoud*	Pleased
محظوظ	*Mahzouz*	Delighted
محزون	*Mahzoun*	Grieved
مکدر	*Mukéddér*	Sorry
مأیوس	*Mé'youss*	Desperate, hopeless

Examples :—

اشتیاقانه مراسلاته مصروف اولان همتکزدن محظوظ اولدم	*Ishtiyákané muraselaté másrouf olán himmetiniz-den mahzouz oldoum*	I am *delighted at* the exertions made by you in affectionately corresponding* (with me)
خواجهلر و همپالری اندن خوشنود و محظوظ اولدیلر	*Khojalar vé hempaleri andan khoshnoud ou mah-zouz oldoular*	His teachers and school-fellows were *pleased* and *delighted with* him
فلان شی شو قدر غروشه اشترا و ارسال بیوردقلرینه دائر بر قطعه تحریرات والالری مآلی مفهومیمز اولمش	*Filán shéi shou kádar grousha ishtira vé irsal bouyourdouklarĭna da'ir bir kĭta tahrirat valaleri mé'eli mefhoumoumouz ol-moush*	I have understood the meaning of a " sublime " letter of yours* *about* your kindly buying and sending such and such things at so many piastres
ذات عالیکزی عافیت اوزره کوردیکمدن غایتله ممنونم	*Zat - i - alinĭzi afĭyet uzeré ghĭeurdughumden ghayetlé memnounoum*	I am extremely *glad* I see you in good health
سزی کوردیکمدن پك ممنونم	*Sizi ghĭeurdughumden pek memnounoum*	I am *glad* to see you
ابوالمجد مقصودینك حاصل اولمسندن مأیوس اولوب زار زار اغلدی	*Abul-Mejd máksoud-ounoun hásĭl olmasindan mé'youss oloup zar zar ághladĭ*	Abul-Mejd *despairing of* his object being attained, cried and groaned.

---

* Turkish epistolary style of writing.

EXERCISE XXX.

Look at these pretty flowers ? He is a good and a learned man. The Turkish language is very useful (فائده‌لی *faïdé'li*), She is a fascinating (دلفریب *dilfirib*) woman. There are many pretty women in London. What is that book about ? It is about geometry (هندسه *hendessé*). Have you read the history (تاریخ *tarikh*) of Turkey (دولت علیه *devlet-i-aliyé*) ? I have read it. The eternal (ابدی *ébedi*) friendship (محبت *mahabet*) existing (درکار *derkiar*) between us. Does he know Oriental (شرقی *sharki*) languages (السنه (pl.) *elsiné*) ? He is a very learned man. How is your (sublime) health (کیف *kéif*) ? Thank you (الحمد لله *elhamd-u-lilláh*), I am very well (ایو *éi*). How is your (noble) (شریف *sherif*) mother (والده (A.) *walidé*) ? All kinds (درلو درلو *turlu turlu*) of various (مختلف *moukhtélif*) individuals (اشخاص (pl.) *eshkhass*) came to the town. He received various presents (هدایا (pl.) *hédaya*) from his friends. He acted (حرکت ایتمك *héréket etmek*) thus after great (عظیم *ázim*) reflection (تفکر *téfekkiur*). He is an old and faithful (صادق *sádik*) servant (امكدار *émekdar*). The king not knowing the worth (قدر *kádr*) and value (قیمت *kéimet*) of an old servant, grew tired (اوصانمق *ousanmak*) of him. You have beautiful silver spoons. Where did you buy them ? I bought them in London of a good silversmith (قیومجی *kouyoumjou*). They are not dear (بهالو *páháli*). What a pretty little watch (ساعت *saat*)! Is it gold? Yes.* The English merchants are very rich (زنكین *zenghin*). Have you ever been in England? I lived there three months (آی *ai*). Do you think it a pretty country (مملكت *memléket*) ? It is a pretty and a healthy (شفالو *shifali*) country. The climate is too damp (دها چوق رطوبتلو *daha chok routoubetli*). The climate (هوا *hawa*) of Turkey is very agreeable (لطیف *latif*). The sky (کوك *ghieuk*) is very clear (براق *berrak*). There are many (چوق *chok*) high (یوكسك *yuksek*) hills (تپه *tepé*) in the neighbourhood (جوار *jiwar*) of Constantinople (استانبول *Iestanbol*).

THE DEGREES OF COMPARISON.

The Comparative.

564. The comparative degree is generally expressed by putting the word with which the comparison is made in the ablative case and leaving the adjective unaltered. The words دها *daha* (more) and زیاده *ziyadé* (more) are sometimes put before the adjective for the sake of emphasis, or to prevent ambiguity. Example :—

---

* Say, " It is gold," it being too abrupt in Turkish to merely answer, " Yes."

سركهدن اكشى	*Sirkéden ekshi*	Sourer than vinegar
شكردن طاتلو	*Shékérden tátlĭ*	Sweeter than sugar
احمد سزدن بویلو (در)	*Ahmed sizden boilou dir*	Ahmed is taller than you
سز بندن زنكين سكز	*Siz benden zenghin siniz*	You are richer than I
بو جوهر بى نظيرى الوب	*Bou jevher bi náziri*	They said : " Take this
كندى الكله سلطان رومه	*alĭp kendi elinlé soultán-*	peerless jewel with thy own
هديه ايدەسن بو هديه	*-i-rouma hédiyé edésin bou*	hand, and make a present (of
ضمننده لطف و كرميله	*hédiyé zimnindé loutf ou*	it) to the king of Roum; and
مأمولكدن زياده مسرور و	*keremilé mémoulinden*	with regard to this jewel,
خندان اولورسن ديديلر	*ziyadé messrour ou khan-*	by his favour and gracious-
	dan oloursoun dédiler	ness you will be *more*
		pleased and *delighted* than
		you expect
ارسلان تلكيدن شجاعتلو	*Arsslan tilkiden she-*	The lion is *braver* than
در	*juaatli dir**	the fox
التون كومشدن ايو در	*Altĭn ghiumishden éi dir*	Gold is *better* than silver
ظن ايتديكمدن كچ در	*Zan etdiyimden ghech*	It is *later* than I thought
	dir	
†سندن دولتلو اولن	*Senden devletli olán ilé*	Do not become a partner
ايله اورتاق اولمه	*ortak olma*	with a *more exalted* man
		than thyself
†محبّ صادق ايو در	*Muhibb-i-sádĭk éi dir*	A faithful friend is *better*
كيشينك اقرباسندن	*kishinin ákrabasĭndan*	than relations
†حق سوز زهردن	*Hákk seuz zéhirden ájĭ*	A true word is *bitterer*
آجيدر	*dir*	than poison.

565. Sometimes the Arabic comparative form of adjectives is used Example :—

حكما ضرر عامدن ضرر	*Hukéma zarar-i-amdan*	Wise men have said,
خاص اولى درديمشلر	*zarar-i-khass evla dir dé-*	" individual harm is *better*
	mishler	than public harm " (*i.e.*
		injury to individuals is
		better than injury to the
		world in general)
بو شخصى تجربه	*Bou shakhssi tejribé*	It is *better* to test this
ايتمك اوليدر	*etmek evla dir*	individual.

---

* The در *dir* may be omitted. † Turkish proverb.

The Superlative.

566. The superlative in general is expressed by the word اك *en* being prefixed to the adjective. The adjective takes the pronominal termination سی or ی (his, hers, its), and the word with which the comparison is made is put in the genitive. Example :—

المالرك اك ايوسی	*Elmalerin en éissi*	The best of the apples, or the best apple
بادشاهه كـلـوب محروسهیی غایتده چرکین دیوب قدح و ذم ایدوب ایتدیلر بادشاهم سنك حرمكده جاریهلرك اك ادناسی اول قزدن حسندار اولمق كرك	*Padishaha ghelip Mahrouséyi ghayetdé chirkin déyup kádh ou zem edip éitdiler Padishahim senin haremindé jariyélerin en ednassi ol kïzdan hussndar olmak gherek*	They came to the king and said that Mahrousé was extremely ugly, and censuring and reviling her, exclaimed : Sire, the *lowest* of the slaves in thy harem must be more beautiful than that girl.

567. The word اك *en*, however, is sometimes omitted. Example :—

قیزلرك ایوسی	*Kïzlarïn éissi*	The best girl
ادملرك بیوكی	*Adámlarïn biyughu*	The biggest man
ات حیوانلرك ایوسی در	*At haïwánlarïn éissi dir*	The horse is the best animal.

568. The superlative is occasionally expressed by employing the comparative in conjunction with such words as جمله *jumlé* or هب *hep* (all). Example :—

جملهسندن شجاعتلو در	*Jumlésinden shejaatli dir*	He is the bravest
بادشاهك بر قزی وار در كه جمیع قزلردن جمیله و حسنه در	*Padishahin bir kïzï var dir ki jémi kïzlardan jémilé vé hassané dir*	The king has a daughter who is the prettiest and most beautiful of all girls.

EXERCISE XXXI.

Your brother is taller than you. Knowledge (علم *'ilm*) is better than wealth (مال *mál*). If you do as I tell you you will be more delighted than you expect. London (لوندره *Londra*) is larger than Paris (پارس *Paris*). Teheran (طهران)

Tehrān) is smaller than Constantinople. The horse is the most useful (فائدهلی *faïdéli*) animal. Silk (ابپك *ipek*) is dearer (بهالو *pâhâlī*) than cotton (پاموق *pâmouk*). Our house is larger than yours, but Mr. So-and-so's (فلان افندی *filân effendi*) is the largest. This is the best book for learning French (فرانسزجه *fransizja*). It is most necessary (الزم *elzem*, Arabic comparative) for those who go to Turkey to know Turkish. It is later than you thought. He knows French better than you.

THE NUMERALS.

The Position of the Numerals.

569. A Turkish or Persian noun of number, when used as an adjective, is always put *before* the noun, but an Arabic noun of number is put after the noun. Example :—

ایکی ادم	*Iki âdâm*	Two men
بش قاری	*Besh kârï*	Five women
اوچ چوجق	*Uch chojouk*	Three children
ایکی واریل باروت و ایکی طوپ و اون ایکی تفنك	*Iki varil barout vé iki top vé on iki tufék*	Two barrels of powder and two cannon and twelve muskets
هفت اقلیم (P.) *	*Heft iklim*	The seven climates
هزاریك روز (P.)	*Hézar yek rouz*	A thousand and one days
صد هزار لاله (P.)	*Sad hézar lalé*	A hundred thousand tulips
قوای خمسه (A.)	*Kouwa-yi-khamsé*	The five senses
بعد زمان بصریه كلوب ها شمنیك خانه سنی سؤال ایدوپ هزار زحمت ایله بولدی	*Bad zeman Bassrayé ghelip Hashiminin khanéssini sual edip hézar zahmet ilé bouldou*	After some time he came to Bassora, and asked for the house of Hashmin, and found it after (with) a *thousand troubles.*

570. When the Turkish and Persian nouns of number are used, the nouns they refer to must be in the singular. Example :—

اوچ كتابم وار در	*Uch kitâbïm var dir*	I have three *books*
بو محاربه ده ایكی بیك بشیوز اوتوز درت ادم مقتول اولدی	*Bou mouharebédé iki bin besh yuz otouz deurt âdâm mâktoul oldou*	In this battle two thousand five hundred and thirty-four *men* were killed

---

* The words marked P. are Persian, those marked A. are Arabic.

بزم محلّهده بيك بش خانه وار	*Bizim mahalédé bin besh khané var*	In our parish there are one thousand and five houses
بو اثر انشا اولنهلی بش يوز سنه در	*Bou essr insha olounali besh yuz sené dir*	It is five hundred years since this monument was erected
دو جهان (.P.) دستی باشندن دوشوب بيك پاره اولدی	*Du jihan* *Tessti báshindan dushup bin paré oldou*	The two *worlds* The tray falling from his head, became (broke into) a thousand *pieces*
بو طرفده يمورطه و طاوق بولنمديغندن سزلره رجا أيدرم يوز دانه طاوق و بيك دانه يمورطه اشترا أيدوب قاطرجی ايله طرفمزه كوندرهسز	*Bou tarafdé yïmourta vé tawouk boulounmadïgh-indan sizleré rija edérim yuz tané tawouk vé bin tané yïmourta ishtira edip kátïrjï ilé tarafimizé ghieunderésiz*	There being no eggs or fowls here, I request you to buy 100 *fowls* and 1000 *eggs*, and send them to me by the muleteer.

The Arabic Numerals.

571. The Turks never make use of the Arabic numerals أحد *ahad* or واحد *wahid* (one), أحدی *ihda* (one) (feminine), and أثنين *issnéin* or أثنی *issni* (two), as adjectives; but they do sometimes in writing employ the other Arabic numbers as adjectives, and when they do so the noun is put in the plural. Example:—

جزائر سبعه	*Jezá'ir-i seba*	The seven *islands* (the name given by the Turks to the Ionian Islands)
أقاليم سبعه (.A.)	*Akálim-i-seba*	The seven *climates*
* قوای خمسه (.A.)	*Kouwa-yi-khamsé*	The five *senses*
جوانب أربع	*Jewanib-i-erba*	The four *sides*
عناصر أربعه	*Anasïr-ï-érbaa*	The four *elements*.

A Noun of Number with an Adjective.

572. If the noun is described by one or more adjectives as well as a

---

* قوا *kuwa* is the Arabic plural of قوّت *kouvvet* (power, faculty).

noun of number, the number, if it be Turkish, is put before the adjective, and if it be Arabic it is put directly after the noun.   Example :—

ايكى بياض يلك	*Iki béyáz yélek*	*Two white* waistcoats
يكرمى قره قويون	*Yirmi kára koyoun*	Twenty black sheep
قواى خمسهء ظاهره	*Kouwa-yi-khamsé-'i-zahiré*	The five physical (apparent) senses.

The Word " Or " between Numerals.

573. The word " or " between two nouns of number in English is omitted in Turkish.   Example :—

ايكى اوچ الما	*Iki uch élma*	Two *or* three apples
بكا قرق اللى ليرا بورجلو در	*Bána kirk elli lira borjli dir*	He owes me forty *or* fifty pounds
بش التى درلو كتاب الوب بزلره ارسال بيورملرى رجامز در	*Besh áltï turlu kitáb álïp bizleré irsal bouyourmaleri rijamiz dir*	I request* you to buy *five or six* kinds of books, and send them to me (us)†
طاغك بر خوش مسيرلك محلنه واردقده كورديكه بش اون آدم بر يرده اوتورمشلر	*Dághïn bir khosh mesirlik mahaliné vardïkda ghieurduki besh own ádám bir yeré otourmoushlar*	Having come to a pleasant promenade amongst the mountains, he saw that *five or ten* men were sitting in a place (there).

574. The Turkish nouns of number are sometimes put after nouns they qualify in appearance when they designate only a part of another number. In this case the noun is put in the genitive, is either singular or plural, and the noun of number takes the pronominal affix of the third person singular (ى or سى).   The Turkish noun of number is, in reality, in such instances, used substantively.   Example :—

درويشلرك برى	*Dervishlerin biri*	} One of the dervishes, or, a dervish
درويشك برى	*Dervishin biri*	
ادملرك برى	*Adámlarïn biri*	} A man, or, one of the men
or ادمك برى	*Adámïn bïrï*	

---

* Literally, " It is our request" ; but it is considered respectful to use " we " for " I," and " our " for " mine."

† " Us " is used for " me."   See preceding note.

The Use of چوق, بعض, برقاچ, وافر and قاچ.

575. After the words چوق *chok* (much, many), وافر *wâfïr* (many), برقاچ *bir kach* (a few), بعض *bâzï* (some), and قاچ *kach* (how many?), the noun may be put in the singular or plural, but is generally put in the former. Example :—

برقاچ سطر يازارم	*Bir kach sâtr yazarïm*	I will write *a few lines*
برقاچ ادملر كلدى	*Bir kach âdâmlar gheldi*	*A few men* came
استانبولده قاچ كوپرى وار	*Isstanbolda kach kieupru var ?*	*How many bridges* are there in Constantinople?
بعض كره صيقى لدوس اسرايسه دكز پك سرت اولور	*Bâzï-kerré sïkï lodoss essérsé dénïz pek sert olour*	*Sometimes* if a strong south-west wind is blowing, the sea gets very rough
برقاچ اى ياننده خدمت ايلدى	*Bir kach aï yanïndé khidmet (hizmet) éilédi*	He was in his service a *few months.*

EXERCISE XXXII.

Please buy me twenty okes of grapes and send them here. You have a great many friends in Constantinople. A great many thousand men were killed in the war (محاربه *mouharebé*) between Turkey and Russia. The Turks fought (غوغا كاوغا ايتمك *kawgha etmek*) better than the Russians (مسقو *mosskof*). Russia is a larger country than Turkey. The Mediterranean (اق دكز *âk dénïz*) is larger than the Black Sea (قره دكز *kâra dénïz*). The position (موقع *mevki*) of Constantinople is most (پك *pek*) beautiful. The Bosphorus (بوغاز *Boghâz*) is more beautiful than the Bay of Naples (ناپولى كورفزى *Napoli kieurfezi*). Give me five or six pounds. I called you five or six times (كره *kerré*), but you did not come. What were you doing? I was writing and did not hear you. Make haste (عجله ايتمك *ajelé etmek*) for (زيرا *zira*) it is later than I thought. He brought two beautiful white roses (كل *ghiul*) from his garden (باغچه *bâgché*). You have five white cows (اينك *inek*), but the best one is ill. In hot countries mutton (قويون اتى *koyoun eti*) is more digestible (خفيف *khafif*) than beef (صيغر اتى *sïghïr eti*), veal (دانا اتى *dana eti*) is worse than beef, but pork (طوكز اتى *domouz eti*) is the worst of all. I like lamb (قوزو اتى *kouzou eti*) better than mutton. Tea (چاى *chaï*) is dearer than coffee (قهوه *kahwé*). Tea is better than wine.

o

The Demonstrative Pronoun.

576. A demonstrative pronoun, used adjectively, precedes both the noun adjective and noun of number, as in English.   Example :—

بو اوچ بیوك باصمه كتاب   *Bou uch biyuk bássma kitáb*   These three large printed books.

The Pronominal Affixes.

577. The pronominal affixes corresponding to my, thy, his, hers, &c., are not always put after the noun to which they refer.   If the noun be followed by an adjective, simple or compound, or another noun with which it is in conjunction, then they are put at the end of the last word. Example :—

كیف عالیكز نصل در   *Keif-i-aliniz nassl dir?*   How is *your high* health?

عید شریفكز مبارك اولسون   *Eid-i-sherifiniz mubarek olsoun*   May *your noble* fête be blessed *

همت عالیسته و كرمنه تحسین و افرین ایلدیلر   *Himmet-i-alisiné vé kériminé tahsin u aferin éilédiler*   They approved and applauded *his august exertions* and graciousness

بر كون عادت معروفهسی اوزره شهرك ایچنده در بدر كزر كن ناكاه بر كمسهیه راست كلوب زاهده خطاب ایلدیكه   *Bir ghun adet-i-marouféssi uzeré shehirin ichindé der béder ghézer ken na-ghiah bir kimséyé rásst ghelip zahïdé khïtáb éilédi ki . . .*   One day, according to *his well-known custom,* going from door to door (begging) in the town, he suddenly met someone who addressed him (the ascetic), saying . .

خاتون خانهنك ایچنده اوتورمقدن جانی صقیلوب بر كون طشره چیقوب چارشویه كزمكه كتدی نا كاه بر صراف جوانی كوروب عاشق اولدی و مشاهدهٔ جمالندن بیصبر و بی ارام اولوب هر كون   *Khátoun khanénin ichindé otourmakdan jáni sïkïlïp bir ghiun táshra chïkïp charshïya ghézméghé ghitdi na-ghiah bir sarraf juwani ghieurup áshïk oldou vé mushahedé-'i-jemalinden bi sábr vé bi aram oloup hér ghiun*   The lady being weary of sitting at home, one day went out to walk in the market-place.   Suddenly she perceived the son of a money-changer and fell in love with him, and *from the contemplation of his beauty* becoming restless and im-

* Used on the occasion of any festival, as we say, " A merry Christmas to you," &c.

دكانی اوكندن كچوب جوانك يوزينه باقوب بر أز تسلى بولوردى	*dukkiani euninden ghechip juwanin yuziné bákïp bir áz téselli boulourdou*	patient she used to pass before his shop every day, and (thus) found a little consolation
سنك صداى مكروهكدن ارباب طبيعت قاچار	*Senin sada-yi-mekrou-hinden erbab-i-tabiat káchar*	People of taste run away from your disgusting voice
عادت قديمهسى اوزره زاهدك خانهسنه غلنجه شو قوشى بكا كباب ايله كوكلم استدى* ديدى	*Adet-i-kádiméssi uzeré zahidin khanésiné ghelinjé shou koushou bána kébáb éilé ghieunulum isstédi dédi*	According *to his old custom*, on his coming to the ascetic's house, he said: "Roast that bird for me, my heart desires it"
پادشاهك بر دختر پاكيزه اخترى وار ايدى جانى صقلوب پنجرهدن طشره بقار كن كوزى فريده دوش اولديغى كمى بيك جان ايله فريده عاشق اولدى فريد دخى پنجرهيه باقوب قزى كورديكى كمى كذلك عاشق اولوب درد عشقلرينه چاره آرامغه باشلديلر	*Padishahin bir dukhter--i-pakizé akhteri var-idi jáni sïkïlïp pénjeréden táshra bákar iken ghieuzu Feridé doush oldoughou ghibi bin ján ilé Feridé áshik oldou Ferid dakhï pénjeréyé bákïp kïzï ghieurdughu ghibi kézalik áshïk oloup derd-i-áshk-larina charé áramagha báshladïlar*	The king *had a beautiful daughter*. Being *ennuyée*, while looking out of the window, her eye fell on Ferid, and she became enamoured of him "with a thousand souls." Ferid, also, looking at the window, and seeing the girl, immediately fell in love, and they began to seek a remedy for the "*illness of their love*"
تبريزده بر پادشاهك عاصم نامنده بر وزير روشن ضميرى وار ايدى كشينك كاسهٔ حياتى لبريز اولمدقجه جام موتى نوش ايلمز	*Tebrizdé bir padishahin Asim naminadé bir vézir roushen-zamiri var idi Kishinin kiassé-'i-hay-ati lebriz olmadoukcha jam-i-mevti noush éilémaz*	In Tebriz there was a king who *had a clear-headed* vizier called Asim Until a person's bowl of life is overflowing he does not drink the glass of death
فريد دخى ينه قالقوب پدرينك و والدهسنك اللرينى اوپوب دعاء خيرلرينى الدى	*Ferid dakhï yiné kálkïp péderinin vé validésinin ellerini eupup dua-i-khaïr-lerini áldï*	Ferid, also rising again, kissed the hands of his father and mother, and received *their good prayers* (*i.e.* their blessing)

---

* The past tense is often used in Turkish where we should use the present.

صورتده خوابده اولديغم
زمان چشم جهانبينم
عالم ظاهردن قيانوب عالم
علويه چشم حقيقت
اثرم اچيلوب انكله
تمثيلات كوناكون و اسرار
حكمت مشحون مشاهده
ايدرم

Souretdé khabdé ol-
doughoum zeman chesshm-
-i-jihanbinim além-i-za-
hirden kâpânĭp além-i-
-ulviyé chesshm-i-hâkiket
essrm âchĭlĭp aninlé tem-
silat ghiunaghiun vé iss-
rar - i - hikmet meshhoun
mushahedé ederim

When I am apparently
asleep, " *my world-seeing* "
eye being closed to the visible
world, *my true eye* being
opened to the higher world,
I see all kinds of examples
and secrets full of wisdom.*

578. A pronominal affix sometimes refers to two or more nouns.
Example : —

بعده احوالـلـريـنـى
سويلوب فقر و فاقهلرندن
شكايت ايلديلر

Badéhou ahvallerini su-
wéyléyip fakr vé fakaler-
inden shikiayet éilédilér

Then they described their
condition and complained of
their poverty and misery

بر كون بابل شهرينه
كلوب آب و هواسندن
غـايت حظ ايدوب
مكث و اقامت ايلدى

Bir ghiun Babil shehi-
riné ghelip âb-ou-hawas-
sinden ghayet hâz edip
mekks-u-ikamet éilédi

One day coming to the
city of Babylon and liking
its air and water he sojourned
there.

579. Besides the pronominal affix appended to a noun the personal
pronoun corresponding to it is sometimes placed before it. This is generally
done to prevent ambiguity or for the sake of emphasizing who is the possessor. Thus, instead of كتابم *kitâbĭm* (my book) you can say بنم كتابم
benim kitâbĭm (my book) in contradistinction to anyone else's. پدرم
péderim or بنم پدرم *benim péderim* (my father). Example :—

بنم پدرم اختيار اولوب
و دار دنياده بندن غيرى
اولادى اولمديغندن هر نه
تكاليف ايلسم دريغ ايلمز

Benim péderim ikhtiyar
oloup vé dar-i-dunyadé
benden ghaïri evladi ol-
madĭghĭndan hér né teklif
éilessém derigh éilémaz

My father being old and
having no other child but
me, whatever I ask he does
not refuse

پس اللهك امريله بنى
شول يكيده نكاح ايله
ديرم اما بوندن اقدم بر
خصوص ايچون پدرم

Pess âllâhĭn emrilé
béni shol yighidé nikiah
éilé derim ama boundan
âkdem bir khousous ĭchĭn

Then, by the will of God,
I will say : Marry me to
that youth. But, for a certain reason, hitherto, my

---

* طوطى نامه (Tales of a Parrot).

جمله وزرا و اركان دولت
اچنده بنم عقديمى بر
خدمته تعليق ايلمشيدى
مادامكى اول خدمت
وجوده كلمياجه بنم عقدم
اولمز

*péderim jumlé vuzara vé
erkian-i-devlet ichindé benim ákdïmï bïr hizmeté
talik éilémishidi madam
ki ol hizmet vujouda ghelméyinjé benim ákdm ol-
maz*

father has made *my marriage*
amongst the viziers and pil-
lars of the State dependent
on a certain service. As long
as that service is not performed *my marriage* will not
come about

بنم بو خوابم خواب
راحت دكلدر

*Benim bou khabim khab-
-i-rahat déïl dir*

This sleep of *mine* is not
the sleep of repose.

كندى *kendi* "Own."

580. In such expressions as My own father, Thy own father, &c., the
pronominal affix is appended to the noun and not to كندو. Example:—

كندى كتابم در
كندى باباكز استدى
ملكهٔ روم كندى
اوتورديغى سرايى اول
نقـاش كلـوب نقش
ايتمسيچون باباسى قيصر
رومدن نياز ايدوب اذن
الدى

*Kendi kitábïm dïr
Kendi bábánïz isstédi
Meliké-'i-roum kendi
otourdoughou serayi ol
nakkásh ghelip nakhsh et-
masï ïchïn bábássï kaïser-
i-roumdan niaz edip izn
áldï*

It is *my own* book
Your *own father* wished it
The queen of Greece re-
quested her father the emperor of Greece to let that
artist come and paint *her
own palace* where she lived,
and obtained his permission

ناكاه بر چفت اهو
ياوريلريله كلوب صو اچچر
كن بر سيل كلوب اهونك
ياوريلرينى الوب كوتورر
كن اركك اهونك كندى
ياوريلرينى سيل سيلوب
سپور ديكنى كورجه
كندسنى صويه اوروب
ياوريلرينى خلاص ايدهيم
ديركن قضا وقدر ايرشوب
ياوريلرى ايله اركى معا
صويه غرق اولديلر اما
ديشى آهو اصلا همت
ايتميوب كندى جاننى
قورتارمغه مشغول اولوب

*Na-ghiah bir chift ahou
yavrïlarïlé ghelip sou
icher-iken bir séil ghelip
ahounoun yavrïlarïnï álïp
gheuturur iken erkek
ahounoun kendi yavrïla-
rïnï séil silip supurdu-
yunu ghieurunjé kendi-
ssini souya wouroup yav-
rïlarïnï khalass edéyim
dér iken káza-ou-káder
eriship yavrïlarï ilé erkéyi
maan souya ghark oldoular
ama dishi ahou ássla him-
met etméyip kendi jánïnï*

Suddenly a couple of
gazelles, with their little
ones, came and were drinking the water, when a tor-
rent came and carried off
their young ones. On the
male gazelle seeing the tor-
rent sweep away *their own
young ones* he threw himself
into the water, saying:
"Let me save them;" but,
by the decree of fate and
destiny, he was drowned
with his young in the water.
But the female gazelle, not

اشندن و ياوريلرندن اعراض ايدوب فرار ايلدى	koutarmagha meshghoul oloup eshinden vé yavrï- larïndan iraz edip firar éilédi	exerting herself in the least, and thinking only of saving her own life, abandoning her mate and her young ones, fled away.

EXERCISE XXXIII.

I knew your late (مرحوم *merhoum*) father. He was a very good man. My father also was a good man. He had a great many camels (دوه *devé*) and horses. How many mares (قسراق *kïssrák*) have you? I shall sell (صاتمق *sátmak*) these three pretty cows. There are two bridges now in Constantinople. One of them is of iron, and the other (بشقهسى *báshkassi*) of wood. There are a great many beautiful large bridges in London. Have you seen them? I have seen most (اكثر *ekser*) of them. How old (قاچ ياشينده *kach yashindé*) is he? He is twenty-five (ياشنده *yashindé*). How many houses are there in this town? More than twenty thousand. Then it must be very big and prosperous (معمور *mamour*). Certainly (البته *elbetté*).

PERSONAL PRONOUNS.

The Omission of Pronouns.

581. In Turkish personal pronouns are generally omitted, except when the sense would not be clear from the context without them. Especially when they are in the nominative, they are never used except for the sake of emphasis, as the meaning is always apparent from the termination of the verb. Thus, "he loves" is سور *sevér*, not او سور *o sevér*, unless you wish to emphasize *he;* سورم *sevérim* is "I love," سورسكز *sevérsiniz* "you love," كلدى *gheldi* "he came." Example:—

بر قاچ ايستردىا ييه جكم	Bir kach isstridiya yéyéjéyim	I will eat a few oysters
اندن ايكى اوچ دانه دها المزميسكز	Andan iki uch tané daha álmazmïsïnïz?	Will you not take a few more of them?
شو كراز بوركندن بر پارچه استرميسكز	Shou kiraz beuréyinden bir parcha isstérmisiniz?	Do you want a piece of that cherry tart?
ايو كورنيور	Eï ghieuruniyor	It looks good
نرهده اوتورر	Nerédé otourour?	Where does he live?
بلمم	Bilmem	I do not know
كوسترىرم	Ghieustéririm	I will show you

بن دخی او طرفدن كيديورم	*Ben dakhĭ o tarafdan ghidiyoroum*	*I* also am going that way
سلطان مصرك بر حسنا غايتده جميله بر قزی وار ایدی تقصاءربانی باغچهلری كزرکن بر يیلان صوقدی پادشاهه خبر ویردیلر پادشاهك عقلی باشندن كتدی زیرا دنیاده اول قزدن غیری اولادی يوق ایدی*	*Soultán-i-Missrin bir hassna ghayetdé jémilé bir kĭzĭ var idi kázai-rabbani bághchéleri ghézériken bir yilán sokdou padishaha kháber vérdiler. Padishahin áklĭ báshĭndan ghitdi zira dunyadé ol kĭzdan ghaïri evladi yoghoudou*	The Sultan of Egypt had a beautiful and extremely handsome daughter. By divine fate, one day while *she* was walking in the gardens a snake bit (*her*). *They* informed the king, and the king's senses went out of his head, for *he* had no child in this world except that daughter.

582. They are frequently understood in the dative and accusative cases. Example :—

ليمون وار در كندی الیکزله صقیكز	*Limon var dir. Kendi elinizlé sĭkĭnĭz*	There is a lemon. Squeeze *it* with your own hand
چای حاضرلدیلر كتورسونلرمی	*Chaï házĭrladĭlar. Ghettirsinlermĭ?*	They have prepared tea. Shall they bring *it*?
نارکیلهیه میلکز وار می اکر كتوررلرسه قنا اولمز	*Narghileyé méiliniz var mi? Eyer ghettirirlérsé féna olmaz*	Are you inclined for a *narghilé* (water-pipe)? If they bring *it*, it will not be bad
بندهکر سودن غیری چایك ایچنه بشقه شی قویمام	*Bendéniz soutdan ghaïri chaïn ichininé báshka shéĭ koïmam*	I put nothing in the tea but milk
چوق كوزل بنده سود ایله ایچرم	*Chok ghiuzel bendé sout ilé icherim*	Very good. I also drink *it* with milk
اخشام طعامنی نزمان كتورسونكر	*Akhsham taamini né zeman ghettirsinlér?*	When shall *they* bring the dinner? [o'clock
ساعت برده كتورسونلر	*Saat birdé ghettirsinlér*	Let them bring *it* at one
بندهکر ظن ایدرم كه دون كیجه ساعتکزی قورمدیكز	*Bendénĭz zan ederim ki dun ghejé saatinizi kourmadiniz*	I think you did not wind your watch up last night
اکر قومش اولیدم شمدی ایشلمز طوررتدی	*Eyer kourmamash olaydim shindi ishlémaz dourourdou*	If I had not wound *it* up it would have stopped

در دكل لازم مـوم	Moum lazim déïl dir.	Candles are not neces-
در مهتاب	Mehtab dir	sary; it is moonlight
كتورسونلرده ياقماسونلر	Ghetirsinlerdé yakma-	Let them bring *them* and
	sinler	not light *them*
چاى طاقميده بورايه	Chaï takïmïdé bouraya	I have brought the tea
كتوردم	ghettirdim	things here
كوزل ايتدكز صباحلين	Ghiuzel etdiniz sabah-	You did quite right.
سز كلمزدن اول حاضر	léin siz ghelmazden evvel	Shall I make *it* in the
ايده يم	házïr edéyim ?	morning before you come?
ابتدا سايسى چاغروب	Ibtida sa'issi chaghïrïp	First of all, call the
سپارش ايدكز	siparish ediniz	groom, and give *him* orders
نه سپارش ايده يم	Né siparish edéyim ?	What shall I order *him*?
سويليكز اير و طاقملره	Suwéyléyeniz éyer vé	Tell *him* to attend to the
دقت ايتسون	takïmlara dikkát etsin	saddles and (other) neces-
		saries
قهوه التى يـرايسه كـز	Kahwé áltï yérisséniz	If you take breakfast, let
كتورسونلر	ghettirsinlér	them bring *it*
خير يمم	Khaïr yémem	No, I shall not take *it*
اشته همماليه كزى	Ishté hámmáliyénïzï	Here is your money (por-
		terage)
باش اوستنه فقط از	Básh usstiné fákát áz	Very good, only you have
ويردكز بر ده بر قهوه	vérdiniz bir dé bir kahwé	given *me* very little. Give
پاره سنى ويركز	parassini vériniz	*me* the price of a cup of
		coffee also
ويردم	Vérdim	I gave (*it to you*)
خير افندم ويرمدكز	Khaïr efendim vérma-	No, Sir, you did not give
	diniz	(*it to me*).

The Employment of مذكور *mezkiour,* مزبور *mezbour,* &c.

583. In writing, the use of personal pronouns in the third person is
avoided by repeating the noun for which they stand accompanied by
one of the words مزبور *mezbour,* مذكور *mezkiour,* مرسوم *mérsoum,* مسطور
mestour, مومى اليه *mouma-iléyh,* مشار اليه *musharun-iléyh,* سابق‌الذكر *sabïk-*
-uz-zikr, سالف‌الذكر *salif-uz-zikr,* مارالذكر *mar-uz-zikr,* سابق البيان *sabik-*
-ul-béyan, and مرقوم *merkoum,* which all mean " the above-mentioned."
Example:—

فلان شيك اشترا و
أرسال اولنمسى شامل
وارد دست خلوصورى
اولان بر قطعه نميقهلرى
مألى معلوم ثناكارى
اولديغى اندە شى مذكور
مظنون وغير مظنون اولان
محللرده آرانلمش ايسهده
بولنمد يغندن اشترا أولوب
أرسال اولنهمديغى بيانيله
استفسار خاطر عاطرلرى
رفتارنده شقه تحرير و
تسيير قلندى

*Filán shéin ishtira vé
irsal olounmassï shamil
varid desst khoulousvéri
olán bir kïta némikéleri
mé'éli maloum-i-senavéri
oldoughou andé shéi mez-
kiour máznoun vé ghaïr-
-i-máznoun olán mahal-
lérdé áranïlmïsh issédé
boulounmadïghïndan ish-
tira oloup irsal olounama-
dïghi beyanilé isstifsar-i-
-khátïr-ï-átïrléri reftar-
indé shoukka tahrir-u-
-tessyir kïlïndï*

This letter has been written and sent to explain to
you that although the mo-
ment I understood the purport of a letter of yours
which has reached me, about
purchasing and sending a
certain thing, it was sought
for in all imaginable and
unimaginable places, *it* (the
aforementioned thing) not
being found has not been
able to be purchased and
forwarded*

ازميرده فلان مكتبده
فرانساوى و انكليزى
السنه لطبفهلرينى
اوكرنمك اوزره نجابتلو
مخدوملرى بو طرفه
كوندردكلرينه دائر وارد
اولان بر قطعه تحريرات
مألى معلومهمز اولمش و
مرقوم افنديلر سلامت
ايلـه كلديلر و مـذكور
مكتبده تويدق مرقوم
افنديلر ذاتلرنده كامل و
عاقل و نازك اولدقلرندن
انشالله پك يقين كونده
مكتب مذكورده چوق
علم و معرفت اوكرنهجكلر

*Ezmirdé filán mekteb-
dé fransavi vé inghlizi
elsiné-'i-latiélerini eugh-
renmek uzeré nejabetli
makhdoumlarï bou tarafé
ghieunderdikleriné daïr
varid olán bir kïta tah-
rirat mé'éli maloumou-
mouz olmoush vé merkoum
effendiler selamet ilé ghel-
dilér vé mezkiour mek-
tebdé koïdouk merkoum
effendilér zatlerindé kiamil vé ákïl vé nazik ol-
douklarindan inshallah pek
yakïn ghiundé mekteb-i-
-mezkiourdé chok ilm u
marifet eurenéjekler*

I have understood the
purport of a letter concerning your sending your noble
sons here to learn the pleasant English and French
languages in a certain school
in Smyrna. And the *said*
gentlemen have arrived
safely, and I have put them
in the *aforementioned* school.
The *abovementioned* (young)
gentlemen being perfect
and intelligent and re-
fined in their persons,
please God, in a short time
they will learn a great deal
of science and knowledge
in the *said* school.†

---

* Copy of a Turkish letter, the involved style of which, even when toned down
enough to be comprehensible in English, is quite oriental.

† This epistolary Turkish style somewhat resembles that adopted by English
lawyers.

584. مذكور *mezkiour,* مزبور *mezbour,* and مرسوم *mersoum* are used when speaking of persons of inferior position. مشاراليه *musharun iléyh* is applied to persons of high rank, and موميّ اليه *mouma iléyh* and مرقوم *merkoum* to people of the middle class. When speaking of inanimate objects, مزبور, مرسوم, مسطور, سابق‌الذكر, مذكور, and مارالذكر are used indiscriminately.

شو قدر غروش قاطرجی احمد ایله بو ستایشورلرینه ارسال اولدیغنه دائر وارد اولان بر قطعه کرمنامه‌لری مآلی معلوم ثناورئ اولمش و مبلغ مبعوث مذكور وصول بولدیغی بیاسنده شقه تحریر و تسییر قلندی	*Shou kădar groush kătĭrjĭ Ahmed ilé bou sitayishvérlériné irsal ol-doughouna daïr varid olăn bir kĭta kéremnaméleri mé'éli maloum-i-sénavéri olmoush vé meblagh-i--mebouss mezkiour vusoul bouldoughou béyanindé shoukka tahrir vé teesyir kĭlĭndĭ*	This note has been written and despatched to explain that a kind letter of yours, which has reached (me) concerning sending so many piastres to me by the muleteer Ahmed, has been understood by me, and the *aforementioned* sent sum has arrived
قبرس ساكنلرندن فلان بازرکاندن ایکیوزآللی بیك غروش باتحویل مطلوباتم اولوب مرقومدن چند دفعه در مطالبه ایدیورایسه‌مده مبلغ مذكورك اعطا و تأدیه‌سنه مخالفت ایلیوب و كچن هفته دخی قرنداشمی قبرس جزیره‌سنده مدیون مرقومدن مبلغ مذكوری اخذ ایتمك اوزره ارسال ایتدیكمده مدیون مرقوم دینی اعطا ایتمدیکندن بشقه قرنداشمه نا روا وناحتی قلم فاحش ایله ستم ایلدیکی معلوم دولتلری بیورلدقده مدیون مرقوم حضور عالیلرینه جلب و مبلغ مذكور	*Kibrus sakinlerinden filăn băzĭrghianden iki yuz elli bin groush bé tahvil mătloubatoum oloup merkoumdan chend defa dir moutalebé idiyoris-sémdĭ meblagh-i-mezkiou-roun ita vu tédiyésiné moukhaléfet éiléyip vé gechen hăfta dakhĭ karn-dashimi kibrus jézirésindé medyoun - i - merkoumdan meblagh-i-mezkiouri akhz etmek uzeréirsal etdiyimdé medyoun-i-merkoum dini ita etmadiyinden băshka karndashimé na - reva vu na-hăkk kelam-i-fahish ilé sitém éilédiyi maloum-i--devletleri bouyouroul-*	I beg to inform you that I have a claim against a certain merchant, a resident of Cyprus, in the shape of a promissory note for 250,000 piastres; and although I applied several times for the *said* sum, he has always refused payment; and last week on my sending my brother to receive the *abovementioned* sum, from the *said* debtor in the island of Cyprus, the said debtor, besides not paying the *aforementioned debt,* abused my brother in false, unseemly, and indecorous language; and I request you to have the

تحصیل وبو قوللرینه قرداشم
قوللری واسطه سیله ارسال
بیورلمق بابنده لطف و
مرحمت افندمکدر

شاه پیلسان عرضحالی
اوقودیغی کبی غضب
ایدوب تیز قتل اولنسون
دیو امر ایلدی اما بر عاقل
و دانا وزیری وار ایدی
ایتدی که پادشاهم
قتل نفس خصوصنده
عجله ایتمك پادشاهلره
مناسب دکلدر بلکه
دیوانه اولمق احتمالی
وار در . . . . ابوالمجدی
مشارن الیه یاننه چاغروب
ای ابوالمجد بو بی معنا
کلام نیچون سویلرسن
دیدی

doukda medyoun-i-mer-
koum huzour-i-alileriné
jelb vé meblagh-i-mezkiour
tahsïl vé bou koullarina
karndashim koullari vas-
sitésilé irsal bouyouroul-
mak bắbïndé loutf-u-mer-
hamet efendimin dir

Shah Pilsan arzuhali
okoudoughou ghibi gházáb
edip téz kátl olounsoun
déyou emr eilédi ama bir
ắkïl ou dana véziri var idi
éitdi ki Padishahim kắtl-
-i-nefss khousousinda ajelé
etmek padishahleré munas-
sib déyil dir belki diwané
olmak ihtimali var dir . .
Abul Mejd musharun iléih
yaniné chaghïrïp éi Abul
Mejd bou bi mana kélam
nïchïn suwéylérsin dédi?

kindness to summon the
abovementioned debtor to
your august presence, and
to obtain the *above* sum,
and forward it to me by my
brother, your servant.

As soon as King Pilsan
read the petition, he got
into a passion, and gave
orders for the immediate
execution (of the writer of
it). But he had a wise and
sensible vizier, who said:
" Sire, in the matter of
taking life, it is not proper
for kings to be in a hurry.
Perhaps he may be mad."
. . He (the *aforementioned*
vizier) called Abul-Mejd
into his presence and said
to him: " Why do you use
this senseless language ?"

Avoidance of the Pronouns "I" and "My."

585. In polite conversation and in letters the use of the pronouns "I" and
"me" is avoided. Such words as بندڭز *bendéniz* (your servant) (or بندلری
bendéleri, * their servant) in talking, and عبدعاجزلری *abd-i-ajizléri* (your
poor slave—humble servant), مخلصلری *mukhlissléri* (your sincere friend),
and داعیلری *daileri* (he who prays for you) are substituted for them.
Example:—

---

* It is more polite to address anyone in the third person plural than in the
second, and to say "their" rather than " your."

بندهكز ايكى بچوق يـيلدر ايرانده ايدم	*Bendéniz iki bouchouk yïl dir irandé idim*	I have been two years and a-half in Persia
بندهكز ايشتمامش ايدم قنغى سنه كتمش ايدكز ايرانه	*Bendéniz ishitmamish idim hánghi sené ghitmish idiniz irané?*	I did not hear of it. Which year did you go to Persia?
بندهكزى فرامـوش بيورديكز	*Bendénizi feramoush bouyourdounouz?*	You have forgotten *me*?
استغفرالله	*Isstaghfirou-'llah!*	God forbid (oh, no)!
معروض چاكرلريدر كه بـو قوللرينك ازميرده شيطـان چارشوسنده متصرف اولديغم بر باب مغازهمى بوندن اون كون مقدم احمد افندیه اون ایكى بیك یوز غروشه فروخت ایتدم و سكز بیك غروشنى بندهكره اعطا ایدوب قصور درت بـیـك یوز غروشه بـر قطعه تحویل ویرمش ایسـهده مزبـور مبلـغ مذكورك تأديه و اعطاسى خصوصنده مخـالـفت ایلدیكندن مراحم عليه مشيرانهلرندن مرجو درکه مدیون مرقومى جلب ایدوب مبلـغ مذكورى تحصیل بیورهرق بو قوللرینه اعطا بیورلمسى بابنده أمر و فرمان من له الامركدر	*Marouz-i-chakérleri dir ki bou koullarinin ezmirdé shéitan charshïsïnda mutésarrif oldoughoum bir báb maghazami boundan on ghiun moukáddem Ahmed Effendiyé on iki bin yuz ghrousha furoukht etdim vé sekkiz bin ghroushounou bendénize ita edip koussourou deurt bin yuz ghrousha bir kïta tahvil vermish issédé mezbour meblagh mezkouroun tédiyé vu itasi khousousïnda moukhaléfet éilediyinden merahïm-i-aliyé mushiranélerinden mérjou dir ki medyoun-i-merkoumou jelb edip meblagh-i-mezkiourou tahsïl bouyourarak bou koullarina ita bouyouroulmasi bábïnda emr u firmán men lahu'l-imrin dir*	My petition (*the petition of your servant*) is that :— Ten days since I sold a shop I own in Smyrna, in the Sheitan market, to Ahmed Effendi for 12,100 piastres, and he paid *your servant* (me) 8,000 piastres; and as, although he gave a bill for the remaining 4,100 piastres, the aforementioned resists paying the said sum, I request you to summon the abovementioned debtor and obtain the said sum, and send it to *your servant* (me).

586. In epistolary Turkish, also, the use of the pronoun " my " by itself is considered objectionable. It is always accompanied by some adjective expressive of humility or affection, such as عاجزانه *ajizané* (poor), بندكانه *bendïghiané* (humble), مخلصانه *mukhlissané* (sincere—pertaining to a

sincere and devoted friend). Thus, instead of اوم *evim* (my house), it is polite to say خانهٔ چاكرانهم *khané-'i-chakeraném* (my humble house); instead of مكتوبم *mektouboum* (my letter), it is better to say مكتوب بندكانهم *mektoub - i - bendéghianém* (my humble (dutiful) letter), and so on. Example :—

| Arabic | *Dunkighiun chakérlerini ziyaret etmek ichin khané--'i-chakéranémé teshrif bouyourmoush issénizdé chakérléri khané-'i-hákï-ranémdé boulounmadigh-imdan hassba'l ijab bir mahala ghitmish oldou-ghoumdan zat - i - devlet-leriné mulakï olama-dïghïmdan moujib-i-hijab u shermsari oloup chakér-leriné dakhï zat valalériné ziyaret etmek farz oldou-ghoundan bou ghiun alla-franka saat beshdé vákït--i-alileri vé musaade-i-.kerimanéleri olour-oussa vákït-i-mezkiour khané--'i-devletlerindé bouloun-malari niazïlé mubarek mizaj-i-sherifleri isstif-sarindé nemiké tahrir u tessyir kïlïndï* | Although when you called at my *humble house* yester-day in order to visit your servant (me), I was not in my *wretched* house,* having been necessitated to go somewhere, and could not meet you ; feeling shame and timidity, and it being my duty to visit you, this letter has been written and despatched to request you to be at home to-day at five o'clock (European time), if you have time and are wil-ling, and to enquire after your sacred noble health |

| Arabic | *Mubarek desst-i-dev-letleri ba leb - i - édeb tákbil oloundoukdan sora rijayi ajizaném dir ki bou ghiunlerdé insha - i - ter kiraatiné mubaderet edé-* | Sir,—After kissing your sacred august hand with the lip of good manners, my *humble* request is that you may have the kindness and generosity to buy a |

---

* This tautology is good Turkish style.

لطفا و احسانا بر قطعه	*jéyimden loutfa vu ihsana*	letter-writer, and by send-
انشا اشترا و كله حك هفته	*bir kǐta insha ishtira vé*	it next week, without fail,
بهر حال ارساليله بو	*ghelejek háfta béher hal*	inspirit and delight your
اوغلكزی احیا و مسرور	*irsalilé bou oghlounouzou*	son, as, in a few days, I am
بیورملری افندم	*ihya vé messrour bouyour-*	going soon to set about read-
	malerĭ effeṇdim	ing a fresh letter-writer.

The Use of the Second and Third Person Plural instead of the Second Person Singular.

587. Formerly, in talking Turkish, everybody was addressed in the second person singular; and even in speaking to royal personages " thou " and "thee " were used. They are still used amongst equals and in familiar discourse, but in speaking to superiors and to any one to whom you wish to be polite, it is better to employ the second person plural, " you." Sometimes in conversation the third person plural is used in addressing any one when you wish to be very respectful; and in epistolary composition it is quite customary to say " theirs" when you mean " yours," as in German. Example :—

صباح شریفکز خیر اولسون	*Sabáh - i - sherifiniz khaïr olsoun*	May *your* noble morning be good (good morning)
صباح شریفلری خیر بولسون	*Sabáh - i - sherifleri khaïr olsoun*	May *their* noble morning be good (good morning to *you*)
كیف عالیلری نصل در	*Kéif-i-alileri nassl dir ?*	How is *their* august health (how are you) ?
كیف عالیكز نصل در	*Kéif-i-aliniz nassl dir ?*	
قلمتراشكزی بكا ويره بلورمیسكز؟	*Kalemtráshĭnĭzĭ bána véré bilirmisiniz ? [niz*	Can *you* give me your penknife ?
درسكزی اوكرنمدكز	*Derssinizi eurenmadi-*	*You* have not learnt *your* lesson [*thy lesson*
درسی اوكرنمدك	*Derssini eurenmadin*	*Thou* hast not learnt
فساج بی صبر و آرام اولوب خاتونه ابرام و حددن زیاده كلام وحشت انجام كوستروب	*Fessaj bi sábr u aram oloup khatouna ibram vé hadden ziyadé kélam-i- -vahshet enjam ghieusterip*	Fessaj becoming im- patient and restless, and importuning the lady, and using unbounded barbarous

اكر بكا رام اولمزسن سنى
هلاك ايدرم ياخود رسواى
عالم ايـدرم صـكـرهسى
پشيمان اولـورسـن ديـو
عظيم قورقو ويردى

*éyer bana ram olmazsin
seni helak ederim yakhod
russvayi alem ederim so-
rassi peshiman (pishmán)
oloursan déyou* ázim kor-
kou vérdi*

language, greatly frightened
her, saying : "If *thou* dost
not become obedient to me
I will destroy *thee* or dis-
grace *thee*, and afterwards
thou wilt be sorry for it"

مرحومه جواب ويرديكه
اولومدن خلاص ايتديكمك
عوضى بو ميدر كه بكا
زنا ايتمك استرسن الله
تعاليدن قورقمازميسن

*Merhoumé jéwáb vérdi
ki eulumden khalass etdiyi-
min ivazi bou mou dour ki
bána zina etmek isstérsin
állâh taaladen korkmaz-
-mïsïn ?*

Merhoumé answered :
"Is this the reward for my
saving *thee* from death,
that *thou* wishest to make
me commit adultery ? Art
thou not frightened of God
(may His name be ex-
alted !) ? "

جوان ايتدى كاشكى
بنى بر دار ايده لردى تك
سنك بلاى عشقكه كرفتار
الميايدم كويا سن بنى
دريادن چيقاروب اتشه
براقدك

*Juwan éitdi keshki béni
bér dar edélerdi tek senin
bilayi-áshkïna ghiriftar
olmayaydim ghiouya béni
deryaden chïkarïp áteshé
brakden*

The youth replied :
"Would to God that they
had hánged me, merely that
I might not have been
overtaken by the calamity
of *thy* love. As it were,
thou hast taken me out of
the sea and left me in fire"

ناكاه قارشولرندن بر تازه
يكيت ظاهر اولوب كلوب
شهزاده نك الين اوپوب
رعـايـت ايـدوب بنى
†خدمتكارلغه قبول ايتكى
بنم آديمه مبارك فال
ديرلر ديدى

*Na-ghiah karshïlarïn-
dan bir tazé yighit zahir
oloup ghelip shezadénin
elïni eupup riayet edip
béni hizmetkiarlïghe† ká-
boul et ki benim adimé
Mubarek Fal dérler dédi*

Suddenly a young man
appeared opposite to them,
and kissed the prince's
hand, and did homage to
him, and said : "Take me
as *thy* servant, for they call
me Mubarak Fal (Blessed
Augury)"

پس فرخ بخت دخى
قالقوب پادشاهه واروب
سلطان مصرك غمنى
طاغتدى و يـر اوپوب اك
همت همايونك بنمله

*Pess Ferroukh Bakht
dakhï kálkïp padishaha
varip Soultán-i-missrin
ghemini dághïtdï vé yér
eupup éyer himmet huma-*

Then Ferrukh Bakht
arose and went to the king,
and dispelled the king of
Egypt's grief, and kissed
the ground, and asked per-

---

* In conversation this is pronounced *deyé.*

† Written *khidmetkiar,* but commonly pronounced *hizmetkiar.*

اولورسه بن قولك واروب
خاتمی چیقاریرم دیواثن
طلب ایلدی سلطان مصر
دخی رخصت وبردی
فرخ بخت همان کلوب
مخلصه سویلینجه مخلص
قالقوب صو کنارنه کلوب
خاتمك دوشدیکی یرده
قوربغه صورتنه کیروب
طالدی و صویك قعرنده
خاتمی بولوب الدی
چیقاردی

*younoun benimilé oloursa
ben kouloun varip khatemi
chĭkarĭrĭm déyou izn taleb
éĭlédi Soultán-ĭ-missr dakhĭ roukhsat vérdi Fer-
roukh Bakht heman ghelip
mukhlissé suwéyléyinjé
Mukhliss kálkĭp sou ke-
nariné ghelip dushduyu
yérdé kourbágha souretiné
ghirip dáldi vé souyoun
karindé khatemi bouloup
áldĭ chĭkardĭ*

mission, saying : "If I
have *thy* imperial authority,
I *thy* servant will go and
get the ring out." The king
of Egypt also gave him
permission. On Ferrukh
Bakht coming at once and
telling Mukhliss, he arose
and went to the water's
edge, and took the form of
a frog in the place where
the ring had fallen, and
plunged in, and found the
signet at the bottom of the
water, and caught hold of
it and brought it out

عنایتلو قرنداشم
حضرتلری اول طرفدن
وابوره راكبا بو طرفه سلامتله
کلدم و فلان مکتبه کیردم
و ترکجه و فرانسزجه اوقومغه
باشلادم امابورا ده استدیکم
کبی ترکجه کتاب
بوله مد یغمدن کرم و
عنایت ایدوب ترکجه
کتابلردن التی درلو کتاب
الوب بزلره ارسال بیورملری
رجامز در افندم

*Inayetlou karndashim
hazretleri ol tarafden
vaporé rakiba bou tarafé
selametlé gheldim vé filán
mektebé ghirdim vé turkjé
vé fransizjé okoumagha
báshladĭm ama bourada
isstédiyim ghibi turkjé
kitáb boulamadighimdan
kérem u inayet edip turkjé
kitáblardan áltĭ turlu
kitáb álĭp bizleré irsal
bouyourmalari rijamiz dir
effendim*

My dear brother, *your*
excellency (*their* excellency), I got on board the
steamer and came here
safely, and entered such and
such a school, and began
studying Turkish and
French. But, as I cannot
find here such Turkish
books as I want, I request
that you, Sir (they), may
have the kindness to buy
six kinds of Turkish books
and send them to me

عنایتلو افندم حضرتلری
بو کون *خدمتکارمز ایله
سزلره اون دانه قاون

*Inayetlou effendim
hazretleri bou ghiun hiz-
metkiarimiẕ ilé sizleré on*

Dear Sir, your excellency
(their excellency†), I have
sent you to-day ten melons

---

* See note page 207.

† This word is now used to almost anyone and in familiar correspondence. It
will be noticed in this letter that the writer sometimes addresses his father in the
second person plural and sometimes in the third person plural.

(Ottoman Turkish)	Transliteration	English
كوندردم وصولنده قبول و صفاك خاطرايله اكل بيورملرك و دائماً صاغلق خبرڭز ايله بزلرى مسرور ايتملرى مرجودر	tané kaoun ghieunderdim vusoulindé káboul vé sáfa-yi-khátïrilé ékel bouyour-malari vé da'ima saghlïk kháberiniz ilé bizleri mess-rour etmaleri merjou dir	by our servant. On their arrival, I beg that you (they) may condescend to accept them and eat them in peace of mind, and that you (they) may always delight me with news of your health
سايهٔ عليهلرينده	Sayé-'i-aliyélérindé	Under *your* (*their*) high shadow (by your kind assistance)
بر قطعه مكتوب والالرى واصل دست ثناكارى اولمش	Bir kïta mektoup-i--valaleri wásïl-i-desst senakiari olmoush	An august letter of *yours* (*theirs*) has reached me (the hand of him who prays for you)
فلان شى شو قدر غروشه اشترا و ارسال بيوردقلرينه دائر بر قطعه تحريرات والالرى مألى مفهوممز اولمش	Filán shéi shou kádar grousha ishtira vé irsal bouyourdouklarina daïr bir kïta tahrirat-i-valaléri mé'éli mefhoumoumouz olmoush	I have understood the meaning of an august letter of yours (theirs) concerning your (their) buying such and such a thing at so many piastres and forward-ing it.

EXERCISE XXXIV.

Light (ياقمق *yakmak*) the candle. I have lit it. Have you lit the fire? I have not lit it yet (دها *daha*). Have you heard the news? I have not heard it. What is it? Russia has declared (اعلان حرب ايتمك *ilan-i-harb etmek*) war. Why has she done so? Give me the newspaper and let me see. I gave it to you. I beg your pardon (عفو ايدر سكز *áfv edérsiniz*); you did not give it to me. Tell me what you see. How is your father's health? How are you? I have received your letter. I request you to buy me a hundred eggs and ten fowls, and send them to me by the steamer (وابور ايله *vapor ilé*). You have made great (ايلرولمك *ilérilémek*) progress in learning Turkish. By your kind assistance (سايهٔ عليهلرينده *sayé-i-aliyélerindé*). I beg of you to buy me some English books, and send them by my servant. Make haste. I am making haste. Has the baker come? Yes, sir. Tell him to come (كلسون *ghelsin*) earlier to-morrow. I will tell him. Why has he not brought the bread? He says it is not ready (حاضر *házïr*). Why is it not ready? It is nine o'clock. While I was walking in the garden I saw a snake (يلان *yilán*), and it bit me. Did you not see it? Yes, Sir. Why did you not kill it (اولدرمك *euldurmek*)? I was frightened

(قورقمق *korkmak*) of it. Where has it gone? It is near the tree. I will go and kill it. Take care (صاقن *sakïn*). It may bite you. Do not be frightened. Behold (أشته *ishté*), I have killed it! I am very glad. Dear Sir, last Tuesday when you (they) visited (زيارت ايتمك *ziyaret etmek*) me I was not at home, and as it is my duty to call on you, if you have time and are agreeable, I will come to-morrow at four o'clock. Dear Sir, I have received your (august) (والالرى *valalari*) letter, and shall be at home to-morrow at four o'clock, and shall be much pleased if you call (تشريف ايتمك *teshrif* etmek*). I humbly request (رجاى عاجزانهم در *rijayi ajizaném dir*) your excellency to give me permission (رخصت *roukhsat*) to go to England (أنكلتره *Inghilterra*). I cannot give you permission. I will speak to the Grand Vizier (صدراعظم *sâdr-ï-âzam*†). Perhaps he will give you permission. The Grand Vizier has given him permission, and he will start (عزيمت ايتمك *azimet etmek*) next Wednesday (چهار شنبه *chéhar-shenbé*).

Relative Pronouns.

588. Relative pronouns are but little used in Turkish (see 151). The Turkish participles are generally employed to express both the relative pronoun and the verb by which it is always followed. The Turkish participles, so to speak, contain the relative pronouns "who," "which," "that," " what," in themselves. This is extremely puzzling to Europeans at first, and constitutes one of the greatest difficulties of the Turkish language. As practice alone will familiarize the student with this peculiarity of the language,—although we have treated this subject already in the first part of this volume,—I think it will be advantageous to subjoin various examples.

صكره كلان كيم ايسه قپويى اول قپار	*Sora‡ ghelan kim issé kapouyi ol kâpâr*	He who comes last, whoever he may be, shuts the door§
فقيرلره ويرن اللهه ويرر	*Fakïréré véren âllâha vérir*	He who gives to the poor gives to God
عيبسز يار استين يارسز قالور ●	*Aïbsiz yar istéyen yarsiz kalïr*	He who wants a faultless friend remains friendless

---

* This word literally means " to honour," but is often used for " to call," or " visit."   † Commonly pronounced *sadrazam*.

‡ Written *sonra,* but generally pronounced *sora* in Constantinople.

§ Turkish proverb.

ياغموردن قاچان طولوبه اوغرادی	*Yaghmourdan káchán dolouya oghradï*	He who fled from rain fell in with hail *
تیز کیدن تیز یورلور	*Téz ghiden téz yoroulour*	He who goes quickly is quickly tired
چوق یاشایان چوق بلمز چوق کزن چوق بلور	*Chok yashayan chok bilmaz chok ghézen chok bilir*	*He who lives* a long time does not know much; *he who* travels a great deal knows a great deal
الله دیین محروم قالمز	*Alláh déyen mahroum kálmaz*	He who calls (on) God is not disappointed
اغلمیان چوجغه ممه ویرمزلر	*Aghlamayan chojougha memé vermazlér*	They do not give the breast to a child *who does not cry*
بهواج دیدیکك کیم در	*Behvaj dédiyin kim dir?*	Who is he *whom thou callest* Behvaj ?
قپوسنه کلنلردن بر کمسه محروم کتمزدی	*Kápïsïna ghelenlerden bir kimsé mahroum ghitmazdï*	Not one of *those who came* to his gate went away disappointed
حتی بر دفعه بر عاشق معشوقنه ایرمسیچون جاننی بیله فدا ایتمشدر	*Hatta bir defa bir áshïk mashoukouna ermasi ichin jánïnï feda etmish dir*	So much so that once he sacrificed his life in order to bring a lover together with his beloved
ایتدیلر که اکر سکا بو التونی ویرنك باشنی دخی کسوب کتوره بلورسك تمام شجاعت ایتمش ارلورس اول زمان قزی سکا ویرز	*Éitdiler ki éyér sana bou áltïnï vérenin báshïnï dakhï kessip ghettiré bilirsin támám shejaat etmish oloursoun ol zeman . kïzï séna veririz*	They said : " If thou canst also cut off the head of *him who gave* thee this gold, and bring it, thou wilt have performed a great piece of bravery, and we will give thee the girl then
بکا ایتدیکك لطف و کرمی بر کمسه برکمسه یه ایتمش دکل در	*Bána etdiyin loutf u kéremi bir kimsé bir kimséyé etmish déil dïr*	The kindness and goodness *which thou hast shown* me, no person has ever shown to another person
حقیقت حاله واقف اولمینلر	*Hákïkát-ï-halé wákïf olmayanlar*	*Those who are not aware* of the true state of the case

---

* Equivalent to our saying, "He fell out of the frying-pan into the fire."

كسيلان باش بر دخى يرينه كلوب صاحبنه خير ايتمز	*Kessilan básh bir dakhï yériné ghelip sahibiné khaïr etmaz*	If a head *which has been cut off* come back again into its place, it does not benefit its owner
زياده‌سیله مال فراوانه مالك ایدی لكن دنیایه اولادی كلمدیكندن غايت محزون القلب اولوب هر راست كلدیكنه سؤال ايدوب درمان اراردى	*Ziyadésilé mál ferawana malik idi lakin dunyayé evladi ghelmadiyinden ghayet mahzoun ul-kálb oloup hér rasst gheldiyiné sual edip derman árardï*	He possessed exceeding great wealth, but no child of his having come into the world he was very sad at heart, and asked *every one whom he met* for a remedy
اصله‌جق ادم صوده بوغلمز	*Asïlajak ádám souda boghoulmaz*	A man *who is to be hanged* is not drowned.

589. Not only are the relative pronoun and the verb expressed by a Turkish participle, but sometimes such prepositions and adverbs as "with," "in," "at," "when," and "where," as well. Example:—

تحصيل علم ايتديكمز مكتب	*Tahsïl-ï-ilm etdiyimiz mekteb*	The school *in which we acquire* knowledge (or acquired knowledge)
كچه‌جكى شهر	*Ghechéjéyi shehir*	The town *through which he will pass*
بر كبچه معهود طاوسك اولدیغى باغچه‌یه كلوب كمند ايله باغچه‌نك ابچنه كيروب طاوسى چیقاردیلر	*Bir ghejé mahoud tawoussoun oldoughou bágchéyé ghelip kémend ilé bágchénin ichiné ghirip tawoussou chïkárdïlar*	One night, coming to the garden *where* (in which) the famous peacock was, and entering the garden with a slip-knot, they took him out
مقدما سویلدیكك زماندہ زياده‌سیله تلاشم اولمغله بر خوشجه دكليه‌مدم ايدى لطف ايدوب بر دخى كل ايله كلدیكى كون	*Moukádemma suwéylédiyin zemandé ziyadésilé telashim olmaghlé bir khoshjé dinléyémadim idi loutf edip bir daha nákl éilé*	At the time *when you told me before*, being greatly alarmed, I could not listen properly. Have the kindness to relate it again
	Gheldiyi ghiun	The day *on which* he came
باباك سویلدیكى او يقلدى	*Bábán suwéylédiyï ev yïkïldï*	The house *which thy father spoke of* has been pulled down.

EXERCISE XXXV.

The news which came to-day is very important (مهم *muhim*). Do you know the name of the town where (in which) he lives? I have forgotten it. Do you remember (در خاطر ايتمك *dér khátïr etmek*) the name of the town where he was born (طوغمق *doghmak*)? Where is the knife with which I cut the meat (ات *et*)? It is on the table. Give it to me. I put it in the cupboard (دولاب *doláb*) where the meat is. What is the name of the garden you were walking (كزمك *ghézmek*) in yesterday? Who is the man you met there (كلمك راست *rásst ghelmek*)? Have the grapes which you ordered (اصمارلمق *ïssmarlamak*) arrived? They came this morning at eight o'clock. Have you found the book you want? The iron-clads (زرهلو كمى *zirhli ghémi*) which were built (انشا اولنمق *insha olounmak*) for the Turkish Government have not left England. They will come to Constantinople in (صكره* *sora*) a few months. The guns (طوب *top*) which came from Prussia (پروسيا *Proussia*) are very good, but they are very dear. Take away (قالدرمق *káldïrmak*) the things which are on the table. Certainly, Sir (باش اوستنه *básh usstuné*). Bring the coffee (قهوه *kahwé*) which I bought (المق *almak*) this morning. Which are the towns that we shall pass through? I will show you on the map (خريطه *kharita* [*harta*]). Thank you (تشكر ايتمك *téshekkiur etmek*). Have you seen the Khan in Constantinople where the Persian (عجمى *ajemi*) merchants live? I went there last year (كچن سنه *ghechen sené*).

THE VERB.

The Position of the Verb in a Sentence.

590. The verb must always be placed at the end of the sentence. Example:—

ديار يمنده بر بازركان	*Diyar·i-yémendé bir*	There *was* a merchant
وار ايدى اسمنه جوهر	*bázirghian var idi issminé*	in the country of Yemen.
شناس ديرلردى دار	*Jevhér-Shinass dérlérdi*	They *called* him Jevhér-
دنياده بر قزندن غيرى	*dar-i-dunyadé bir kïzïn-*	Shinass. He *had* no one
كمسنسى يوق ايدى بر	*dan ghaïri kimséssi yogh*	in the world except one
كون جوهر شناس صحرٱده	*oudou bir ghiun Jevhér-*	daughter of his. One day
كزر كن ناكاه برٱدم باشى	*-Shinass sahrada ghézér*	while walking in the wil-

* See note page 210.

كوردى الينه الوب باقدى

بر قاچ كون صبر ايدەلم

خدمدن برى شاهزادەيه بو قز هند پادشاهلرندن فلان پادشاهك قزيدر ديدى شاهزاده اولساعت* دونوپ باباسنه نقل ايلدى اكر پادشاهه خبر كوندروپ قزينى بكا اليويرمزسك كندى كنديمى هـلاك ايدرم ديدى

اول غلام اول طفل بيكناهى بوغازليوپ قاننى مرحومەنك جامەسنه بولشدردى و قانلى بچاغى مرحومەنك ياصدىغى التنه قودى

بيــروت واپــورى يازيجيسى فلان ايله بر قطعه مكتوبكرى الدم و پك فرحلندم و كوندردككز شام فستغى وصول بولدى و پك خوشلندم افندم برادرم بر كوفه قاوون يازيجى مرسوم ايله أرسال ايتدم قبول ايدەرك خبرينى بزه اشعار بيورەسز افندم

---

iken na-ghiah bir ádám báshi ghieurdu eliné álíp bákdí

Bir kach ghiun sábr edélim

Khademden biri shah-zadéyé bou kíz hind padi-shahlerinden filán padi-shahin kízí dír dédi shah-zadé ol saat deunup bábá-sina nákl éilédi éyer pa-dishaha kháber ghieun-derip kízíní bána álíver--mazsin kendi kendimi helak ederim dédi

Ol ghoulam ol tifl bi-ghiunahi bogházlayíp ká-níní Merhouménin jamé-siné boulashdirdi vé kánlí bíchághí · Merhouménin yassdíghí áltíné kodou

Béirout vaporou yazí-jíssí filán ilé bir kíta mektoubounouzou áldím vé pek férahlendem vé ghieundérdiyiniz sham físstíghí vusoul bouldou vé pek khoshlandam, ef-fendin, beradérim bir kiufé kawoun yazíjí mer-soum ilé irsal etdim káboul edérek khábberini bizé ishiar bouyourasiz effen-dim

---

derness, he suddenly *saw* a man's head, and, taking it up in his hand, he *looked* at it

Let us have patience for a few days

One of the servants *said* to the prince: "This girl is the daughter of king So-and-so, one of the kings of India." The prince imme-diately returned and *told* his father, and *said:* "If you do not send word to the king and obtain his daugh-ter for me I *will destroy* myself"

That slave boy cut the throat of the innocent child and *smeared* Merhoumé's clothes with the blood, and *put* the bloody knife under Merhoumé's pillow

I *have received* a letter of yours by So-and-so, the clerk of the Beyrout steamer, and I was much delighted; and the Syrian · pistachio nuts *have arrived* which you sent, and I was much pleased. I *have sent* you, my (dear) brother, a basket of melons by the aforemen-tioned clerk. Please *condes-cend to accept* them and to send me word about them.

---

* Sometimes written thus instead of ساعت اول.

The Agreement of the Verb with the Nominative.

591. In general the verb must agree with its nominative in number and person, but sometimes when the nominative is in the third person plural the verb is put in the third person singular. Example:—

پس دهقان اوياندیغی کیی قویننده جوهری بولهمیوب بلدیکه سیاحلر المشدر	*Pess dihkan ouyandighi ghibi koïnïnda jevhéribou- lamayïp bildi ki séyyah- ler álmïshdïr*	Then the peasant, as soon as he woke, not being able to find the jewel in his breast pocket knew that the *travellers* had *taken* it
اول کلعذار دخی ارزوی سیر کلزار ایدوب بر قاچ جاریهلر ایله واروب بر درخت سایهدارك التده نظر قرار ایلدی اطرافه نظر ایدر کن مبارك کوزلری بر کله راست کلدیکه سرو سرکشی کیی باش چکوب جملهدن ممتاز و بهجت حسنله سر افراز اولمش	*Ol ghiulizar dakhï ar- zouyi séir-i-ghiulzar edip bir kach jariyéler ilé varip bir dirakht-i-sayédarin áltïnda kárar éilédi. Et- rafé názar edér iken mu- barek ghieuzléri bir ghiulé rásst gheldi ki serv-i-sér- keshi ghibi básh chekip jumléden mumtaz vé beh- jet hussnlé sér efraz ol- moush*	That rosy-cheeked (dam- sel) also wishing to walk in the rose-garden came with a few of her slave-women and sat down under a shady tree. Whilst looking around her sacred *eyes fell* on a rose, which holding its head like a proud cypress tree was distinguished above all, and gloried in its beauty
کذبلری ظاهر اولوب یوزلری قره اولدی	*Kezbleri zahir oloup yuzleri kára oldou*	Their lies becoming manifest, their *faces be- came* black*
چوجقلر درسلرینی اوقوسون	*Chojouklar dersslerini okousoun*	Let the *children read* their lesson
دوستلرمز کلمیه جك	*Dosstlérimiz ghelméyé- jek.*	Our *friends will not come.*

592. If the nominative, however, in the third person plural, is understood, the verb must be in the third person plural, as otherwise the sense would not be clear. Example:—

اول پادشاهك بر عاقل و دانا وزیری وار ایدی ادینه کامبین دیرلردی	*Ol padishahin bir ákïl ou dana véziri var idi adiné Kiambin dérlerdi*	That king had a sensible and wise vizier. *They called* him Kiambin

---

* A Turkish idiomatic way of saying that they were disgraced.

(Ottoman Turkish)	*Zeman - i - evveldé bir*	In olden times an indi-
زمان اوّلده بر شخص	*shakhss nissf - ul - léildé*	vidual used to leave his
نصف الليلده خانه‌سندن	*khanésinden táshra chĭkĭp*	home at midnight and walk
طشره چیقوب کیجه ایله	*ghejé ilé shehirin ichindé*	about the city by night.
شهرك ایچنده کزردی	*ghézérdi na-ghiah bir*	Suddenly one night one of
ناکاه بر کیجه احباسندن	*ghejé ahibbasinden birissi*	his friends met him, and
بریسی قارشوسنه کلوب	*karshĭsina ghelip ashinalik*	before saluting him began
آشنالق ایتمزدن مقدم	*etmazden moukáddem seni*	blaming and reproaching
سنی خانه‌کدن قوغدیلرمی	*khanénden koghdoularmi*	him, saying : " *Have they*
بویله بیوقت کیجه	*beuilé biwakĭt ghejé ichin-*	*turned thee out* of thy house
ایچنده دیوانه کبی یالكز	*dé diwané ghibi yaliniz*	(that) thou walkest about
چارشو و بازارده کزرسن	*charshĭ vé bazardé ghézer-*	alone at an untimely hour
دیو طعن و تشنیع ایتمکه	*sin déyou tan u teshni*	by night like a madman in
باشلادی	*etméyé báshladĭ?*	the streets and markets ? "

A Verb with several Nominatives.

593. If a verb has several nominatives, which are all expressed and are all in the third person, the verb may be in the third person singular, even if one or more of the nominatives be in the plural.   Example :—

باباك و اناك ازمیره کتدی	*Bábán vé ánan Ez-miré ghitdi*	Thy father and mother *have gone* to Smyrna
کوناکون تحف و هدایالر کلوب طاغلر کبی یغلدی	*Ghiunaghium tuhéf u hedayalér ghelip dághlar ghibi yĭghĭldĭ*	All kinds of *presents* and *gifts* came and *were heaped up* like mountains
اول جزیره نك میشه‌لکنده بر عظیم ارسلان توطن ایدوب اول حوالینك سباع و بهایمی کندویه رام اولمشیدی	*Ol jézirénin méishéli-yindé bir ázĭm arsslan téwattun edip ol hawa-linin sebba vu bahaïmi kendouyé ram olmoush oudou*	A large lion had taken up his abode in an oak forest of that island and the *wild animals* and *beasts of prey* of that neighbourhood *had become* obedient to him.

594. When a verb has several nominatives, one in the second and others in the third person, singular and plural, the verb must be in the second person plural.

سن و دوستتك و اوشاغك اوچكز سویلدكز	*Sen vé dosstoun vé oushághĭn uchunuz su-wéylédiniz*	Thou and thy *friend* and thy *servant*, all three of you, *said* it.

595. If a verb have several nominatives and one of them be in the first person, singular or plural, the verb must be in the first person plural. Example :—

بن و قرنداشم پك سوندك	*Ben vé karndashim pek sevindik.*	I and my brother were very glad.

The Use of the Auxiliary Verb.

596. An auxiliary Turkish verb applying to two or more Arabic or Persian words is not repeated. Example :—

بيام عافيت وصحتلرى ثناكارلرينى فرحان بيورملرى تمناسنده شقه تحرير و تسيير قلندى

Péyam-i-afiyetu-sïhatleri senakiarlerini férhan bouyourmalari témennasindé shoukka tahrir u tessyir kïlïndï

The (this) letter *was written* and *sent* to request you to gladden your humble servant with tidings of your health and freedom from sickness ,

ارسال بيوردقلرى ايكى كوفه قاون هديهكز وصول بولهرق پك ممنون و محظوظ اولدم

Irsal bouyourdouklarï iki kiuffé kawoun hédiyéniz vusoul boularak pek memnoun-ou-mahzouz oldoum

Your present of two baskets of melons arriving, I *was* very *pleased* and *delighted*

پس مختار اول مزارك يانه كلوب مرور و عبور ايدن مسلمين و مسلماتدن ديلنوردى

PessMukhtarolmezarin yaniné ghelip murour-ou-oubour eden Musslimin vé musslimatden dilenirdi

Then Mukhtar came near that burying-ground and begged from the male and female Muslims who *passed*

ايتديكى ايشه توبه و استغفار ايتدى

Etdiyi ishé teubé vu isstighfar etdi

He *repented* of the act he had done and *asked pardon* (of God)

زبان تركيى اوقومقده ايلرو كيتديكمدن حظ و افتخار ايتملرى مأمولنده

Zebán-i-turkiyi okoumakda iléri ghitdiyimden ház ou iftikhar etmaleri mémoulïnda

In the hope that you *will be glad* and *proud* of my having progressed in the study of the Turkish language

لايق دكل در كه جميع عمريكى عورتكله كچورهسن بارى كوندز كار و كسب ايله

Layïk déyil dir ki jémi eumrunu avretinlé ghechirésin bari ghiunduz kiar-ou-kessb éilé

It is not proper that thou shouldst pass all thy life with thy wife. At any rate, in the day *work* and *earn*

شاه بهواجك انسانيتنه و لطف و مروتنه تحسين و افرين ايدرم	Shah Behvajin insani- yeté vé loutf ou muru- vetiné tahsin ou aferin ederim	I *admire and applaud* Shah Behvaj's kindness and his goodness and gra- ciousness
تقصيراتنه باقميوب هم *بورجني ادا و هم زيادهسيله احسان ايتدى	Táksïratina bákmayïp hem borjounou éda vé hem ziyadésilé ihsan etdi	Not considering his de- fects, he both *paid* his debt and *made* him very many *presents*
عازمك صحبتندن فارغ اولميوب دائما لطيفه و صحبت و انعام بغايت ايدر ايدى	Azimin suhbetinden fa- righ olmayip da'ima la- tifé vé suhbet vé inam bé ghayet edér idi	He did not give up the society of Azim and always *joked* and *associated* with him and *bestowed* many favours on him.

The Omission of در *dir*.

597. In talking the verb در *dir* (is) is very often left out. Example :—

كيفى يرنده	Kéifi yérindé	He (is) in good health
هوا سيجاق	Hawa sïják	The weather (is) hot
روزكار يوق	Rouzghiar yok	There (is) no wind
اقندى وار مى	Akïndï var mi ?	(Is) there any current ?
بو كون جمعه	Bou ghiun juma	To-day (is) Friday
كيفك ايو مى	Kéifin éi mi ?	(Is) thy health good ?
كوپريدنمى كچهلم يوخسه قايقله قارشويه كچهلم	Kieuprudenmi ghéché- lim yokhsa káïghla kar- shïya ghechélim ?	Shall we pass ovér the bridge or go over in a boat?
كوپرى دها ايو قايق تهلكهلو در	Kieupru daha éi káïk téhlikéli dir	The bridge (is) best. A boat (is) dangerous.

598. But when repeating the words of another person در must not be omitted, unless the sentence quoted be interrogative.

The Verb of Facility.

599. By adding the verb ويرمك *vérmek* to the root of any verb another verb is formed which expresses doing the same action, but in a very off-hand way. This verb is termed the verb of facility. If the root of the original

---

* Sometimes written thus in old books instead of بورجنى.

verb end in a consonant it takes a vowel ﺱ after it, and if it end in a vowel the syllable ﯼ must be added to it. Thus we have ﯾﺎﭘﯿﻮﺭﻣﻚ *yapivérmek* (to make or do with ease), ﺳﻮﯾﻠﻪﯾﯿﻮﺭﻣﻚ *suwéyléyivérmek* (merely to say, just to say), ﺑﺎﻗﯿﻮﺭﻣﻚ *bakivérmek* (just to look), ﯾﻮﺭﻭﯾﯿﻮﺭﻣﻚ *yuruyu-vérmek* (just to walk), ﮔﻠﯿﻮﺭﻣﻚ *ghelivérmek* (to come quickly), ﺑﻮﻟﯿﻮﺭﻣﻚ *boulouvérmek* (to find quickly). Example:—

ﺑﺎﻗﯿﻮﯾﺮ	*Bắkĭvér*	Just look
ﺳﻦ ﺗﺮﻙ ﺩﯾﺎﺭ ﺍﯾﺪﺭﺳﻦ	*Sen terk-i-diyar edérsin*	If you leave the country
ﺑﻦ ﺳﻨﻰ ﯾﺎﻟﻜﺰ ﻗﯿﻮﯾﺮﻣﻢ	*ben seni yalĭnĭz koyouvér-*	I shall not just let you go
ﺍﻟﺒﺘﻪ ﺑﻨﺪﺧﻰ ﺑﯿﻠﻪ ﻛﺘﻤﻠﻮﯾﻢ	*mam elbetté ben dakhĭ bilé*	alone. Of course, I also
	ghitméliyim	must even go too
ﺑﻦ ﺳﻨﻚ ﻛﻨﺪﻯ ﻗﻮﻟﻜﻢ	*Ben senin kendi koulou-*	I am thy own servant,
ﻗﺰﯾﻢ ﺩﺧﻰ ﺟﺎﺭﯾﻪﻛﺪﺭ	*noum kĭzĭm dakhĭ jariyén*	my daughter also is thy
ﻫﻤﺎﻥ ﻧﻪ ﻛﻮﻧﻪ ﻣﺮﺍﺩ	*dir heman né ghiuné mou-*	slave. Just marry her this
ﺷﺮﯾﻔﻜﺰ ﺍﻭﻟﻮﺭﺳﻪ ﻧﻜﺎﺡ	*rad-i-sherifiniz oloursa*	minute, in any way thou
ﺍﯾﺪﯾﻮﯾﺮﻚ	*nikiah edivérin*	pleaseth.

The Position of an Emphasized Word.

600. The word which one wishes to give prominence to is put as near the verb as possible. Example:—

ﺩﻭﻥ ﭘﺎﺩﺷﺎﻩ ﻋﺰﯾﻤﺖ ﺍﯾﺘﺪﻯ	*Dun padishah azimet etdi*	The king started yester-day
ﭘﺎﺩﺷﺎﻩ ﺩﻭﻥ ﻋﺰﯾﻤﺖ ﺍﯾﺘﺪﻯ	*Padishah dun azimet etdi*	The king started yester-day
ﺩﻭﻥ ﻛﺎﺗﺐ ﻣﻜﺘﻮﺑﻰ ﯾﺎﺯﺩﻯ	*Dun kiatib mektoubou yazdĭ*	Yesterday the clerk wrote the *letter*
ﻣﻜﺘﻮﺑﻰ ﻛﺎﺗﺐ ﺩﻭﻥ ﯾﺎﺯﺩﻯ	*Mektoubou kiatib dun yazdĭ*	The clerk wrote the letter *yesterday*.

The Conditional* Mood.

601. After the words ﻫﺮ ﻧﻘﺪﺭ *hér nékádar* (although), ﻫﺮ ﻧﻪ *hér né* (whatever), ﻫﺮ ﻗﻨﻐﻰ *hér kánghĭ* (whichever), ﻧﻪ ﺯﻣﺎﻥ *né zemán* and ﻧﻪ ﻭﻗﺖ *né wákĭt* (when), ﻫﺮ ﻧﻪ ﺯﻣﺎﻥ *hér né zemán* and ﻫﺮ ﻧﻪ ﻭﻗﺖ *hér né wákĭt* (when-ever), ﺍﻛﺮ *éyér* (if), ﺍﻛﺮﭼﻪ *éyérchi* and ﻛﺮﭼﻪ *yérchi* (although), ﻓﺮﺿﺎ *faraza*

---

* The conditional corresponds to what is called in European grammars the subjunctive.

and كه طوتهلم *tutalim ki* (supposing that), and كيم *kim* and نه *né* (not used interrogatively) the verb is put in the conditional. قنغى *kánghǐ* (which) when followed by the pronominal affixes س, كز, مز, and not used in an interrogative sentence, also requires the verb which follows it to be in the conditional. Example :—

* قنغيسى كلورسهدٖ كلسون	*Kánghǐssǐ ghelirsé ghelsin*	Whichever of them *may come*, let him come
وزير عاصم موكللرٖ تنبيه ايتمش ايديكه كلفشان نه سويلرسه و نه كونه حركت ايدرسه بكا افادٖ ايدك و وزيرك دخى نقدر شىء معلومى اولورسه پادشاهه افادٖ ايتمك مرادى ايدى	*Vézir Asim muvékkéleré tenbih etmish idiki Ghiulfishan né suvéylérse vé né ghiuné héréket edérsé bána ifadé eden vé vézirin dakhǐ nékádar shéi maloumou ouursapadishaha ifadé etmek mouradi idi*	Vizier Asim had directed the agents (saying) "Let me know *what* Ghiulfishan says and *how* he behaves;" and it was also the vizier's intention to communicate to the king *whatever* things came to his knowledge
هر كيم قوپاررسه بندن نه مقصودى وار ايسه حاصل ايدرم	*Hér kim koparǐrsa benden né maksoudou var issé hássǐl ederim*	*Whoever plucks it* (the flower) *whatever* he *may desire* of me I will grant it
اول شيخِ كامل انلرٖ مرحمت ايدوب و بر وافر مراقبهدهنصكرٖ قوينندن درت دانه مهر چيقاردى و بو مهرلردن هر بريكز بر دانهسنى باشكزٖ ديككز هر نه محلدٖ باشكزدن دوشرايسه اول موضعى قازٖسز هر كسك مهرى دوشديكى يردٖ نصيبى موجود در و اكر بريكزك نصيبنه كندو رضاكريكز ايله ايكيكز ياخود ديكريكز اشتراكيله قناعت ايدرسكز اول	*Ol shéikh-i-kiamil onlara merhamet edip vé bir wafir murakebéden sora koïninden deurt tané muhur chǐkardǐ vé bou muhurlerden hér biriniz bir tanéssini báshǐnǐza dikiniz hér né mahaldé báshǐnǐzdan dushurissé ol mevzǐï kázésǐz hér kessin muhuru dushduyu yérdé nássǐbǐ mevjoud dour vé éyér birinizin nássǐbǐna kendou rizaleriniz ilé ikiniz yakhod dighéri-*	That good sheikh having pity on them after long meditation took out four seals from his breast and said: "Each of you take one of these seals and set it on your head. *In whatever* place it *falls* from your head, dig up that place : in the place where each one's seal falls, his lot (fate) is there. And, *if* two of you or others of you, by your own free will in common are satisfied with what

---

* These pronouns which govern the conditional of the verb generally take دٖ *dé* (also) after the verb.

دخی جائز در و اكر هر برمز كندیمزه مخصوص نصیبمزى استرز دیرسكز هر كسه مخصوص مهر هر قنده دوشرسه اول محلى قازمق كرك در دیدی	niz ishtirak ilé kánaét edérsiniz ol dakhï ja'iz dir vé éyér hér birimiz kendimizé makhsouss nás-sïbïmïzï issteriz dérséniz hér kessé makhsouss mu-hur hér kandé dushursé ol mahali kázmak gherek dir dédi	falls to the lot of one of you, there is no objection. And if you all say each one of us wants specially what falls to each of us, you must dig up the place *wherever* each one's special seal falls "
اما ایرتسی كون طاوسك ضایع اولدیغی پادشاهك معلومى اولدیغى كبى ارانمسى ایچون امر ایلدی و هر كیم طاوسى بولسه یاخود حیات و مماتندن خبر ویرسه بیك آلتون مژدكانه ویرم دیو وعد ایلدی	Ama irtéssi ghiun tawoussoun zayï oldou-ghou padishahin malou-mou oldoughou ghibi áranmassi ichin emr éïlédi vé hér kim tawous-sou boulsa yakhod hayat vé mématinden kháber versé bin altïn muzhdé-ghiané vérerim déyou vad éïlédi	But the following day, as soon as it came to the knowledge of the king that the peacock was lost, he gave orders for its being looked for, and made a promise, saying : " *Who-ever* shall find the peacock, or give information respect-ing its being alive or dead, I will give (him) a thousand gold pieces " as the bearer of good tidings
اكر ادڭ شریفكز اولورسه	Éyér izn-i-sherifïniz oloursa	*If* you *give* your (noble) permission
اكر انلرك سعى و همتى اولمسیدى عاقبت هلاك اولمسى امر مقرر ایدى	Éyér anlerin saï vu himmeti olmasaydï akibet tamainden helak olmassi emr mukarrér idi	*If* they had not *striven* and *used their influence* for him, his destruction would have been certain, owing to his avarice
قسمت ازلیه هر نه ایسه اكا راضى ایم	Kissmet-i-ézeliyé hér né issé ana rázï yim	Eternal fate—*whatever* it may be—I am satisfied with it
اكر سن كندى كرمكدن بكا مرحمت ایدوب هر نه لایق كوررسك اكا راضیم فرضا بنى بو حبسدن ازاد ایلیوب صالى ویریدك	Éyér sen kendi kere-minden bána merhamet edip hér né layïk gheurur-sén ana rázïyim faraza béni bou habssden azad	*If* thou *hast pity* on me, I shall be satisfied with *anything* you *think* proper. *Supposing* (for instance) you *liberate* me from this prison,

بن دخى وأروب هميجنسم
و اقرانم ايله بستانلرده
كزوب ينه سنك خدمتكه
كلسم جهان جهان ممنون
و خندان اولوردم

éiléyip sálĭ vérsén ben dakhĭ varip hemjinssim vé ákranim ilé bosstanlerdé ghézip yiné senin hizmetiné ghelsém jihan jihan memnoun ou khanédan olourdoum

and I go and roam in the gardens with my fellows and companions, and then *come* back into thy service, I should be extremely obliged and delighted

و نقدر اسراف و اتلاف
دخى اولورسه ينه مالنه
هيچ نقصان كلمز

Vé né kádar issraf u itilaf dakhĭ oloursa yiné málina hich noksan ghelmaz

And however much extravagance and waste there may be, yet there is never any deficiency in his wealth

هر كيم يقين كلورسه
اكر بو قز بكا نصيب
اولورسه   كنديمى
بتخانه نك   ايچنده
قربان ايده يم

Hér kim yakĭn ghelirsé Éyér bou kĭz bána nássĭb oloursa kendimi poutkhanénin ichidé kourbán edéyim

Whoever comes near *If* this girl *fall* to my lot, I will sacrifice myself in the temple

بو حادثه بندن صادر
اولمامش . . . . . هر نقدر
سزلر بندن صادر اولدى
صانديكر ايسه

Bou hadissé benden sádĭr olmamoush . . . . . her né kádar sizler benden sádĭr oldou sandiniz issé

This calamity did not emanate from me . . . . . *although* you *imagined* it did emanate from me

هر نه وقت طلب
بيورلورايسه حضوركده حاضر
ايز شمدى اذنكز ايله
كتمك استرز

Hér né wákĭt taleb bouyouroulouroussa huzourounda házĭr ĭz shindi izniniz ilé ghitmek issteriz

Whenever it is required, we shall be ready in your presence. Now, with your permission, we wish to go.

The Optative.

602. Words which express a wish, such as كاشكى كاشكه *kiashki* (*keshki*) (would that), اللّه ويرسون *álláh versin*, اللّه ويرسونكه *álláh versinki*, and اللّه ويره *álláh veré* (God grant that), اللّه ويربدى *álláh veréydi* (would to God that), require the verb which follows to be in the optative. The expression تا كه *ta ki* (in order that) also takes the optative after it. Example:—

بن محبوبمى تجربه
ايتمزدن مقدم سن بكا

Ben mahbouboumou tejribé etmezden moukáddem

Before I put my lover to the test, explain (it) to me,

بیان ایله تاکه بندخی انی تجربه ایدهیم	sen bána béyan éilé taki ben dakhï onou tejribé édéyim	in order that I may try him
کاشکی بونده اولمش اوله ایدی	Keshki bundé olmoush olaydi!	Would that he had been here!
کور تاکه جانکی خلاص ایدهسن	Ghiur taki jánïnï khalass edésin	See (take care) that thou savest thy life
قفسده بر جفت قمری وار ایدی دیشی قمری ارکگنه دیدی کاشکی بنم دخی المده صندال و کلاب اولیدی سنک ایاغنه یوز سورر و دوکردم	Kéfessdé bir chift koumrou var idi dishi koumrou erkéyiné dédi ki keshki benïm dakhï elimdé sándál vé ghiuláb olaydi senin ayaghiné yuz surér vé deukérdim	There were a couple of doves in a cage. The female dove said to her mate: "Oh that I also had sandal wood and rose water: I would rub my face against your foot and pour them out."

603. A word which expresses a wish, an order, a request, an intention, doubt or astonishment, followed by "that" expressed or understood, generally requires the verb which follows and depends on it to be in the optative. Example:—

سکا نصیحتم بو در که شمدیلك مراده نائل اولوب ذوق وصفا ایدهسن	Sana nássïhatim bou dour ki shindilik muradé na'il oloup zevk u sáfa edésin	My advice to thee is that thou shouldst now attain thy wish and enjoy thyself
استمم کـه طورهسن شمدیکی حالده بیورك بعده بر وقت واسعده سویلرم	Isstémem ki dourasïn shindiki haldé bouyouroun badéhou bir wákït vasïdé suwéylerim	I do not wish you to stop. Go now, and by-and-by when we have plenty of time I will tell you
اویله جزم ایتدمکه بو شهردن قالقوب آخر ولایته کیدهایم	Euilé jezm etdim ki bou shehirden kálkip akhïr vilayeté ghidéyim	I have resolved that I will leave this city and go to another country
سزلردن رجا ایدرم که معرفتلریکزی اظهار ایدوب قزم زهرهنك قنده ایدوکرن* بکا اعلام ایدهسز دیدی	Sizlerden rija ederim ki marifetlerinizi izhar edip kïzïm Zuhrénin kandé eduyunu bána ilam edésiz dédi	He said: "I beg of you to show your skill and let me know where my daughter Zuhré is"
جاوش صحت خابه†	Chaoush sïhat khábe-	The sergeant getting

---

* Sometimes thus written instead of ايدوكنی.

† Sometimes thus written instead of خبرينی.

الوب مراد ايتديكه كيرو
دونه

ايتدى بلكه بو مقامده
ارسلان اولميه فرضا
ارسلانك اولديغى صورتده
دخى لطف حتى ايله
كتديكى يرده بر حادثه يه
اوغرامش اوله بلكه كلميه
و كلديكى صورتده دخى
بر حيله ايله الندن خلاص
اولمق ممكن در

*rini álïp murad etdi ki
ghéri deuné*

*Éitdi belki bou mekám-
dé arsslan olmaya faraza
arsslanin oldoughou sou-
retdé dakhï loutf-i-hák ilé
ghitdiyi yérdé bir hadiss-
éyé oghramish ola belki
ghelméyé vé gheldiyi souretdé dakhï bir hilé ilé elin-
den khalass olmak mumkïn
dir*

news of the truth *intended
to turn* back

He said : "*Perhaps there
may* be no lion in the place,
and also supposing there be,
by the favour of God, he
may have met with an accident where he has gone.
Perhaps he may not come,
and, in case he does come, it
is possible to escape from
him by some *ruse*"

The Optative used for the Imperative.

604. The optative is often used instead of the imperative, and the
imperative for the optative also. Example :—

بو كون اشتدم كه
وجودكزه صتمه خسته لغى
عارض اولمش الله بلور
كه كندو وجودمده اولمش
قدر كدر ايتدم همان
جناب اللـه وجودكزه
عافيت احسان بيورسون
آمين افندم ساعتده
ايكى دانه يمك ايچون
اون ايكى دانه حب
كوندردم وجودكزده
صيجاقلق اولمديغى وقتده
يهسكز افندم

*Bou ghiun ishïtdim ki
vujoudounouza sïtma
khásstalïghï ariz olmoush
állàh bilir ki kendi vujou-
doumda olmoush kádar ké-
dér etdim heman jenab ál-
láh vujoudounouza afiyet
ihsan bouyoursoun Amin
Effendim saatdé iki tané
yémek ichin on iki tané
hap ghieunderdim vujou-
dounouzda sïjáklïk olma-
doughou wákïtda yéyé-
siniz effendim*

I have heard to-day that
you have been attacked by
fever. God knows that I am
as sorry as if I were attacked.
God grant you health Sir.
I have sent you twelve pills,
two be taken every hour.
Take (eat) them when there
is no heat in the body

واپور تذكره سنى دخى
لفا كوندردم واپور
مغازه سندن آلوب
خانه كزده حفظ ايده سز

*Vapor tezkerésini dak-
hï lefan ghieunderdim
vapor maghazasindan álip
khanénizdé hifz edésiz*

I have also sent the
ticket for the steamer, en-
closed. Get it from the
office of the steamer and
keep it in your house

بو قولكزى صاغلق خبركز ايله مسرور بيوره‌سز	*Bou koulounouzou saghlïk khâbrïniz ilé messrour bouyourasïz*	*Make* your servant (me) delighted by tidings of your health
بر كوفه قاون ارسال ايتدم قبول ايده‌رك خبرينى بزله اشعار بيوره‌سز	*Bir kiufé kawoun irsal etdim kâboul edérek khâberini bizleré ishiar bouyourasïz*	I have sent (you) a basket of melons. Please accept them, and *let me hear* about them
شقه‌مزك وصولنده هر حالده اوچ سپد افيون الوب طرفمزه ارسال ايده‌سز و اهمال ايتميسز زيرا بو طرفده فلان اغا ايله قونطوراتو ايتدم	*Shoukkamizin* vusoulounda hér haldé uch séped afyon âlip tarafimizé irsal edésiz vé ihmal etméyésiz zira bou tarafdé filân âghâ ilé kontrato etdim*	On the arrival of my note, send me three baskets of opium, without fail, and do not neglect (it), for I have made a contract with Mr. So-and-so

✝ غروش ٥٠٠٠ يالكز بشبيك غروش	*Ghroush* 5,000 *Yalïnïz besh bin ghroush*	Piastres 5,000 Only five thousand piastres

استانبولده شريكمز فلان اغا	*Istanbolda sherikimiz filân âghâ*	Mr. So-and-so, our partner in Constantinople
اشبو پوليچه‌مزى كورديككزده قبول ايده‌رك ناطق اولديغى يالكز بشبيك غروشى بش كون وعده‌سى دخولنده فلان كمسنه‌يه بلا اذا اعطا ايده‌رك پوليچه‌مزى خلاص ايده‌سز	*Ishbou polichamizi ghieurduyunuzdé kâboul edérek nâtïk oldoughou yalïnïz besh bin ghroushou besh ghiun vadéssi dukhoulinda filân kimessnéyé bila ‡éza ita edérek polichamizi khalass edésiz*	On your seeing this bill of exchange of mine, accept it, and on its becoming due, after the term of five days, pay the five thousand piastres it speaks of to Mr. So-and-so, without giving any trouble,‡ and *save* (honour) my bill.

---

* The Turks often say " our " when they mean " my."

✝ The above is a copy of a Turkish bill of exchange.

‡ The word اذا *éza* literally means " molestation," but here it is used to signify that the writer wishes his partner to pay without giving the person to whom the bill is payable any trouble or bother.

The Optative Used for the Conditional.

605. The optative is very often used instead of the conditional and the conditional instead of the optative.

هر نه وقت بر كمسه
جد و جهد ايله بزم
دامنمزى طوته بز انك
تقيدنى ضايع ايتميوب
بهر حال انى مقصودنه
ايرشديريرز

Hér né wâkït bir kimsé jed - u - jehd ilé bizim damenimizi touta biz onoun tékayudunu zayï etméyip béhér hal onou maksoudouna erishdirirz

Whenever any one strenuously strives to take hold of our garment, we do not let his care be in vain, but without fail cause him to attain his wishes

بو مرضدن بكا خلاص
يوق در اكر خلاص اوليدم
سكا انواع احسان ايدردم
لكن وفاتمدن صكره وارث
سلطنتم اولان كمسنه سنى
البته قتل ايتمسى امر
مقرر در

Bou marazden bana khalass yok dour éyér khalass olaydim sana envaï ihsan edérdim lakin vefatimden sora variss-i-sâltanâtim olân kimessné seni elbetté kâtl etmassi emr mukarrér dir

There is no saving me from this illness. *If I were saved* I would bestow all kinds of things on thee; but after my death it is quite certain, of course, that the person who is heir to my authority will kill you

بو حادثه بندن صادر
اولمامش در اكر بندن
صادر اوليدى اقرار ايدوب
بو بيتله اعتذار ايدردم

Bou hadissé benden sâdïr olmamïsh dïr éyér benden sâdïr olaydi ikrar edip bou béitlé itizar edérdim

This accident did not emanate from me. *If it had emanated* from me, I would have confessed it, and excused myself with the verse—

كامجوى دخى ريا
طريقنه كتممش اوليدى
بو بلايه كرفتار اولمزدى

Kiamjouï dakhï riya tarikiné ghitmamish olaydi bou belayé ghiriftar olmazdi

If Kiamjoui *had not gone* into the path of hypocrisy, he would not have met with this calamity.

كرك *gherek.*

606. در كرك *gherek dir* (it is necessary), which corresponds to the French expression *il faut*, requires the verb to which it refers to be in the conditional or optative.

بندخى اولسم كرك در

Ben dakhï eulsém gherek dir

I also *must* die

اوغلم بركيجه خانه نك

Oghloum bir ghejé

One night my son dis-

ایچندن غایب اولدی بو	khanénin ichinden kai‘b*	appeared from the house.
قدر زماندر ارادم اصلا نام	oldou bou kádar zemán-	I have been looking for him
و نشاننی بولمدم شمدی	dir áradĭm ássla nam	for a long time, but have
دخی طشرویه ارامغه كتسم	u nishánĭnĭ boulmadoum	never found any trace of
كرك در	shindi dakhĭ táshraya	him. I *must* now *go* and
	áramagha ghitsém gherek	seek him also in the pro-
	dir	vinces.

The Past and Present Optative when used.

607. If a verb depend on another verb which requires the optative after it, if the first verb be in the present or future tense, the second must be in the present of the optative, and if the first verb be in the past tense, the second must be in the past optative. Example :—

استرم كه يابەسن†	Issterim ki yapésin	I *wish* thee *to do it*
استدم كه يابەايدی	Isstédim ki yapéydi	I *wished* that he *should do it* (or, I wished him to do it).

The Optative used Interrogatively.

608. The optative is sometimes used interrogatively instead of the future indicative. Example :—

يازەيم ‡	Yazéyim ?	Shall I write ?
چارشویه كیدەلمی	Charshĭya ghidélimmi ?	Shall we go to the market ?
اما يارين بهزادە نه	Ama yarĭn Behzadé né	But what answer shall I
جواب ويرەيم	jawáb véréyim ?	give to Behzad to-morrow ?
بن نه ديەيم	Ben né déyéyim ?	What shall I say ?
نیجه صبر ايدەيم	Nijé sábr edéyim ?	How shall I have pa- tience ?
معقول اولن ينه اول	Makoul oldn yiné ol	What is advisable, how-
طفلی تجربه ايتمكدر اما	tifli tejribé etmek dir ama	ever, is to test that child ;

---

* Written *gha'ib*, but usually pronounced *kai‘b* by the Turks.

† Such sentences as these do occur in Turkish, but it is more elegant to use the declinable participles instead of كه, &c.

‡ Of course such sentences as these are elliptical, and really means, "Do you wish *that* I may *write* ?" "Do you wish that we may go ?" &c.

| نه وجهله تجربه ايدهلم | *né véjhlé tejribé edélim ?* | but in what way shall we test him ? |

The use of the word ديو *déyou* or *déyé.*

609. When one verb follows another on which it depends and with which it is connected by "that" expressed or understood, the use of the relative pronoun كه *ki* between them is frequently avoided by employing the word ديو *déyou* (saying). Very often, also, the infinitive of the verb in English is rendered by introducing this word.

قاضى به:ادك بورننى كسيكز ديو حكم ايتدى	*Kázï Behzadin bourou-nounou kessiniz déyou hukm etdi*	The Kazi decreed that they should cut off Behzad's nose (literally, the Kazi gave judgment, saying: "Cut off Behzad's nose")
مدت عمرمده بويله سركش عورت كورمدم ديو سويلدى	*Muddet - i - eumrumdé beuilé serkesh avret ghieurmadim déyou suvéylédi*	She told (him) that she* had never in all her life seen such a haughty woman
فرعى دخى خواجه منصوزك يقاسنه يابشوب سن بنم خانهمده نه كزرسن و نه ايشك وار در ديوب بربر ايله عظيم مجادله ايتديلر	*Feri dakhï Khoja Man-souroun yakasina yapïshïp sen benim khanémdé né ghézérsen vé né ishin var déyip bir bir ilé ázïm majadelé etdilér*	Feri also collared Khoja Mansour, and *asked him why he was walking* about his house, and what business he had there? and a great quarrel arose between them
هر بريكز خاتونمدر ديو دعوا ايدرسكز	*Hér biriniz khátounoum dour déyou dava edérsiniz*	Each of you maintains that she is your wife
كرم ايله بزى خدمتكه قبول ايله ديو نياز ايتملريله فرخ بنت باباسنك امكدارلرندن ظن ايدوب قبول ايلدى	*Kérem ilé bizi hiz-metiné káboul éilé déyou niaz etmalerilé Ferroukh Bakht bábásïnïn émek-darlerinden zan edip káboul éilédi*	On their *asking him to* kindly admit them into his service, Ferrukh Bakht accepted them, thinking they were his father's old servants

---

* Notice that in Turkish, in such sentences as this, the words of the speaker are repeated as spoken in the first person.

بر کون صو کنارنده اوتوررکن پرماغندن خاتم صوبه دوشدی مکرخاتمه زیادهسیله علاقهسی وار أیدی محاصبلرینه غواصلر کتورك چیقارسونلر دیو أمر ایتدی	*Bir ghiun sou kénarindé otourour-iken parmaghin- den khatem souya dushdu méyér khatémé zïyadésilé alakassi var-idi musahib- leriné ghávwásslar ghet- tirin chĭkarsĭnlar déyou emr etdi*	One day, while sitting by the water-side, a ring fell from his finger into the water. He, however, had a great affection for the ring, and *ordered* his cour- tiers *to bring* divers and let them take it out
سلطان مصره واروب خاتمی بن بولورم دیو افاده ایدهسك	*Soultán-i-missré varip khatemi ben boulouroum déyou ifadé edésin*	Go to the king of Egypt and *announce* to him *that thou wilt find* the ring
بو اوغلانی بزه ویر دیو نیاز ایتدکلرنده	*Bou oghláni bizé vér déyou niaz etdiklerindé*	On their *requesting* him *to give* them this lad
کابل شهرنه گلدیلر و عقل و هنرده یکانه یز دیو ادعا ایدوب زهرهیی طلب ایتدیلر	*Kaboul shehiriné ghel- dilér vé ákl vé hunérdé yekané yiz déyou iddia edip zuhréyi taleb etdilér*	They came to the city of Cabul, and *claiming to be* unique in intellect and ability, demanded Zuhré (in marriage)
قزك محمورهیی وزیره ویرهسن دیو فرمان بیوردی	*Kĭzĭn Mahmouréyi vé- ziré vérésin déyou firmán bouyourdou*	He ordered (him) *to give* his daughter Mahmouré to the vizier.

The Definitive and Indefinite Object of the Verb.

610. Every transitive verb must have an object. This object or accusative is either definitive or indefinite, distinguished in English by the use of
articles " the " or " a," or the absence of both. The Turks having no definitive article express whether the object is definitive or indefinite in a different
way. If the object of the verb be definite it takes either ى or سی after it
(according as it ends in a consonant or a vowel). If it be indefinitive it
remains unchanged and has the same form as the nominative. Example :—

مکتوب الدم	*Mektoub áldĭm*	I have received *a* letter
مکبوبی الدم	*Mektoubou áldĭm*	I have received *the* letter
بالق طوتمق	*Bálĭk toutmak*	To catch *fish* (in general) or a fish
بالغی طوتمق	*Báligĭ toutmak*	To catch the (particular) fish (referred to before)

(Ottoman Turkish)	Transliteration	English
صو كنارنده بالق طوتمق ايله اكلنيورلرايدى ديرى طوتيلان بالقلرى بر لكن ايچنه قيوب وزيرك اوكنه كتورديلر	Sou kénarindé bálïk toutmagh-ilé éleniorléridi diri toutoulán bálïklarï bir léyen ichiné koyoup vézirin euniné ghettirdilér	They were amusing themselves at the water side by *catching fish*. The fish which were caught alive they put in a dish and brought them before the vizier
اول كيجه بر سارق اشيا سرقت ابتمك ايچون بهزادك خانهسنه كيروب بر كوشهده پنهان اولوب فرصت كوزهتردى باغجيلر حمارى كورنجه ارسلان ظن ايدوب جمله سى بردن بر اغاجك اوزرينه چقديلر	Ol ghejé bir sárïk eshya sirkát etmek ichin Behzadin khanésiné ghi- rip bir kiushédé pinhan oloup fursat ghiuzédirdi Bághjiler himari ghieu- runjé arsslan zan edip jumléssi birden bir ághá- gïn uzeriné chïkdïlar	That night a thief en- tered Behzad's house to steal *things*, and hiding himself in a corner watched for *an* opportunity The gardeners on seeing *the* ass thought he was *a* lion, and all of them at once climbed up a tree.

611. Proper names, personal, demonstrative and interrogative pronouns as well as nouns accompanied by an affix must by their nature be definite, and therefore always take the ى or سى in the accusative.   Example:—

(Ottoman Turkish)	Transliteration	English
اخر كار ديوه غالب اولوب زهرهيى الوب كتوردى	Akhïrkiar divé ghálib oloup Zuhréyi álïp ghet- tirdi	At last he conquered the demon and took *Zuhré* and brought her (here)
كيمى كوردكز	Kimi ghieurdunuz?	*Whom* did you see?
ابراهيمى كوردم	Ibrahimi ghieurdum	I saw Abraham
هاشمى جاريه يى ياننه دعوت ايليوب سازيكى چال ديو نياز ايدنجه جاريه دخى سازنى الينه الوب مضراب اوردى	Hashimi jariyéyi yaniné davet éileyip sázïnï chál déyou niaz edinjé jariyé dakhï sázïnï eliné álïp mizrab wourdou	On Hashimi calling *the* slave woman to his side and requesting* her to play *her* lute, she took *her* lute in *her* hand and performed.

The Use of the Past Tense for the Present.

612. Very often in Turkish the verb is put in the past tense when we should put it in the present. " Do you understand?" in Turkish is اكلادكمى *annadinmi* (have you understood?) and the answer " I understand," is

---

* Literally, requesting her, saying, "Play *thy* lute."   See 609.

always اكلادم *annadim* (I have understood). I am glad is سوندم *sevindim* not سونيورم *seviniyoroum*, and so forth. Example :—

سن نصل سن	*Sen nassl sin ?*	How art thou?
ايوايم شكر	*Éyiyim shukr*	Very well, thank you
ممنون اولدم	*Memnoun oldoum*	I am glad (to hear it)
بك چوق خوشلاندم	*Pek chok khoshlandim*	I am very much pleased
تذكرهٔ محبتكز مفهومی	*Tezkeré-i-mahabetiniz*	I have understood your
معلوم اولهرق بو وجهله	*mefhoumou maloum olarak*	friendly letter and am much
تبريك و تسعيده واقع	*bou véjhlé tebrik ou téssi-*	pleased by your taking the
اولان همتكزدن ممنون	*dé wákĭ olán himmetiniz-*	trouble to congratulate and
اولدم	*den memnoun oldoum*	felicitate me
درس بتدی	*Derss bitdi*	The lesson is over.

Verbs which Govern the Dative.

613. Verbs which express a direction or a striving after something require the name of a person or thing which follows to be in the dative. Amongst these verbs are the following :—

ارشمك	*erishmek*, to attain, reach		سويلمك	*suwéylémek*, to speak to, to tell
اورمق	*wourmak*, to strike		صغنمق	*sighĭnmak*, to take refuge in
اوكرتمك	*euretmek*, to teach		صورمق	*sormak*, to ask, enquire
باشلامق	*báshlamak*, to begin		طارلمق	*dárĭlmak*, to get angry with
باغشلامق	*bághĭshlamak*, to forgive, spare		طيانمق	*dayanmak*, to rest on
باقمق	*bákmak*, to look		كوسترمك	*ghiusstérmek*, to show
بكزمك	*benzémek*, to resemble		وارمق	*varmak*, to go
بنمك	*binmek*, to mount		يابشمق	*yapĭshmak*, to stick to, adhere to
بيلدرمك	*bildirmek*, to inform		يارامق	*yaramak*, to be of use to, to be good for
چالشمق	*chálĭshmak*, to strive, work		يتشمك	*yetishmek*, } reach, attain
دوشمك	*dushmek*, to fall		يتمك	*yetmek*, } to.
دونمك	*deunmek*, to turn			
ديمك	*démek*, to say			
رجا ايتمك	*rija etmek*, to request			

Example :—

اغاجك اوزرندن فرياده باشلادی *Âghájĭn uzerinden fer-yadé báshladĭ*   He began crying out from the top of the tree

باغك ايچنده بولديغى شئى يمكه باشلادى	*Bághĭn ichindé boul-doughou shéi yéméyé báshladĭ*	He *began* eating the things he found inside the garden
باشنى اول تيغ هلاكه اوروب همان بدنندن جدا ايلدى	*Báshĭnĭ ol tigh-i-hela-ké wouroup heman bede-ninden juda éilédi*	He *struck* his head *against* that " sword of destruc-tion " (that fatal sword) and immediately severed it from his body
البته بر مراده ارشمك ايچون بكا خدمت ايدرسن	*Elbetté bir muradé erishmek ichin bána hiz-met edérsin*	Of course you serve me in order *to attain* an object
روم پادشاهنك قزينه بكزر	*Roum Padishahinin Kĭzina benzér*	She *resembles* the daughter of the king of Greece
بر مراديكز وار ايسه لطف ايدوب بن قولكه سويليه سز	*Bir muradiniz var issé loutf edip ben koulouna suwéyléyésiz*	If you have any wish have the kindness to *tell* me your (humble) servant
دردكز بردن بازركانك اوينه واروب قزى كورك	*Deurdunuz birden bá-zĭrghianin eviné varip kĭzĭ ghieŭrun*	The four of you *go to* the merchant's house at once and see the girl
پادشاه بو قزى المسون زيراً اكر الهجى اولورسه امور مملكته باقميوب مصالح سلطنت واحوال مملكت بالكليه پريشان اولور	*Padishah bou kĭzĭ ál-masĭn zira éyér álajak olourssa oumour-i-memlék-eté bákmayip mássalih-i--sáltanát u ahwal-i-mem-léket bil kuliyé perishan olour*	Let the king not take the girl ; for, if he take her, he will not *attend* to the busi-ness of the country, and the affairs of the Government, and the condition of the country will be ruined
فغفورك اياغنه دوشديلر	*Faghfouroun ayaghina dushdulér*	They *fell at* the feet of Faghfour.

614. Many verbs formed with the auxiliary verb ايتمك *etmek* and Arabic verbal nouns govern the dative. As سؤال ايتمك *sual etmek* (to ask), عفو ايتمك *afv etmek* (to pardon), نظر ايتمك *nâzr etmek* (to look), &c. Example :—

سرت سركه كندى قابنه ضرر ايدر	*Sert sirké kendi kábĭna zarar edér*	(Too) sharp vinegar *in-jures* its own cruet

عورتك مروتنه تعجب ايتدی	Avretin muruvetiné taajub etdi	He was *surprised at* the woman's kindness
دشمننه مرحمت ايتدی	Dushmeniné merhamet etdi	He *had mercy on* his enemy
اطرافه نظر ايدركن	Etrafé názar edér ken	While *looking around*
بکا زياده مال وعده ايتديلر	Bána ziyadé-mál vad etdilér	They *promised me* great wealth
فى الحقيقه سکا کوکلمدن محبت ايلدم	Fi'l hákika séna ghiunulumden mahabet éilédim	Really I *loved* you from my heart
سليمه سالمه نصيحته شروع ايتديکى کبی بی صبرو ارام اولوب کندوی اعلام ايتدی	Selimé Salimé nássihaté shurou etdiyi ghibi bi sábr ou aram oloup kendiyi ilam etdi	As soon as Selimé *began* to give Salim advice, he became impatient and restless, and made himself known
کندی کندينی اولديردی ديسم بنم کلامه کيم اعتماد ايدر برهمن قزه طمع ايدوب شهزادهیی اولديردی ديرلر	Kendi kendini euldurdu disém benim kélamimé kim itimad edér Brahmin kiza tama edip shehzadéyi euldurdu dérler	If I say that he killed himself, who will *believe* what I say? They will say: "He *coveted* the Brahmin girl and killed the prince."

615. Compound verbs formed with Arabic active participles also govern the dative, as راضی اولمق *razï olmak* (to consent), سبب اولمق *sébeb olmak*, or باعس اولمق *baïss olmak* (to cause), غالب اولمق *ghalib olmak* (to vanquish), تابع اولمق *tabi olmak* (to obey). Example :—

کوچك بيوکه تابع اولور	Kiuchuk buyuké tabi olour	The small *obey the* great
جادونك اياغنه دوشوب پادشاهك قزنه عاشق اولديغنی سويلدی	Jadunun ayaghiné dushup padishahin kizné áshïk oldoughounou suwéylédi	He fell at the feet of the witch and told her that he *had fallen in love with* the king's daughter
غضب همايونکزه نه سب اولدی	Gházáb-i-houmayounounouzané sébeb oldou?	What caused your imperial wrath ?
رومه داخل اولوب تختگاه قسطنطنيه يه داخل اولديلر	Roumé dakhil oloup takhtghiah kosstaniyéyé dakhil oldoular	They went into Byzantium and entered Constantinople
زيرك دخی دزدارزاده يه غالب کلدکده لطيفه ايدوب رنجيده ايدردی	Zéirek dakhï Duzdarzadéyé ghálib gheldekdé latifé edip renjidé edérdi	Zéirek having *beaten* Duzdarzadé, joked and tormented him.

Verbs which govern the Ablative.

616. Verbs which express separation or distance from a thing govern the ablative, such as the following :—

أزمق *ázmak*, to grow beyond all bounds, to become depraved, rebellious

أشمق *áshmak*, to pass over or beyond [tired of

أوصانمق *ousánmak*, to grow sick of,

بزمك *bézmek*, to get tired of, lose one's taste for

چكلمك *chekilmek*, to withdraw, retire

چكنمك *chekenmek*, to be loth, to scruple

چيقمق *chĭkmak*, to go out

سويلمك *suwéylémek*, to speak (of)

صاقنمق *sakĭnmak*, to take care

صورمق *sormak*, to ask (from)

قاچمق *káchmak*, to fly (from)

قوپمق *kopmak*, to arise, take place

قورتارمق *kourtarmak*, to save (from)

قورتلمق *kourtoulmak*, to be saved from

قورقمق korkmak, to fear, be frightened of

كچمك *ghechmek*, to pass (through)

كلمك *ghelmek*, to come (from).

Example :—

اللهدن قورقان ادملردن قورقماز	*Alláhdan korkan ádám-lardan korkmaz*	He who *fears* God does not *fear* men
يولدن ازدق	*Yoldan ázdĭk*	We *strayed from* the road
قوجهمش دلكى اغدن قورقماز	*Kojamish tilki ághdan korkmaz*	An old fox does not *fear* the net
توتوندن قورتلمق ايچون اتش ايچنه دوشمه	*Toutoundan kourtoul-mak ichin átesh ichiné dushma*	Do not fall into the fire in order to *avoid* the smoke
ياغمـوردن قاچان طولويه اوغرادى	*Yaghmourdan káchan dolouya oghradi*	He who *ran away from* the rain fell in with the hail
كارونك اوكنده اولان دوهيسى كـوپـريـسدن كچورهمديلر	*Kiarbawin eunundé olán dévéyi kieupruden gechiré-médiler*	They could not get the camel which was in the front of the caravan to *pass over* the bridge

---

* If قورقمق is followed by an infinitive, the latter may be either in the dative or ablative. Example, كتمكه قورقارم *ghitmeyé korkarim*, or كتمكدن قورقارم *ghit-mekden korkarim* (I am frightened to go).

هر نه شيدن اوصانورسه	Hér né shéiden ousá- nĭrsa	Whatever he gets *tired* *of*.

617. Numerous compound verbs govern the ablative, such as خوف
ایتمك *khavf etmek* (to fear), اجتناب ایتمك *ijtinab etmek* (to avoid),
احتذار ایتمك *ihtizar etmek* (to keep from), تجاوز ایتمك *téjavuz etmek* (to
overstep, trespass), حظ ایتمك *ház etmek*, and خوشلنمق *khoshlanmak* (to
like, be pleased with), دربغ ایتمك *dirigh etmek* (to withhold, refuse),
عاخز قالمق *ajiz kálmak* (to be incapable of), واز كچمك *vaz gechmek* (to
give up), فراغت ایتمك *feraghát etmek* and فارغ اولمق *farigh olmak* (to
abandon, to do without), محروم قالمق *mahroum kálmak* (to be disappointed
of, deprived of), اكاه اولمق *aghiah olmak* (to be aware of), &c. Example:—

اول مكاندن فرار ایتدی	Ol mekianden firar etdi	He *fled from* that place
بر كون بابل شهرینه كلوب آب و هواسندن غایت حظ ایدوب مكث و اقامت ایلدی	Bir ghiun Babil she- hiriné ghelip áb ou hawa- sinden ghayet ház edip mekss u ikamet éilédi	One day he came to the city of Babylon and *liking* the air and water of it (*i.e.*, its climate) settled (there)
بن اولادمدن فارغ اوله‌مم	Ben evladimden farigh olamam	I cannot *do without* my child
اخركار ما‌یوس اولوب ارامقدن فراغت ایتدیلر	Akhĭrkiar mé'youss oloup áramakdan feraghát etdiler	At last they lost hope and *gave up* looking for (her)
بر كیجه سرایدن غائب اولدیلر	Bir ghejé seraïdan káïb oldoular	One night they *dis- appeared from* the palace
شهوت ایله نظر ایتمكدن حذر قیله‌سن	Shehvet ilé názar et- mekden hézer kĭlasĭn	*Keep from* looking at her sensually
سندن *رجا ایدرم كه بكا باقمیه‌سن	Senden rija ederim ki bána bákmayasin	I *beg of* you not to look at me
عورت جنسسندن اجتناب ایدر	Avret jinssinden ijtinab edér	He *avoids* womankind.

618. Passive verbs govern either the dative or the ablative. Example:—

دلكی طوزاغه طوتلدی	Tilki touzágha toutoul- dou	The fox was *caught in* (or by) a trap.
دونكی اجمالمزده	Dunki ijmalimizdé isha-	As we pointed out in our

---

* رجا ایتمك *rija etmek* may also take the dative.

اشارت ايدلديكى اوزره	*ret edildiyi uzeré russiya*	yesterday's summary, the
روسيه ديپلوماتلرينك	*diplomatlerinin el-halet-u-*	greatest anxiety of the
الحالة هذة الك بيوك	*-hazihi en biyuk telashleri*	Russian diplomatists at
تلاشلرى تركمنلره روسيه	*turkmenleré russiya or-*	present is to deny the news
اردولرينك يكيدن مغلوب	*doularinin yéniden magh-*	that the Russian armies
اولمش اولدقلرى خبريني	*loub olmoush oldouklari*	have been again *defeated by*
تكذيب خصوصنده در	*khâberini tekzib khoussous-*	the Turcomans.*
	sinda dir	

EXERCISE XXXVI.

He is frightened (قورقمق *korkmak*) of you. When did he begin to learn Turkish? Two years ago (اول *evvel*). What did he tell you? He told me that he begun to study (اوقومق *okoumak*) Turkish three years ago. Does he resemble (بكزمك *benzémek*) his brother? He does not resemble his brother, but he resembles his father. Who taught you French (فرانسزجه *fransîzja*)? He struck his head against the wall (ديوار *duwar*). He and his brother and sister have started for Smyrna. I and my father lived in Adrianople (ادرنه *Edirné*) many years. I like (حظ ايتمك *hâz etmek*) the climate (اب وهوا *âb ou hawa*) of Italy (اتاليا *Italia*) very much. I should like to go there very much. If you come to Italy I shall be very glad. I prefer to live in England, although its climate is not so agreeable (لطيف *latif*). If I were rich I would live in London (لوندره *Londra*). Would that I were there now! If I could talk English I would go at once (بردن *birden*). Have patience (صبر ايتمك *sâbr etmek*). If I receive news from your father shall I write to you? If you are at leisure (اشكز يوق ايسه *ishiniz yoghoussa*), let us take a walk. With pleasure (مع الممنونيه *ma elmemnouniyé*). Where shall we go? Shall we go to the market (چارشو *charshî*)? He avoids womankind. Shall I light (ياقمق *yakmak*) the fire? He requested me to light the fire, but I cannot find the lucifers (كبريت *kibrit*). If you look (ارامق *âramak*) for them, you will find them. Whoever comes. When you go to Paris buy some books for me. I beg you not to forget. I shall not forget. What do you wish me to do? I want you to write to me every week. You do not attend (دقت ايتمك *dikkât etmek*) to what I say. Has your friend consented to what you proposed (تكليف ايتمك *teklif etmek*)? He has not consented yet (دها *daha*). The English have beaten (غالب اولمق *ghâlib olmak*) the Zulus (زولولر *zouloular*). I am very glad. Are you glad? Of course (طبيعتيله *tabiatileh*).

---

* Extract from a Turkish newspaper.

ايسه *issé.*

619. ايسه *issé,* the third person singular of the defective verb ايم *im,* sometimes has no verbal signification at all, and is equivalent to "as for," "as regards." Example:—

قزازك بر حلّاج دوستى	*Kázézin bir hallác*	The silk-merchant had a
وار ايدى بر كون انك	*dosstou var idi bir ghiun*	friend, a carder. One day
خانهسنه واروب اوينك	*anin khanésiné varip*	he went to his house, and
ايچنى كوناكون نعمتلرايله	*evinin ichini ghiunaghiun*	on seeing it full of comforts
مشحون و اثواب و اثقالى	*nimetlerilé meshhoun vé*	and a great quantity of
حددن افزون كوريجك	*esswáb vé esskáli hadden*	clothes and luggage, he was
قزاز بونك احوالنه	*efzoun ghieurijek kazéz*	much surprised at his con-
تعجّب ايدوب كندى	*bounoun ahvaliné taajub*	dition, and said to himself:
كندويه ايتدى بن شب	*edip kendi kendiyé éitdi*	"I am going night and day
و روز پادشاهلره و بكلره	*ben sheb-u-rouz padishah-*	to kings and lords, and
واروب انلرهلايق شيلر	*leré vé béyleré varip an-*	making things fit for them.
ايشلرم بوحلّاج ايسه پنبه	*lará layïk shéiler ishlérim*	*As for* this carder, he has
و يوك اتاركن بوقدر ماله	*bou hallác issé penbé vé*	got so much wealth by
مالك اولمش بن ايسه	*yun átarken bou kádar mála*	carding cotton and wool,
فقر و فاقهدن جان	*malik olmoush ben issé fakr*	while (*as for* me) I am
ويريبورم	*u fakéden ján vériyioroum*	dying of poverty and want"
اول كون ارسلانك	*Ol ghiun arsslanin ya-*	That day, by the side of
ياننده ندماندن قورد ايله	*nindé nudémaden kourt ilé*	the lion there were (only) the
شغال بولندى انلرك ايسه	*shaghál bouloundou anlarin*	wolf and the jackal from
جبلتى شرّ و شقاوت	*issé jibilleti sher ou shé-*	amongst his associates; and
اوزره اولديغندن شيرى	*kavet uzeré oldoughoundan*	*as for them,* their nature
اصلا خيره دلالت	*shiri ássla khairé delalet*	being evil and bad, they
ايتمزلردى	*etmazlerdi*	never led the lion into good.

The Participles.

620. اولان *olan,* the present active participle of the verb اولمتى *olmak,* is sometimes left out after an Arabic active participle. Example:—

مدينه ازميرده لب	*Médiné-'i-ezmirdé leb-*	A house of mine *situated*
درياده كأين بر باب	*-i-déryadé ka'in bir báb*	on the sea-shore in the
مغازه عاجزانهم	*maghaza-i-ajizaném*	town of Smyrna
Instead of كأين اولان	*Ka'in olán*	*Being situated.*

621. Very often the nouns to which active and passive participles refer are understood, and the participles then being used as nouns are declined like them. All the participles can be used as substantives in the nominative; but the present active, however, is the only one which can be used as the object of a verb, direct or indirect. Example :—

سو سنی سونی	*Sev seni seveni*	Love (the person) who loves you
قپوسنه كلنلردن كمسه محروم كتمزدی	*Kápĭssĭna ghelenlerden kimsé mahroum ghitmazdi*	Not one *of those who* came to his gate went away disappointed
هر كشی یه لایق اولان بو در كه كندی حال و شاننی بیلوب حددن تجاوز ایلممك كركدر	*Hér kishiyé layĭk olán bou dour ki kendi hal ou shánĭnĭ bilip hadden téjavuz éilémemek gherek dir*	The *thing which is proper* for everyone is that he must know his place and rank, and not go beyond his bounds
بنی صایانك قولی ایم بنی صایمیانك سلطانی ایم	*Béni sayanin koulouyoum béni sayamayanin soultáni yĭm*	I am the slave of the *man who* esteems me, and the lord of the *man who* has no esteem *for* me
كوزدن اوزاق اولان كوكلدن دخی اوزاق	*Ghieuzden ouzák olán ghieunulden dakhĭ ouzák*	He who is far *from* the eye; (is) also far from the heart
كورك استدیكی ایكی كوز	*Kieurun isstédiyi iki ghieuz*	The *thing which* the blind man wishes for is two eyes
هپیسندن بختلو در بشكده اولان	*Hepisinden bakhtli dĭr beshikdé olán*	The *happiest* (man) of all is *the one who* is in his cradle
چوق یاشایان چوق بلمز چوق كرن چوق بیلور	*Chok yashayan chok bilmaz chok ghézen chok bilir*	The *man who has lived* long does not know much, but the *man who has travelled* much knows a great deal.

622. Active participles are preceded by the nouns they govern directly or indirectly in the objective case, the same as the verb they belong to, and passive participles also, except the noun they describe. Example :—

راحت استین ادم صاغر كور دلسز اولملو	*Rahat isstéyen ádám sághĭr kieur dilsiz olmálĭ*	The man *who wishes for* comfort ought to be deaf, blind, and dumb

خدمت ایتمكی اوكرنمین افندیلك دخی ایتمز	*Hizmet etméyi euren- méyen effendilik dakhï et- maz*	He who has *not learnt to do service* cannot act well as a master
طوز اتمك بیلمین اتدن كوتو در	*Touz ekmek* bilméyen itden keutu dur*	He who does not *recog- nise bread and salt* is worse than a dog
عجبا بو بغداى نه جنس قومك زماننده بتمشدر و بونك سرى ندر و بونى بر بلور آدم یوقمیدر	*Ajeba bou boghdaï né jinss-i-kavmin zemáninda bitmish dir vé bounoun siri nédir vé bounou bir bilir ádám yokmoudour*	I wonder at the period of what kind of people this corn grew, and what is the secret of this, and whether there is not a *man who knows this ?*

623. Arabic and Persian participles are also preceded by the nouns they
govern in the objective case. Example :—

چوغه طالب اولان ازه یتشیر	*Chogha talib olán áza yetishir*	He who wants (too) much attains but little
استفسار خـــاطـــر ثناورانهمى شامل بر قطعه كرمنامهلرى وامل دست عاجزى اولدى	*Isstifsar-i-kháťïr-i- -senaveranémi shamil bir kïta kéremnaméleri wássïl desst ajïzi oldou*	A gracious letter of yours *containing enquiries* about my health has reached my humble hand.

Verbal Nouns and Infinitives.

624. Verbal nouns of Turkish origin are treated like other nouns.
Those ending in مه and مقلق or مكلك are capable of being declined (see
156, 157) in the singular, but have no plural ; and they also take pronominal affixes, as یازماكز *yazmaniz* (your writing), كلمسى *ghelmassi* (his
coming), سومكلیم *sevmekliyim* (my loving). The perfect and future verbal
nouns (ending in دق or دك and جق or جك respectively) also take pronominal affixes, and then can be declined, as كدیكى *ghitdiyi* (his having
gone), الما یدیكم *elma yédiyim* (my having eaten apples), استانبوله كیدهجكلرى
Isstanbola ghidéjekleri (their being about to go to Constantinople). When
Turkish verbal nouns are used in conjunction with other nouns the Turkish
construction alone is possible. As كونش طوغمسى *ghiunesh doghmassi* (sun-
rise). Example:—

---

* Written *etmek* but pronounced *ekmek*.

باباسنك فرمانى اوزره
كمال مرتبه رعايت
ايدوب يمده و ايجمده
طورمده و اوتورمده بر
ساعت ياندن ايرمزدى

بنم اتش عشقده
ياندیغم یتر
بعد اليوم بن سنكله
الفت ايتميوب اخرة
*كتمم ايو در

طوطى قزى اولقدرمدحه
مبالغه ايلديكه جاماسب
شاه بالصرور قولاقدن عاشق
اولدى و ايتدى اى زبان
آور اسوده لكمز وار ايكن
بزى نه عجب درده كرفتار
ايلدك امدى بزه لازم
اولديكه اول دختر پاكزه
اخترى الهوز اكر مدح
ايتديكك قدر حسندار
دلبر ايسه سكا حددن
زياده لطف و كرم ايدرم
و الا مدح ايتديكك قدر
اولمزايسه سكا نه عقاب
ايده جكمى بن بلورم

زبان اورد ايتدى
بادشاهم بن قولك قزك
كوزللكنى بيلورم و انشاالله
تعالى بادشاهمك

Bâbâsĭnĭn fèrmânĭ uzeré kemal mertebé riayet edip yemédé vé ichmédé dourmada ve otourmada bir saat yaninden aïrmazdi

Benim átesh-i-áshkda yandighim yetér

Bad el yavm ben seninlé ulfet etméyip akhiré ghitmam éi dir

Touti kĭzĭ ol kádar medhé mubalagha éilédi ki Jamaseb shah bĭ-z--zarour koulakdan áshĭk oldou vé éitdi éi Zebanavér `assoudéliyimiz var iken bizi né ajb derdé ghiriftar éilédin imdi bizé lazim oldou ki ol dukhtér--i-pakizé akhteri álayĭz--éɣer medh etdiyin kádar hussndar dilbér issé séna hadden ziyadé loutf ou kérem ederim vé illa medh etdiyĭn kádar olmazissa sana né ikáb edéjéyimi ben bilirim

Zebán Avérd éitdi padishahim ben kouloun kĭzĭn ghiuzellighini bilirim vé inshállâh taala padi-

According to her father's command she showed him great consideration, and did not leave him one hour (in) *eating, drinking, standing, or sitting*

My being burnt in the fire of love is sufficient

Henceforth, it is well that I should not associate with thee and go to another (literally, *my going* is well)

The parrot extolled the girl so much that king Jamaseb fell in love with her necessarily from hearsay, and he said: "Oh! Zeban-aver, I was in a state of tranquillity, and you have made me a prey to what a strange malady! It is now become necessary for me to obtain that splendid girl. If she be as lovely and attractive as you say, I will overwhelm you with grace and favour; but if she is not, I know how I shall punish you (literally, I know my being about to make what punishment)

Zeban Avérd said: "Sire, I (your humble servant) know the girl's beauty, and I have no

---

* Often written thus, but كتمام is better.

مشربنجه اوله‌جغنه شیهٔم
یوقدر لکن پادشاهمدن
مرادم بو در که اول قزك
بر متكلمه دیشی طوطیسی
وار در اسمنه سخن پرور
دیرلر بنده‌کز کوچكدنبری
بر یرده بیومشز سرور و
انــدوهــده انیــس
غمكسارمدر انك ایله بر
قفسه قیوب مسرور
بیورمکزی نیاز ایدرم

shahimin meshrebinjé ola-jaghina shuphém yok dour lakin padishahimden mura-dam bou dour ki ol kïzïn bir mutékellimé dïshi tou-toussou var dir issminé Sukhn Pérvér dérlér ben-déniz kiuchukdenberu bir yerdé buyumushiz surour vé endouhdé eniss ghem-kiussarim dir anin ilé bir kéfessé koyoup messrour bouyourmamaxizi niax ederim

doubt—please God (may he be exalted!)—about her being to your majesty's taste. But what I desire of your majesty is this:—That girl has a talking female parrot whom they call Sukhn Pervér. She has been my 'grief-dispel-ling' companion in joy and in sorrow from my child-hood. I beg of you *to put* me in a cage with her and make me happy"

قاشنمقلق طرناق استر

Káshïnmaklïk tïrnak isstér

Scratching requires nails (*i.e.*, to be able to scratch one's-self nails are requisite)

بنده‌لرینك مرقوم
سورینك اجراسی مطلق
ذات والارینك تشریفنه
منوطدر بو بابده لطفاً و
تنزلاً بر ساعت اول
تشریف والاریله مشرف
بیورلمقلغمز بادیٔ‌تحششیه
اولمشدر

Merkoum bendélerinin sourounoun ijrassi mout-lák zat valalerinin teshri-finé menout. dour bou bábda loutfa ou ténezzula bir saat evvel teshrif vala-lerilé musherref boyou-roulmaklighimiz badi-'i-tashiyé olmoushdour

The above-mentioned feast of your humble ser-vant being held, depends entirely on your coming (And), this postscript has been written (to ask you) to honour me by kindly and condescendingly coming an hour before

اولنم امر مقرر در

Eulmém emr-i-mukar-rér dir

My dying is certain

اشبو پولیچه‌مزی
کوردیكکزده
فقیرلرك تسلیسی
اولمدر
فلان شیك اشترا و
ارسال اولنمسی
باره‌یی طرف حقیرانه‌مه
ارسال بیورملری نیازمدر

Ishbou polichamizi ghieurduyunuzdé

Fakïrlerin tésellissi eulmé dir

Filán shéin isshtira vu irsal olounmassi

Parayi taraf-i-hákïra-némé irsal bouyourmaléri niazimdir

On your seeing this bill of exchange of mine (ours)

The consolation of the poor is *dying*

The *buying* and *sending* of a certain thing

I request *your sending* the money to me.

Arabic Verbal Nouns.

625. Arabic verbal nouns are declinable and take affixes in the same way as other Turkish nouns, but, when they are in conjunction with other nouns, either the Turkish or Persian mode of construction may be used; as امور اداره‌ٔ *idaré-'i-oumour* or امور اداره‌سی *oumour idaréssi* (the management of affairs). Example:—

مبلغ مذکوری مدیون مرقومدن ملایمت و یاخود مخالفتنده جبرا تحصیلنه صرف همت بیورملری مرجو در	*Meblagh - i - mezkiourou medyoun - i - merkoumdan mulayémet vé yakhod mukhaléfetindé jebra tahsïliné sarf-i-himmet bouyourmaléri merjou dour*	I request your *kindly taking* the trouble of obtaining the said sum from the aforementioned creditor by fair means, or, in case of *his opposing* it, by force
بو طرفده فلان کمسنه‌دن مطلوبات والارینك تحصیلنه ثناورلری وکیل نصب بیورلدیغنه دائر وارد اولان بر قطعه وکالتنامه‌لری	*Bou tarafdé fïlán kimessnéden mátloubat-i--valalérinin tahsïlïna senavérleri vékil nássb bouyourouldoughouna daïr warid oldán bir kïta vékialetnaméléri*	A power of attorney which has come respecting *my having been appointed* agent for the *collecting* of your claims against a certain person here
اقدمجه سپارش والارك اولان شی فلان ایله طرف عالیلرینه فرستاده اولنمش ایسه‌ده وصول خبرینی الهمدیغمدن مراق و اندیشه‌ده قالدم	*Akdemjé siparish - i - valaleri oldán shéi fïlán ilé taraf-i-alïleriné frisstadé olounmoush oussadé vusoul kháberini álamadighimdan merak ou endishédé káldïm*	Although the thing you ordered some time ago has been sent by So-and-so, not having received *the news of the arrival* (of it) I am in doubt and anxiety
باعث تحریر سند اولدر که	*Baïss-i-tahrir-i-sened ol dir ki . . .*	The reason for *writing* this document is that . . .

Verbal Nouns ending in دق or دك.

626. Verbal nouns ending in دق or دك (*i.e.*, the perfect verbal nouns) accompanied by the pronominal affixes and the word وار *var* are occasionally used in a very peculiarly Turkish fashion to express the past tense of a verb. Example:--

بو رسمی کورديككز وار می	Bou ressmi ghieurdu-yunuz var mi?	Have you ever seen this picture?
کورديکم يوق	Ghieurduyum yok	I have never seen it
روز و شب اصلا خاطرمدن مهجور اولديغی يوق در	Rouz ou sheb ássla khátírïmdan méhjour ol-doughou yok dour	Night and day she has never been out of my mind
جميع عاشق معشوغنه واصل اولديغی يوق در	Jémi áshïk mashou-ghouna wássïl oldoughou yok dour	Every lover has not ob-tained his beloved one.

Infinitives Used as Nouns.

627. Turkish infinitives are frequently used as nouns, and when so employed can be declined like substantives, except that they have no genitive and no plural. They cannot, however, take pronominal affixes as verbal nouns do. Example:—

کشی کندوبی مدح ايتمك ايو شی دکلدر	Kishi kendiyi medh et-mek éi shéi déil dir	*Praising one's-self* (to praise one's self) is not a good thing
عورت قسمنده بيوفا چوق اولور لکن اکثری بيوفا اولمقدن جملهسی بيوفا اولمق لازم کلمز	Avret kissmindé bivefa chok olour lakin ekseri bivefa olmakdan jumlési bivefa olmak lazim ghel-maz	There are many faithless ones amongst womankind; but from most of them *being* faithless, it does not neces-sarily follow *that all of them are* faithless
اويله عاشغی بر مراد ايتمك محضا انسانيتدر	Euilé áshïghï bér mu-rad etmek mahza insaniyet dir	*To cause such a lover to attain his wish is merely humanity*
مشقته صبر ايتمك راحت کتورر	Meshakáta sábr etmek rahat ghettirir	*Having patience* in afflic-tion brings comfort
قزيمی ويرمکی اژدرك اولمسنه تعليق ايتمشدم	Kïzïmï verméyi ézh-dérin eulmassiné talik et-mishdim	I had made the *giving* of my daughter depend on the death of the dragon
اوق اتمق علمنده ماهرم	Ok átmak ilmindé ma-hér im	I am skilful in the *art of archery* (*throwing arrows*)
احبابنك کيفيت احوالنی تجربه ايتمکده	Ahibbanin kéifiyet-i--ahwalini tejribé etmekdé	In testing the state of friends, the ancient sages

R 2

حكماءَ متقدمين بر طريق دخى وضع ايتمشلر در تاكه آنكله انسانك احوال درونى نمايان اولور	*hukemay-'i-mutékaddemin bir tarik dakhĭ wáz et- mishler dir taki aninlé insanin ahval-i-derounou numayan olour*	have laid down a method also whereby the state of a man's heart (interior) be- comes clear
تركى لساننى تحصيل ايتمك هر حالده فائدهٔ كثيرهٔ ئىى موجب اولديغنى پك اعلا درك ايتديكمدن بو كونلرده لسان مذكورى تحصيله بدأ و مباشرت ايدهجكم مصمم اولدم	*Turki lissanini tahsĭl etmek hér haldé faïdé-'i- -kessiré-'i-yi mujib ol- doughounou pek ala derk etdiyimden bou ghiunlerdé lissan-i-mezkiourou tah- sĭla bed ou mubashiret edéjéyim mussammen ol- doum*	Having clearly perceived that *acquiring* the Turkish language is the cause of much advantage in any case, I have lately resolved that I will set about learn- ing the aforesaid language
معشوقكه كتمك وقتى اولدى	*Mashoughouna ghitmek wákĭtĭ oldou*	It is time to go to thy lover (literally, *the time of to go*)
اغلمق ايله ايش بتمز	*Âghlamagh-ilé ish bit- maz*	The business will not be concluded by crying
بو درده اولمكدن غيرى چاره يوقدر	*Bou derdé eulmekden ghaïri charé yokdour*	There is no remedy for this evil but *dying* (to die).

628. Turkish infinitives, verbal nouns, and participles govern nouns and pronouns which are always put before them, as صو ايچمك *soü ïchmek* (to drink water), صو ايچمه *sou ichmé* (drinking water), يمش يين *yémish yéyen* (he who eats fruit), بورايه كلهجكلرى *bouraya gheléjekleri* (their being about to come here), شراب ايچمسى *sherab ichmassi* (his drinking wine). Example :—

اوزوم اشترا ايتمسنه دائر مكتوب	*Uzum ishtira etmassiné daïr mektup*	A letter about one *buying* grapes
ايكى صندق حلب فستغى ارسال ايتملرى رجاسنده شقه تحرير و تسيير قلندى	*Iki sándĭk haleb fisstĭ- ghĭ irsal etmaleri rijas- sindé shoukka tahrir ou tessyir kĭlĭndĭ*	This note has been writ- ten and despatched to re- quest *you to send two boxes* of Aleppo pistachio nuts.

629. The English infinitive is sometimes rendered in Turkish by the future participle. Example :—

استخلاف ايده‌جك كمسه‌سى يوق ايدى	Isstïkhláf edéjek kim-séssi yoghoudou	He had no one *to succeed* him
اكره‌جق وقت دكل در	Anghirajak wákït déil dir	It is not a time *to bray*
اكلنه‌جك زمان دكل در	Elenéjek zemán déil dir	It is not a time *to tarry.*

The Gerunds.

630. Gerunds are very little used in conversation, but in written Turkish, on the contrary, they are continually employed. Short sentences consisting of only a few words and but one verb, are adopted in speaking ; but, long sentences formed of a large number of subordinate ones, strung together by the gerunds, are preferred by the Turks when writing. An attempt was made a few years ago to introduce short sentences after the European model, but this style has never yet taken firm root. It is to be hoped it will eventually, as it is far more clear and practical than the regular old-fashioned long-winded obscure sentences. We subjoin some specimens of the use of these gerunds in the narrative and epistolary style, in which it is particularly affected. Example :—

بر كون حجره‌سندن چيقوب شهرك اطرافنى سير ايدر كن بر باغچه كنارينه كلوب ايچريسنه نظر ايدنجه كورد*يكه بو باغچه‌نك اورطه‌سنده بر حوض و كنارنده بر زرين تخت قوريلوب اوزرنده صاحبة الجمال و بر دختر ملك خصال †اوتورر كه به‌جت و لطافتده نظيرى كورلمامش	Bir ghiun hujrésinden chïkïp shehirin etrafini séir edér ken bir bághché kénariné ghelip ichérisiné názar edinji ghieurdu ki bou bághchénin ortasindé bir hawouz vé kénarindé bir zerin takht kourouloup uzerindé sahibé el jemal vé bir dukhter melek khïsal otourour ki behjet vé latafetdé názïrï ghieurul-mamish	One day he *left* his cell, and *while walking* around the city he *came* to the edge of a garden, and, *on his looking* in, he saw in the centre of it a pond, and on the edge of it a golden throne *erected*, and on it a beautiful and angelic girl, whose equal in beauty and agreeableness had not been seen
بيچاره ابوالمجد بو دلبر ماه جمالى كوردكده كيم	Bicharé Abul-Mejd bou dilbér mah-i-jemali ghie-	On poor Abul Mejd *seeing* this moon of beauty,

---

* This که must be omitted when translating into English.

† More commonly spelt اوطورر.

در ديو سؤال ايلدكده
سهريمزك پادشاهنك
قزيدر ديديلر أبوالمجدك
عقلى باشندن كيدوب
اول دم درون دلدن
عاشق اولدى

urdikdé kim dir déyou sual éilédekdé shehirimizin padishahinin kĭzĭ dir dédiler Abul-Mejd ăklĭ băshĭndan ghidip ol dem deroun-i-dilden ăshĭk oldou

and *asking* who she was, they said :* "She is the daughter of the king of our city." Abul Mejd's senses went out of his head, and that instant he fell in love from the interior (bottom) of his heart

عمرم اولدقچه انك
حسن و جمالنى سويلسم
بيكده برينى سويلمك
ممكن دكل در

Eumrum oldoukcha anin hussn-u-jemalini suwéyléssém bindé birini suwéylémek mumkin déil dir

If I talk about her beauty and loveliness *as long as I live*, it is impossible to tell one-thousandth part of it

هند پادشاهلرندن بر
پادشاهك اوغلى اطراف
مملكتى كزوب سير ولايت
ايتمكله نيچه غرايب و
عجايبه واقف اولوركن بر
كون يولى. بر بتخانهيه
اوغرادى

Hind padishahlerinden bir padishahin oghlou etraf-i-memléketi ghézip séir - i - vilayet etmeghlé niché gharaïb vé ajaibé wăkĭf olourken bir ghiun yolou bir poutkhanéyé oghradi . . .

The son of one of the kings of India *travelled* round the country and (*while*) *becoming acquainted* with all kinds of wonderful and strange things, his road one day passed by a temple . . .

اى همشيرهبكا بر يره
مسافرته كتمك اقتضا
ايلدى شو صنديقلرك
ايچنده اولان بنم ذى
قيمت اشيامدر كندى
خانهمده قويوب كتمكه
خوف ايتدم بن كلنجيه
دك بونلر سنك يانكده
امانت طورسون

Ei hemshiré bana bir yeré musafereté ghitmek iktiza éilédi. Shou săndĭklarin ichindé olăn benim zi kéimet eshyamdir. Kendi khanémdé koyoup ghitméyé khavf etdim. Ben ghelinjiyé dek bounlar senin yanindé emanet doursoun

Oh! sister, it is requisite for me to travel somewhere. What is in those boxes is valuable things of mine. I am frightened *to put* them in my own house and go. Let them remain in trust with thee *until* I *come*

درحال ينه فرطنه ساكن
اولوب ملايم روزكار اسوب
اول سفينهىى بر شهرك
كنارنه كتوردى

Dér hal yiné firtina sakin oloup mulayim rouzghiar essip ol séfinéyi bir shehirin kénariné gheutturdu

At once the storm again *subsiding*, and a gentle wind *blew* and brought that ship near a city

---

* I sacrifice the English style in order to keep to the Turkish and make it comprehensible to the learner.

بر قاچ كوندنصكره
نسيب دخى سپاهينك
شهرينه كلوب كزرك
قهوه‌خانه‌يه واروب مقدما
حسيب ايله دوست
اولان يكتر نسيبي كوروب
كمال مرتبه حسيبه
بكزديكندن حسيب
قياس ايدوب اشنالق
ايلديلر

مستحق سلطنت
اولنحيه قدر

جوهرشناسك قزى بر
كون مذكور صنديغى
اچوب پدرينك
تحفه‌لرينى سير ايدركى
مزبور حقه قزك الينه
كيردى

اول درت يوز حكمانك
رأيى بونك اوزرينه جارى
اولديكه بر مجلس پر ساز
ترتيب ايده‌لر اول
شهزاده‌يى كندى اقرانى
اولان اطفال ايله اول
مجلسه بشكلر ايله كتوروب
قويه‌لر سازلر چالندقجه
شهزاده حركت ايدرسه
لايق سلطنت در ديديلر
و اكر ايتمزايسه دكلدر

ايتدى شمدنصكرچابك
دستى عزل ايده‌لم زيرا
منصبك علتى شغل و
عملدر شغل و عمل
اولميانجه بر ادمى منصبه

*Bir kach ghiunden sora
Nessib dakhi sipahinin
sheheriné ghelip ghezérek
kahwé-khanéyé warip mu-
kádemma Hassib ilé dosst
olán yighitler Nessibi
ghieurup kémal mertébé
Hassibé benzédiyinden
Hassib kiyass edip ashin-
alik éilédilér*

*Mustahák - i - sáltanát
olounjouya kádar*

*Jevkérshinassin kïzï bir
ghiun mezkiour sándïghï
achip péderinin teuhfé-
lerini séir edérken mez-
bour hokka kïzïn eliné
ghirdi*

*Ol deurt yuz hukémanin
ré'yi bounoun uzeriné jari
oldouki bir mejliss pur
sáz tertib idéler ol shehza-
déyi kendi ákrani olán
itfal ilé ol mejlissé beshik-
ler ilé ghettirip koyalar
sázlar chálendïkja sheh-
zadé heréket edérsé layïk-
-i-sáltanát dir dédiler vé
éyér etmarsé dé'il dir*

*Éitdi shindensora Cha-
bik-Dessti ázl edélim zira
mánsïbïn illeti shoughl ou
aml dir shagl ou ámel
olmayïnjï bir ádámi mán-*

After a few days Nessib
also *came* to the sepoy's
town, and *walking* about
and *coming* to the coffee-
house, the young men who
had been friends with
Nessib saw him, and *think-
ing* he was Nessib, *as he
greatly resembled* him,
bowed to him

Until he is fit for govern-
ing

The daughter of Jevher-
shinass one day *opened* the
aforementioned box, and
(while) *looking* at her father's curiosities the said
casket fell into her hands

The opinion (decision)
of those four hundred sages
was to the effect that they
should arrange a musical*
party, and bring the prince
and the children who were
his equals in age, with their
cradles, to that assembly;
(and) they said, "If the
prince moves in accordance
as the lutes are played, he
is worthy to govern, and if
he does not, he is not"

He said: "Now, let us
dismiss Chabik-Desst, for
the reason for an appoint-
ment is work and occupa-
tion. *Unless* (until) there

---

* Literally, a party or company full of lutes.

قویمتی عینله اعمایه اییبنه ویرمکه بکزر	*sibé koïmak aïnlé amayé aïné vermeyé benzér*	be work and occupation, putting a man into an office is exactly like giving a mirror to a blind man."

The Omission of the Auxiliary Verb.

631. When compound verbs are used, the gerund of the auxiliary may be omitted once or twice in the sentence, one auxiliary gerund then applying to two or more verbal nouns.   Example :—

| بو قوللری اوچیوز اللی بیك غروشلتی انجیر فلان قپودانك سفینه سنه تحمیل ایدرك در سعدتده شریك چاكرانه،مزه كوندرلمش ایسه،ده مزبور سفینه ازمیردن حركت و چناق قلعه،سنه اوچ میل قالهرق و بر شدید هوایه تصادف ایدرك باشدن قره اوتورمش و ایچنده،كی اولان جمله انجیرلر تلف اولنمش | *Bou koulleri uch yuz elli bin ghroushlouk enjir filán kápoudánïn séfiné-siné tahmil edérek der-i--saadetdé sherik-i-cha-kéranémizé ghieunderil-mish issédé mezbour séfiné ezmirden héreket vé cha-nak-kalésiné uch mil kálarak vé bir shédid hawayé tésáddouf edérek báshdan kára otourmoush vé ichindéki olán jumlé enjirler télef olounmoush* | I, your humble servant, put 350,000 piastres' worth of pearls on board Captain So-and-so's ship, and sent them to my humble partner in Constantinople. The said vessel *started* from Smyrna, and at three miles distance from the Dar-danelles, *falling in with* stormy weather, ran aground, and all the pearls in her were destroyed |
| بر كون خوجه منصور سفر تجارته عزیمت و جمیع لوازماتنی ترتیب و خاتوننی جناب رب العالمینه امانت ایدوب یوله روانه اولدی | *Bir ghiun Khoja Man-sour séfer-i-tijareté ázi-met vé jémi levazimatini tertib vé khátounounou jenáb reb-ul-aleminé ema-net edip yola revané oldou* | One day Khoja Mansour *determining* to travel on business, and *arranging* all things necessary, *bade* his wife *good-by*, and started on the road. |

EXERCISE XXXVII.

My going to London is not necessary. If you go to London, I request you to buy me a dictionary (لغت كتابی *loughat-kitábi*). He has no children to inherit (وارث اولمتی *wariss olmak*) his property (مال *mál*). It is not a time to laugh (كولمك *ghiulmek*). Have you ever seen that girl? I have never seen her. One day my brother went out, and while walking about the city met an old beggar (ديلنجى *dilenji*). I shall not forget what you tell me as long as I live. The king had no one to succeed (استخلاف *isstikhlaf*) him. It is well that you should leave Turkey and go to Egypt (مصر *Missr*). It is well that I should go.* The storm (فرطنه *firtina*) subsided (ساكن اولمق *sakin olmak*), and a gentle (ملايم *mulayim*) breeze blew (اسمك *essmek*). I took (قياس ايتمك *kiyass etmek*) you for Mr. So-and-so, and saluted (اشنالق ايتمك *ashinalik etmek*) you, as you resemble (بكزمك *benzémek*) him exactly (كمال مرتبه *kémal mertébe*). I request you to obtain† (تحصيل *tahsil*) the said sum. The sending of the money is difficult. His dying is quite certain. As soon as my letter reaches (واصل اولمق *wássil olmak*) you, go to my friend and tell him what has happened. His coming here is not necessary. To die is better than to be disgraced (رسواى عالم اولمق *russvay-alem olmak*). Acquiring (تحصيل *tahsil*) art (فنون *fenoun*) and science (علوم *uloum*) is difficult. The arrival (ورود *vuroud*) of Mahmoud (محمود *Mahmoud*) Pacha in Aleppo (حلب *Halep*). As soon as you hear (خبرينى المق *kháberini álmak*) of Ali Pasha's coming to Constantinople, it will be well for you to write him a petition (عرضحال *arzuhal*). I have a house situated on the sea-shore at Smyrna. A man who wants happiness must be contented (قانع اولمق *káni olmak*) with little. As for me, I am contented with very little.

The Adverb.

632. Adverbs are used to qualify verbs, adjectives, or other adverbs. In Turkish they always go before these said words. Example:—

يارين كل	*Yarin ghel*	Come to-morrow
مصاحبك اول كلماتندن غايت حظ ايدردى	*Ol mussahibin kélimatinden ghayet ház edérdi*	He extremely liked the words of that courtier
ايرتسى كون بر مغارەيه كلدى	*Irtéssi ghiun bir magharayé gheldi*	The next day he came to a cave
اخشامه دكين كزدى	*Akhshama déyin ghézdi*	He walked until evening
وزيرك اندن غير أولادى اولمديغندن قتى خوب و اوضاع نا معقولى اكا دلفريب كورينورردى	*Vézirin ondan ghaïri evladi olmadighindan káti khob vé evza-i-na-makoulou ana dilfirib ghieurunurdu*	The vizier having no other children but him, he appeared very handsome to him, and his senseless ways fascinating

---

* My going is well.　　† Say, "Your obtaining."

بك كوزل چیچك	*Pek ghiuzel chichek*	A *very* pretty flower
ادم ادمی صالت بر کره الدادر	*Adám ádámĭ sált bir kerré áldadir*	One *only* deceives a man *once*
الما كندی اغاجندن ایراق دوشمز	*Elma kendi ághájĭndan irák dushmaz*	An apple does not fall *far* from its own tree
بونلر قتی چوق زمان بو منوال اوزره ذوق وصفا ایدرلردی	*Bounlar kátĭ chok zemán bou minval uzeré zevk ou sáfa edérlérdi*	They (these) enjoyed themselves in this way a *very long* time.

Avoidance of "Yes" and "No."

633. In reply to a question, it is not grammatically incorrect to answer simply " Yes " or " No," using the words اوت *evvet* or بلی *béli* (Yes) and یوق *yok* or خیر *khair** (no) ; but it is more courteous and more customary to repeat the words used by the interrogator, or, at any rate, the word which the question specially refers to.   Example :—

پوسته کلدیمی	*Possta gheldĭmmi ?.*	Has the post arrived ?
اوت افندم کلدی	*Evvet effendim gheldi*	Yes, Sir (it has come)
خیر افندم کلمدی	*Khaïr effendim ghelmadi*	No, Sir (it has not come)
بو می سزك رسمكز	*Bou mou sizin ressminiz ?*	Is *this* your drawing ?
بو	*Bou*	Yes (this).

EXERCISE XXXVIII.

Let us walk quickly, for it will rain before long.   Have you brought the book I spoke of ?   Yes.   Did you get it from *London ?*   Yes.   Does it rain ?   Yes, Sir.   No, Sir.   Did it snow yesterday ?   Yes, Sir.   Is your friend ill ?   No.   Is *this* your writing (یازی *yazĭ*) ?   No.   That is a very pretty flower.   I must leave Smyrna the day after to-morrow (اولبرکون *o bir ghiun*).   Is it necessary that you should go so soon ?   Yes, Sir.   Is it true that you lost your money ?   Yes, Sir. Did you lose it in the street (صوقاق *sokák*) ?   Yes.   How long‡ is this cloth (بز

---

* خیر *khaïr* is more polite than یوق *yok.*

† The interrogative particle می is placed after the word on which the emphasis is laid.

‡ Either نه بو *né boï,* or نه بویده *ne boïdé,* or نه اوزنلقده *né ouzounloukda.*

béz) ? How far (نقدر اوزاق né kádar ouzák) is Adrianople (ادرنه Édirné) from here ? Three hours' journey (اوچ‌ساعتلق يولدر uch saatlik yol dour). Shall we reach it before night ? Yes. Have you received the news of the victory (مظفریت mouzáfferiyet) ? Yes. Have you written to the Minister of Public Instruction (معارف ناظری maarif nazĭrĭ) ? Yes. Did he reply ? No. Probably (غالبا gháliba) he will reply (جواب ويرمك jéwáb vermek) next (كله‌جك ghelejek) week. He was formerly (سابقا sabĭka) a professor in the military (حربی harbi) school. Perhaps (بلكه belki) he has forgotten me. What do you sell these pears at ? Fifty paras. It is very dear. No, sir, it is very cheap (اوجوز oujouz). Give me three okes. Have you any wild ducks (يبان اوردكی yabán ewrdéyi) ? Yes. How much do you sell them at ? Thirty piastres. Do you like wild ducks ? Yes. Flowers are the ornament (زينت zinet) of a garden. Do you not think so ? Yes. The taste (طاعت tát) of meat and vegetables (سبزوات ايله ات et ilé sebzévat). Did you know that Ahmed (احمد Ahmed) wrote a letter yesterday to his father ? Did you know that he would write ? Yes.

The Preposition.

634. A preposition or postposition often refers to more than one word in a sentence. Example :—

طاغك بر خوش
مسيره‌لك محلنه واردقده
كورديكه بش اون آدم بر
يرده اوتورمشلر اوكلرينه بر
دستی قومشلر طعام و
شراب و ماكولاتدن هر نه
استرلر سه اول دستيدن
چقاروب يييوب ذوق
ايدرلر ايدی

Dághĭn bir khosh mes-sirélik mahaliné vardĭkda ghiewrduki besh on ádám bir yérdé otourmoushlar eunleriné bir tessti ko-moushlar taam vé sherab vé mékoulatden hér né iss-térlérsé ol tesstiden chĭka-rĭp yéyip zevk edérlér idi

On his coming to a pleasant open ground amongst the mountains, he saw that five or ten men were sitting in one place, and in front of them they had put a dish, and whatever they wished for in the way of (from) food or wine or eatables they got out of that dish, and ate and enjoyed themselves

بر بيوفانك عشقيله كار
و كسبدن دور اولمق
معقول دكلدر

Bir bivéfanin áshkĭlé kiar-ou-kessbden dour ol-mak makoul déʿil dir

To neglect business (to be far from work and earning) for the love of a faithless (creature) is not sensible

بو قزی بو قدر مال و
جهاز ایله کیم الیرسه
ملکمده طورمسون بر اخر
ولایته کتسون دیدی

Bou kĭzĭ bou kádar mál
ou jihaz ilé kim alĭrsa
mulkumdé dourmasĭn bir
akhĭr vilayeté ghitsin dédi

He said : " Whoever takes this girl *with* so much property and wealth,* let him not stop in my dominions ; let him go to another country"

خانهنك ایچنده اولان
اموال و اثقالدن هر نه وار
ایسه آلوب ولایت
اصلیهسنه کلدی

Khanénin ichindé olán
emwal ou esskáldan hér né
var issé álĭp vilayet-i-
-assliyésiné gheldi

He took whatever wealth and property there was in the house, and came to his native country

مدح و توصیفه باشلادی

Medh ou távsĭfé básh-
ladĭ

He began *to praise and describe* (her)

بلخ شهرنده درت
یاران وار ایدی که ذوق و
راحتده و شدت و محنتده
قطعا بربرلرنـدن دور
اولمزلردی

Balkh shehirindé deurt
yaran var idi ki zevk ou
rahatdé vé shiddet ou mih-
netdé káta birbirlérinden
dour olmázlardĭ

In the city of Balkh there were four companions who *in pleasure and happiness*, and *in affliction* and *sorrow*, were never apart from one another

باقی عمرلرینی فرح و
شادی ایله کچوردیلر

Bákĭ eumrlerini ferah
u shadi ilé ghechirdilér

They passed the rest of their lives in (*with*) joy and gladness

هربارکه اعیان مملکت
و ارباب دولتدن کمسهلر
بو قزی استرلر ویرمزدی و
عقل و فراستده کامل
اولمینه بن قزیمی ویرمم
دیردی

Hér bar ki ayan-i-mem-
léket ou erbáb-i-devletden
kimséler bou kĭzĭ isstérlér
vermazdi vé ákl ou feras-
setdé kiamil olmayana
ben kĭzĭmĭ vermem dérdi

Whenever *any of the* grandees *or* rich men wanted the girl, he did not give her, and he used to say : "I will not give my daughter to any one who is not perfect in intellect and sagacity."

The Conjunction.

635. The conjunctions شايد که *shayedki* (lest, may be that, peradventure), مبادا که *mébada ki* (for fear that, God forbid that), حاشا که *Hasha ki* (God forbid that !), مگر *méyer* or مگر که *méyer ki* (unless), require the verb which

---

* جهاز *jihaz* is a marriage portion, consisting of furniture, jewels, &c.

follows them to be in the optative; and مادامكه *madam ki* (since, as) sometimes takes the optative and sometimes the indicative after it. Example :—

حكما اتفاق ايتديلر كه بو اژدرهانك هلاكنه قوت بشريه طاقت كتوره‌مز مكر بر آدم مرغ هفت رنك قوشك باشنى يمش اوله

Hukema ittifák edilér ki bou azhdérhanin helayiné kouvvet - i - beshriyé táket ghettirémaz méyer bir ádám mergh-i-heftrengh koushoun báshini yémish ola

The wise men agreed that human power was not equal to the destruction of this dragon *unless* a man had eaten the head of the bird "Mergh-heft-rengh" (the bird of seven colours)

بنم سكا بو نصيحتلردن مقصودم بو در كه معشوغكه كتمكه مسامحه اوزره اولميەسن شايد خواجه سعيد كله

Benim sana bou nássihatlerden máksoudoum bou dour ki mashoughouna ghitméyé musamaha uzeré olmayasïn shayed Khoja Saïd ghelé

My object in giving you this advice is that you should not be dilatory in going to your lover, *lest* Khoja Said come

عورت كندى كندويه ايتديكه شمدى عجله ايدوب قاچرسم شايد كه قپلان پشمان اولوب كيرو دونه و اردمدن غلوب يتشه

Avret kendi kendiyé éitdi ki shimdi (shindi) ajelé edip kácharsam shayed ki káplán pishmán oloup ghéri deuné ve ardimden ghelip yetïshé

The woman said to herself : "If I make haste and run away, *peradventure* the leopard repenting (of his promise) *may turn* back, and following me *overtake* me

*ركاب همايونكه عرضحال ايتمكه خوف ايدرم كه شايد قوللرينه باعت برودت اوله

Rikiab-i-humayounouna arzuhal etméye khavf ederim ki shayed koullarina ba'iss-i-bouroudet ola

I am frightened to lay a petition at thy feet *lest* it may be the cause of coolness towards me.

بر طبيب بو جراخته مرهم صارامز مكر خداى متعال كندى كرمندن لطف و احسان ايليه

Bir tabib bou jérahata mérhem saramaz méyer khuda-yi mataal kendi kéreminden loutf ou ihsan éiléyé

A doctor cannot apply an ointment to this wound *unless* God (may He be exalted!) vouchsafe and grant it from His perfect grace.

حاشا كه سنك وجود شريفكه خيانت ايدوب اهانت ايتمش اولم

Hasha ki senin vujoud-i-sherifiné khiyanet edip ihanet etmish olam

God forbid that I should betray thee (thy noble body) and insult thee !

---

* The word ركاب *rikiab* literally means "stirrup," but here corresponds to "feet."

636. In general conjunctions are put at the beginning of the phrases which they connect with something preceding. But دخى *dakhi* and ده *dé* (also) are put *after* the word which is emphasized, as مكتوب دخى لوندرەدن *Londradan dakhĭ mektup áldĭm* (I have also received a letter from London), لوندرەدن مكتوب دخى الدم *Londradan mektub dakhĭ áldĭm* (I have received from London a *letter also*). Examples:—

قز غلامك يوزینی کوردیکی کبی درون دلدن عاشق اولدی وغلام دخی قزك افتاب حسنی کوروب عقلی باشندن زائل اولدی	*Kĭz ghulámin yuzunu ghieurduyu ghibi deroun- -i-dilden áshĭk oldou vé ghulám dakhĭ kĭzĭn afi- tab-i-hussnunu ghieurup áklĭ báshĭndan zaĭl oldou*	As soon as the girl saw the face of the youth she fell in love from the bottom (interior) of her heart, and the *youth also* seeing the girl's sun of beauty, lost his senses *
سندخی اوغلمه نصیحت ایله دیو نیاز ایلدی	*Sendakhĭ oghlouma nássihát éilé déyou niaz éilédi*	He requested *him†* *also* to advise his son (literally he requested him saying: "Thou *also* advise my son"
پدرى زاهدى وزیر ایدوب دایهسنی دخی حرمده اولان جمله جاریهلر اوزرینه باش تعیین ایتدی	*Pédéri zahidi vézir edip dayésini dakhĭ haremdé olán jumlé jariyélér uze- riné básh tayin etdi*	He made his father Zazid vizier and appointed his nurse also head over all the slaves in the harem
قپویی اچهجق وقتده حکمت خدا قپودخی طشرەدن دق اولندی	*Kápĭyĭ ‡ achajak wá- kĭtdé hikmet-i-khuda ká- pĭudakhĭ táshradan dak oloundou*	When she was about to open the door, by the mys- terious ways of Providence, the door also was knocked at from outside
احبانك کیفیت احوالنی تجربه ایتمکده حکماء متقدمین برطریق دخی وضع ایتمشلردر	*Ahĭbbanin kéifiyet-i- ahvalini tejribé etmekdé hukema-i-mutékaddémin bir tarik dakhĭ wáz et- mishlerdir*	In testing the state of friends the ancient sages have laid down a method also

* Literally, his senses disappeared from his head.

† When دیو *déyou* is employed the words of the person referred to are repeated without alteration of the pronoun or person of the verb, precisely as they were uttered.

‡ More commonly pronounced *kapouyou*.

بنم دخی مقصودم اشتر	Benim dakhĭ máksou-	Also my object is that
سندخی بو وجهله مراد	doum ishté sendakhĭ bou	thou also mayst attain (thy)
ايرشهسن	vejhlé muradé erishésin	wish in this way.

637. The conjunction تا *ta* (until) is sometimes used in conjunction with the gerund ending in نجه, which is then put in the dative, and takes the adverb دك *dek,* or دكين *déyin,* or قدر *kadar* after it. The same meaning may be expressed by putting the gerund in the negative without the dative postposition, and omitting دك, دكين, or قدر. Thus, تا او يازنجهيهدك كتمكز *ta o yazinjéyédek ghitmaniz* and تا او يازميانجه كتمكز *ta o yazmayinjé ghitmaniz* both mean exactly the same thing, viz., " Do not go until he writes."

Example :—

نياز ايدرم كه تا بن	Niaz ederim ki ta ben	I request that she may
كلنجهيه دك حرم	ghelinjéyédek harem - i -	do service in thy Imperial
همايونننده خدمت	-humayounounda hizmet	harem until I come.
ايلسون	éilésin	

كه ki.

638. The conjunction كه *ki* is sometimes used in Turkish after such words as ديمك *démek,* سويلمك *suwéylémek,* رجا ايتمك *rija etmek,* &c., in such a way as to correspond to our inverted commas put over words quoted. In such cases it must be omitted when translating into English ; and, in citing words, when writing or speaking Turkish, precisely the same pronouns and the same tenses and persons of the verbs must be employed as those used by the person who uttered them. Thus the sentence, " He said he would come next week " must be put in Turkish thus, ديد يكه كلهجك هفته كلورم *dédi ki gheléjek háfta ghelirim,* which literally means, " He said, ' I will come next week.' " In conversation, however, it is more usual to omit كه, and then the words quoted are put *before* such words as صورمق, سويلمك, ديمك, &c. ; but in this case, also, when the words of another are reported they must be repeated precisely as uttered, without the change of pronouns and tenses and persons of the verbs we introduce. Example :—

پس بعد زمان زاهدك	Pess bad- i-zamán zahi-	Then, after some time,
دخی حجدن سلامت	din dakhĭ hájdan sélamet	the ascetic also coming
ايله كلوب كورديكه نه	ilé ghelip ghieurdu ki né	safely (back) from the pil-
قوش وار و نه اوغلی وار	koush var vé né oghlou	grimage saw that there was
و نه دايه وار سبحان الله	var vé né daya var	neither the bird, nor his

بونلر نیجه اولدی دینجه
خاتون اغلیهرق زاهدك
یوزینه باقوب بنم افندم
باشك صاغ اولسون
جملهسی كوچدیلر انلرك
فرتندن بو حاله كرفتار
اولوب كول یوزم كهربایه
دوندی دیدی

*subhana 'lláh bounlar nijé
oldou dénjé khátoun
ághlayarak zahidin yuzuné
bákip benim effendim bá-
shǐn sagh olsoun jumléssi
gheuchduler onlarin firkát-
indan bou halé ghiriftar
oloup ghiul yuzum kehru-
bayé deundu dédi*

son, nor his nurse (there).
On his saying, " Oh God !
what has become of them ? "
the woman cried, and looking into the ascetic's face,
said, "Well, never mind.*
They have all decamped.
Owing to my separation
from them, I have got into
this state, and my rosy face
has turned to (the colour of)
amber"

برکون بر قره قولق اول
یره اوغرایوب كوردیكه بر
جای خوش و مقام
دلكش و موضع دلارام
غایتله طبیعتی حظ
ایدوب انده توطن ایتمكه
نیت ایلدی میمون قره
قولق انده كوروب دیدیكه
قره قولق بو خباثت و
قباحت نه درکه ایدرسن
و نیچون كندی حدكی
بیلمیوب ایاغك
یورغانندن طشره اوزادرسن

*Bir ghiun bir kára
koulák ol yéré oghrayip
ghieurdu ki bir jayi-khosh
vé mékám-i-dilkesh vé
mevzǐ-ǐ-dilaram ghaᵧetlé
tabiati ház edip anda té-
wattoun etméyé niyet éǐlé-
di. Maïmoun·kára koulák
andé ghieurup dédi ki
kára koulák 'bou khabaset
u kábahat né dir ki edér-
sin vé nichin kenđi 'hadini
bilméyip ayaghin your-
ghánǐndan táshra ouzá-
dǐrsǐn ?*

One day a lynx, coming
to that place, saw it (was)
an agreeable spot, a charm-
ing situation, and a delight-
ful position. (His nature)
liking it very much he determined to settle there.
The monkey, seeing the
lynx there, said : " Lynx,
what is this villany and ras-
cality thou art perpetrating ?
and why dost thou not know
thy station and not stretch
thy foot out beyond thy
quilt ?"†

اوازبلند ایله جاغردیكه
كیرو طور عجله ایتمه سكا
بر سوزم واردر

*Awaᵤ-i-bulend ilé cha-
ghǐrdǐ ki ghéri dour ajelé
etma sana bir seuzum var
dir*

She cried out with a loud
voice: "Stand back! do not
be in a hurry, I have a word
to say to thee "

بر ساعت مقداری
ملاحظه ایدوب بعده

*Bir saat mǐkdari mula-
haza edip badahu báshǐnǐ*

He reflected for the space
of an hour and then raised

---

* The expression باشك صاغ اولسون means literally, " May your head be
healthy," but is used in a consolatory way, and corresponds to " Never mind."

† This is a Turkish idiom expressive of any one presuming too far.

باشنی قالدیروب دیدیکه
اول قزی پریلر قاپوب
فلان جزیره ایچنده بر
قوی یرده حفظ ایتمشلر
در انا وارمغه بنی آدمك
قدرتی یتشمز

káldĭrip dédi ki ol kĭzĭ
périler kapip filan jéziré
ichindé bir kavi yerdé hifz
etmishler dir ana varma-
gha beni ádámĭn koudreti
yetishmaz

his head and *said :* "The
fairies have carried off that
girl and have secured her
in a strong place in such-
and-such an island. The
power of mankind is not
sufficient to go to her"

قردخی دیدیکه
شمدیدنصره جمله خلق
بنم شوملغمه و نحوستمه
حمل ایدرلر معقولی بو
در که بندخی کندیمی
قربان ایده‌یم

Kĭz dakhĭ dédiki shim-
didensora jumlé khalk be-
nim shoumloughouma vé
nouhoussetimé haml edér-
lér makoulou bou dour ki
ben dakhĭ kendimi kour-
bán edéyim

The girl also said :
"Henceforth all the peo-
ple will attribute (this) to
my malign and unlucky in-
fluence. The best thing for
me to do is to sacrifice myself also"

ماه شکر سؤال ایتدیکه
نیجه در اول حکایه

Mah-shékér su'al etdi
ki nijé dir ol hikiayé ?

Mah - Shékér asked :
"What (how) is that tale?"
(in good English, Mah-
Sheker asked what that
tale was)

قتی اواز ایله دیدیکه
بنم* اخرت قرنداشم
اولەسن

Kátĭ awaz ilé dédi ki
benim akhĭret karndashĭm
olasĭn

She told him in a loud
voice to be her adopted
brother (literally she told
him : "Be my adopted bro-
ther ")

طوطی چاغردیکه ای
عبیده بز سنك خانەکه
کلوب سکا مهمان اولمشز
نیچون بزمله صحبت
ایتمزسن

Touti chaghĭrdĭki éi
Abidé biz senin khanéné
ghelip sana mihman ol-
moushouz nichin bizimlé
suhbet etmazsin?

The parrot cried out :
"Abidé, we have come to
thy house and become thy
guests, why dost thou not
associate with us ?"

بر اعرب خلیفه‌یه
کلوب دیدیکه یا امیر
المؤمنین حج ایتمكه
عزیمت ایلدم لکن اقچەم
یوقدر

Bir Arab khaliféyé
ghelip dédiki ya emir-ul-
-mou'menin háj etméyé
ázimet éilédim lakin ák-
chém yokdour

An Arab came to the
caliph and *said* that he had
determined to perform the
pilgrimage, but that he had
no money.

---

* اخرت *akhĭret* means the future state ; but in this place and on similar
ccasions it is used as an adjective, and means "adopted."

يوخسه *yokhsa,* " Or."

639. The conjunction يوخسه *yokhsa* (or) is used instead of ياخود when there is a doubt expressed, which is indicated by the use of the interrogative particle می *mi.*

كتمكه اذن وارميدر يوخسه يوقميدر	*Ghitméyé izn varmĭ dir yokhsa yokmoudour?*	Have (I) permission to go *or* not?
فى الحقيقه بنم محبوبم عاقـلـمـيـدر يـوخـسـه احمقمبدر معلومم دكل	*Fi'l hák̆iké benim mah- bouboum ák̆ĭlmĭdĭr yokhsa ahmakmidir maloumoum déil*	Really, I do not know whether my beloved is in- telligent *or* stupid.

EXERCISE XXXIX.

He only deceived (الداتمق *áldatmak*) me once.   The *savans* (علما *oulema*) agreed that a man could not speak so well unless he had studied Arabic.   Do not light the fire until I come.   I cannot receive the tobacco (توتون *tutun*) I ordered (اصمارلمـق *issmarlamak*) from Salonica (سلانيك *Sélanik*) until the steamer (واپور *vapor*) arrives. Do not start till he writes.   He said that he would write to me in three weeks.   He asked me if I were well.   I said I was very well.   I will write to you, but you also must write to me.   She is a handsome, well-behaved (ادبلو *édebli*), and modest (محجوب *mahjoub*) girl.   What is the length (طول *toul*) of the Red Sea (بحراحمر *Báhr-i-ahmér*)?   Who is governor (حاكم *hakim*) of the island (جزيره *jéziré*) of Malta (مالطه *Malta*)?   Is he a countryman of yours?   No. Have you ever travelled (سياحت ايتمك *séyahet*) in India (هندستان *hindisstan*)? Yes.   Have you read many Turkish books?   No; I do not know whether they are good or bad.   I do not know whether my friend is sincere (صادق *sádĭk*) or insincere (بيوفا *bivéfa*).   There is no resource (چاره *charé*) but to leave (ترك *terk*) the country (ديار *diyar*).   I do not know whether it is good or bad.   Is he an honest (اهل عرض *ehl-i-irz*) man?   Yes.   Do you know the reason of his coming here?   Yes, but I cannot tell you.   We cannot begin dinner until Mr. So-and-so arrives.   I doubt that he will comé.   He is* sure (امر مقرر در *emr-i-moukarrér dĭr*) to come.   Do you think your brother will come?   He said he would come.   I said we would wait (بكلمك *beklémek*).   He said he was going to India, but he has not gone yet (دها *daha*).   I shall be very sorry if he goes.   If he went I should be glad.   Would that I were going too (دخی *dakhĭ*).   If you wish you can go.   I wish (كاشكی *keshki*) that I was as learned as (قدر *kadar*) you.   I want (استمك *isstémek*) you to buy me two okes of tobacco.   Bring me six okes of grapes.

---

* Say, "His coming is sure."

You told me yesterday not to buy grapes. He said he would pay (پاره ویرمك *para vérmek*). I told him not to come on Sunday (بازار کوني *Bazar ghiunu*). I asked him if he would come on Tuesday (سالی کوني *Sáli ghiunu*). I was sure (ابو بلمك *éi bilmek*) he would come, as he said he would.

Order of the Words in a Turkish Sentence.

640. The proper position of the verb is at the end of the sentence; but, still, in common conversation, when short phrases are used, it occasionally (especially when in the imperative) is followed by its object. Example:—

ال پارهکزی	*Âl paranizi*	Take your money
صویی صچراتمه	*Souyou sïchrátma*	Do not splash the water
وارکتور اول ادمی	*Var ghettir ol ádámi*	Go and bring that man
کوزکی اچ قوغارم سنی	*Ghieuzunu ach koghárïm seni*	Mind what you are about (or) I will dismiss you
ال سنا یکرمی پاره دها	*Âl séna yirmi para daha*	Here, take twenty paras more.

641. In a simple sentence the order of the words is as follows:—1st, the subject; 2nd, the noun or pronoun which is the object of the verb; 3rd, the verb. Example:—

فلان افندی بر کوزل او صاتون الدی	*Filán effendi bir ghiuzel ev sátïn áldï*	Mr. So-and-so has bought a nice house
سلطان مصر رخصت ویردی	*Soultán-ï-missr roukhsát vérdi*	The king of Egypt gave permission.

642. If the verb have a direct and indirect object, viz., a noun in the accusative and another in the dative, or a noun in the accusative and another in the ablative, the noun in the accusative is generally put nearest to the verb. Occasionally, however, the dative comes after the accusative; but the accusative is almost always put after the ablative. Example:—

اکر علاج ایده بلورایسهکز قزی سکا ویروب سنی کندیمه داماد ایدرم	*Éyér ilaj edé bilirissé-niz kïzï sana verip seni kendimé damad ederim*	If thou canst cure her, I will give the *girl to thee* and make *thee* son-in-law *to myself*
بر کون بر ادم کندی خانهسنی بر اخر ادمه فروخت ایلدی	*Bir ghiun bir ádám kendi khanésini bir akhïr ádáma furoukht éilédi*	One day a man sold his own *house to* another *man*

s 2

اولدخی بر التون اوجنه قریدی	Ol dakhĭ bir áltĭn awoujouna koìdou	He also put *a piece of* gold into his *hand*
بزلره اوچ سپد افیون کوندرهسز*	Bizleré uch séped afyon ghieunderésiz	Send *us* three *baskets* of opium
بادیکه شهزاده یه اصلنی سویلمدکچه اولمز	Bildi ki shehzadéyé ásslini suwéylémédikché olmaz	He knew that it would be impossible until he told *the prince* the *origin* (cause) of it
سیار اول طبیبه اولاد ضمننده ارزوسنی نقل ایدوب و بکا برعلاج ایله دیو عظیم نیاز ایتدی	Seyyar ol tábibé evlad zimnindé arzousounou nákl edip vé bána bir ilaj éilé déyou ázĭm nĭyaz etdi	Seyyar told that *doctor* his *desire* with reference to children and urgently requested him to give him a remedy
قزینی اول جوانه نکاح ایلدی	Kĭzĭnĭ ol juwané nikiah éilédi	He married *his daughter* to that young man
کرم و لطف ایدوب بنی انامه و بابامه کتورک	Kérem ou loutf edip béni anama vé bábáma ghettirin	Have the kindness to take *me* to *my mother and father* *
جناب حقه شکر ایلدی دوستندن بر هدیه الدی	Jenáb hákka shukr éilédi Dosstoundan bir hédiyé áldĭ	He gave *thanks to God* He received a *present from* his *friend*
شیر بونلردن بو کلامی ایشتدیکی کیی غضبی ساکن اولدی	Shir bounlardan bou kélami ishitdiyi ghibi gházábĭ sakin oldou	As soon as the lion heard these words from them his anger was appeased
اول محلی فریده کوستردیلر	Ol mahali feridé ghieusstérdiler.	They showed that *place* to Ferid
قزیمی ویرمکی اژدرهانک اولمسنه تعلیق ایتمشدم یوخسه بویله اولممش اولیدی قزیمی اول یکیده ویردم	Kĭzĭmĭ verméyi éžhdérhanin eulmasiné talik etmishdim yokhsa beuilé olmamish olaydi kĭzĭmĭ ol yighidé vérerdim	I made giving my daughter depend on the death of the dragon; or, had it not been so, I would give my daughter to that youth.

643. Adverbs of time generally come at the beginning of the sentence before everything; if there be an adverb or an adverbial phrase expressing the place where the action takes place it comes next, and if there be another

* It will be seen from the above examples that there is considerable latitude allowed as regards the relative positions of the dative and accusative.

adverb or adverbial expression indicating the way in which the act is performed, that follows. The adverb or adverbial phrase of manner may also come before the adverb or adverbial phrase of place. Example :—

بو كون فرانسز وابورايله بر قطعه مكتوب مرغوبلريني الدم	*Bou ghiun fransĭz va-* *porilé bir kĭta mektoub* *merghoublerini āldīm*	*To-day* I received a welcome letter of yours *by the* *French steamer*
بوكون خدمتكارمز ايله سزلره اون دانه قاوون كوندردم	*Bou ghiun hizmetkiar* *imiz ilé sizleré on tané* *kawoun ghieunderdim*	I sent you *to-day* ten melons *by my servant*
بر كون عـادت معروفهسى اوزره شهرك ايچنده در بدر كزركن	*Bir ghiun adet-i-ma-* *rouféssi uzeré shehirin* *ichindé der béder ghézer-* *ken*	*One day* going from door to door in the town *according to his usual custom*
بعد زمان سالما غانما ازربيجانه كلوب داخل اولديلر	*Bad-i-zemán saliman* *ghániman azerbéijané* *ghelip dakhil oldoular*	*After some time* they came in safety, loaded *with* *spoil*, to Azerbéijan and entered it.

Emphatic Words.

644. If one wishes to draw attention to a word it is put as near the verb as possible, and thus the ordinary order of the words in a sentence is sometimes interfered with, and we see the nominative coming after the accusative, and so on. Example :—

خاتمى بن قولك بولورم	*Khatemi ben koulloun* *boulouroum*	*I* your servant will find the ring
سكا كيم ويردى	*Sana kim vérdi ?*	*Who* gave it to you ?
همشيرهسى جميلهيى بوكا نكاح ايلدى	*Hemshiréssi Jemiléyi* *bouna nikiah ĕĭlédi*	He married his sister Jemilé to *this one*
قزى باباسى بكا ويردى	*Kĭzĭ bábássĭ bána* *vérdi*	Her father gave the girl *to me*
بكا قزى والدهسى ويردى	*Bána kĭzĭ walidéssi* *vérdi*	*Her mother* gave the girl to me
زاهد اره يرده شاشوب قزى قنغيسنه ويرهجكنى بلمدى	*Zahid ara yerdé shaship* *kĭzĭ kánghĭsĭna veréjeyeni* *bilmadi*	The ascetic in the meantime getting confused did not know *to which of them* he should give his daughter

سن چلبی بن چلبی   *Sen chelébi ben chelébi*   If thou art a gentleman,
اتی کیم قاشر   *átï kim káshïr ?*   and I be a gentleman, *who* will groom the horse.

EXERCISE XL.

I received a present from my uncle last (کچن *ghechen*) week. The pasha gave money to the poor (فقیرلر *fakïrler*). She showed the house to me. To whom did your friend sell his house? He sold it last year to my father. To-morrow I shall hunt (اولامق *ávlamak*) with my own dogs (تازی *tázï*) in the neighbourhood (جوار *jiwar*) of Belgrade (بلغراد *Belégrad*). I wish (کاشکی *keshki*) that I were going with you. Come with me, if you like (استملك *isstémek*). I should like (حظ ایتملك *ház*) very much (پك *pek*), but I am busy (ایشم وار *.*). When you see Mr. So-and-so give him my compliments (مخصوص سلام *makhsouss selam*). I will. Did you know that he was ill? No. Has he caught (المق *almak*) cold? A cold wind is blowing (اسملك *essmek*). Do you know where he lives (اوطورمق *otourmak*)? He lives in such-and-such a street (صوقاق *sokák*). Is it far (اوزاق *ouzák*) from here? I will show you his house. The sun has begun to rise (طوغمق *doghmak*). The weather is very mild (ملایم *mulayim*). Do you know that it hailed (طولو یاغمق *dolou yaghmak*) yesterday? It (the ice) (بوز *bouz*) is thawing (اریملك *erimek*) now. I hope that it will clear up (احلمق *achilmak*). If you want to send your letter by to-day's mail (پوسته *possta*), you must make haste (عجله ایتملك *ajelé etmek*). Shall I seal it (مهورلملك *muhurlémek*)? Yes. Take this letter at once (همان *heman*) to the post (پوسته *possta*), and pay for it. First of all (ابتدا *ibtida*), show me some rings (یوزك *yuzuk*). Who gave you this ring? I bought it. Do not begin to read till I come. I cannot receive the grapes I ordered from Smyrna until the steamer arrives. He cried out to me not to be in a hurry (عجله ایتملك *ajelé etmek*), and that he had a word to say to me (سکا بر سوزم وار *sana bir seuzum var*). It is a long time (خیلی *khaïli*) since he went (کیدهلی *ghidéli*); perhaps he may come soon (یقینده *yakïndé*). He had never been able (قادر *kadïr*) to earn (تحصیل تهصیل ایتملك *tahsïl etmek*) one halfpenny more (زیاده *ziyadé*) than was sufficient (کفایت ایتملك *kéfayet etmek*) for the day. As soon as the peasant (دهقان *dihkan*) awoke, not finding his jewel in his breast (قوین *koïn*), he knew that the travellers (سیاح *seyyah*) had taken it. He said to himself: if I tell them and demand (طلب *taleb*) the jewel, it is probable that I shall not be able to get it. After a few days they came to Greece, and the peasant presented (صونمق *sunmak*) a petition, and made known (اعلام ایتملك *ilam etmek*) his case (احوال *ahwal*) to the king (صلطان *soultán*) of Greece (روم *Roum*). The king of Greece had the travellers (کتورتملك *ghettirtmek*)

brought before him, and interrogated (سويلتمك *suwéyletmek*), and they flatly (بالْك)
denied it (انكار ايتمك *inkiar etmek*). Well (هله *helé*), they put the travellers in
prison (حبس ايتمك *habss etmek*). But the king of Greece reflected (عظيم فكر‌ه
âzĭm fikré gheldi ki), perhaps, if I punish (مجازات ايتمك *mujazat etmek*)
these three individuals (شخص *shakhss*) merely (مجرد *mujerred*) on (ايله) their
word (قول *kávl*), perhaps I may torment (رنجيده ايتمك *renjidé etmek*) innocent
(بكناه *bighiunah*) men* unjustly (نا حق *na hák*). It is related (نقل اولنمق *nákl*
olounmak) that, in olden times (زمان اولد‌ه *zemán-i-evveldé*) there was a merchant
in the city of Damascus (دمشق *Damaskh*) who was the possessor (صاحب *sahib*)
of immense (فراوان *firavan*) wealth. The said merchant had a virtuous daughter
(پاكيزه كريمه *pakizé kerimé*) called (نامنده *namindé*) Dilfuruz, exactly (تمام *támám*)
sixteen years (اون التی یاشنده *own áltĭ yashindé*) of age. One day in spring
(ايام بهارد‌ه *eyyam i bahardé*), while the vineyards (باغ) and gardens (بستان *bosstan*)
were decked (مزين *muzéyen*) with flowers (شكوفه ايله *shughiufé ilé*), that rose-
cheeked damsel (كلعذار *ghiulizar*), wishing to walk in the rose-gardens (ارزوی سير
arzouyi-séïr ghiulzar edip), came into the garden (باغ *bagh*) with a few
female slaves (جاريه *jariyé*), and sat down under a shady tree (سايه‌دار درخت
sayédar dirakht). While looking around (اطرافه *etrafé*) her eyes fell (راست كلمك
rasst ghelmek) on a rose, which raised (جلمك *chekmek*) her head like a proud
cypress (سرو سركش *serv sérkesh*) tree, and was distinguished (سمتاز *mumtaz*) from
all by her beauty. . . But the rose being exceedingly (كمال مرتبه *kémal mertebé*)
high up (یوكسكده *yuksekdé*), it was not possible to pluck (قوپارمتی *koparmak*) it.

* Omit "men."

TURKISH PROVERBS.

دل قلیجدن چوق اولدرر

Dil kĭlĭjdan chok eul-durur

The tongue kills more than the sword

چوغه طالب اولان ازه یتشور

Chogha talib oldn dza yetishir

He who demands too much gets but little

چوق یاشایان چوق بیلمز چوق کزن چوق بیلور

Chok yashayan chok bilmaz chok ghézen chok bilir

He who has lived long does not know much; he who has travelled much knows much

دلی اولدرکه زنکیندر و لکن فقرا کبی کچینور

Déli oldirki zenghin dir vé lakin foukera ghibi ghechenir

He is a madman who being rich lives as if he were poor

حق سوز زهردن آجیدر

Hăk seuz zéhirden ájĭ dir

A true word is bitterer than poison

حیوان اولور سمری قالور انسان اولور آدی قالور

Haïwăn eulur seméri kălĭr insan eulur adi kălĭr

(If) a horse dies his saddle remains behind him; if a man dies his name remains

دشمن قارنجه ایسه فیل کبی ظن ایله

Dushmen kărĭnjé issé fil ghibi zan eilé

If an enemy be (as small as) an ant, think him like an elephant

دلکی الدانلمز

Tĭlki áldanĭlmaz

A fox is not deceived

حدمت ایتمکی اوکرنمین افندیلك دخی ایتمز

Hizmet etméyi euren-méyen efendilik dakhĭ etmaz

He who does not learn how to serve, will also not know how to act as a master

دیکندن کل بتر کلدن دیکن

Dikenden ghiul bitér ghiulden diken

The rose grows from the thorn, and the thorn from the rose

توتوندن قورتلمق ایچون اتش ایچنه دوشمه

Tutunden kourtoulmak ichin átesh ichiné dushma

Do not fall into the fire to escape from the smoke

تنبله هر کون بیرامدر

Tenbelé hér ghiun Bay-ram dir

To the lazy man every day is a fête (Bayram)

بیك ایشت بر سویله

Bin ishit bir suwéylé

Hear a thousand times, speak once

بیك تاسه بر بورج اودەمز

Bin tássé bir borj eudé-maz

A thousand sorrows do not pay a debt

بو كونكى يمورطه يارينكى طاوقدن يكدر	*Bou ghiunki yĭmourta yarĭnkĭ tawoukdan yekdir*	To-day's egg is better than to-morrow's fowl
تهى دست قپويه وارسن افندى اويور ديرلر الكده پيشكش اولسه افندم بيور ديرلر	*Téhi desst kápĭya varsan effendi ouyour dérlér elindé bir pishkesh olsa effendim bouyour dérlér*	If you come to the door empty handed, they say to you: "The master is asleep." If you have a present in your hand, they say: "Master, come in"
تيز كيدن تيز يورلور	*Téz ghiden téz yoroulour*	He who goes quickly is quickly tired
ايولك ايله دكزه براق دكز بيلمز ايسه خالق بيلور	*Éilik éilé dénizé brak déniz bilmaz issé khalĭk bilir*	Do good and cast it into the sea. If the sea does not recognise it, the Creator will
ايولك بيلمين آدم ادم صايلماز	*Éilik bilméyen ádám ádám sayilmaz*	A man who does not recognise kindness is not accounted a man
بخشيش آتك ديشنه باقلماز	*Bakhshish átĭn dishiné bákĭlmaz*	The teeth of a gift horse are not looked at
بر ايو شراب ودلبر عورت ايكى طاتلو زهردر	*Bir éi sherab vé dilbér avret iki tátlĭ zéhir dir*	A good wine and a fascinating woman are two sweet poisons
بقال برادم ايچون دكان اچماز	*Bákkál bir ádám ichin dukkian achmaz*	A grocer does not open a shop for one man
بكلره اينانمه صويه طيانمه كچ كونه اينانمه عورت سوزينه الدانمه اتك يوركنه طيانمه	*Beyleré inanma souya dayanma ghech ghiuné inanma avret seuzuné áldanma átĭn yuréyiné dayanma*	Do not believe in the great, do not lean on water, do not trust in the dying day, do not believe in a woman's word, and do not trust to the courage of your horse
بنى صايانك قولى ايم بنى صايميانك سلطانى ايم	*Béni sayanin koulou youm béni saymayanin soultánĭ yĭm*	I am the slave of him who hath consideration for me, and the lord of him who hath no consideration for me

اغلامیان چوجغه ممه ویرمزلر	*Âghlamayan chojougha mémé vermézler*	They do not give the breast to a child who does not cry
اکری اوتور طوغری سویله	*Éghri otour doghrou suwéylé*	Sit crooked, speak straight (truth)
الچق یرده دپه جك کندوسنی طاغ صانور	*Âlchak yerdé tepéjek kendissini dâgh sanïr*	A little hill in a low place thinks itself a mountain
الله دیین محروم قالماز	*Âllâh déyen mahroum kâlmaz*	He who calls on God is not disappointed
الما کندی اغاجندن ایراق دوشمز	*Élma kendi âghâjindan irâk dushmaz*	The apple does not fall far from its own tree
انسان انسانك اینه سی در	*Insan insanin aïnéssi dir*	Man is the mirror of man
تقدیر تدبیری بوزار	*Tâkdïr tedbiri bozar*	Man proposes, and God disposes
اوغری اول خرمز اول انصافی الدن قومه	*Oghrou ol khïrsïz ol insâfi elden koma*	Be a robber, be a thief, (but) do not put conscience aside
اولوم قره دوه در که هر قپوده چوکر	*Eulum kâra devé dir ki hér kâpïdé cheuker*	Death is a black camel which kneels down at everybody's door
ایشنی بیلن اشنی بیلن آشنی بیلن فقیر اولمز	*Ishini bilen eshini bilen âshini bilen fakïr olmaz*	He who knows his business, he who knows his companion, and he who knows his food, does not get poor
ایکی رئیس برکمی باترر	*Iki ré'iss bir ghémi bâtïrïr*	Two captains sink the ship
اصله جق ادم صوده بوغلماز	*Assilajak âdâm souda boghoulmaz*	A man who is to be hanged will not drown
ادم ادمه کرکدر	*Adâm âdâma gherek dir*	Man is necessary to man
ات حولر کاروان کچر	*It havlar kiarvan ghechér*	The dog barks, (but) the caravan passes on
اتلن اوق کیرو دونمز	*Atïlan ok ghéri deunmaz*	The arrow which has been cast comes not back

اخشام ايسه يات صباح ايسه كيت	*Âkhsham issé yat sabâh issé ghit*	Sleep in the evening, and bestir thyself in the morning
ادم ادمى صالت بر كره الدادر	*Âdâm âdâmĭ sâlt bir kerré âldadir*	One only deceives a man once
ادم اولدر كه اقراردن دونمز	*Âdâm ol dir ki ikrarin- den deunmaz*	He is a man who does not turn from what he has said
ارق طاوقدن سميز توريت اولمز	*Arĭk tawoukdan sémiz tirid* olmaz*	You cannot make a fat broth from a lean fowl
جان جانك يولداشيدر	*Ján jánĭn yoldashĭ dĭr*	The soul is the companion of the soul
دل ادمى بيان ايدر	*Dil âdâmĭ béyan edér*	The tongue proclaims the man
دلينك يوركى اغزنده در عاقلك دلى يوركنده در	*Délinin yuréyi âgh- zĭnda dir âkĭlĭn dili yu- réyindé dir*	The heart of the fool is in his tongue, the tongue of the wise man is in his heart
دوست ايله يه ايچ الش ويريش ايتمه	*Dosst ilé yé ich âlĭsh verish etma*	Eat and drink with a friend, but do no trade with him
دوست فنا وقتده بيلنور	*Dosst féna wâkĭtda bilenir*	A friend is known in bad times
دوسته جوق واران اكشى صورت كورر	*Dossta chok varan ekshi souret ghieurur*	He who goes too often to a friend sees a sour face (gets sour looks)
دوست بيك ايسه از در دشمن بر ايسه جوقدر	*Dosst bin issé âz dĭr dushmen bir issé chok dour*	A thousand friends are but little; one enemy is a great deal
راحت استين آدم صاغر كور دلسز اولملو	*Rahat isstéyen âdâm saghĭr kieur dilsiz olmalĭ*	A man who wants comfort must be deaf, blind, and dumb
روزكاره توكرن يوزينه توكرر	*Rouzghiaré tukiuren yuzuné tukiurur*	He who spits at the wind spits in his own face

---

* Old-fashioned spelling for ترید *tirid*, the name of a dish consisting of broth or gravy with bread in it.

زحمتسز بال ينمز	*Zahmetsiz bál yénmez*	Without trouble one eats no honey
زحمتسز بر شی اولمز	*Zahmetsiz bir shéi olmaz*	Nothing is achieved without trouble
زمانه اويمق كرك در	*Zemáné ouïmak gherek dir*	One must accommodate himself to the times
سرت سركه كندى قابنه ضرر ايدر	*Sert sirké kendi kábïna zarar edér*	Strong vinegar injures its own vessel
سر ويرمك اولور سر ويرمك اولماز	*Sér vermek olour sir vermek olmaz*	You may give up your head, but you must not give up a secret
صبر ايلمك شاذلق اناختريدر	*Sábr éilémek shazlik anakhtari dir*	Patience is the key of joy
صقال باشه قربان اولسون	*Sakkál básha kourbán olsoun*	Sacrifice your beard to save your head
طاتلو دل يردن ييلانى چيقارر	*Tátlï dil yérden yïlánï chïkarïr*	A sweet tongue draws the snake forth from the earth
طاغ طاغه اولاشماز انشان انسانه اولاشور	*Dágh dágha oulashmaz insan insané oulashïr*	Mountain does not meet mountain, but man meets man
طوتلمين اوغرى بكدن طوغرى	*Toutoulmayan oghrou beyden doghrou*	A thief who has not been caught is honester than a bey (in the eyes of the world)
طوز اتمك بلمين اتدن كوتو در	*Touz ekmek bilméyen itden kieutu dir*	He who does not recognise bread and salt is worse than a dog
عاشغه بغداد اوزاق دكل	*Ashïgha Baghdad ouzák déil dir*	Bagdad is not far to a lover
طوغرى سويليني طقوز شهردن سوررلر	*Doghrou suwéyléyeni dokouz shehirden surérlér*	He who tells the truth is turned out of nine cities
عيبسز يار استين يارسز قالور	*Aypsiz * yar isstéyen yarsiz kalïr*	He who wants a faultless friend remains friendless
فائده ضررك قرنداشيدر	*Fa'idé zararin karndashï dïr*	Advantage is the brother of injury

---

* Generally pronounced *aypsiz* although written *aybsiz.*

قرەیە صابون دلیه اوكوت نه ایلسون	*Káraya saboun déliyé uyut né éilésin?*	What good is soap to a nigger, or advice to a fool ?
قضا كلدكده دانش كوزی كور اولور	*Káza gheldikdé danish gheuzu kieur olour*	When fate overtakes us the eye of wisdom becomes blind
قورت تویىی دكشدرر خویىی دكشدرمز	*Kourt tuyunu déyish-dirir khouyounou déyish-dirmaz*	The wolf changes his coat, but he does not change his nature
قوردی اورماندن آچلق چیقارر	*Kourdou ormándan achlik chikarir*	Hunger brings the wolf out of the wood
قوزغونه یاوریسی بلبل كلور	*Kouzghouna yavrissi bulbul ghelir*	The young of the raven appears to it a nightingale
كدی بولنمدیغی یرده سیچانلر باش قالدرر	*Kédi boulounmadighi yérdé sichánler básh kál-dirir*	The mice raise their heads where the cat is not to be found
كسەمدیكك الی اوپ	*Kessémédiyin eli eup*	Kiss the hand which you cannot cut off
كلمك ارادت كیتمك اجازت	*Ghelmek iradet ghitmek ijazet*	The will only is wanted to come, permission is wanted to go
كلی استین دیكنلری دخی استمك كرك	*Ghiulu isstéyen diken-leri dakhi isstémek gherek*	He who wants the rose must want the thorns also
كوپكسز چوبانك قیوىی قورت الور	*Kieupeksiz chobánin koyounou kourt álir*	The wolf steals the sheep of the shepherd who has not a dog
كندیندن دوشن اغلامز	*Kendinden dushen ágh-lamaz*	He who falls of himself does not cry
كچوك بیوكه تابع اولملو	*Kuchuk buyuké tabi olmali*	The little must obey the great
كور قوشك یواسىی تكری یاپار	*Kieur kouzhoun yiwas-sini tangri yapar*	God builds the nest of the blind bird
كورك استدیكی ایكی كوز در	*Kieurun isstédiyi iki ghieuz dir*	What the blind man de-sires is two eyes
كوز بر پنجره در كوكله باقار	*Ghieuz pénjeré dir ghieunulé bákar*	The eye is a window which looks into the heart

كوزدن اوزاق اولان اولان
كوكلدن دخى اوزاق

Ghieuzden ouzak olan ghiunulden dakhĭ ouzak

He who is far from the eye is also far from the heart

كوزمزى اچالم يوخسه اچارلر

Ghieu.umuẓu achalim yokhsa acharlar

Let us open our eyes, or they will open them for us

كوملك قفتاندن يقيندر

Ghieumlek káftándan yakĭndĭr

The shirt is nearer to us than the coat (kaftan)

كونه كوره كورك كيمك كرك

Ghiuné ghieuré kieurk ghémek gherek

You must put on furs according to the weather

كيشينك حرمتى كندى النده در

Kishinin hurmeti kendi elindé dir

The respect one gets depends on one's self

لاقردى ايله پلاو اولماز

Lakĭrdĭ ilé pilaw olmaz

Pilaw is not made by talking

مالمز يوغيسه عرضمز اولسون

Málĭmĭz yoghooussa irzimiz olsoun

If we have not wealth, let us have honour

محبت ايكى باشدندر

Mahabet iki báshdan dĭr

Love must be on two sides

محب صادق ايو در كيشينك اقرباسندن

Mouhib-i-sádĭk éi dir kishinin ákrabassĭndan

A faithful friend is better than one's relations

مفت سركه بالدن طاتلو در

Muft sirké báldan tátlĭ dĭr

Vinegar which one gets for nothing is sweeter than honey

ميخانه‌جى غزل المز

Méykhanéji ghazl ál-maz

A wine-shop keeper does not take songs (as payment)

نصل كه ياشارسق اويله اولورز

Nasl ki yasharsak euilé euluruz

As we live, so shall we die

نه اكرسن انى بچرسن

Né ekeérsen onou bichérsin

Whatever you sow, that will you reap

ويرن الى كمسه كسمز

Véren eli kimsé kessmez

No one cuts the hand which gives

هپسندن بختلو در بشكده اولان

Hepsinden éi dir beshikdé oldn

He is most fortunate who is in his cradle

هر اغاجك كولكه‌سى وار

Her ághájĭn ghiul-ghéssi var

Every tree has its shadow

هر اغلمه‌نك كولمه‌سى وار

Her ághlamanĭn ghiul-massĭ var

Every cry has its laugh

يوركدن يوركه يول وار	*Yurekden ̯uréyé yol var*	There is a road from heart to heart
يورغانڭه كوره اياغكی اوزات	*Yourghắnĭna ghieuré ayaghini ou̯ắt*	Stretch out your legs according to the length of your quilt
ياغموردان قاچان طولویه اوغرادی	*Yaghmourdan kắchan dolouya oghradi*	He who fled from the rain fell in with the hail
یا زور یا زر یا شهردن سفر	*Ya zor ya zér ya she-hirden séfér*	You must have either power or money, or walk out of the town
یاتان ارسلاندن دری دلكی یكدر	*Yatan arsslandan diri tilki yekdir*	A live fox is better than a dead lion
هر عسردن صكره یسر وار در	*Hér ussurden sora yussr var dir*	After every suffering comes a joy
قاری اوی یاپار قاری اوی یقار	*Kắrĭ evi yapar kắrĭ evi yĭkar*	A wife makes a house, (or) a wife breaks a house
اتکزی ابتدا صاغلم قازغه بغلیكز صكره جناب حقه حواله ایدكز	*Atĭnĭzĭ ibtida saghlem kắzĭgha bắghlayĭnĭz sora jenắb - i - ḥắkka hawalé ediniz*	First tie your horse fast to a post, and then put your trust in God.*

---

* This is a Turkish saying equivalent to Cromwell's celebrated utterance, "Put your trust in Providence, but keep your powder dry."

لوندره شهرنده وایمان افندینك مطبعه سنده
طبع اولنمشدر

ERRATA.

Page 6, paragraph 19. For ‏دوق‎, read ‏ذوق‎.

  ,,   7,   ,,   30. Instead of ‏عرب‎, read ‏غرب‎.

  ,,   10. The note at the bottom refers to paragraph 49 and not to 50.

  ,,   11, paragraph 59. For "*On* the same," read "*By* the same."

  ,,   12,   ,,   61. For *kieukieu*, read *kieuku*.

  ,,   59, note. For See 156, read See 153.

  ,,   60,   ,,   ,,   ,,

  ,,   63,   ,,   For See 156 and 211, read See 153 and 211.

  ,,   65, paragraph 242. Instead of ‏سويله مديككزدن‎, read ‏سويله مديككردن‎.

  ,,   67, note ‡. For See 228, read See 233.

  ,,   69, paragraph 255. Instead of *yazmélĭ*, read *yazmalĭ*.

  ,,   69, Exercise IX.   ,,   *gheldimim*, read *gheldimmi*.

  ,,   89, note §. For ‏كيم‎, read ‏كيم‎.

  ,,   201, line 5. For *senavéri*, read *senakiari*.

  ,,   202, line 16. For *teesyir*, read *tessyir*.

  ,,   202, line 23. For *idiyorissémdĭ*, read *idiyorissémdé*.

  ,,   203, lines 19 and 21. For *Abul-Mejd*, read *Abul-Mejdi*.

  ,,   205, line 15. For *olamadĭghĭmdan*, read *olamadĭghĭm*.

  ,,   205, line 22. For *musaade*, read *mussaadé*.

  ,,   205, last line. For ‏ايده جكمدن‎, read ‏ايده جكمزدن‎.

  ,,   206, line 20. For ‏بولسون‎, read ‏اولسون‎.

  ,,   207, line 5. For *oloursan*, read *oloursoun*.

  ,,   207, line 14. For ‏الميايدم‎, read ‏اولميايدم‎.

Published by **BERNARD QUARITCH**, 15 Piccadilly.

Forming One Volume, 8vo., Double Columns, cloth, price £2.

REDHOUSE'S
ENGLISH-TURKISH & TURKISH-ENGLISH
DICTIONARY.

NEW AND IMPROVED EDITION.

REVISED AND ENLARGED BY

DR. CHARLES WELLS.

OPINIONS OF THE PRESS.

الجوائب **EL JEWAÏB.** (Constantinople.) *March 3rd*, 1880.

[LITERAL TRANSLATION.]

"It is not unknown that in the year 1857 was printed in London a dictionary in Turkish and English, and *vice-versâ*, its author being Mr. Redhouse, one of the celebrated English scribes who have studied the Turkish language and excelled in it. But the aforementioned book did not contain all words. Hence this edition has been edited and improved by Dr. Charles Wells, one of the celebrated English writers who have studied the Turkish language and become famous in it. And he has added numerous words to this book, and glorious advantages '(فوائد جليلة),' and this book of his has been prepared properly and solidly. And it is divided into two parts : the first part, English words and their translation into Turkish ; and the second, *vice-versâ*. And the number of pages in the first is 382, and the number of pages in the second 500. And the above-mentioned Dr. Wells was the Secretary of General Kemball, when he came to these parts in 1876, on behalf of the English Government, to settle the dispute which had arisen between the Sublime Porte and Persia respecting the frontier question. And what he (Dr. Wells) has done now will immensely facilitate the two languages to those who wish to learn them, both Turks and Englishmen."

TIMES. (London.) *March 17th.*

" At a time when so many Englishmen are engaged in Turkey in various capacities, official or commercial, and when tourists are likely more than ever to abound, we must welcome the appearance of a new and enlarged edition of Mr. Redhouse's useful work. It is just a quarter of a century ago, at the hottest of the Crimean war, that Mr. Redhouse, as he tells us, in the preface to the first edition of this dictionary, published a ' Vade-mecum of the Ottoman Colloquial Language,' on the occasion of the formation of the Turkish Legion ; and he then promised to prepare ' for the information of those who may wish afterwards to penetrate deeper into the arcana of this really beautiful tongue, a series of more complete and scientific works.' The dictionary was the first fruits of this enterprise. To say that it was popular and unpretending in character is to say that it was well directed towards the object to be attained—the readiest instruction of Englishmen totally unacquainted with any Eastern tongue. There can be no greater mistake than to suppose that for a popular or elementary work on any subject, a high standard of attainment is not necessary in the author, or that the man of learning will be too learned for those whom he has to instruct. Modern experience is entirely against this view, and no one who is acquainted with educational books in the present day can fail to perceive that it is just the most accomplished scholars who, thoroughly understanding their subject, have presented it most simply and effectively. Such a mastery is eminently necessary to a writer who would deal with the cultivated Osmanli language, which we know as ' Turkish,' since this language is a conglomerate of three different forms of speech, representing, singularly enough, three of the great races into which the inhabitants of the Old World have been divided by ethnologists. The main stock of words and the grammar are Turkish, but almost every word expressing an abstract idea, or belonging to the domains of philosophy, theology, law, politics, or science, is of Arabic origin. There is also a considerable infusion of Persian words, particularly in matters touching Court or ceremonial. To learn Turkish thoroughly the student must first give a long period to the language of the

Prophet, from which the Turkish transplants not only words, but the elaborate mechanism of the Arabic language. Mr. Redhouse brought to his task the large and accurate knowledge which belongs to the author of the 'Grammaire Ottomane.' The present revised and enlarged edition has been prepared by Mr. Charles Wells, formerly professor at the Imperial Naval College, Constantinople, and late private secretary to Sir Arnold Kemball on the Turco-Persian Frontier Commission. In his preface to this edition, Mr. Wells says:—'While preserving all the valuable matter contained in the first edition, I have attempted to increase its usefulness by the addition of a considerable number of words omitted originally for want of space, or which have been coined by the Turks during the last twenty years to meet the requirements of their advancing civilization. . . . . The English-Turkish portion being scarcely copious enough to enable a Turk to read an English book, or an Englishman to write or speak on all subjects in Turkish, I have introduced a large number of fresh words into it, and I have also, to some extent, augmented the Turkish-English part. Thus the present edition will be found to contain several thousand more words than the original work published twenty-five years ago.'"

DAILY NEWS. *April* 17*th.*

"In his prefatory essay the editor, who enjoys a high reputation as a Turkish scholar, and who served as the private secretary of Sir Arnold Kemball on the Turco-Persian Frontier Commission, sets forth some interesting facts in connection with the strange neglect of the study of Turkish language by our officials and diplomatists. Contrary, we believe, to popular belief, it is neither Arabic nor Persian in origin. It is in its foundations and present structure a language of Tartar descent, the Turks having come from Central Asia. It is, indeed, as distinct from Arabic and Persian as Anglo-Saxon from Latin and Greek, though the Arabic characters have in modern times been adopted, and the Constantinople dialect is largely adulterated with Arabic and Persian words. Nevertheless, Turkish is more or less used in official circles from Tunis to the walls of China, and is actually the Court language of Persia, in many provinces of which country it is spoken as much as the native tongue. The reader of Mr. Wells's introduction will agree that it is somewhat remarkable that in a country so involved in Turkish engagements as Great Britain so little effort should be made to train officials or others in a knowledge of the language. As a rule we learn that our officials in Cyprus, in Constantinople, and in fact throughout the Turkish dominions, are dependent for communication upon Levantine interpreters, who seldom or never know either English or Turkish properly, and who speak the latter unidiomatically and with a vulgar accent peculiarly distasteful to the ears of educated Osmanlis. Mr. Wells advocates with good reason the establishment of a professorship of Turkish in one of our Universities, believing that acquaintance with the native tongue is not merely useful in communicating ideas, but indispensable to an accurate study and comprehension of the character and institutions of the people. It is a significant commentary on the facts noted that Russian and Austrian officials all learn Turkish at their respective Universities before going to Turkey, and that the Governments in both cases have numerous good Turkish scholars in their service. On the other hand, the number of Englishmen who can read and write Turkish is, we are assured, so small that they can be 'counted on the fingers of one hand.' For other interesting facts connected with Turkish literature we must refer the reader to Mr. Wells's essay."

THE MORNING POST. *April 28th.*

"The dictionary has been carefully edited by Dr. Charles Wells, also celebrated as a careful student of the Turkish language and letters. It is a grave error to suppose that the Turks have no literature, for, on the contrary, they have produced many notable poets and historians, and a dictionary of their language is obviously necessary, especially at the present time, when public attention is so frequently directed towards Turkey and her affairs."

LAND AND WATER. *March 27th.*

"In the times when a long sea voyage, beset with dangers, or a difficult land journey, 800 miles of which had to be performed on horseback, was necessary to reach the Ottoman dominions, it was not surprising that we knew little or nothing of Turkey or the Turks, and they still less of us. But in these days, when Constantinople can be reached by rail or steam in a week or so, it is extraordinary that we know so little of the Osmanlis, and that their character, their manners, and especially their language and literature, are a sealed book to us. This would be regrettable under any circumstances, but now that we have in a manner identified ourselves with Turkey, assumed the administration of a part of it, and undertaken the protectorate of its Asiatic provinces, it is most indispensable that we should remedy this anomalous state of things. We have a large amount of diplomatic, administrative, and commercial business to transact with the Turks, and if the reforms we advocate in Asia Minor be adopted we shall have still more; and yet there are not half-a-dozen Englishmen in existence who can read and write Turkish, and but very few who can even talk it decently. One great obstacle which has prevented our countrymen from acquiring Turkish has no doubt been the extreme difficulty of that language, and the want of good books and efficient instructors. The Turkish language is of Tartar origin, and its original framework was very simple, but the Turks have introduced so many Arabic and Persian words into their language that it is necessary to learn nearly all the words in those two tongues, and something of their grammars, to be able to read or write a Turkish letter or book. Many years of hard study and peculiar aptitude are indispensable to master this agglomeration of three languages, and to add to the arduousness of the task, hitherto the books written on Turkish have been extremely defective and full of errors. Apart from the usefulness of a knowledge of this language for diplomatic and business purposes, it is well worth studying for itself, as it is extremely curious, has a beneficial influence on the training of the mind, and possesses a literature which, though not equal to the Arabic or Persian, is extremely original and piquant, and can boast of authors of real genius and ability. Turkish poets and historians are well worthy of perusal, and are justly renowned in the East. Few Europeans, however, even know of their existence, and few indeed are those who have read their works. This ignorance on our part is easily accounted for when we consider that we have no professorship of Turkish at any of our Universities, and no other means afforded anywhere in England for imparting instruction in the Turkish language or literature. Austria has an Oriental Academy for preparing her officials for the East, France a similar institution, and at St. Petersburg, Leipsic, Pesth, and other places on the Continent professors of Turkish have long been appointed. In Turkey no facilities are afforded to a foreigner at any college or institution for acquiring Turkish, and if he goes there, not having previously studied, he will rarely acquire more than a very imperfect acquaintance with the colloquial tongue, and the written language probably never. There are no Turks, knowing English well, who teach their language, and the Armenians and other Christians who undertake to do so are not generally well educated either in English or Turkish. The importance of having a staff of Englishmen, well acquainted with the Turkish language and qualified to transact our business in the East, can hardly be exaggerated, and if, as is asserted, the system of student-interpreters, inaugurated at Constantinople by the late Foreign Secretary, is not the best possible, we would urge the Government to consider the suggestions which the editor of the work before us makes on the subject, as he evidently speaks from long experience in connection with the acquisition of Turkish gained both in England and Turkey. Dr. Wells proposes that we should have an Oriental Academy or a professor of Turkish at one of our Universities to prepare candidates for student-interpreterships, which he recommends should be given as rewards to gentlemen who show aptitude for learning Turkish. One great help in learning a language is a good dictionary, but a correct and copious lexicon is still a rarity in almost all languages. Some thirty years ago Mr. Redhouse rendered a great service to Oriental students by producing a really sound Turkish-and-English and English-and-Turkish dictionary. It was the best in Europe. But the last thirty years in the life of Turkish literature have witnessed a wonderful change. Thousands of new words have been

coined to meet the wants created by increased communication with the
European diplomatic, scientific and business world. Many words have
acquired new shades of meaning, and the language has thus been greatly
enriched and developed. Moreover, Mr. Redhouse omitted geographical
names in both parts of the dictionary, which are particularly requisite in
reading Turkish, as the Turks have no capital letters to distinguish proper
names, and thus the name of a place, if not found in the dictionary, is not
even recognisable as such, and in many cases there is not the slightest
resemblance to European names of places to assist one in arriving at the
meaning. For example, no one would guess that 'Habsh' means
Abyssinia, or 'Missr' Egypt, 'Sham' Syria, 'Chanak Kaléssi' the
Dardanelles, or 'Dijlé' the Tigris. Dr. Wells has shown great learning
and ability in supplying these great wants, viz., the insertion of newly-
created words and geographical names, and this volume is now a good
standard dictionary he Turkish language, and worthy to take its place
beside the best works of the same nature for European languages. But
although several thousands of useful words have been added, we recommend
these improvements being still further extended in a future edition, although
it would involve great labour. Future students will have a great advantage
over their predecessors by possessing this improved lexicon, and their thanks,
as well as those of all interested in the spread of the knowledge of this language, are due to Dr. Wells, who has given them the benefit of years of
study and observation in examining the current Turkish language and
literature. We are glad to hear, also, that he will publish in a few months
an entirely new grammar, the want of a good work of that kind having been
very severely felt, and a great barrier to the acquisition of this most difficult
but important tongue."

PUBLIC OPINION. *February 7th.*

"Viewing Dr Wells' production as a typical dictionary, it would have
demanded high commendation at our hands. But it is designed especially
with a view of protecting that numerous class of persons who are scarcely
aware of the difficulties inseparable from the study of modern Turkish, and
have not rendered themselves thoroughly familiar with the Arabic language,
or at least with the modes of thought a nation of Shemitic descent habitually
employs, and interprets into the dialects which are used by the speakers
and writers, a series of ideas characteristic of the diplomacy of Western
Europe. How Dr. Wells has mastered the difficulties of the Turkish language, in itself containing a *stirps* of original Arabic words, mingled with
a number of vocables derived from sources which, whatever they are, are
not Shemitic, we can scarcely imagine. Let us, therefore, take one of his
articles alone, just with a view of showing his method. Taking the word
'copy' in the dictionary, we have it as 'model of writing,' *mèshk*;
'writing exercise,' *karalama*; 'sample of scholar's writing,' *tä'lim*; 'of

a book,' *nusskha*; 'of a writing,' *suret*; 'of a drawing,' *'ayn* and *urnek.*
It is curious that the word *printer's copy* should be omitted from this list,
as it has a different signification from any of the above forms. Turning to
the active verb 'to copy,' we have for 'imitate' *taklid et*; 'to imitate'
(a writing) *suretini-almak, chikarmak,* or *yàzmak*; 'to imitate' (a drawing) *aynini-almak* or *urneghini-almak.* We see by the above comparison
that a series of ideas expressed in the English by the solitary word 'copy'
are in Turkish capable of expression by a number of collateral words. The
greater copiousness of the Turkish is now manifest, and this copiousness,
although it redounds to the dignity of the language which is capable of
expression in certain various manners, nevertheless gives an amount of
difficulty to the scholar which is of itself scarcely easy of acquirement to
the neophyte. If the Turkish language has the advantage of copiousness, it
has also that of brevity. Phrases which in Western Europe can only be
expressed each by a periphrasis or a prosopopœia are capable of being written
in Turkish with extreme brevity. For instance, the phrase, 'the book
which I have written' can be expressed in Turkish in two words, viz.
yazdighim kitab. Personal and relative pronouns, conjunctions, and other
parts of speech constantly recurring in European languages are almost
entirely dispensed with, by the help of certain peculiar inflections of which
the verb is capable. This naturally saves space. Dr. Wells has had a big
task, as Redhouse's Dictionary has long become the classical authority on
the subject of Turkish. He has exactly struck the keynote of real Oriental-
ism, and the difficulties of the language which he has so well mastered, and
which might have appalled many other less hardy students, have been so
entirely vanquished, that he has managed to produce not only the best
practical dictionary of the Turkish language, but also the best treatise on
the methods of Turkish orthoepy and pronunciation. This work will
always be the best as it is the most solid dictionary of Turkish, and the
editor has performed his appointed task nobly and well."

ILLUSTRATED LONDON NEWS. *March 6th.*

" The Turkish language, whatever may be the fate of the Ottoman Empire,
is likely to be worth studying for purposes of travel and commerce in the
East. A new edition, revised and enlarged, of the standard English-and-
Turkish and Turkish-and-English Dictionary, by J. W. Redhouse, is published in these days. The editor is a very competent person, Dr. Charles
Wells, formerly Professor in the Imperial Naval College at Constantinople,
and late private secretary to Lieutenant-General Sir Arnold Kemball in the
Special Commission to settle the frontier between Turkey and Persia. He
is also the author of an essay on political economy in Turkish, and of some
translations from the Turkish literature. The publisher of the new edition
of Redhouse's Dictionary is Mr. Bernard Quaritch, of Piccadilly."

8

BRIEF: THE WEEK'S NEWS. *February 6th.*

" The events of recent years have created a demand in England for works upon the Turkish language. A new edition of Mr. Redhouse's Dictionary— originally compiled in the time of the Crimean War, and hitherto the best book of its kind, but long since out of print—has, therefore, been prepared by Dr. Charles Wells, the most accomplished Anglo-Turkish scholar of the day. Much more copious than the first edition, and supplying the numerous deficiencies in that work which time and experience have discovered, it will mark a new epoch in the study of a language still of great political importance."

PRINTING TIMES AND LITHOGRAPHER. *January 15th.*

" The Emperor Francis Joseph has conferred the gold medal for science and art on Mdlle. Camilla Ruzicka Ostoic for a new Turkish-and-German Dictionary which the authoress recently published. This reminds us that a new and greatly-improved edition of Redhouse's Turkish-and-English Dictionary has just been edited by Dr. Charles Wells and printed by Messrs. Wyman & Sons, for Mr. Bernard Quaritch of Piccadilly. But who ever heard of any similar mark of recognition being bestowed upon a man of letters or a compiler in this country ! "

A RABIC DICTIONARY : AN ARABIC-ENGLISH AND ENGLISH-ARABIC DICTIONARY, by JOSEPH CATAFAGO, of Aleppo, Syria, 2 vols. sm. 8vo. Vol. I. xii. & 316 pp. Vol. II. viii. & 744 pp. double columns, *much matter compressed into a small space, all the Arabic words with the pronunciation in Roman letters,* cloth, £2. 1865.

This work is the FIRST Arabic and English Dictionary ever published.

Vol. I, consisting of pp. xx and 466, is now ready. The entire work will comprise over 1000 pp., compressed into a portable volume, and representing the only Arabic-English and English-Arabic Dictionary now in existence.

" On the whole the work is a most acceptable contribution to Oriental literature ; and the English and Arabic part especially will be an invaluable aid to travellers in the East, and to all Englishmen who have occasion to study Arabic."--ATHENÆUM, Jan. 29, '59.

A RABIC GRAMMAR : FARIS' PRACTICAL GRAMMAR OF THE ARABIC LANGUAGE, with Interlineal Reading Lessons, Dialogues and Vocabulary, by FARIS EL-SHIDIAC, a Native of Mount Lebanon, Syria ; 12mo. the new edition by the Rev. H. A. WILLIAMS, Professor of Arabic at Cambridge, cloth, 5s. 1866.

The best Grammar for learning Arabic, equally of service to travellers in the East and to young Scholars. The Rudiments of Grammar extend to 64 pp., the Exercises to 68, the Dialogues to 12, the Vocabulary to 62 pp. All the Arabic words have the Vowel-points and the pronunciation.

BERNARD QUARITCH, 15 PICCADILLY, LONDON.

759862

Printed in Great Britain by
Amazon.co.uk, Ltd.,
Marston Gate.